After Philosophy

After Philosophy

End or Transformation?

edited by
*Kenneth Baynes, James Bohman, and
Thomas McCarthy*

The MIT Press, Cambridge, Massachusetts, and London, England

Second printing, 1987

This book was set in Baskerville by DEKR Corporation and printed and bound by Halliday Lithograph in the United States of America.

Library of Congress Cataloging-in-Publication Data

After philosophy.

Includes bibliographies and index.
1. Philosophy, Modern—20th century. I. Baynes, Kenneth. II. Bohman, James.
III. McCarthy, Thomas A.
B804.A33 1987   190'.9'04   86-10498
ISBN 0-262-02254-0
ISBN 0-262-52113-X (pbk.)

Contents

II
The Transformation of Philosophy: Systematic Proposals

Sources and Acknowledgments

Acknowledgment is made to the following sources for permission to reprint the essays in this volume:

Richard Rorty, "Pragmatism and Philosophy," from *Consequences of Pragmatism* (Minneapolis: University of Minnesota Press, 1982), xii–xlvii. By permission of the author and the University of Minnesota Press.

Jean-François Lyotard, *La Condition postmoderne: rapport sur le savoir* (Paris: Editions de Minuit, 1982). Translated as *The Postmodern Condition: A Report on Knowledge* (Minneapolis: University of Minnesota Press, 1984), xxii–xxv, 16–19, 26–27, 30–31, 37–41, 64–67. By permission of the University of Minnesota Press. Translation by Geoff Bennington and Brian Massumi.

"Questions of Method: An Interview with Michel Foucault," *Ideology and Consciousness* 8 (1981), 3–14. By permission of Humanities Press and *Ideology and Consciousness*. Translation by Alan Bass.

Jacques Derrida, "Les Fins de l'homme," from *Marges de la philosophie* (Paris: Editions de Minuit, 1972). Translated as "The Ends of Man" in *Margins of Philosophy* (Chicago: University of Chicago Press, and London: Harvester Press, 1982). By permission of the University of Chicago Press and Harvester Press. Translation by Alan Bass.

Donald Davidson, "The Method of Truth in Metaphysics," *Midwest Studies in Philosophy* II (1977), 244–254. By permission of the author and the University of Minnesota Press.

Michael Dummett, "Can Analytical Philosophy Be Systematic, and Ought It to Be?" from the proceedings of the 1975 Stuttgart Hegel Conference, published in *Hegel-Studien,* supplement 19 (1977), 305–327. By permission of the proceedings.

Hilary Putnam, "Why Reason Can't Be Naturalized," *Synthese* 52 (1982), 1–23. By permission of the author and D. Reidel Publishing Company. Originally delivered as the second Howison Lecture at the University of California on April 30, 1981.

Karl-Otto Apel, "The Problem of Philosophical Foundations in Light of a Transcendental Pragmatics of Language," *Man and World* 8 (1975), 239–275. Revised version published as "Das Problem der philosophischen Letztbegründung im Lichte einer transzendentalen Sprachpragmatik," in *Sprache und Erkenntnis: Festschrift für Gerhard Frey,* edited by B. Kanitschneider (Innsbruck: Institut für Sprachwissenschaft der Universität Innsbruck, 1976). By permission of the author and Martinus Nijhoff Publishers. Translation by Karl Richard Pavlovic, modified for this edition, as well as the original German by the author.

Jürgen Habermas, "Philosophie als Platzhalter und Interpret," from *Moralbewusstsein und kommunikatives Handeln* (Frankfurt: Suhrkamp, 1983). Translated as "Philosophy as Stand-In and Interpreter" in *Moral Consciousness and Communicative Action* (Cambridge, Massachusetts: MIT Press, 1987). By permission of the author and MIT Press. Translation by Christian Lenhardt. This essay is based on a talk given at a conference on "Comparative Perspectives on Transcendental and Dialectical Modes of Justification" held in Stuttgart in June 1981 under the auspices of the International Hegel Society.

Hans-Georg Gadamer, *Vernunft im Zeitalter der Wissenschaft* (Frankfurt: Suhrkamp, 1976). Excerpts from the essays translated as "Hermeneutics as a Theoretical and Practical Task" and "Hermeneutics as Practical Philosophy" in *Reason in the Age of Science* (Cambridge, Massachusetts: MIT Press, 1983), pp. 91–93, 97–98, 100, 103–115. By permission of the author and MIT Press. Translation by Frederick Lawrence.

Hans-Georg Gadamer, foreword to the second edition of *Wahrheit und Methode* (Tübingen: Mohr, 1965). Translated as *Truth and Method* (New York: Seabury Press, and London: Sheed and

Ward, 1970), xvi–xxvi. By permission of the author, Continuum Publishing Company, and Sheed and Ward Ltd. Translation by G. Barden and J. Cumming, modified for this edition.

Paul Ricoeur, "On Interpretation," from *Philosophy in France Today*, edited by Alan Montefiore (Cambridge: Cambridge University Press, 1983). By permission of Cambridge University Press. Translation by Kathleen McLaughlin.

Alasdair MacIntyre, "Relativism, Power, and Philosophy," the Presidential Address delivered before the 81st Annual Eastern Division Meeting of the American Philosophical Association in New York, New York, December 29, 1984, in *Proceedings and Addresses of the American Philosophical Association* (Newark, Delaware: APA, 1985), 5–22. By permission of the author and the American Philosophical Association.

Alasdair MacIntyre, postscript to the second edition of *After Virtue* (Notre Dame, Indiana: University of Notre Dame Press, and London: Duckworth, 1984), 265–272. By permission of the University of Notre Dame Press and Duckworth Publishing Company.

Hans Blumenberg, "Anthropologische Annäherung an die Aktualität der Rhetorik," in *Wirklichkeiten in denen wir leben* (Stuttgart: Reclam, 1981), 104–136. First published in Italian in *Il Verri* (Milan) 35/6 (1971), 49–72. By permission of the author. Translation by Robert M. Wallace for this edition.

We also thank Charles Taylor for his original contribution.

General Introduction

To outside observers it might well seem odd that philosophy should presently be so preoccupied with its own continued existence. To initiates, especially the historically well-traveled among them, this self-questioning will have a more familiar ring. Agonizing over the "wherefore" and "whither," and even the "whether," of philosophy has been a staple of Western philosophical discourse since the time of Socrates and Plato. One might even argue, and with good reason, that periods in which self-doubt ran deepest were often periods of extraordinary philosophical creativity. And yet it would be a mistake to think that everything is as it always has been. The rise of the modern sciences of nature removed — forever, it seems — vast domains from the authority of philosophical reflection. The ensuing turn to the subject, the "mirror of nature," appears now to have been only a temporary stopgap, which could remain effective only until the human sciences and the arts grew strong enough to claim their proper domains from philosophy as well. Since that began to happen in the last century, there has been a more menacing ring to the repeated announcements of the end of philosophy — from Marx and Nietzsche to historicism and the sociology of knowledge.

The most recent refuge of philosophy, language, is proving no safer a haven from this onslaught, as most of the authors represented in this volume will argue. One did not, of course, have to wait until today to perceive the dangers inherent in the linguistic turn. The intrication of language in forms of life and lifeworlds, practices and conventions, taken-for-granted backgrounds and cultural traditions already prompted Wittgenstein's therapeutic farewell to philosophy as well as Heidegger's more dramatic overcoming. Many of the arguments advanced here are, in fact, echoes of or variations upon themes already developed in their work. Indeed Wittgenstein and Heidegger might well have been represented here, as might Quine, Goodman, and many others. There is an unavoidable element of arbitrariness in a collection such as this. We did decide to include thinkers from the French and German worlds as well as the Anglo-American, for it would not have been possible to comprehend the current end-of-philosophy debates without them. For the same reason we tried to include representatives of the principal positions in the debates — poststructuralism and postanalytic philosophy, hermeneutics and critical theory. Because it did not seem possible to capture the changes taking place in all the various subdisciplines of philosophy, we picked authors and essays that addressed themselves to core philosophical questions of "truth" and "reason." And, with some misgivings, we chose to include more recent developments of important lines of thought rather than their original formulations — Gadamer and Derrida, for instance, rather than Heidegger; Davidson and Putnam rather than Quine; Rorty and Dummett rather than Wittgenstein; Foucault and Lyotard rather than Nietzsche. For the rest, it was largely a matter of our collective judgment as to which were the most important voices in contemporary discussions concerning whether philosophy should be brought to an end or transformed and continued.

As this formulation of what is at issue suggests, the thinkers we have chosen all take the view — in very different ways certainly — that philosophy is at a turning point, that things philosophical cannot simply go on as they have. It is in this sense that they are all thinking "after Philosophy" — with a capital *P,* as Rorty has put it. For some, like Rorty and Derrida, this means after philosophy, period: the Platonic tradition has "outlived its usefulness." For others, like Habermas, philosophy is to be *aufgehoben,* as Marx put it, into a form of social inquiry. For still others, like Gadamer and Ricoeur, it means philosophy's continuation through its transformation into philosophical hermeneutics; or, in the case of MacIntyre and Blumenberg, into a kind of philosophical historiography. And finally, for some, like Davidson and Dummett, philosophy continues in the altered yet not unfamiliar form of a theory of meaning.[1]

In the long run this proliferation of approaches to philosophy may turn out to be quite fruitful; in the short run it has produced confusion and consternation in the absence of a coherent overview of the issues that separate them. This volume was put together in the belief that what may at times seem like a Tower of Babel does, in fact, have the makings of a genuine philosophical conversation. If it is to be carried on as such, there is need for a clearer delineation of what is really in dispute among the different parties to the conversation. We hope partly to fill that need in the remainder of this general introduction and by the introductory remarks and suggestions for further reading that precede each essay. We have grouped the selections to reflect relevant family resemblances. The groupings are admittedly rough, and in the case of the second, perhaps even artificial. But they are merely a convenience and not at all intended to substitute for an identification of the issues. To this we now turn, with all due apologies for the unavoidable sketchiness and oversimplification of what follows. It will have served its purpose if the contemporary cacophony begins to sound more like a meaningful dialogue concerning the options for doing, or not doing, philosophy today.

Kant's thought provides a convenient reference point for identifying some of the general themes in the "whither philosophy?" discussions today, for they are often presented as critiques of or variations upon Kantian themes. Thus, those calling for an end to philosophy typically support this with a critique of strong conceptions of *reason* and of the autonomous rational subject. To the necessity that characterizes reason in the Kantian view, they oppose the contingency and conventionality of the rules, criteria, and products of what counts as rational speech and action at any given time and place. To its universality they oppose the irreducible plurality of incommensurable language games and forms of life, the irremediably "local" character of all truth, argument, and validity — to the a priori the empirical, to certainty fallibility, to invariance historical and cultural variability, to unity heterogeneity, to totality the fragmentary, to self-evident givenness ("presence") universal mediation by differential systems of signs, to the unconditioned a rejection of ultimate foundations in any form — transcendental conditions of possibility no less than metaphysical first principles.

Interwoven with this critique of reason is a critique of the *sovereign rational subject* — atomistic and autonomous, disengaged and disembodied, and, at least on some views, potentially and ideally self-transparent. It is high time we took to heart, our postphilosophers urge, the lessons of Darwin and Marx, Nietzsche and Freud, Wittgenstein and Heidegger. It is no longer possible to deny the influence of the unconscious on the conscious, the role of the preconceptual and nonconceptual in the conceptual, the presence of the irrational — the economy of desire, the will to power — at the very core of the rational. Nor is it possible to ignore the intrinsically social character of "structures of consciousness," the historical and cultural variability of categories of thought and principles of action, their interdependence with the changing forms of social and material reproduction. And it is equally evident that "mind" will be misconceived if it is opposed to "body," as will theory if it is opposed to practice: the subject of knowledge is essentially embodied and practically engaged with the world; and the products of our thought bear ineradicable traces of our purposes and projects, passions and interests. In short, the epistemological and moral subject has been definitively decentered and the conception of reason linked to it irrevocably desublimated. Subjectivity and intentionality are not prior to but a function of forms of life and systems of language; they do not "constitute" the world but are themselves elements of a linguistically disclosed world.

Closely connected with these critiques of reason and the rational subject is a critique of the associated picture of *knowledge as representation,* according to which the subject stands over against an independent world of objects that it can more or less accurately represent. On the view of the postphilosophers, subject and object cannot be set off from one another in this way. We can make no sense of the idea of a linguistically naked "given" that is interpreted in various more or less adequate ways, of an invariant "content" that is incorporated into different "schemes" — the final dogma of empiricism, as Davidson calls it. The object of knowledge is always already preinterpreted, situated in a scheme, part of a text, outside which there are only other texts. On the other hand, the subject of knowledge belongs to the very world it wishes to interpret. As Taylor, following Heidegger, puts it: The condition of our forming disinterested representations of the world is that we be already engaged with it. And the kinds of representations we form will depend on the kinds of dealings we have with it. Underlying propositional knowledge, then, is a largely inarticulate and unarticulatable grasp of the world that we have as agents within it — agents, as Merleau-Ponty has shown, who are essentially embodied and the locus of orientations and desires that we never fully grasp or control. Thus the idea of a knowing subject disengaged from the body and from the world makes no more sense than the idea of self-transparence; there is no knowledge without a background, and that background can never be wholly objectified.

Another strand in the end-of-philosophy argument can be traced back to Nietzsche's emphasis on the rhetorical and aesthetic dimensions of language. Thus a number of critics seek to undercut philosophy's traditional *self-delimitation from rhetoric and poetics* as reflected in the standard oppositions between logos and mythos, logic and rhetoric, literal and figurative, concept and metaphor, argument and narrative. Pursuing Nietzsche's idea that philosophical texts are rhetorical constructs, they take aim at philosophy's self-understanding of its discourse in purely logical, literal — that is to say, nonrhetorical — terms. They argue that this is achieved only at the cost of ignoring or suppressing the rhetorical strategies and elements of metaphor and other figurative devices that are nevertheless always at work in philosophical discourse. And they seek actively to dispel the illusion of pure reason by applying modes of literary analysis to philosophical texts, exploiting the ten-

sions between reason and rhetoric within them so as to undermine their logocentric self-understanding. This approach
makes evident the figurative dimensions of philosophical texts,
the effects of dominant metaphorics upon them, the role
played by rhetorical considerations in determining the elements and order of philosophical texts, the presence in them
of indirect communications that often speak against their manifest content — in general, the rhetorical-poetic surplus of
meaning intrinsic to the literary dimension of philosophical
texts and the consequent need to study them in rhetorical-
poetical terms.

It would be a mistake to think that all or even most of the
above points would be denied by those who call for a transformation rather than an end of philosophy. All of the thinkers
represented in this volume have made the "linguistic turn."
That is no longer an issue. The question now is where that
turn leads. For mainstream philosophical analysis one influential answer has been: to the semantics of ideal or natural
languages. The answers given by most of our authors read
otherwise: to the *pragmatics* of natural languages — that is, to
a study of language in use, of linguistic practices, sometimes
understood in a quite restricted sense (as in Dummett's "theory
of force"), sometimes extended to a general theory of linguistic
communication (Apel's transcendental pragmatics), sometimes
expanded to a general study of "language games" (Lyotard's
"agonistics of language"); to the *politics* of language in use —
for example, to the genealogy of power/knowledge constellations (Foucault), to the critique of ideologies rooted in social
injustice (Habermas), or to a hermeneutics of suspicion (Ricoeur); to the *rhetoric* and *poetics* of language as they figure, for
example, in the project of a philosophical hermeneutics (Gadamer, Ricoeur), or in the practice of deconstructing Western
metaphysics (Derrida), or in the narrative understanding of
epistemological and moral crises (MacIntyre). In short, whatever their other differences, there is widespread (though not
universal) agreement among the various parties to the debate
that the linguistic turn must be more broadly conceived. In
both its Wittgensteinian and Heideggerian versions, it leads
inevitably to the pragmatics, politics, rhetoric, and poetics of

language in use — thus undercutting the hierarchical oppositions upon which traditional conceptions of Philosophy were based. For some this signals the end of philosophy; for others, the need for a new systematic conception of philosophy; for still others, the need to transform philosophy into philosophical hermeneutics.

Having identified some of the general themes central to contemporary discussions about what comes after Philosophy, it is time we turned to the differences separating the three streams of thought we have distinguished in grouping our selections.

1. Notwithstanding the repeated denunciation of philosophers who believe in a priori knowledge and self-evident givenness, in necessity and certainty, in totality and ultimate foundations, there are relatively few of them around today. Whatever disagreements may separate the philosophers represented here, all of them are fallibilists and finitists. None claims self-certifying necessity for philosophical insight.[2] Where then do the real issues lie?

While all are agreed in their opposition to the "Platonic conception of Truth" and in their belief that "truth is of this world," there is strong disagreement as to whether this immanence is the whole story and as to what conclusions can be drawn from it. Putnam, for instance, argues that our notions of truth and reason are marked by transcendence as well. On the one hand, we can have no idea of standards of rationality wholly independent of historically concrete languages, cultures, practices; on the other hand, reason serves as a regulative idea with reference to which we can criticize the traditions we inherit. Though never divorced from social practices of justification, it can never be reduced to any given set of practices. Truth is *idealized* rational acceptability. Essentially the same view is defended by Apel and Habermas, among others.

Again, while all start from the pluralism of language games and forms of life, not all agree that this is an *irreducible* pluralism of *incommensurable* language games. In fact, the notion of incommensurability has come under very severe attack from several angles. Davidson argues that our general method of interpretation makes it impossible to discover whether others have radically different conceptual schemes. Gadamer suggests that hermeneutic dialogue and the achievement of mutual understanding across cultures and epochs are a repeated practical demonstration that reason, though always embodied in language, always transcends the particularity of specific languages. With a kind of modest Hegelianism (that is, Hegel without the teleological progress of reason), MacIntyre maintains that claims involving alternative conceptual schemes can be evaluated in terms of the history of an argument: the case for the rational superiority of any particular scientific, moral, or epistemological theory can be made only by showing that it is the best so far, that it transcends the limitations of its competitors, avoiding their defects while incorporating their strengths. Historicism, he argues, does not imply relativism. Habermas endorses these arguments and adds the claim that there are, as a matter of fact, cross-cultural universals of cognition, speech, and action, which can be captured in fallible, but nevertheless general reconstructions of species-wide competences. There is no need to tie universality to necessity and certainty; forswearing these marks of the a priori in no way precludes searching for empirical and hypothetical, yet universal theories of basic human competences.

2. Similarly, despite the repeated attacks on it, Cartesianism is something of a straw man in contemporary philosophy. Having all made the linguistic turn, none of our authors regards the subject of knowledge and action as punctual, atomistic, disembodied; none understands rational autonomy in terms of an ideal of total disengagement; none appeals to immediate, intuitive self-presence as the basis of self-knowledge; and none regards full self-transparence as a sensible ideal of self-knowledge. Where then do the real issues lie?

For the end-of-philosophy thinkers the twilight of Cartesian-Kantian subjectivity means the end of "Man" and of the philosophical humanism that draws its life from that conception. For our other authors this situation represents rather a challenge to rethink our idea of the rational subject and to recast accordingly our received humanistic ideals. Among hermeneutic philosophers this typically takes the form of an "ontology of finitude" (Ricoeur) or an anthropology of the human being as a *Mängelwesen,* a creature of deficiencies (Blumenberg). Ricoeur understands his project as an attempt to continue-through-transforming the modern tradition of reflective philosophy. Human existence can be viewed only mediately, in the mirror of the objects and acts, symbols and signs in which it is manifested. "Reflection" is then construed as an essentially hermeneutic enterprise, mediated through the interpretation and critique of "signs scattered in the world." It is only through appropriating these texts and text analogues, through making them our own, that we better understand ourselves. In a similar vein, Gadamer insists that consciousness is always more *Sein* than *Bewusstsein;* our historical being precedes and grounds any abstract separation between the subject and the object of knowledge. Philosophical hermeneutics merely raises to reflective awareness the basic human capacity for intelligent communication with one's fellow beings, for achieving mutual understanding in language. As such it is preceded by and remains bound up with a certain kind of practical action. It is, in Gadamer's view, a continuation of practical philosophy by other means. Taylor argues that overcoming epistemology does not amount to overcoming philosophy *tout court.* It points, rather, to a continuation-through-transformation of the "tradition of self-critical reason." Reflection on the indispensable conditions of intentionality reveals that we are first and foremost embodied agents in a world. Our propositional knowledge of the world is grounded in our dealings with it; and there can be no question of totally objectifying the prior grasp gained as agents within it. The task of philosophy is the unending one of articulating this background, disclosing what it involves, and thus making partial detachment and revision possible. Philosophy as a self-clarification of the conditions of intentionality leads to a better understanding of what we are as knowing agents; it thereby provides insight into the anthropological questions associated with our moral concerns.

In all these variations on the hermeneutic theme, we encounter a traditional philosophical claim in somewhat different forms: reflection on the conditions of knowing, understanding, speaking leads to a deeper and more adequate self-understanding, one with moral-practical implications. Opposed to this are the various end-of-philosophy arguments to the effect that there is nothing there that could be better understood; the idea that there is a true meaning to be discovered is rejected on the grounds of the essential undecidability of meaning. This is usually connected with a replacement of the ideal of self-understanding by that of self-making, with a Nietzschean aestheticization of the self, the watchwords of which are innovation and experimentation, dissemination and proliferation, creative language use in the search for interesting self-redescriptions — the self as a work of art. As Taylor points out, "Whoever is ultimately right, the dispute has to be fought on the terrain of the [defenders of reason]. The Nietzschean position stands or falls with a certain construal of knowledge — that it is relative to various, ultimately imposed, 'regimes of truth,' to use Foucault's expression. This has to show itself to be a superior construal to that which emerges from the exploration of the conditions of intentionality."

As compared with hermeneutic transformations, the thinkers we have grouped together as "systematic" have, on the whole, a somewhat different conception of "knowing better what we are," but one equally opposed to the aesthetics of self-making. In very different ways, they all see philosophy as continuing by other means some aspect of the "Kantian" project (in a very broad sense that includes, for instance, Fregean variations). For Davidson it is a matter of constructing, on the basis of a Tarskian approach to truth, an empirical theory of meaning that "recovers the structure of our ability to speak and understand a language," as part of the more general project of a "unified theory of speech and action." For Dummett the fundamental task of philosophy, underlying all the others, is to construct a "theory of understanding," that is, an account of what someone knows when he or she knows a language — without assuming, as Davidson does, a nonepistemic notion of truth. For Putnam philosophy is "almost coextensive with a theory of rationality," which, dealing as it does with an irreducibly normative notion, has to proceed by seeking a reflective equilibrium between individual judgments, maxims, and a general "theory" or conception of rationality. For Apel philosophy as transcendental pragmatics seeks to reconstruct the (pragmatic) conditions of possibility of intersubjectively valid critique and argumentation, that is, of rational practice par excellence. For Habermas, finally, philosophy "originates in reflection on the reason embodied in cognition, speech, and action," and it issues in reconstructive theories of these basic species competences. Despite the unmistakable differences, there are strong family resemblances among these conceptions, particularly when compared with conceptions of Nietzschean or hermeneutic lineage: (a) The idea of reconstructing — giving an account of the structure of — basic human abilities, constitutive of what we think of as human reason, turns up again and again, as do (b) the idea that this is not an a priori but an empirical task — fallible, criticizable, revisable in light of the evidence afforded by the actual exercise of these abilities — and (c) the idea that because what is to be reconstructed is essentially normative in nature, the type of "empirical" theory called for is fundamentally distinct in kind from natural-scientific theories and incorporates modes of thinking traditionally regarded as "philosophical."

3. Another complex of issues separating end-of-philosophy thinkers from transformation-of-philosophy thinkers can be grouped around what we have referred to as the politics of language. In undercutting the "Platonic conception" of reason, truth, and language, post-Nietzschean philosophers have stressed their lowly origins in struggle and conflict, in arbitrariness and contingency, in a *will* to truth that is essentially involved with power and desire. They are, in Rorty's phrase, no more nor less than "tools for coping," and as such they are essentially *relative to* variable and contingent purposes and interests rather than means for rising above them. The result, in Foucault's view, is that they are always bound up in power/knowledge constellations, "regimes of truth" in which "effects of veridiction" are interwoven with "effects of jurisdiction."

None of the philosophers we have identified as proponents of a transformation of philosophy any longer defends "Platonic" conceptions of reason, truth, and language. Their transformations consist precisely in recasting these notions to fit their different conceptions of human finitude and fallibilism. On the other hand, not all of them take into consideration the complex of problems alluded to in the phrase "the politics of language." Among those who do, the strategy is by and large to admit the complicity of truth with power and constraint, with privilege and exclusion, but to argue that this complicity is not always vicious in nature and that where it is, the situation is not beyond remediation. Thus, for instance, Habermas and Apel argue that knowledge is always and inextricably — indeed constitutively — bound up with fundamental human interests and that it is upon this very basis that concepts of reason, truth, and language are to be reconstructed. Hermeneutic thinkers generally grant that the variable configurations of language and practice, with their shifting horizons of meaning, are by no means innocent of purposes and interests, power and desire — that the very idea of such innocence makes no sense at all. They typically argue, however, that this by no means obviates the distinctions between truth and falsity, right and wrong, justice and injustice, nor does it make them simply equivalent to what is de facto acceptable at a given time and place. Gadamer, for instance, argues that genuine hermeneutic understanding, because it involves serious dialogue seeking rational agreement about *die Sache selbst,* the matter under discussion, brings to light unjustifiable preconceptions and prejudgments rooted in structures of domination. Ricoeur argues that the hermeneutics of trust — aimed at recollecting and restoring the fullness of meaning — has to be practiced alongside a hermeneutics of suspicion aimed at demystifying meanings by unmasking the unavowed forces concealed within them. In addition to rational reconstruction and hermeneutic interpretation, Habermas sees a need for a critique of ideology aimed at identifying and explaining systematic distortions of language that are rooted in pathologies of individual and social life. To oversimplify somewhat: These authors agree with the post-Nietzscheans in rejecting ideas of reason, truth, and language as innocent of power and desire, but they argue in differing ways that the normative notion of rational acceptability can also be applied to needs and interests, constraints and prescriptions, thus allowing for post-Platonic conceptions of validity in which it is neither divinized nor naturalized.

4. Another constellation of issues separating our groups of thinkers has to do with the rhetoric and poetics of language. Many postphilosophers follow a Nietzschean strategy of undercutting philosophy's traditional self-delimitation from non-philosophy, so as to reactivate the disruptive effects of language that this was meant to contain. They argue that the exclusion of rhetoric and poetry was achieved only at the cost of ignoring or suppressing or concealing the literary effects that have nevertheless pervaded philosophical discourse, from Plato's allegory of the cave onward. Once the impossibility of a Platonic conception of logos is acknowledged and the omnipresence of the rhetorical dimensions of language recognized, philosophical discourse can no longer be misconceived as logical *rather than* literary, literal *rather than* figurative, argumentative *rather than* rhetorical — in short, it can no longer be conceived of as philosophical in any emphatic sense of the term. The sovereignty of rhetorical analysis, which is concerned with the qualities and effects of texts in general, extends to the would-be independent realm of philosophical texts as well.

By contrast, hermeneutic philosophers typically argue that interpretive modes, metaphorical elements, narrative structures, and the like can be incorporated into a transformed conception of rational discourse — and indeed much of the writing of Gadamer, Ricoeur, MacIntyre, Blumenberg, and others has aimed to do just that. On the other hand, those we have identified as systematic philosophers tend, on the whole, to renew the arguments for the primacy of literal and, at the more organized levels of speech, scientific discourse — in a broad sense of the term "scientific," to be sure, but one involving nonetheless the idea of rigorous argumentation. These are very thorny issues, and they are far from being resolved. As Blumenberg points out, rhetoric was assigned its subordinate position in the Platonic tradition on the supposition that the Truth was available to us. It was sophism to suggest the impossibility of Truth and to replace it with what people could be persuaded to accept as true or with what people could be seduced into accepting by the beauty of language. Philosophy was thereby lodged in a perpetual cold war with rhetoric and aesthetics. It is no wonder, then, that at the present conjuncture, when some form of Ricoeur's ontology of finitude is accepted by all parties to the debate, Philosophy should find itself on the defensive. An approach to knowledge and morality that takes the knowability of the True and the Good as its point of departure is bound to be hard pressed when we have to surrender as unrealistic the rationalist principles of sufficient reason in favor of what Blumenberg calls "the axiom of all rhetoric, the principle of insufficient reason." Like the other thinkers grouped with him under the rubric "hermeneutics," Blumenberg is out not only to deconstruct the notions of Reason and Truth but also to reconstruct them in a way fitting for *Mängelwesen* such as we are, that is, to construct notions keyed not to "definitive certainties" and "eternal truths" but to "agreements subject to later revocation." His invocation of rhetoric in this connection signals the view that the modes of reasoning suited to our anthropological situation will essentially involve figurative devices — metaphor, above all — that are not simply surrogates for missing concepts that could in principle be supplied, and rhetorical structures that are not simply embellishments for structures of rigorous argument that are in principle available. A theory of reasoning proper to creatures such as we, a theory of how we arrive at and maintain agreements subject to later revocation through persuasion rather than through force, will have to include an account of the essential functions of myth and metaphor, narrative and interpretation.

While most hermeneutic philosophers would agree with most of this, in one form or another, the philosophers we have characterized as systematic typically (but not universally) regard the figurative uses of language as parasitic upon the literal, and hence as derivative in some sense; and they typically insist that where rationality is concerned, standards of rhetorical success have to be subordinated to those of logical consistency, probative force, argumentative cogency, and the like. Even if rhetorical elements of language are present and at work in philosophy, they must be harnessed, as far as possible, for purposes of argumentation — in a suitably broad sense —

and subordinated to its exigencies. What is at stake in these disagreements is more than the age-old boundaries between logic and rhetoric and poetics; it is a question of redrawing the entire map of reason.

5. One final set of issues dividing the different approaches to the end/transformation of philosophy deserves notice here: the role of theory in philosophy generally, and philosophy's relation to the human sciences particularly. The end-of-philosophy thinkers clearly oppose the continuation of theoretical philosophy, by any means. Foucault's genealogy, Derrida's deconstruction, and Lyotard's paralogism are all explicitly proposed as practices and not theories. As for the human sciences, they are typically dismissed by thinkers in this group as merely would-be sciences or worse. They tend to look instead to literature, the arts, and aesthetic criticism for inspiration. Foucault is something of an exception to this rule, who at the same time proves it. Unlike most other postphilosophers, he has devoted a great deal of energy to analyzing the origins and philosophical foundations of the "sciences of man" — but only for the purpose of unmasking the power/knowledge connections they embody and disguise. In fact, one of the principal aims of Foucault's genealogy is to construct a "nominalist critique," by way of historical analysis, of the fundamental ideas in terms of which we have constituted ourselves as subjects and objects of knowledge. By constructing histories of the "objectification of objectivities," he seeks to disassemble the apparent unity of the seemingly self-evident concepts with which social scientists usually begin. In this sense genealogy, the successor discipline to philosophy, is a kind of critical-philosophical historiography.

Hermeneutically inclined philosophers typically conceive of their thought as a continuation of *practical*, not theoretical, philosophy. Of course, practical philosophy too has a "theoretical" moment, in a broad sense, for it raises basic practical abilities to the level of reflective awareness — in the case of hermeneutics, the ability to reach mutual understanding in language; but this theoretical moment remains tied to the practice it reflects — unlike, say, the classical metaphysics of nature or the Kantian metaphysics of experience. As for the role of the human sciences in this reflective project, hermeneutical philosophers tend to be critical of the "objectifying" human sciences — those, roughly speaking, that try to model themselves after the natural sciences. Like the postphilosophers, they generally regard this attempt to objectify the subject as self-defeating and link it as well to the interest in extending instrumental control over the individual and society. Because the object domain of social inquiry is linguistically prestructured, antecedently constituted by the interpretive activities of its members, social investigators can gain access to it only via their own interpretive activities. Since their being in the world precedes any subject-object representation of it, they cannot claim for themselves the status of neutral, extramundane observers who can view the social world from the outside and study it with the methods of objectivating science. The human sciences are essentially hermeneutic enterprises; when we forget this, or seek to soar above it on the wings of methodology, the results are at best bogus and more often dangerous.[3]

Those philosophers we have grouped as systematic have a different attitude toward the continuation of theoretical philosophy. Davidson, on one interpretation of his work, would see it transformed into a unified theory of speech and action; Dummett into a theory of meaning that is a theory of understanding natural languages; Apel into a transcendental pragmatics of communication; Putnam, on one interpretation, into a theory of rationality; and Habermas into a reconstruction of the various species competences that together comprise rationality. In quite different ways, these might all be read as continuations-through-transformation of theoretical philosophy, in a post-Kantian sense to be sure. As to the role of the human sciences in these undertakings, the views are quite mixed and we shall not attempt to summarize them here. Habermas's position is worth noting, however, since he alone proposes a transformation of theoretical philosophy *into* a peculiar form of mixed discourse — reconstructive science — that is empirically based and hypothetical in character while remaining universalist in ambition. He also argues, against Foucault for instance, that the transformation of philosophy as critique can only be accomplished in conjunction with social *theory* of a certain form. Like the Marxian critique of ideology or the Freudian account of rationalization, the practice of disassembling pseudo-objectivities requires, in his view, a general theoretical background.

This hasty tour through the maze of contemporary controversy regarding the end of philosophy indicates that it turns on paradigmatically philosophical disagreements about familiar philosophical issues, such as the following:

Can the notion of argumentative reason be loosened up enough to incorporate the rhetorical and figurative aspects of philosophical discourse, while being kept tight enough to allow for its demarcation from, say, literature or nonargumentative forms of persuasion?

Does philosophy have a responsibility to develop a nonredundant theory of truth? What are the relationships between truth and meaning? truth and reason?

Is there today any viable distinction between theoretical and practical philosophy? Can we make sense of continuing-through-transforming one or the other or both? If so, what role can the human sciences play in this transformation?

What remains of the notion of philosophical critique? Can it be replaced by genealogy? deconstruction? ideology critique? philosophical historiography?

Can the hermeneutic conception of philosophical self-understanding as rooted in and oriented to practice be sustained against the aestheticization of discourse about the self? What role do the arts and sciences play in this project of self-understanding?

Such eminently philosophical questions are central to the fate of philosophy "after Philosophy."

One of the essays included in this volume is an original contribution (Taylor); two have not appeared previously in English (Blumenberg, Habermas); and two have been retranslated for this volume (Apel, Gadamer). Several others, while previously available, have not yet had the wide circulation they deserve.

The editors would like to thank the numerous colleagues and friends who commented on earlier drafts of the introductions to the essays, and Robert Wallace for also translating the essay by Blumenberg. Though all three editors actively collaborated on each introduction, Kenneth Baynes assumed primary responsibility for those on Rorty, Derrida, Putnam, Apel, Gadamer, Ricoeur, and Taylor; James Bohman for those on Lyotard, Foucault, Davidson, Dummett, Habermas, MacIntyre, and Blumenberg; and Thomas McCarthy for the general introduction.

Notes

1. Davidson's thought has been subject to somewhat different interpretations by, for instance, Richard Rorty on the one hand and British philosophers like Gareth Evans and John McDowell on the other. See, for example, the discussion by Frederick Stoutland cited in the suggested readings for Davidson. It has also been argued that Davidson's present view of his program is quite different from the view he advanced earlier in "Truth and Meaning" (1967). Without claiming to have resolved such questions of interpretation, we have simply decided to represent the views of "Davidson I" in this volume — whether or not there is a "Davidson II."

2. Apel does make one important exception to the principle of fallibilism: some pragmatic presuppositions, he argues in a transcendental vein, are unavoidable presuppositions of critical and argumentative discourse. Thus philosophical doubt only makes sense within a pragmatic framework that is itself beyond doubt.

3. Ricoeur is something of an exception to this, as he allows for an interplay between hermeneutic and objectifying approaches to the social world and sees both involved in such critical enterprises as Freudian psychoanalysis. In fact, he insists that the continuation of the philosophy of reflection by other means — the means of hermeneutic phenomenology — must remain in constant "dialogue" with the human sciences.

I

The End of Philosophy

1

Richard Rorty

Introduction

In *Philosophy and the Mirror of Nature* (1979) Richard Rorty argued that the Western philosophical tradition, at least since the seventeenth century, has been seduced by the metaphor that the mind mirrors the world. This metaphor, in turn, has inspired the view that philosophers, as those who investigate the structure of mind or the conditions of knowledge, stand in the privileged position not only of assessing the accuracy of our mental representations but also of assigning to the various kinds of representations (scientific, moral, aesthetic) their respective cultural and social importance. That is, the task of the philosopher is not only to determine whether our theories of discourses are true but also to define the proper relation between discourses about the True, the Good, and the Beautiful. Further, Rorty argued, despite important variations and more or less successful (though never completely successful) attempts to escape that metaphor, this conception continues to underlie not only "transcendental philosophy" from Kant to Apel but also "rational psychology" from Descartes to Fodor and "naturalized epistemology" from Hume to Quine. In one way or another these projects all attempt to identify invariant rules governing any recognized scientific ("normal") discourse or to single out one form of discourse (for example, physics) as paradigmatic for all in the hope that in this way agreement (and hence, rationality) could be secured in the future. As Rorty puts it, they all share "the urge to see social practices of justification as more than just such practices" (*Philosophy and the Mirror of Nature,* 390).

Rorty's rejection of this conception of philosophy involves both internal criticisms of its failure to fulfill its own claims and an attempt to evoke an alternative model that he refers to variously as "pragmatism," "hermeneutics," and "edifying discourse." Rather than the reconstruction of transcultural and ahistorical rules under which rational consensus might be achieved, Rorty calls for the proliferation of new forms of discourse (386); instead of "accurate representation," he speaks of "the successful accomplishment of a practice" (319); in place of the professional philosopher-king, he offers the "informed dilettante" (317); and instead of the quest for Truth, he regards the search for new forms of self-description as our most important task (359). Postphilosophical, pragmatist philosophers no longer strive to transcend the limitations of convention and contingency by seeking "natural starting points" of thought prior to all cultural traditions. Recognizing that language and knowledge are tools for coping with reality and that categories and criteria are always relative to purposes and interests, they practice a kind of culture criticism — comparing, contrasting, weighing, and integrating the multifarious vocabularies of different epochs, cultures, and practices in search of new and "better" ways of talking and acting. They see the Platonic tradition as "having outlived its usefulness"; they realize that no appeal to intuition or reference is going to get us off the "literary-historical-anthropological-political merry-go-round"; and thus they are aware that any new vocabulary that might arise from their activity is not the result of "rigorous arguments" — for there are no invariant criteria according to which such arguments might proceed: "Criteria are temporary resting places constructed for utilitarian ends."

Rorty's pragmatist philosophers no longer see themselves as a secular priesthood or community of superscientists. Operating in zones where the absence of a neutral vocabulary and of an agreement on criteria makes scientific argument impossible, where reflective rather than determinate judgment is called for, they are a species of literary intellectual who seek not agreement in propositions but the creation of new vocabularies.

Thus, the vision Rorty holds out for a "postphilosophic culture" is one of creative inquiry freed from the bad faith evidenced in the search for ultimate foundations or final justification, a "conversation" from which no one is excluded and in which no one, especially not the philosopher, holds a privileged position. The sole aim would be to keep the conversation going, or, as he puts it, "to let a hundred flowers bloom."

The present selection provides one of Rorty's most succinct statements of his version of pragmatism. At the same time it contains a reply to recent critics, especially advocates of the "new theory of reference" or "referential semantics." He divides his critics into two groups — "technical realists" (Kripke, Putnam, and Dummett) and "intuitive realists" (Nagel, Cavell, and Stroud). "Technical realists" are those who believe that recent developments in the philosophy of language can be used to resolve traditional philosophical disputes. Putnam's use of referential semantics to refute radical skepticism and Dummett's rejection of metaphysical realism by way of a critique of bivalence are examples. Rorty suggests that, in both cases, at crucial points in their exposition (the distinction between natural and nominal kinds in referential semantics; the distinction between those statements for which bivalence obtains and those for which it does not in Dummett), argument gives way to intuition. "Intuitive realists," however, defend an equally unacceptable position. Certainly we have various deep-seated intuitions about the world (for example, the difference between I-Thou and I-It experiences); the question for Rorty, however, is whether we should regard such intuitions as insights into the mystery of the world or as products of our social conventions and practices. Rorty sees in this question the still more basic question of what philosophy is (or should be): Should philosophy attempt to clarify and preserve some of our deepest intuitions even when they come into conflict with each other, or should it seek to engender new "self-descriptions" freed from the metaphysical impasses of our past? Of course, whether these are the principal options available to philosophy depends, at least in part, on how well Rorty has characterized the present scene, including the various perspectives presented in this volume.

Suggested Readings

Bernstein, Richard. "Philosophy in the Conversation of Mankind," *Review of Metaphysics* 33 (1980), 745–776.

Bernstein, Richard. *Beyond Objectivism and Relativism.* Philadelphia: University of Pennsylvania Press, 1983.

Brodsky, Gary. "Rorty's Interpretation of Pragmatism," *Transactions of the Charles S. Peirce Society* 18 (1982), 311–337.

Caputo, John D. "The Thought of Being and the Conversation of Mankind: The Case of Heidegger and Rorty," *Review of Metaphysics* 36 (1983), 661–685.

Edel, Abraham. "A Missing Dimension in Rorty's Use of Pragmatism," *Transactions of the Charles S. Peirce Society* 21 (1985), 21–38.

Hacking, Ian. "Is the End in Sight for Epistemology?" *Journal of Philosophy* 77 (1980), 579–588.

Hollinger, Robert, ed. *Hermeneutics and Praxis.* Notre Dame: University of Notre Dame Press, 1985.

Kim, Jaegwon. "Rorty on the Possibility of Philosophy," *Journal of Philosophy* 77 (1980), 588–597.

MacIntyre, Alasdair. "Philosophy, the 'Other' Disciplines, and Their Histories," *Soundings* 65 (1982), 127–145.

Rorty, Richard. "Realism and Reference," *The Monist* 59 (1976), 321–340.

Rorty, Richard. *Philosophy and the Mirror of Nature.* Princeton: Princeton University Press, 1979.

Rorty, Richard. "Transcendental Arguments, Self-Reference and Pragmatism," in *Transcendental Arguments and Science,* ed. P. Bieri, R. P. Horstmann, and I. Krüger, 77–103. Dordrecht: Reidel, 1979.

Rorty, Richard. "A Reply to Dreyfus and Taylor," *Review of Metaphysics* 34 (1980), 39–46.

Rorty, Richard. *Consequences of Pragmatism.* Minneapolis: University of Minnesota Press, 1982.

Rorty, Richard. "Contemporary Philosophy of Mind," *Synthese* 53 (1982), 323–348.

Rorty, Richard. "Postmodern Bourgeois Liberalism," *Journal of Philosophy* 80 (1983), 583–589.

Rorty, Richard. "The Historiography of Philosophy," in *Philosophy in History,* ed. R. Rorty, J. B. Schneewind, and Q. Skinner, 49–75. Cambridge: Cambridge University Press, 1984.

Rorty, Richard. "Habermas and Lyotard on Postmodernity," in *Habermas on Modernity,* ed. R. Bernstein, 161–176. Cambridge, Massachusetts: MIT Press, 1985.

Rorty, Richard. "Solidarity and Objectivity," in *Post-Analytic Philosophy*, ed. J. Rajchman and C. West, 3–19. New York: Columbia University Press, 1985.

Rorty, Richard, ed. *The Linguistic Turn*. Chicago: University of Chicago Press, 1967.

Ross, Stephen D. "Skepticism, Holism and Inexhaustibility," *Review of Metaphysics* 35 (1982), 529–556.

Schwartz, Robert. "Review of *Philosophy and the Mirror of Nature*," *Journal of Philosophy* 80 (1983), 51–67.

Sleeper, R. W. "Rorty's Pragmatism," *Transactions of the Charles S. Peirce Society* 21 (1985), 9–20.

Sosa, Ernest. "Nature Unmirrored, Epistemology Naturalized," *Synthese* 55 (1983), 49–72.

Warnke, Georgia, "Hermeneutics and the Social Sciences: A Gadamerian Critique of Rorty," *Inquiry* 28 (1985), 339–357.

Pragmatism and Philosophy

Richard Rorty

Platonists, Positivists, and Pragmatists

A pragmatist theory says that truth is not the sort of thing one should expect to have a philosophically interesting theory about. For pragmatists, "truth" is just the name of a property that all true statements share. It is what is common to "Bacon did not write Shakespeare," "It rained yesterday," "E equals mc^2," "Love is better than hate," "*The Allegory of Painting* was Vermeer's best work," "2 plus 2 is 4," and "There are nondenumerable infinities." Pragmatists doubt that there is much to be said about this common feature. They doubt this for the same reason they doubt that there is much to be said about the common feature shared by such morally praiseworthy actions as Susan leaving her husband, America joining the war against the Nazis, America pulling out of Vietnam, Socrates not escaping from jail, Roger picking up litter from the trail, and the suicide of the Jews at Masada. They see certain acts as good ones to perform, under the circumstances, but doubt that there is anything general and useful to say about what makes them all good. The assertion of a given sentence — or the adoption of a disposition to assert the sentence, the conscious acquisition of a belief — is a justifiable, praiseworthy act in certain circumstances. But, *a fortiori*, it is not likely that there is something general and useful to be said about what makes all such actions good — about the common feature of all the sentences that one should acquire a disposition to assert.

Pragmatists think that the history of attempts to isolate the True or the Good, or to define the word "true" or "good," supports their suspicion that there is no interesting work to be done in this area. It might, of course, have turned out otherwise. People have, oddly enough, found something interesting to say about the essence of Force and the definition of "number." They might have found something interesting to say about the essence of Truth. But in fact they haven't. The history of attempts to do so, and of criticisms of such attempts, is roughly coextensive with the history of that literary genre we call "philosophy" — a genre founded by Plato. So pragmatists see the Platonic tradition as having outlived its usefulness. This does not mean that they have a new, non-Platonic set of answers to Platonic questions to offer, but rather that they do not think we should ask those questions anymore. When they suggest that we not ask questions about the nature of Truth and Goodness, they do not invoke a theory about the nature of reality or knowledge or man which says that "there is no such thing" as Truth or Goodness. Nor do they have a "relativistic" or "subjectivist" theory of Truth or Goodness. They would simply like to change the subject. They are in a position analogous to that of secularists who urge that research concerning the Nature, or the Will, of God does not get us anywhere. Such secularists are not saying that God does not exist, exactly; they feel unclear about what it would mean to affirm His existence, and thus about the point of denying it. Nor do they have some special, funny, heretical view about God. They just doubt that the vocabulary of theology is one we ought to be using. Similarly, pragmatists keep trying to find ways of making antiphilosophical points in nonphilosophical language. For they face a dilemma: If their language is too unphilosophical, too "literary," they will be accused of changing the subject; if it is too philosophical it will embody Platonic assumptions that will make it impossible for the pragmatist to state the conclusion he wants to reach.

All this is complicated by the fact that "philosophy," like "truth" and "goodness," is ambiguous. Uncapitalized, "truth" and "goodness" name properties of sentences, or of actions and situations. Capitalized, they are the proper names of objects — goals or standards that can be loved with all one's heart and soul and mind, objects of ultimate concern. Similarly, "philosophy" can mean simply what Sellars calls "an attempt to see how things, in the broadest possible sense of the term, hang together, in the broadest possible sense of the term." Pericles, for example, was using this sense of the term when he praised the Athenians for "philosophizing without unmanliness" (*philosōphein aneu malakias*). In this sense, Blake is as much a philosopher as Fichte, Henry Adams more of a philosopher than Frege. No one would be dubious about philosophy, taken in this sense. But the word can also denote something more specialized, and very dubious indeed. In this second sense, it can mean following Plato's and Kant's lead, asking questions about the nature of certain normative notions (for instance, "truth," "rationality," "goodness") in the hope of better obeying such norms. The idea is to believe more truths or do more good or be more rational by knowing more about Truth or Goodness or Rationality. I shall capitalize the term "philosophy" when used in this second sense, in order to help make the point that Philosophy, Truth, Goodness, and Rationality are interlocked Platonic notions. Pragmatists are saying that the best hope for philosophy is not to practice Philosophy. They think it will not help to say something true to think about Truth, nor will it help to act well to think about Goodness, nor will it help to be rational to think about Rationality.

So far, however, my description of pragmatism has left an important distinction out of account. Within Philosophy there has been a traditional difference of opinion about the Nature of Truth, a battle between (as Plato put it) the gods and the giants. On the one hand there have been Philosophers like Plato himself who were otherworldly, possessed of a larger hope. They urged that human beings were entitled to self-respect only because they had one foot beyond space and time. On the other hand — especially since Galileo showed how spatio-temporal events could be brought under the sort of elegant mathematical law that Plato suspected might hold only for another world — there have been Philosophers (for instance, Hobbes, Marx) who insisted that space and time make up the only Reality there is, and that Truth is Correspondence to *that* Reality. In the nineteenth century this opposition crystallized into one between "the transcendental philosophy" and "the empirical philosophy," between the "Platonists" and the "positivists." Such terms were, even then, hopelessly vague, but every intellectual knew roughly where he stood in relation to the two movements. To be on the transcendental side was to think that natural science was not the last word — that there was more Truth to be found. To be on the empirical side was to think that natural science — facts about how spatio-temporal things worked — was all the Truth there was. To side with Hegel or Green was to think that some normative sentences about rationality and goodness corresponded to something real, but invisible to natural science. To side with Comte or Mach was to think that such sentences either "reduced" to sentences about spatio-temporal events or were not subjects for serious reflection.

It is important to realize that the empirical philosophers — the positivists — were still doing Philosophy. The Platonic presupposition that unites the gods and the giants, Plato with Democritus, Kant with Mill, Husserl with Russell, is that what the vulgar call "truth" — the assemblage of true statements — should be thought of as divided into a lower and an upper division, the division between (in Plato's terms) mere opinion and genuine knowledge. It is the work of the Philosopher to establish an invidious distinction between such statements "It rained yesterday" and "Men should try to be just in their dealings." For Plato the former sort of statement was second-rate, mere *pistis* or *doxa*. The latter, if perhaps not yet *epistēmē*, was at least a plausible candidate. For the positivist tradition that runs from Hobbes to Carnap, the former sentence was a paradigm of what Truth looked like, but the latter was either a prediction about the causal effects of certain events or an "expression of emotion." What the transcendental philosophers saw as the spiritual, the empirical philosophers saw as the emotional. What the empirical philosophers saw as the achievements of natural science in discovering the nature of Reality, the transcendental philosophers saw as banausic, as true but irrelevant to Truth.

Pragmatism cuts across this transcendental/empirical distinction by questioning the common presupposition that there is an invidious distinction to be drawn between kinds of truths. For the pragmatist, true sentences are not true because they correspond to reality, and so there is no need to worry what sort of reality, if any, a given sentence corresponds to — no need to worry about what "makes" it true. (Just as there is no need to worry, once one has determined what one should do, whether there is something in Reality which makes that act the Right one to perform.) So the pragmatist sees no need to worry about whether Plato or Kant was right in thinking that something nonspatio-temporal made moral judgments true, nor about whether the absence of such a thing means that such judgments are "merely expressions of emotion" or "merely conventional" or "merely subjective."

This insouciance brings down the scorn of both kinds of Philosophers upon the pragmatist. The Platonist sees the pragmatist as merely a fuzzy-minded sort of positivist. The positivist sees him as lending aid and comfort to Platonism by leveling down the distinction between Objective Truth — the sort of true sentence attained by "the scientific method" — and sentences that lack the precious "correspondence of reality" which only that method can induce. Both join in thinking the pragmatist is not really a philosopher, on the ground that he is not a Philosopher. The pragmatist tries to defend himself by saying that one can be a philosopher precisely by being anti-Philosophical, that the best way to make things hang together is to step back from the issues between Platonists and positivists, and thereby give up the presuppositions of Philosophy.

One difficulty the pragmatist has in making his position clear, therefore, is that he must struggle with the positivist for the position of radical anti-Platonist. He wants to attack Plato with different weapons from those of the positivist, but at first glance he looks like just another variety of positivist. He shares with the positivist the Baconian and Hobbesian notion that knowledge is power, a tool for coping with reality. But he carries this Baconian point through to its extreme, as the positivist does not. He drops the notion of truth as correspondence with reality altogether, and says that modern science does not enable us to cope because it corresponds, it just plain enables us to cope. His argument for the view is that several hundred years of effort have failed to make interesting sense of the notion of "correspondence" (either of thoughts of things or of words to things). The pragmatist takes the moral of this discouraging history to be that "true sentences work because they correspond to the way things are" is no more illuminating than "it is right because it fulfills the Moral Law." Both remarks, in the pragmatist's eyes, are empty metaphysical compliments — harmless as rhetorical pats on the back to the successful inquirer or agent, but troublesome if taken seriously and "clarified" philosophically.

Pragmatism and Contemporary Philosophy

Among contemporary philosophers, pragmatism is usually regarded as an outdated philosophical movement — one that flourished in the early years of this century in a rather provincial atmosphere and has now been either refuted or *aufgehoben*. The great pragmatists — James and Dewey — are occasionally praised for their criticisms of Platonism (for example, Dewey on traditional conceptions of education, James on metaphysical pseudoproblems). But their anti-Platonism is thought by analytic philosophers to have been insufficiently rigorous and by nonanalytic philosophers to have been insufficiently radical. For the tradition that originates in logical positivism the pragmatists' attacks on "transcendental," quasi-Platonist philosophy need to be sharpened by more careful and detailed analysis of such notions as "meaning" and "truth."[1] For the anti-Philosophical tradition in contemporary French and German thought that takes its point of departure from Nietzsche's criticism of both strands in nineteenth-century Philosophical thought — positivistic as well as transcendental — the American pragmatists are thinkers who never really broke out of positivism and thus never really broke with Philosophy.[2]

I do not think that either of these dismissive attitudes is justified. On the account of recent analytic philosophy that I offered in *Philosophy and the Mirror of Nature*,[3] the history of that movement has been marked by a gradual "pragmaticization" of the original tenets of logical positivism. On the account of recent "Continental" philosophy that I hope to offer in a book I am writing on Heidegger,[4] James and Nietzsche make parallel criticisms of nineteenth-century thought. Further, James's version is preferable, for it avoids the "metaphysical" elements in Nietzsche that Heidegger criticizes, and, for that matter, the "metaphysical" elements in Heidegger that Derrida criticizes. On my view, James and Dewey were not only waiting at the end of the dialectical road that analytic philosophy traveled, but are waiting at the end of the road that, for example, Foucault and Deleuze are currently traveling.

I think that analytic philosophy culminates in Quine, the later Wittgenstein, Sellars, and Davidson — which is to say that it transcends and cancels itself. These thinkers successfully, and rightly, blur the positivist distinctions between the semantic and the pragmatic, the analytic and the synthetic, the linguistic and the empirical, theory and observation. Davidson's attack on the scheme/content distinction,[5] in particular, summarizes and synthesizes Wittgenstein's mockery of his own *Tractatus*, Quine's criticisms of Carnap, and Sellar's attack on the empiricist "Myth of the Given." Davidson's holism and coherentism shows how language looks once we get rid of the central presupposition of Philosophy: that true sentences divide into an upper and a lower division — the sentences that correspond to something and those that are "true" only by courtesy or convention.

This Davidsonian way of looking at language lets us avoid hypostatizing Language in the way in which the Cartesian epistemological tradition, and particularly the idealist tradition that built upon Kant, hypostatized Thought. For it lets us see language not as a *tertium quid* between Subject and Object, nor as a medium in which we try to form pictures of reality, but as part of the behavior of human beings. On this view, the activity of uttering sentences is one of the things people do in order to cope with their environment. The Deweyan notion of language as tool rather than picture is right as far as it goes. But we must be careful *not* to phrase this analogy so as to suggest that one can separate the tool, Language, from its users and inquire as to its "adequacy" to achieve our purposes. The latter suggestion presupposes that there is some way of breaking out of language in order to compare it with something else. But there is no way to think about either the world or our purposes except by using our language. One can use language to criticize and enlarge itself, as one can exercise one's body to develop and strengthen and enlarge it, but one cannot see language-as-a-whole in relation to something else to which it applies, or for which it is a means to an end. The arts and the sciences, and philosophy as their self-reflection and integration, constitute such a process of enlargement and strengthening. But Philosophy, the attempt to say "how language relates to the world" by saying what *makes* certain sentences true, or certain actions or attitudes good or rational, is, on this view, impossible.

It is the impossible attempt to step outside our skins — the traditions, linguistic and other, within which we do our thinking and self-criticism — and compare ourselves with something absolute. This Platonic urge to escape from the finitude of one's time and place, the "merely conventional" and contingent aspects of one's life, is responsible for the original Platonic distinction between two kinds of true sentence. By attacking this latter distinction, the holistic "pragmaticizing" strain in analytic philosophy has helped us see how the metaphysical urge — common to fuzzy Whiteheadians and razor-sharp "scientific realists" — works. It has helped us be skeptical about the idea that some particular science (say physics) or some particular literary genre (say Romantic poetry, or transcendental philosophy) gives us that species of true sentence which is not *just* a true sentence, but rather a piece of Truth itself. Such sentences may be very useful indeed, but there is not going to be a Philosophical explanation of this utility. That explanation, like the original justification of the assertion of the sentence, will be a parochial matter — a comparison of the sentence with alternative sentences formulated in the same or in other vocabularies. But such comparisons are the business of, for example, the physicist or the poet, or perhaps of the philosopher — not of the Philosopher, the outside expert on the utility, or function, or metaphysical status of Language or of Thought.

The Wittgenstein-Sellars-Quine-Davidson attack on distinctions between classes of sentences is the special contribution of analytic philosophy to the anti-Platonist insistence on the ubiquity of language. This insistence characterizes both pragmatism and recent "Continental" philosophizing. Here are some examples:

Man makes the word, and the word means nothing which the man has not made it mean, and that only to some other man. But since man can think only by means of words or other external symbols, these might turn around and say: You mean nothing which we have not taught you, and then only so far as you address some word as the interpretant of your thought . . . . the word or sign which man uses is the man himself . . . . Thus my language is the sum-total of myself; for the man is the thought. (Peirce)[6]

Peirce goes very far in the direction that I have called the de-construction of the transcendental signified, which, at one time or another, would place a reassuring end to the reference from sign to sign. (Derrida)[7]

. . . *psychological nominalism*, according to which *all* awareness of sorts, resemblances, facts, etc., in short all awareness of abstract entities — indeed, all awareness even of particulars — is a linguistic affair. (Sellars)[8]

It is only in language that one can mean something by something. (Wittgenstein)[9]

Human experience is essentially linguistic. (Gadamer)[10]

. . . man is in the process of perishing as the being of language continues to shine ever brighter upon our horizon. (Foucault)[11]

Speaking about language turns language almost inevitably into an object . . . and then its reality vanishes. (Heidegger)[12]

This chorus should not, however, lead us to think that something new and exciting has recently been discovered about Language — for instance, that it is more prevalent than had previously been thought. The authors cited are making only *negative* points. They are saying that attempts to get back behind language to something that "grounds" it, or that it "expresses," or to which it might hope to be "adequate," have not worked. The ubiquity of language is a matter of language moving into the vacancies left by the failure of all the various candidates for the position of "natural starting points" of thought, starting points that are prior to and independent of the way some culture speaks or spoke. (Candidates for such starting points include clear and distinct ideas, sense data, categories of the pure understanding, structures of prelinguistic consciousness, and the like.) Peirce and Sellars and Wittgenstein are saying that the regress of interpretation cannot be cut off by the sort of "intuition" that Cartesian epistemology took for granted. Gadamer and Derrida are saying that our culture has been dominated by the notion of a "transcendental signified" that, by cutting off this regress, would bring us out from contingency and convention and into the Truth. Foucault is saying that we are gradually losing our grip on the "metaphysical comfort" that that Philosophical tradition provided — its picture of Man as having a "double" (the soul, the Noumenal Self) who uses Reality's own language rather than merely the vocabulary of a time and a place. Finally, Heidegger is cautioning that if we try to make Language into a new topic of Philosophical inquiry we shall simply recreate the hopeless old Philosophical puzzles that we used to raise about Being or Thought.

This last point amounts to saying that what Gustav Bergmann called "the linguistic turn" should not be seen as the logical positivists saw it — as enabling us to ask Kantian questions without having to trespass on the psychologists' turf by talking, with Kant, about "experience" or "consciousness." That was, indeed, the initial motive for the "turn,"[13] but (thanks to the holism and pragmatism of the authors I have cited) analytic philosophy of language was able to transcend this Kantian motive and adopt a naturalistic, behavioristic attitude toward language. This attitude has led it to the same outcome as the "Continental" reaction against the traditional Kantian problematic, the reaction found in Nietzsche and Heidegger. This convergence shows that the traditional association of analytic philosophy with tough-minded positivism and of "Continental" philosophy with tender-minded Platonism is *completely* misleading. The pragmaticization of analytical philosophy gratified the logical positivists' hopes, but not in the fashion that they had envisaged. It did not find a way for Philosophy to become "scientific," but rather found a way of setting Philosophy to one side. This postpositivistic kind of analytic philosophy thus comes to resemble the Nietzsche-Heidegger-Derrida tradition in beginning with criticism of Platonism and ending in criticism of Philosophy as such. Both traditions are now in a period of doubt about their own status. Both are living between a repudiated past and a dimly seen post-Philosophical future.

The Realist Reaction (I): Technical Realism

Before going on to speculate about what a post-Philosophical culture might look like, I should make clear that my description of the current Philosophical scene has been deliberately oversimplified. So far I have ignored the antipragmatist backlash. The picture I have been sketching shows how things looked about ten years ago — or, at least, how they looked to an optimistic pragmatist. In the subsequent decade there has been, on both sides of the Channel, a reaction in favor of "realism" — a term that has come to be synonymous with "antipragmatism." This reaction has had three distinct motives: (1) the view that recent, technical developments in the philosophy of language have raised doubt about traditional pragmatist criticisms of the "correspondence theory of truth," or, at least, have made it necessary for the pragmatist to answer some hard, technical questions before proceeding further; (2) the sense that the "depth," the human significance, of the traditional textbook "problems of philosophy" has been underestimated, that pragmatists have lumped real problems together with pseudoproblems in a feckless orgy of "dissolution"; (3) the sense that something important would be lost if Philosophy as an autonomous discipline, as a *Fach*, were to fade from the cultural scene (in the way in which theology has faded).

This third motive — the fear of what would happen if there were merely philosophy, but no Philosophy — is not simply the defensive reaction of specialists threatened with unemployment. It is a conviction that a culture without Philosophy would be "irrationalist" — that a precious human capacity would lie unused, or a central human virtue no longer be exemplified. This motive is shared by many philosophy professors in France and Germany and by many analytic philosophers in Britain and America. The former would like something to do that is not merely the endless, repetitive, literary-historical "deconstruction" of the "Western metaphysics of presence" that was Heidegger's legacy. The latter would like to recapture the spirit of the early logical positivists, the sense that philosophy is the accumulation of "results" by patient, rigorous, preferably co-operative work on precisely stated problems (the spirit characteristic of the younger, rather than of the older, Wittgenstein). So philosophy professors on the Continent are casting longing glances toward analytic philosophy — and particularly toward the "realist" analytic philosophers who take Philosophical problems seriously. Conversely, admirers of "Continental" philosophy (of Nietzsche, Heidegger, Derrida, Gadamer, Foucault) are more welcome in American and British departments of comparative literature and political science than in departments of philosophy. On both continents there is fear of Philosophy's losing its traditional claim to "scientific" status and of its relegation to "the merely literary."

I shall talk about this fear in some detail later, in connection with the prospects for a culture in which the science/literature distinction would no longer matter. But here I shall concentrate on the first and second motives I just listed. These are associated with two fairly distinct groups of people. The first motive is characteristic of philosophers of language such as Saul Kripke and Michael Dummett, the second with less specialized and more broadly ranging writers like Stanley Cavell and Thomas Nagel. I shall call those who turn Kripke's views on reference to the purposes of a realistic epistemology (such as Hartry Field, Richard Boyd, and, sometimes, Hilary Putnam) "technical realists." I shall call Cavell and Nagel (and others, such as Thompson Clarke and Barry Stroud) "intuitive realists." The latter object that the pragmatists' dissolutions of traditional problems are "verificationist": that is, pragmatists think our inability to say what would count as confirming or disconfirming a given solution to a problem is a reason for setting the problem aside. To take this view is, Nagel tells us, to fail to recognize that "unsolvable problems are not for that reason unreal."[14] Intuitive realists judge verificationism by its fruits, and argue that the pragmatist belief in the ubiquity of language leads to the inability to recognize that philosophical problems arise precisely where language is inadequate to the facts. "My realism about the subjective domain in all its forms," Nagel says, "implies a belief in the existence of facts beyond the reach of human concepts."[15]

Technical realists, by contrast, judge pragmatism wrong not because it leads to superficial dismissals of deep problems, but because it is based on a false, "verificationist" philosophy of language. They dislike "verificationism" not because of its metaphilosophical fruits, but because they see it as a misunderstanding of the relation between language and the world. On their view, Quine and Wittgenstein wrongly followed Frege in thinking that meaning — something determined by the intentions of the user of a word — determines reference, what the word picks out in the world. On the basis of the "new theory of reference" originated by Saul Kripke, they say, we can now construct a better, non-Fregean picture of word-world relationships. Whereas Frege, like Kant, thought of our concepts as carving up an undifferentiated manifold in accordance with our interests (a view that leads fairly directly to Sellars's "psychological nominalism" and a Goodman-like insouciance about ontology), Kripke sees the world as already divided not only into particulars but into natural kinds of particulars and even into essential and accidental features of those particulars and kinds. The question "Is 'X is ϕ' true?" is thus to be answered by discovering what — as a matter of physical fact, not of anybody's intentions — 'X' refers to and then discovering whether that particular or kind is ϕ. Only by such a "physicalistic" theory of reference, technical realists say, can the notion of "truth as correspondence to reality" be preserved. By contrast, the pragmatist answers this question by inquiring whether, all things (and especially our purposes in using the terms 'X' and 'ϕ') considered, X is ϕ' is a more useful belief to have than its contradictory, or than some belief expressed in different terms altogether. The pragmatist agrees that if one wants to preserve the notion of "correspondence with reality" then a physicalistic theory of reference is necessary — but he sees no point in preserving that notion. The pragmatist has no notion of truth that would enable him to make sense of the claim that if we achieved everything we ever hoped to achieve by making assertions we might still be making *false* assertions, failing to "correspond" to something.[16] As Putnam says,

The trouble is that for a strong antirealist [that is, a pragmatist] *truth* makes no sense except as an intra-theoretic notion. The antirealist can use truth intra-theoretically in the sense of a "redundancy theory" [that is, a theory according to which "*S* is true" means exactly, only, what "*S*" means] but he does not have the notion of truth and reference available extra-theoretically. But extension [reference] is tied to the notion of truth. The extension of a term is just what the term is *true of*. Rather than try to retain the notion of truth via an awkward operationalism, the antirealist should reject the notion of extension as he does the notion of truth (in any extra-theoretic sense). Like Dewey, he can fall back on a notion of 'warranted assertibility' instead of truth.[17]

The question that technical realism raises, then, is: Are there technical reasons, within the philosophy of language, for retaining or discarding this extratheoretic notion? Are there nonintuitive ways of deciding whether, as the pragmatist thinks, the question of what '*X*' refers to is a sociological matter, a question of how best to make sense of a community's linguistic behavior, or whether, as Hartry Field says, "one aspect of the sociological role of a term is the role that term has in the psychologies of different members of a linguistic community; another aspect, *irreducible to the first* [italics added], is what physical objects or physical property the term stands for."[18]

It is not clear, however, what these technical, nonintuitive ways might be. For it is not clear what data the philosophy of language must explain. The most frequently cited datum is that science *works, succeeds* — enables us to cure diseases, blow up cities, and the like. How, realists ask, would this be possible if some scientific statements did not correspond to the way things are in themselves? How, pragmatists rejoin, does *that* count as an explanation? What further specification of the "correspondence" relation can be given that will enable this explanation to be better than "dormitive power" (Molière's doctors' explanation of why opium puts people to sleep)? What, so to speak, corresponds to the microstructure of opium in this case? What is the microstructure of "corresponding"? The Tarskian apparatus of truth-conditions and satisfaction-relations does not fill the bill, because that apparatus is equally well adapted to physicalist "building-block" theories of reference like Field's and to coherentist, holistic, pragmatical theories like Davidson's. When realists like Field argue that Tarski's account of truth is merely a place holder, like Mendel's account of "gene," which requires physicalistic "reduction to non-semantical terms,"[19] pragmatists reply (with Stephen Leeds) that "true" (like "good" and unlike "gene") is not an explanatory notion.[20] (Or that, if it is, the structure of the explanations in which it is used needs to be spelled out.)

The search for technical grounds on which to argue the pragmatist-realist issue is sometimes ended artificially by the realist assuming that the pragmatist not only (as Putnam says) follows Dewey in "falling back on a notion of 'warranted assertibililty' *instead* of truth" but uses the latter notion to *analyze the meaning* of "true." Putnam is right that no such analysis will work. But the pragmatist, if he is wise, will not succumb to the temptation to fill the blank in

S is true if and only if S is assertible ———

with "at the end of inquiry" or "by the standards of our culture" or with anything else.[21] He will recognize the strength of Putnam's "naturalistic fallacy" argument: Just as nothing can fill the blank in

A is the best thing to do in circumstances C if and only

if ——— so, *a fortiori*, nothing will fill the blank in

Asserting S is the best thing to do in C if and only if ———.

If the pragmatist is advised that he must not confuse the *advisability of asserting* S with the *truth* of S, he will respond that the advice is question begging. The question is precisely whether "the true" is more than what William James defined it as: "the name of whatever proves itself to be good in the way of belief, and good, too, for definite, assignable reasons."[22] On James's view, "true" resembles "good" or "rational" in being a normative notion, a compliment paid to sentences that seem to be paying their way and that fit in with other sentences that are doing so. To think that Truth is "out there" is, on their view, on all fours with the Platonic view that The Good is "out there." To think that we are "irrationalist" insofar as it does not "gratify our souls to know/That though we perish, truth is so" is like thinking that we are "irrationalist" just insofar as it does not gratify our moral sense to think that The Moral Law shines resplendent over the noumenal world, regardless of the vicissitudes of spatio-temporal lives. For the pragmatist, the notion of "truth" as something "objective" is just a confusion between

(I) Most of the world is as it is whatever we think about it (that is, our beliefs have very limited causal efficacy)

and

(II) There is something out there in addition to the world called "the truth about the world" (what James sarcastically called "this tertium quid intermediate between the facts *per se*, on the one hand, and all knowledge of them, actual or potential, on the other").[23]

The pragmatist wholeheartedly assents to (I) — not as an article of metaphysical faith but simply as a belief that we have never had any reason to doubt — and cannot make sense of (II). When the realist tries to explain (II) with

(III) The truth about the world consists in a relation of "correspondence" between certain sentences (many of which, no doubt, have yet to be formulated) and the world itself

the pragmatist can only fall back on saying, once again, that many centuries of attempts to explain what "correspondence" is have failed, especially when it comes to explaining how the final vocabulary of future physics will somehow be Nature's Own — the one that, at long last, lets us formulate sentences that lock on to Nature's own way of thinking of Herself.

For these reasons the pragmatist does not think that, whatever else philosophy of language may do, it is going to come up with a definition of "true" that gets beyond James. He happily grants that it can do a lot of other things. For example, it can, following Tarski, show what it would be like to define a truth-predicate for a given language. The pragmatist can agree with Davidson that to define such a predicate — to develop a truth-theory for the sentences of English, for example — would be a good way, perhaps the only way, to exhibit a natural language as a learnable, recursive structure and thus to give a systematic theory of meaning for the language.[24] But he agrees with Davidson that such an exhibition is *all* that Tarski can give us, and all that can be milked out of Philosophical reflection on Truth.

Just as the pragmatist should not succumb to the temptation to "capture the intuitive content of our notion of truth" (including whatever it is in that notion that makes realism tempting), so he should not succumb to the temptation held out by Michael Dummett to take sides on the issue of "bivalence." Dummett (who has his own doubts about realism) has suggested that a lot of traditional issues in the area of the pragmatist-realist debate can be clarified by the technical apparatus of philosophy of language, along the following lines:

In a variety of different areas there arises a philosophical dispute of the same general character: the dispute for or against realism concerning statements within a given type of subject-matter, or, better, statements of a certain general type. [Dummett elsewhere lists moral statements, mathematical statements, statements about the past, and modal statements as examples of such types.] Such a dispute consists in an opposition between two points of view concerning the kind of meaning possessed by statements of the kind in question, and hence about the application to them of the notions of truth and falsity. For the realist, we have assigned a meaning to these statements in such a way that we know, for each statement, what has to be the case for it to be true . . . . The condition for the truth of a statement is not, in general, a condition we are capable of recognizing as obtaining whenever it obtains, or even one for which we have an effective procedure for determining whether it obtains or not. We have therefore succeeded in ascribing to our statements a meaning of such a kind that their truth or falsity is, in general, independent of whether we know, or have any means of knowing, what truth-value they have . . . .

Opposed to this realist account of statements in some given class is the anti-realist interpretation. According to this, the meanings of statements of the class in question are given to us, not in terms of the conditions under which these statements are true or false, conceived of as conditions which obtain or do not obtain independently of our knowledge or capacity for knowledge, but in terms of the conditions which we recognize as establishing the truth or falsity of statements of that class.[25]

"Bivalence" is the property of being either true or false, so Dummett thinks of a "realistic" view about a certain area (say, moral values, or possible worlds) as asserting bivalence for statements about such things. His way of formulating the realist-vs.-antirealist issue thus suggests that the pragmatist denies bivalence of all statements, the "extreme" realist asserts it for all statements, while the level-headed majority sensibly discriminate between the bivalent statements of, for instance, physics and the nonbivalent statements of, say, morals. "Bivalence" thus joins "ontological commitment" as a way of expressing old-fashioned metaphysical views in up-to-date semantical language. If the pragmatist is viewed as a quasi-idealist metaphysician who is ontologically committed only to ideas or sentences and does not believe that there is anything "out there" that makes any sort of statement true, then he will fit neatly into Dummett's scheme.

But, of course, this is not the pragmatist's picture of himself. He does not think of himself as *any* kind of a metaphysician, because he does not *understand* the notion of "there being——— out there" (except in the literal sense of 'out there' in which it means "at a position in space"). He does not find it helpful to explicate the Platonist's conviction about The Good or The Numbers by saying that the Platonist believes that "There is truth-or-falsity about———, regardless of the state of our knowledge or the availability of procedures for inquiry." The "is" in this sentence seems to him just as obscure as the "is" in "Truth is so." Confronted with the passage from Dummett cited above, the pragmatist wonders how one goes about telling one "kind of meaning" from another and what it would be like to have "intuitions" about the bivalence or nonbivalence of kinds of statements. He is a pragmatist just because he doesn't have such intuitions (or wants to get rid of whatever such intuitions he may have). When he asks himself, about a given statement S, whether he "knows what has to be the case for it to be true" or merely knows "the conditions that we recognize

as establishing the truth or falsity of statements of that class,"
he feels as helpless as when asked, "Are you really in love, or
merely inflamed by passion?" He is inclined to suspect that it
is not a very useful question, and that at any rate introspection
is not the way to answer it. But in the case of bivalence it is not
clear that there is another way. Dummett does not help us see
what to count as a good argument for asserting bivalence of,
say, moral or modal statements; he merely says that there are
some people who do assert this and some who don't, presumably having been born with different metaphysical tempera-
ments. If one is born without metaphysical views — or if,
having become pessimistic about the utility of Philosophy, one
is self-consciously attempting to eschew such views — then one
will feel that Dummett's reconstruction of the traditional issues
explicates the obscure with the equally obscure.

What I have said about Field and about Dummett is intended
to cast doubt on the "technical realist's" view that the pragmatist-realist issue should be fought out on some narrow,
clearly demarcated ground within the philosophy of language.
There is no such ground. This is not, to be sure, the fault of
philosophy of language, but of the pragmatist. He refuses to
take a stand — to provide an "analysis" of "S is true," for
example, or to either assert or deny bivalence. He refuses to
make a move in *any* of the games in which he is invited to take
part. The *only* point at which "referential semantics" or "bivalence" becomes of interest to him comes when somebody tries
to treat these notions as explanatory, as not *just* expressing
intuitions but as doing some work — explaining, for example,
"why science is so successful."[26] At this point the pragmatist
hauls out his bag of tried-and-true dialectical gambits.[27] He
proceeds to argue that there is no pragmatic difference, no
difference that makes a difference, between "it works because
it's true" and "it's true because it works" — any more than
between "it's pious because the gods love it" and "the gods love
it because it's pious." Alternatively, he argues that there is no
pragmatic difference between the nature of truth and the test
of truth and that the test of truth, of what statements to assert,
is (except maybe for a few perceptual statements) not "com-

parison with reality." All these gambits will be felt by the realist to be question begging, since the realist intuits that some differences can be real *without* making a difference, that sometimes the *ordo essendi* is *different* from the *ordo cognoscendi*, sometimes the nature of X is *not* our test for the presence of Xness. And so it goes.

What we should conclude, I think, is that technical realism collapses into intuitive realism — that the *only* debating point the realist has is his conviction that the raising of the good old metaphysical problems (are there *really* universals? are there *really* causally efficacious physical objects, or did we just *posit* them?) served some good purpose, brought something to light, was important. What the pragmatist wants to debate is just this point. He does not want to discuss necessary and sufficient conditions for a sentence being true, but precisely *whether* the practice that hopes to find a Philosophical way of isolating the essence of Truth has, in fact, paid off. So the issue between him and the intuitive realist is a matter of what to make of the history of that practice — what to make of the history of Philosophy. The real issue is about the place of Philosophy in Western philosophy, the place within the intellectual history of the West of the particular series of texts that raise the "deep" Philosophical problems that the realist wants to preserve.

The Realist Reaction (II): Intuitive Realism

What really needs debate between the pragmatist and the intuitive realist is *not* whether we have intuitions to the effect that "truth is more than assertibility" or "there is more to pains than brain states" or "there is a clash between modern physics and our sense of moral responsibility." *Of course* we have such intuitions. How could we escape having them? We have been educated within in intellectual tradition built around such claims — just as we used to be educated within an intellectual tradition built around such claims as "If God does not exist, everything is permitted," "Man's dignity consists in his link with a supernatural order," and "One must not mock holy things." But it begs the question between pragmatist and realist to say that we must find a philosophical view that "captures" such intuitions. The pragmatist is urging that we do our best to *stop having* such intuitions, that we develop a *new* intellectual tradition.

What strikes intuitive realists as offensive about this suggestion is that it seems as dishonest to suppress intuitions as it is to suppress experimental data. On their conception, philosophy (not merely Philosophy) requires one to do justice to *everybody's* intuitions. Just as social justice is what would be brought about by institutions whose existence could be justified to every citizen, so intellectual justice would be made possible by finding theses that everyone would, given sufficient time and dialectical ability, accept. This view of intellectual life presupposes either that, contrary to the prophets of the ubiquity of language cited above, language does *not* go all the way down or that, contrary to the appearances, all vocabularies are commensurable. The first alternative amounts to saying that some intuitions, at least, are *not* a function of the way one has been brought up to talk, of the texts and people one has encountered. The second amounts to saying that the intuitions built into the vocabularies of Homeric warriors, Buddhist sages, Enlightenment scientists, and contemporary French literary critics are not really as different as they seem — that there are common elements in each which Philosophy can isolate and use to formulate theses that it would be rational for all these people to accept, and problems which they all face.

The pragmatist, on the other hand, thinks that the quest for a universal human community will be self-defeating if it tries to preserve the elements of every intellectual tradition, all the "deep" intuitions everybody has ever had. It is not to be achieved by an attempt at commensuration, at a common vocabulary that isolates the common human essence of Achilles and the Buddha, Lavoisier and Derrida. Rather, it is to be reached, if at all, by acts of making rather than of finding — by poetic rather than Philosophical achievement. The culture that will transcend, and thus unite, East and West, or the Earthlings and the Galactics, is not likely to be one that does equal justice to each, but one that looks back on both with the amused condescension typical of later generations looking back at their ancestors. So the pragmatist's quarrel with the intuitive realist should be about the *status* of intuitions — about their *right* to be respected — as opposed to how particular intuitions might be "synthesized" or "explained away." To treat his opponent properly, the pragmatist must begin by admitting that the realistic intuitions in question are as deep and compelling as the realist says they are. But he should then try to change the subject by asking, "And what should we *do* about such intuitions — extirpate them, or find a vocabulary that does justice to them?

From the pragmatist point of view the claim that the issues that the nineteenth century enshrined in its textbooks as "the central problems of philosophy" are "deep" is simply the claim that you will not understand a certain period in the history of Europe unless you can get some idea of what it was like to be preoccupied by such questions. (Consider parallel claims about the "depth" of the problems about Patripassianism, Arianism, etc., discussed by certain Fathers of the Church.) The pragmatist is even willing to expand his range and say, with Heidegger, that you won't understand the West unless you understand what it was like to be bothered by the kinds of issues that bothered Plato. Intuitive realists, rather than "stepping back" in the historicist manner of Heidegger and Dewey, or the quasi-anthropological manner of Foucault, devote themselves to safeguarding the tradition, to making us even more deeply Western. The way in which they do this is illustrated by Clarke's and Cavell's attempt to see "the legacy of skepticism" not as a question about whether we can be sure we're not dreaming but as a question about what sort of being could ask itself such a question.[28] They use the existence of figures like Descartes as indications of something important about *human beings*, not just about the modern West.

The best illustration of this strategy is Nagel's way of updating Kant by bringing a whole series of apparently disparate problems under the rubric "Subjective-Objective," just as Kant brought a partially overlapping set of problems under the rubric "Conditioned-Unconditioned." Nagel echoes Kant in saying,

It may be true that some philosophical problems have no solution. I suspect that this is true of the deepest and oldest of them. They show us the limits of our understanding. In that case such insight as we can achieve depends on maintaining a strong grasp of the problem instead of abandoning it, and coming to understand the failure of each new attempt at a solution, and of earlier attempts. (This is why we study the works of philosophers like Plato and Berkeley, whose views are accepted by no one.) Unsolvable problems are not for that reason unreal.[29]

As an illustration of what Nagel has in mind, consider his example of the problem of "moral luck" — the fact that one can be morally praised or blamed only for what is under one's control, yet practically nothing is. As Nagel says,

The area of genuine agency, and therefore of legitimate moral judgment, seems to shrink under this scrutiny to an extensionless point. Everything seems to result from the combined influence of factors, antecedent and posterior to action, that are not within the agent's control.[30]

Nagel thinks that a typically shallow, verificationist "solution" to this problem is available. We can get such a solution (Hume's) by going into detail about what sorts of external factors we do and don't count as diminishing the moral worth of an action:

This compatibilist account of our moral judgments would leave room for the ordinary conditions of responsibility — the absence of coercion, ignorance, or involuntary movement — as part of the determination of what someone has done — but it is understood not to exclude the influence of a great deal that he has not done.[31]

But this relaxed, pragmatical, Humean attitude — the attitude that says that there is no deep truth about Freedom of the Will and that people are morally responsible for whatever their peers tend to hold them morally responsible for — fails to explain why there has been *thought* to be a problem here:

The only thing wrong with this solution is its failure to explain how skeptical problems arise. For they arise not from the imposition of an arbitrary external requirement, but from the nature of moral judgment itself. Something in the ordinary idea of what someone does must explain how it can seem necessary to subtract from it anything that merely happens — even though the ultimate consequence of such subtraction is that nothing remains.[32]

But this is not to say that we need a metaphysical account of the Nature of Freedom of the sort that Kant (at least in some passages) seems to give us. Rather,

in a sense the problem has no solution, because something in the idea of agency is incompatible with actions being events or people being things.[33]

Since there is, so to speak, nothing *else* for people to be but things, we are left with an intuition — one that shows us "the limits of our understanding," and thus of our language.

Contrast, now, Nagel's attitude toward "the nature of moral judgment" with Iris Murdoch's. The Kantian attempt to isolate an agent who is not a spatio-temporal thing is seen by Murdoch as an unfortunate and perverse turn that Western thought has taken. Within a certain post-Kantian tradition, she says,

Immense care is taken to picture the will as isolated. It is isolated from belief, from reason, from feeling, and is yet the essential center of the self.[34]

This existentialist conception of the agent as isolated will goes along, Murdoch says, with "a very powerful image" of man that she finds "alien and implausible" — one that is "a happy and fruitful marriage of Kantian liberalism with Wittgensteinian logic solemnized by Freud."[35] On Murdoch's view,

Existentialism, in both its Continental and its Anglo-Saxon versions, is an attempt to solve the problem without really facing it: to solve it by attributing to the individual an empty lonely freedom .... What it pictures is indeed the fearful solitude of the individual marooned upon a tiny island in the middle of a sea of scientific facts, and morality escaping from science only by a wild leap of will.[36]

Instead of reinforcing this picture (as Nagel and Sartre do), Murdoch wants to get behind Kantian notions of will, behind the Kantian formulation of an antithesis between determinism and responsibility, behind the Kantian distinction between the moral self and the empirical self. She wants to recapture the vocabulary of moral reflection that a sixteenth-century Christian believer inclined toward Platonism would have used: one in which "perfection" is a central element, in which assignment of moral responsibility is a rather incidental element, and in which the discovery of a self (one's own or another's) is the endless task of love.[37]

In contrasting Nagel and Murdoch, I am not trying (misleadingly) to enlist Murdoch as a fellow pragmatist nor (falsely) to accuse Nagel of blindness to the variety of moral consciousness that Murdoch represents. Rather, I want to illustrate the difference between taking a standard philosophical problem (or cluster of interrelated problems such as free will, selfhood, agency, and responsibility) and asking, on the one hand, "What is its essence? To what ineffable depths, what limit of language, does it lead us? What does it show us about *being human*?" and asking, on the other hand, "What sort of people would see these problems? What vocabulary, what image of man, would produce such problems? Why, insofar as we are gripped by these problems, do we see them as deep rather than as *reductiones ad absurdum* of a vocabulary? What does the persistence of such problems show us about *being twentieth-century Europeans*?" Nagel is certainly right, and splendidly lucid, about the way in which a set of ideas, illustrated best by Kant, shoves us toward the notion of something called "the subjective" — the personal point of view, what science doesn't catch, what no "stepping back" could catch, what forms a limit to the understanding. But how do we know whether to say, "So much the worse for the solubility of philosophical problems, for the reach of language, for our 'verificationist' impulses," or whether to say, "So much the worse for the Philosophical ideas that have led us to such an impasse"?

The same question arises about the other philosophical problems that Nagel brings under his "Subjective-Objective" rubric. The clash between "verificationist" and "realist" intuitions is perhaps best illustrated by Nagel's celebrated paper "What Is It Like to Be a Bat?" Nagel here appeals to our intuition that "there is something that it is like" to be a bat or a dog but nothing that it is like to be an atom or a brick, and says that this intuition is what contemporary Wittgensteinian, Rylean, anti-Cartesian philosophy of mind "fails to capture." The culmination of the latter philosophical movement is the cavalier attitude toward "raw feels" — for example, the sheer phenomenological qualitative ipseity of pain — suggested by Daniel Dennett:

I recommend giving up incorrigibility with regard to pain altogether, in fact giving up *all* "essential" features of pain, and letting pain states be whatever "natural kind" states the brain scientists find (if they ever do find any) that normally produce all the normal effects . . . . One of our intuitions about pain is that whether or not one is in pain is a brute fact, not a matter of decision to serve the convenience of the theorist. I recommend against trying to preserve that intuition, but if you disagree, whatever theory I produce, however predictive and elegant, will not be in your lights a theory of pain, but only a theory of what I illicitly choose to *call* pain. But if, as I have claimed, the intuitions we would have to honor were we to honor them all do not form a consistent set, there can be no true theory of pain, and so no computer or robot could instantiate the true theory of pain, which it would have to do to feel real pain . . . . The inability of a robot model to satisfy all our intuitive demands may be due not to any irredeemable mysteriousness about the phenomenon of pain, but to irredeemable incoherence in our ordinary concept of pain.[38]

Nagel is one of those who disagree with Dennett's recommendation. His antiverificationism comes out most strongly in the following passage:

. . . if things emerged from a spaceship which we could not be sure were machines or conscious beings, what we were wondering would have an answer even if the things were so different from anything we were familiar with that we could never discover it. It would depend on whether there was something it was like to be them, not on whether behavioral similarities warranted our saying so . . . .

I therefore seem to be drawn to a position more 'realistic' than Wittgenstein's. This may be because I am drawn to positions more realistic than Wittgenstein's about everything, not just the mental. I believe that the question about whether the things coming out of the spaceship are conscious *must* have an answer. Wittgenstein would presumably say that this assumption reflects a groundless confidence that a certain picture unambiguously determines its own application. That is the picture of something going on in their heads (or whatever they have in place of heads) that cannot be observed by dissection.

Whatever picture I may use to represent the idea, it does seem to me that I know what it means to ask whether there is something it is like to be them, and that the answer to that question is what determines whether they are conscious — not the possibility of extending mental ascriptions on evidence analogous to the human case. Conscious mental states are real states of something, whether they are mine or those of an alien creature. Perhaps Wittgenstein's view can accommodate this intuition, but I do not at the moment see how.[39]

Wittgenstein certainly *cannot* accommodate this intuition. The question is whether he should be asked to: whether we should abandon the pragmatical "verificationist" intuition that "every difference must *make* a difference" (expressed by Wittgenstein in the remark "A wheel that can be turned though nothing else moves with it, is not part of the mechanism"),[40] or instead abandon Nagel's intuition about consciousness. We certainly *have* both intuitions. For Nagel, their compresence shows that the limit of understanding has been reached, that an ultimate depth has been plumbed — just as the discovery of an antinomy indicated to Kant that something transcendental had been encountered. For Wittgenstein, it merely shows that the Cartesian tradition has sketched a compelling picture, a picture that "held us captive. And we could not get outside it, for it lay in our language and language seemed to repeat it to us inexorably."[41]

I said at the beginning of this section that there were two alternative ways in which the intuitive realist might respond to the pragmatist's suggestion that some intuitions should be deliberately repressed. He might say either that language does not go all the way down — that there is a kind of awareness of facts that is not expressible in language and that no argument could render dubious — or, more mildly, that there is a core language that is common to all traditions and that needs to be isolated. In a confrontation with Murdoch one can imagine Nagel making the second claim — arguing that even the kind of moral discourse that Murdoch recommends must wind up with the same conception of "the isolated will" as Kantian moral discourse. But in confrontation with Dennett's attempt to weed out our intuitions Nagel must make the first claim. He has to go all the way and deny that our knowledge is limited by the language we speak. He says as much in the following passage:

If anyone is inclined to deny that we can believe in the existence of facts like this whose exact nature we cannot possibly conceive, he should reflect that in contemplating the bats we are in much the same position that intelligent bats or Martians would occupy if they tried to form a conception of what it was like to be us. The structure of their own minds might make it impossible for them to succeed, but we know they would be wrong to conclude that there is not anything precise that it is like to be us . . . . We know they would be wrong to draw such a skeptical conclusion because we know what it is like to be us. And we know that while it includes an enormous amount of variation and complexity, and *while we do not possess the vocabulary to describe it adequately*, its subjective character is highly specific, and in some respects describable in terms that can be understood only by creatures like us [italics added].[42]

Here we hit a bedrock metaphilosophical issue: Can one ever appeal to nonlinguistic knowledge in philosophical argument? This is the question of whether a dialectical impasse is the mark of philosophical depth or of a bad language, one that needs to be replaced with one that will not lead to such impasses. *That* is just the issue about the status of intuitions, which I said above was the real issue between the pragmatist and the realist. The hunch that, say, reflection upon anything worthy of the name "moral judgment" will eventually lead us to the problems Nagel describes is a discussable question — one upon which the history of ethics can shed light. But the intuition that there is something ineffable that it is like to be us — something one cannot learn about by believing true propositions but only by *being* like that — is not something on which anything could throw further light. The claim is either deep or empty.

The pragmatist sees it as empty — indeed, he sees many of Nagel's discussions of "the subjective" as drawing a line around a vacant place in the middle of the web of words and then claiming that there is something there rather than nothing. But this is not because he has independent arguments for a Philosophical theory to the effect that (in Sellars's words) "All awareness is a linguistic affair" or that "The meaning of a proposition is its method of verification." Such slogans as these are not the result of Philosophical inquiry into Awareness or Meaning, but merely ways of cautioning the public against the Philosophical tradition. (As "No taxation without representation" was not a discovery about the nature of Taxation, but an expression of distrust in the British Parliament of the day.) There are no fast little arguments to show that there are no such things as intuitions — arguments that are themselves based on something stronger than intuitions. For the pragmatist, the *only* thing wrong with Nagel's intuitions is that they are being used to legitimize a vocabulary (the Kantian vocabulary in morals, the Cartesian vocabulary in philosophy of mind) that the pragmatist thinks should be eradicated rather than reinforced. But his *only* argument for thinking that these intuitions and vocabularies should be eradicated is that the intellectual tradition to which they belong has not paid off, is more trouble than it is worth, has become an incubus. Nagel's dogmatism of intuitions is no worse, or better, than the pragmatist's inability to give noncircular arguments.

This upshot of the confrontation between the pragmatist and the intuitive realist about the status of intuitions can be described either as a conflict of intuitions about the importance of intuitions or as a preference for one vocabulary over another. The realist will favor the first description, and the pragmatist, the second. It does not matter which description one uses, as long as it is clear that *the issue is one about whether philosophy should try to find natural starting points that are distinct from cultural traditions, or whether all philosophy should do is compare and contrast cultural traditions.* This is, once again, the issue of whether philosophy should be Philosophy. The intuitive realist thinks that there is such a thing as Philosophical truth because he thinks that, deep down beneath all the texts, there is something which is not just one more text but that to which various texts are trying to be "adequate." The pragmatist does not think there is anything like that. He does not even think that there is anything isolable as "the purposes that we construct vocabularies and cultures to fulfill" against which to test vocabularies and cultures. But he does think that in the process of playing vocabularies and cultures off against each other, we produce new and better ways of talking and acting — not better by reference to a previously known standard, but just better in the sense that they come to *seem* clearly better than their predecessors.

A Post-Philosophical Culture

I began by saying that the pragmatist refused to accept the Philosophical distinction between first-rate truth-by-correspondence-to-reality and second-rate truth-as-what-it-is-good-to-believe. I said that this raised the question of whether a culture could get along without Philosophy, without the Platonic attempt to sift out the merely contingent and conventional truths from the Truths which were something more than that. The last two sections, in which I have been going over the latest round of "realist" objections to pragmatism, have brought us back to my initial distinction between philosophy and Philosophy. Pragmatism denies the possibility of getting beyond the Sellarsian notion of "seeing how things hang together" — which, for the bookish intellectual of recent times, means seeing how all the various vocabularies of all the various epochs and cultures hang together. "Intuition" is just the latest name for a device that will get us off the literary-historical-anthropological-political merry-go-round which such intellectuals ride, and onto something "progressive" and "scientific" — a device that will get us from philosophy to Philosophy.

I remarked earlier that a third motive for the recent anti-pragmatist backlash is simply the hope of getting off this merry-go-round. This hope is a correlate of the fear that if there is nothing quasiscientific for philosophy as an academic discipline to do, if there is no properly professional *Fach* that distinguishes the philosophy professor from the historian or the literary critic, then something will have been lost that has been central to Western intellectual life. This fear is, to be sure, justified. If Philosophy disappears, something will have been lost that was central to Western intellectual life — just as something central was lost when religious intuitions were weeded out from among the intellectually respectable candidates for Philosophical articulation. But the Enlightenment thought, rightly, that what would succeed religion, would be *better*. The pragmatist is betting that what succeeds the "scientific," positivist culture that the Enlightenment produced will be *better*.

The question of whether the pragmatist is right to be so sanguine is the question of whether a culture is imaginable, or

desirable, in which no one — or at least no intellectual —
believes that we have, deep down inside us, a criterion for
telling whether we are in touch with reality or not, when we
are in the Truth. This would be a culture in which neither the
priests nor the physicists nor the poets nor the Party were
thought of as more "rational" or more "scientific" or "deeper"
than one another. No particular portion of culture would be
singled out as exemplifying (or signally failing to exemplify)
the condition to which the rest aspired. There would be no
sense that beyond the current intradisciplinary criteria —
which, for example, good priests or good physicists obeyed —
there were other, transdisciplinary, transcultural, ahistorical
criteria, which they also obeyed. There would still be hero
worship in such a culture, but it would not be worship of heroes
as children of the gods, as marked off from the rest of mankind
by closeness to the immortal. It would simply be admiration of
exceptional men and women who were very good at doing the
quite diverse kinds of things they did. Such people would not
be those who knew a Secret, who had won through to Truth,
but simply people who were good at being human.

A fortiori, such a culture would contain nobody called "the
Philosopher" who could explain why and how certain areas of
culture enjoyed a special relation to reality. Such a culture
would, doubtless, contain specialists in seeing how things hung
together. But these would be people who had no special "problems" to solve nor any special "method" to apply, abided by no
particular disciplinary standards, had no collective self-image
as a "profession." They might resemble contemporary philosophy professors in being more interested in moral responsibility than in prosody, or more interested in the articulation of
sentences than in that of the human body, but they might not.
They would be all-purpose intellectuals who were ready to
offer a view on pretty much anything, in the hope of making
it hang together with everything else.

Such a hypothetical culture strikes both Platonists and positivists as "decadent." The Platonists see it as having no ruling
principle, no center, no structure. The positivists see it as having no respect for hard fact, for that area of culture — science
— in which the quest for objective truth takes precedence over

emotion and opinion. The Platonists would like to see a culture guided by something eternal. The positivists would like to see one guided by something temporal — the brute impact of the way the world is. But both want it to be *guided*, constrained, not left to its own devices. For both, decadence is a matter of unwillingness to submit oneself to something "out there" — to recognize that beyond the languages of men and women there is something to which these languages, and the men and women themselves, must try to be "adequate." For both, therefore, Philosophy as the discipline that draws a line between such attempts at adequacy and everything else in culture, and so between first-rate and second-rate truth, is bound up with the struggle against decadence.

So the question of whether such a post-Philosophical culture is desirable can also be put as the question: Can the ubiquity of language ever really be taken seriously? Can we see ourselves as never encountering reality *except under a chosen description* — as, in Nelson Goodman's phrase, making worlds rather than finding them?[43] This question has nothing to do with "idealism" — with the suggestion that we can or should draw metaphysical comfort from the fact that reality is "spiritual in nature." It is, rather, the question of whether we can give up what Stanley Cavell calls the "possibility that one among endless true descriptions of me tells who I am."[44] The hope that one of them will do just that is the impulse which, in our present culture, drives the youth to read their way through libraries, cranks to claim that they have found The Secret that makes all things plain, and sound scientists and scholars, toward the ends of their lives, to hope that their work has "philosophical implications" and "universal human significance." In a post-Philosophical culture some other hope would drive us to read through the libraries and to add new volumes to the ones we found. Presumably it would be the hope of offering our descendants a way of describing the ways of describing we had come across — a description of the descriptions that the race has come up with so far. If one takes "our time" to be "our view of previous times," so that, in Hegelian fashion, each age of the world recapitulates all the earlier ones, then a post-

Philosophical culture would agree with Hegel that philosophy is "its own time apprehended in thoughts."[45]

In a post-Philosophical culture it would be clear that that is *all* that philosophy can be. It cannot answer questions about the relation of the thought of our time — the descriptions it is using, the vocabularies it employs — to something that is not just some alternative vocabulary. So it is a study of the comparative advantages and disadvantages of the various ways of talking that our race has invented. It looks, in short, much like what is sometimes called "culture criticism" — a term that has come to name the literary-historical-anthropological-political merry-go-round I spoke of earlier. The modern Western "culture critic" feels free to comment on anything at all. He is a prefiguration of the all-purpose intellectual of a post-Philosophical culture, the philosopher who has abandoned pretensions to Philosophy. He passes rapidly from Hemingway to Proust to Hitler to Marx to Foucault to Mary Douglas to the present situation in Southeast Asia to Gandhi to Sophocles. He is a name dropper, who uses names such as these to refer to sets of descriptions, symbol systems, ways of seeing. His specialty is seeing similarities and differences between great big pictures, between attempts to see how things hang together. He is the person who tells you how all the ways of making things hang together hang together. But since he does not tell you about how all *possible* ways of making things hang together *must* hang together — since he has no extrahistorical Archimedean point of this sort — he is doomed to become outdated. Nobody is so passé as the intellectual czar of the previous generation — the man who redescribed all those old descriptions, which, thanks in part to his redescription of them, nobody now wants to hear anything about.

The life of such inhabitants of Snow's "literary culture," whose highest hope is to grasp their time in thought, appears to the Platonist and the positivist as a life not worth living — because it is a life that leaves nothing permanent behind. In contrast, the positivist and the Platonist hope to leave behind true propositions, propositions that have been shown true once and for all — inheritances for the human race unto all generations. The fear and distrust inspired by "historicism" — the emphasis on the mortality of the vocabularies in which such supposedly immortal truths are expressed — is the reason why Hegel (and more recently Kuhn and Foucault) are *bêtes noires* for Philosophers, and especially for spokesmen for Snow's "scientific culture."[46] (Hegel himself, to be sure, had his Philosophical moments, but the temporalization of rationality that he suggested was the single most important step in arriving at the pragmatist's distrust of Philosophy.)

The opposition between mortal vocabularies and immortal propositions is reflected in the opposition between the inconclusive comparison and contrast of vocabularies (with everybody trying to *aufheben* everybody else's way of putting everything) characteristic of the literary culture, and rigorous argumentation — the procedure characteristic of mathematics, what Kuhn calls "normal" science, and the law (at least in the lower courts). Comparisons and contrasts between vocabularies issue, usually, in new, synthetic vocabularies. Rigorous argumentation issues in agreement in propositions. The really exasperating thing about literary intellectuals, from the point of view of those inclined to science or to Philosophy, is their inability to engage in such argumentation — to agree on what would count as resolving disputes, on the criteria to which all sides must appeal. In a post-Philosophical culture this exasperation would not be felt. In such a culture criteria would be seen as the pragmatist sees them — as temporary resting places constructed for specific utilitarian ends. On the pragmatist account, a criterion (what follows from the axioms, what the needle points to, what the statute says) *is* a criterion because some particular social practice needs to block the road of inquiry, halt the regress of interpretations, in order to get something done.[47] So rigorous argumentation — the practice that is made possible by agreement on criteria, on stopping places — is no more *generally* desirable than blocking the road of inquiry is generally desirable.[48] It is something that it is convenient to have if you can get it. If the purposes you are engaged in fulfilling can be specified pretty clearly in advance (finding out how an enzyme functions, preventing violence in the streets, proving theorems), then you *can* get it. If they can not (as in the search for a just society, the resolution of a moral dilemma, the choice of a symbol of ultimate concern, the quest for a "postmodernist" sensibility), then you probably cannot, and you should not try for it. If what you are interested in is *philosophy*, you *certainly* will not get it — for one of the things that the various vocabularies for describing things differ about is the purpose of describing things. The philosopher will not want to beg the question between these various descriptions in advance. The urge to make philosophy into Philosophy is the urge to make it the search for some final vocabulary, which can somehow be known in advance to be the common core of, the truth of, all the other vocabularies that might be advanced in its place. This is the urge that the pragmatist thinks should be repressed, and that a post-Philosophical culture would have succeeded in repressing.

The most powerful reason for thinking that no such culture is possible is that seeing all criteria as no more than temporary resting places, constructed by a community to facilitate its inquiries, seems morally humiliating. Suppose that Socrates was wrong, that we have *not* once seen the Truth, and so will not, intuitively, recognize it when we see it again. This means that when the secret police come, when the torturers violate the innocent, there is nothing to be said to them of the form "There is something within you that you are betraying. Though you embody the practices of a totalitarian society that will endure forever, there is something beyond those practices that condemns you." This thought is hard to live with, as is Sartre's remark:

Tomorrow, after my death, certain people may decide to establish fascism, and the others may be cowardly or miserable enough to let them get away with it. At that moment, fascism will be the truth of man, and so much the worse for us. In reality, things will be as much as man has decided they are.[49]

This hard saying brings out what ties Dewey and Foucault, James and Nietzsche, together — the sense that there is nothing deep down inside us except what we have put there ourselves, no criterion that we have not created in the course of creating a practice, no standard of rationality that is not an appeal to such a criterion, no rigorous argumentation that is not obedience to our own conventions.

A post-Philosophical culture, then, would be one in which men and women felt themselves alone, merely finite, with no links to something Beyond. On the pragmatist's account, positivism was only a halfway stage in the development of such a culture — the progress toward, as Sartre puts it, doing without God. For positivism preserved a god in its notion of Science (and in its notion of "scientific philosophy"), the notion of a portion of culture where we touched something not ourselves, where we found Truth naked, relative to no description. The culture of positivism thus produced endless swings of the pendulum between the view that "values are merely 'relative' (or 'emotive,' or 'subjective')" and the view that bringing the "scientific method" to bear on questions of political and moral choice was the solution to all our problems. Pragmatism, by contrast, does not erect Science as an idol to fill the place once held by God. It views science as one genre of literature — or, put the other way around, literature and the arts as inquiries, on the same footing as scientific inquiries. Thus it sees ethics as neither more "relative" or "subjective" than scientific theory, nor as needing to be made "scientific." Physics is a way of trying to cope with various bits of the universe; ethics is a matter of trying to cope with other bits. Mathematics helps physics do its job; literature and the arts help ethics do its. Some of these inquiries come up with propositions, some with narratives, some with paintings. The question of what propositions to assert, which pictures to look at, what narratives to listen to and comment on and retell, are all questions about what will help us get what we want (or about what we *should* want).

The question of whether the pragmatist view of truth — that it is not a profitable topic — is itself *true* is thus a question about whether a post-Philosophical culture is a good thing to try for. It is not a question about what the word "true" means, nor about the requirements of an adequate philosophy of language, nor about whether the world "exists independently of our minds," nor about whether the intuitions of our culture are captured in the pragmatists' slogans. There is no way in which the issue between the pragmatist and his opponent can be tightened up and resolved according to criteria agreed to by both sides. This is one of those issues that puts everything up for grabs at once — where there is no point in trying to find agreement about "the data" or about what would count as deciding the question. But the messiness of the issue is not a reason for setting it aside. The issue between religion and secularism was no less messy, but it was important that it got decided as it did.

If the account of the contemporary philosophical scene offered here is correct, then the issue about the truth of pragmatism is the issue that all the most important cultural developments since Hegel have conspired to put before us. But, like its predecessor, it is not going to be resolved by any sudden new discovery of how things really are. It will be decided, if history allows us the leisure to decide such issues, only by a slow and painful choice between alternative self-images.

Notes

1. A. J. Ayer, *The Origins of Pragmatism* (San Francisco: Freeman, Cooper, 1968) is a good example of the point of view.

2. For this attitude, see Habermas's criticism of Peirce in *Knowledge and Human Interests* (Boston: Beacon Press, 1968), chap. 6, esp. p. 135.

3. Richard Rorty, *Philosophy and the Mirror of Nature* (Princeton: Princeton University Press, 1979).

4. To appear in the Cambridge University Press *Modern European Philosophy* series.

5. See Davidson, "On the Very Idea of a Conceptual Scheme," *Proceedings and Addresses of the American Philosophical Association*, 47 (1973–74): 5–20. See also my discussion of Davidson in chap. 6 of *Philosophy and the Mirror of Nature* and in "Transcendental Arguments, Self-Reference and Pragmatism" (*Transcendental Arguments and Science*, ed. P. Bieri, R.-P. Horstmann, and L. Krüger [Dordrecht: Reidel, 1979]), pp. 77–103.

6. *Collected Papers of Charles Sanders Peirce*, ed. Charles Hartshorne, Paul Weiss, and Arthur Burks (Cambridge, Massachusetts: Harvard University Press, 1933–58), 5.313–314.

7. Jacques Derrida, *Of Grammatology* (Baltimore: Johns Hopkins University Press, 1976), p. 49.

8. Wilfrid Sellars, *Science, Perception and Reality* (London: Routledge and Kegan Paul, 1967), p. 160.

9. Ludwig Wittgenstein, *Philosophical Investigations* (New York: Macmillan, 1953), p. 18.

10. Hans-Georg Gadamer, *Philosophical Hermeneutics* (Berkeley: University of California Press, 1976), p. 19.

11. Michel Foucault, *The Order of Things* (New York: Random House, 1973), p. 386.

12. Martin Heidegger, *On the Way to Language* (New York: Harper and Row, 1971), p. 50.

13. See Hans Sluga, *Frege* (London: Routledge and Kegan Paul, 1980), introduction and chap. 1, for a discussion of Frege's neo-Kantian, antinaturalistic motives.

14. Thomas Nagel, *Mortal Questions* (Cambridge: Cambridge University Press, 1979), p. xii.

15. Nagel, *Mortal Questions,* p. 171.

16. See Hilary Putnam's definition of "metaphysical realism" in these terms in his *Meaning and the Moral Sciences* (London: Routledge and Kegan Paul, 1978), p. 125.

17. Hilary Putnam, *Mind, Language and Reality* (Cambridge: Cambridge University Press, 1975), p. 236.

18. Hartry Field, "Meaning, Logic and Conceptual Role," *Journal of Philosophy,* 74 (1977): 398.

19. Field, "Tarski's Theory of Truth," *Journal of Philosophy,* 69 (1972): 373.

20. Putnam attributes this point to Leeds in his *Meaning and the Moral Sciences,* p. 16. Field would presumably reply that it *is* explanatory because we use people's beliefs as indicators of how things are in the world. (See "Tarski's Theory of Truth," p. 371, and also Field, "Mental Representations," in *Readings in Philosophical Psychology,* ed. Ned Block, vol. 2 [Cambridge, Massachusetts: Harvard University Press, 1981], p. 103, for this argument.) The pragmatist should rejoin that what we do is not to say, "I shall take what Jones says as, *ceteris paribus,* a reliable indication of how the world is," but rather to say, "I shall, *ceteris paribus,* say what Jones says."

21. Many pragmatists (including myself) have not, in fact, always been wise enough to avoid this trap. Peirce's definition of truth as that to which inquiry will converge has often seemed a good way for the pragmatist to capture the realists' intuition that Truth is One. But he should not try to capture it. There is no more reason for the pragmatist to try to assimilate this intuition than for him to accept the intuition that there is always One Morally Best Thing to Do in every situation. Nor is there any reason for him to think that a science in which, as in poetry, new vocabularies proliferate without end, would be inferior to one in which all inquirers communicated in The Language of United Science. (I am grateful to discussions with Putnam for persuading me to reject the seductions of Peirce's definition — although, of course, Putnam's reasons for doing so are not mine. I am also grateful to a recent article by Simon Blackburn, "Truth, Realism, and the Regulation of Theory," *Midwest Studies in Philosophy,* 5 [1980]: 353–371, which makes the point that "It may be that the notion of improvement [in our theories] is sufficient to interpret remarks to the effect that my favorite theory may be wrong, but not itself sufficient to justify the notion of a limit of investigation" [p. 358].)

22. William James, *Pragmatism and the Meaning of Truth* (Cambridge, Massachusetts: Harvard University Press, 1978), p. 42.

23. James, *Pragmatism*, p. 322.

24. Note that the question of whether there can be a "systematic theory of meaning for a language" is ambiguous between the question "Can we give a systematic account of what the user of a given natural language would have to know to be a competent speaker?" and "Can we get a philosophical semantics that will provide a foundation for the rest of philosophy?" Michael Dummett runs these two questions together in a confusing way when he says that Wittgenstein's metaphilosophical view that philosophy cannot be systematic presupposes that there can be no "systematic theory of meaning" (Dummett, *Truth and Other Enigmas* [Cambridge, Massachusetts: Harvard University Press, 1978], p. 453). Dummett says, rightly, that Wittgenstein has to admit that "the fact that anyone who has a mastery of any given language is able to understand an infinity of sentences of that language . . . can hardly be explained otherwise than by supposing that each speaker has an implicit grasp of a number of general principles governing the use in sentences of words in the language" (p. 451) and thus is committed to such a "systematic theory." But by granting that this is the only explanation of the fact in question, one is not committed to thinking, with Dummett, that "philosophy of language is the foundation for all the rest of philosophy" (p. 454). One might, with Wittgenstein, *not* see philosophy as a matter of giving "analyses," and thus might deny the presupposition of Dummett's claim that "the correctness of any piece of analysis carried out in another part of philosophy cannot be fully determined until we know with reasonable certainty what form a correct theory of meaning for our language must take" (p. 454). This latter remark is Dummett's only explication of the sense in which philosophy of language is "foundational" for the rest of philosophy. As I tried to argue in chap. 6 of *Philosophy and the Mirror of Nature*, the fact that philosophical semantics grew up in the bosom of metaphilosophy does not mean that a mature and successful semantics — a successful "systematic theory of meaning for a language" — would necessarily have any metaphilosophical import. Children often disown their parentage. Dummett is certainly right that Wittgenstein's work does not "provide a solid foundation for future work in philosophy" in the sense in which the positivists hoped (and Dummett still hopes) that Frege's work does (p. 452). But only someone antecedently convinced that semantics must give philosophers guidance about how to "analyze" would blame this lack of a foundation on the fact that Wittgenstein fails to "provide us with any outline of what a correct theory of meaning would look like" (p. 453). Wittgenstein believed, on nonsemantical grounds, that philosophy was not the sort of thing that had foundations, semantical or otherwise. [The Dummett essay is reprinted in this volume, pp. 189–215. — *Eds.*]

25. Dummett, *Truth and Other Enigmas*, p. 358.

26. On the claim that pragmatism cannot explain why science works (elaborated most fully in a forthcoming book by Richard Boyd), see Simon Blackburn, "Truth, Realism, and the Regulation of Theory" (cited in n. 21 above), esp. pp. 356–360. I agree with Blackburn's final conclusion that "realism, in the disputed cases of morals, conditionals, counterfactuals, mathematics, can only be worth defending in an interpretation which makes it noncontroversial" (p. 370).

27. This bag of tricks contains lots of valuable antiques, some bequeathed to the pragmatist by Berkeley *via* the British Idealists. This association of pragmatism with Berkeley's arguments for phenomenalism has led many realists (Lenin, Putnam) to suggest that pragmatism is (a) just a variant of idealism and (b) inherently "reductionist." But an argument for Berkeleian phenomenalism requires not only the pragmatic maxim that things are what they are known as, but the claim (deservedly criticized by Reid, Green, Wittgenstein, Sellars, Austin, and others) that we can make sense of Berkeley's notion of "idea." Without this latter notion, we cannot proceed further in the direction of the British Idealist claim that "reality is spiritual in nature." Failure

to distinguish among Berkeley's premises has led to a great deal of realist rhetoric about how pragmatists think reality is "malleable," do not appreciate the brutishness of the material world, and generally resemble idealists in not realizing that "physical things are externally related to minds." It must be confessed, however, that William James did sometimes say things that are susceptible to such charges. (See, for example, the disastrously flighty passage at p. 125 of *Pragmatism*. Dewey occasionally wandered down the same garden path.) As for reductionism, the pragmatist reply to this charge is that since he regards all vocabularies as tools for accomplishing purposes and none as representations of how things really are, he cannot possibly claim that "*X*'s *really are Y*'s," although he *can* say that it is more fruitful, for certain purposes, to use *Y*-talk than to use *X*-talk.

28. See Thompson Clarke, "The Legacy of Skepticism," *Journal of Philosophy*, 69 (1972): 754–769, esp. the concluding paragraph. This essay is cited by both Cavell and Nagel as making clear the "depth" of the tradition of epistemological skepticism.

29. Nagel, *Mortal Questions*, p. xii.

30. Nagel, *Mortal Questions*, p. 35.

31. Nagel, *Mortal Questions*, pp. 35–36.

32. Nagel, *Mortal Questions*, p. 36.

33. Nagel, *Mortal Questions*, p. 37.

34. Iris Murdoch, *The Sovereignty of Good* (New York: Schocken, 1971), p. 8.

35. Murdoch, *Sovereignty of Good*, p. 9.

36. Murdoch, *Sovereignty of Good*, p. 27.

37. Murdoch, *Sovereignty of Good*, pp. 28–30.

38. Daniel Dennett, *Brainstorms* (Montgomery, Vermont: Bradford Books, 1978), p. 228.

39. Nagel, *Mortal Questions*, pp. 192–193.

40. Wittgenstein, *Philosophical Investigations*, 1, sect. 271.

41. Wittgenstein, *Philosophical Investigations*, 1, sect. 115.

42. Nagel, *Mortal Questions*, p. 170.

43. See Nelson Goodman, *Ways of Worldmaking* (Indianapolis: Hackett, 1978). I think that Goodman's trope of "many worlds" is misleading and that we need not go beyond the more straightforward "many descriptions of the same world" (provided one does not ask, "And what world is *that*?"). But his point that there is no way to compare descriptions of the world in respect of adequacy seems to me crucial, and in the first two chapters of this book he makes it very vividly.

44. Stanley Cavell, *The Claim of Reason* (Oxford: Oxford University Press, 1979), p. 388.

45. Hegel, *Philosophy of Right*, trans. T. M. Knox (Oxford: Oxford University Press, 1952), p. 11. This passage, like the famous one that follows ("When philosophy paints

its grey in grey, then has a shape of life grown old. By a philosophy's grey on grey it cannot be rejuvenated but only understood. The owl of Minerva spreads its wings only with the falling of the dusk.") is not typical of Hegel and is hard to reconcile with much of the rest of what he says about philosophy. But it perfectly represents the side of Hegel that helped create the historicism of the nineteenth century and that is built into the thinking of the present-day literary intellectual.

46. The opposition between the literary and the scientific cultures that C. P. Snow drew (in *The Two Cultures and the Scientific Revolution* [Cambridge: Cambridge University Press, 1959]) is, I think, even deeper and more important than Snow thought it. It is pretty well coincident with the opposition between those who think of themselves as caught in time, as an evanescent moment in a continuing conversation, and those who hope to add a pebble from Newton's beach to an enduring structure. It is not an issue that is going to be resolved by literary critics learning physics or physicists reading the literary quarterlies. It was already drawn in Plato's time, when physics had not yet been invented, and when Poetry and Philosophy first squared off. (I think, incidentally, that those who criticize Snow along the lines of "not just *two* cultures, but many" miss his point. If one wants a neat dichotomy between the two cultures he was talking about, just ask any Eastern European censor which Western books are importable into his country. The line he draws will cut across fields like history and philosophy, but will almost always let physics in and keep highbrow novels out.The nonimportable books will be the ones that might suggest new vocabularies for self-description.)

47. There are, of course, lots of criteria that cut across all divisions between parts of culture — for instance, the laws of logic, the principle that a notorious liar's reports do not count as evidence, and the like. But these do not possess some special authority by virtue of their universality, any more than the set consisting of the fulcrum, the screw, and the lever is privileged by virtue of contributing to every other machine.

48. Peirce said that "the first rule of reason" was "Do not block the way of inquiry" (*Collected Papers*, 1.135). But he did not mean that one should always go down any road one saw — a point that comes out in his emphasis on "logical self-control" as a corollary of "ethical self-control." (See, for example, *Collected Papers*, 1.606.) What he was getting at in his "rule of reason" was the same point as he makes about the ubiquity of language — that we should never think that the regress of interpretation can be stopped once and for all, but rather realize that there may always be a vocabulary, a set of descriptions, around the corner that will throw everything into question once again. To say that obedience to criteria is a good thing *in itself* would be like saying that self-control is a good in itself. It would be a species of Philosophical puritanism.

49. Jean-Paul Sartre, *L'Existentialisme est un humanisme* (Paris: Nagel, 1946), pp. 53–54.

2

Jean-François Lyotard

Introduction

For the past decade the term "postmodern" has been used in so many different ways and with so many different senses as to render precise specification of its meaning impossible. Frequently coupled with such other fashionable "post-" terms as "postempiricist," "postmetaphysical," "poststructuralist," and "postindustrialist," it expresses a consciousness of fundamental changes in culture and society that are no less real for all their obscurity and ambivalence (see Huyssen, Jameson). The contours of this shift seem clearest in literature and the arts, where postmodernism contrasts with the aesthetics of classical modernism. To take the clearest case, in architecture the repudiation of the glass and steel functionalism of the International Style typically takes the form of a play of historical allusion, eclectic pastiche, appropriation of local traditions, and a return to ornamentation and decoration. But even in literature and the arts there is an unresolved ambivalence between the "end" and the radicalized continuation of modernism. (As will become evident, this ambivalence holds for Lyotard's use of the term as well.)

Matters are even less clear when one turns to postmodern thought in philosophy and social theory. Here the points of contrast are rather different: basic categories, principles, and institutions of the modern West. Since the late 1970s — in part via French poststructuralism, especially its reception in the

United States — the modernism/postmodernism constellation
in aesthetics has been connected with the modernity/postmod-
ernity constellation in social theory. For our purposes it is the
specification of modern Western culture as fundamentally rationalist and subjectivist that provides the key point of contrast;
for postmodernism in philosophy typically centers on a critique
of the modern ideas of reason and the rational subject. It is
above all the "project of the Enlightenment" that has to be
deconstructed, the autonomous epistemological and moral subject that has to be decentered; the nostalgia for unity, totality,
and foundations that has to be overcome; and the tyranny of
representational thought and universal truth that has to be
defeated. Like many of his French contemporaries, Lyotard
regards Nietzsche as the model for this all-out, frontal attack
on Western logocentrism. Unlike many of them, however, he
uses Wittgenstein (rather than Heidegger) to develop his version of it. And this Nietzscheanized Wittgenstein allows him to
appropriate certain key themes from postempiricist philosophy
of science (particularly Feyerabend's epistemological anarch-
ism) in his characterization of the postmodern condition of
savoir.

Lyotard chooses as the focus of his analysis not the "will to
power" or "instrumental reason" but the "principle of legitimacy," and he characterizes this principle in terms of "narrativity." In this perspective, modernity is marked by the
breakdown of narrative knowledge in the wake of the advance
of scientific knowledge. The radical suspicion of narrative and
the opposition of scientific to "prescientific" knowledge resulted in a paradox: How was modern science itself to be
legitimated, when by its very nature it rejected all narrative
legitimations? The resolution of this paradox was the creation
of a form of discourse characteristic of modernity in general
and of modern philosophical thought in particular: "Metadis-
courses," appealing to "metanarratives" (with their associated
philosophies of history), were constructed to take the place of
ordinary narratives in the language game of legitimation.

For Lyotard the term "modern" can be applied in this sense
to any form of knowledge that legitimates itself through a
metadiscourse of this kind, that is, through the appeal to some

grand metanarrative such as the progress of Reason and Freedom, the unfolding of Spirit, the emancipation of Humanity.
By contrast, a discourse is postmodern if it is "incredulous
toward metanarratives." In place of the metanarratives of truth
and freedom, postmodern discourse may be defined by a series
of contrasts Lyotard invokes in the call to arms at the close of
his essay "What Is Postmodernism?": "Let us wage war on
totality; let us be witnesses to the unpresentable; let us activate
differences and save the honor of the name" (1984, 87).

To effect this incredulity toward metanarratives, Lyotard
turns to the "pragmatics of language," specifically to Wittgenstein and his treatment of linguistic practices as language
games. On his reading, language is not a unitary phenomenon
but a heterogeneous and heteromorphous play of incommensurable and irreducible language games, each with its own local
and specific rules. We cannot judge one by the criteria of the
other; all we can do is "gaze in wonderment at the diversity of
discursive species." From his Nietzschean standpoint Lyotard
stresses the competitive and rhetorical aspects of language
games — the game as a contest in which each utterance is a
"move" and each player seeks to "displace" the others with new
and unexpected countermoves: "To speak is to fight in the
sense of playing, and speech acts fall within the domain of
general agonistics" (*The Postmodern Condition,* 10). For him, as
for Foucault, a principal aim of discourse analysis is to reveal
the "metaprescriptives," institutional and otherwise, that filter
and privilege particular types of statements in particular discourse formations. His continuing commitment to the aesthetics of high modernism is reflected in his transfer of the ideology
of innovation and experimentation to the domain of knowledge: Paralogical discourse analysis not only identifies these
metaprescriptives but "petitions" the players to accept different
ones on the grounds that this will generate new ideas. Lyotard's
notion of an agonistics of language, with its polytheism of
values and its emphasis on creative language use, stands in
stark contrast to the universal pragmatics of philosophers like
Apel and Habermas who want to "complete" the Enlightenment
and "transform" philosophy rather than to end them.

Lyotard is insistent that the legitimation of knowledge involves questions of justice as well as questions of truth; accordingly, he draws practical conclusons from his shift in perspective and points, however vaguely, toward a new conception of politics. "The nineteenth and twentieth centuries have given us as much terror as we can take. We paid a high enough price for the nostalgia for the whole and the one, for the reconciliation of the concept and the sensible" ("What Is Postmodernism?" 1984, 81–82). In the place of this nostalgia and this terror he proposes a kind of post-Marxist, radically democratic and pluralistic "micropolitics" (Benhabib) based essentially on "paralogy" — the undermining of established language games through an activation of differences, through constant innovation and experimentation. Its principles are not the universality of reason and the need for consensus but the irreducibly local character of all discourse, argumentation, and legitimation and the need to undermine established agreements; its intellectual forms are not the unifying and grounding metadiscourse and the grand metanarrative but a multiplicity of small narratives and local meta-arguments; its underlying notion of justice appeals not to consensus but to "the recognition of the specificity and autonomy of the multiplicity of entangled language games, the refusal to reduce them; with a rule which nevertheless would be a general rule: let us play . . . and let us play in peace" (cited in Wellmer, 341). The release of the creative potentials of language is for Lyotard the only real alternative to the anonymous domination of the principle of "performativity" in all spheres of life.

With his combination of elements from postempiricist epistemology, modern aesthetics, and postutopian political liberalism (Wellmer), it is not surprising that Lyotard has found a defender in Richard Rorty. In an article responding to Habermas's criticisms of Foucault and Lyotard, Rorty characterizes the disagreement between those who call for a transformation of philosophy and those who call for an end of philosophy as follows: "The French writers whom Habermas criticizes are willing to drop the opposition between 'true' and 'false' consensus, or between 'validity' and 'power,' in order not to have to tell a metanarrative to explicate 'true' and 'valid'" (Rorty,

35). Critics have argued that this amounts to a renunciation of philosophy and results in the collapse of pragmatics into rhetoric. But Lyotard is willing to accept these consequences; he sees no need for philosophy to ground itself, "to be a discourse of legitimation with respect to its own status." Unlike other end-of-philosophy thinkers, however, he considers it one of the tasks of postmodern thought to formulate new ideals of justice and truth beyond the false ideals of emancipation and consensus.

Suggested Readings

Barthes, John. *The Literature of Exhaustion.* Northridge: Lord John Publishing, 1982.

Benhabib, Seyla. "Epistemologies of Postmodernism: A Rejoinder to Jean-François Lyotard," *New German Critique* 33 (1985), 103–126.

Berman, Marshall. *Everything That Is Solid Melts into Air.* New York: Simon and Schuster, 1982.

Bourdieu, Pierre, and J. C. Passeron. "Sociology and Philosophy in France Since 1945: Death and Resurrection of a Philosophy without a Subject," *Social Research* 34 (1983), 166–212.

Bürger, Peter. *Theory of the Avantgarde.* Minneapolis: University of Minnesota Press, 1984.

Descombes, Vincent. *Modern French Philosophy.* Cambridge: Cambridge University Press, 1980.

Foster, Hal. "(Post)modern Polemics," *New German Critique* 33 (1984), 67–78.

Foster, Hal, ed. *The Anti-Aesthetic.* Port Townsend: Bay Press, 1983.

Honneth, Axel. "Der Affekt Gegen den Allgemeinen: Zur Lyotards Konzept der Postmoderne," *Merkur* 38 (December 1984), 893–902.

Huyssen, Andreas. "Mapping the Postmodern," *New German Critique* 33 (1984), 5–52.

Jameson, Frederick. "The Politics of Theory: Ideological Positions in the Postmodernism Debate," *New German Critique* 33 (1984), 53–67.

Jencks, Charles. *The Language of Postmodern Architecture.* New York: Rizzoli International, 1977.

Jencks, Charles. *Late-Modern Architecture.* New York: Rizzoli International, 1980.

Lyotard, Jean-François. *Discours, figure.* Paris: Klucksieck, 1971.

The End of Philosophy

Lyotard, Jean-François. *Dérive à partie de Marx et Freud*. Paris: Union Générale d'édition, 1973.

Lyotard, Jean-François. *Economie libidinale*. Paris: Editions Minuit, 1974.

Lyotard, Jean-François. "Analyzing Speculative Discourse as Language Game," *Oxford Literary Review* 4 (1981), 59–67.

Lyotard, Jean-François. *The Postmodern Condition*. Minneapolis: University of Minnesota Press, 1984. With an introduction by Frederic Jameson.

Lyotard, Jean-François. "What Is Postmodernism?" appendix to *The Postmodern Condition*, 71–84. Minneapolis: University of Minnesota Press, 1984.

Lyotard, Jean-François, and Jean-Loup Thébaud. *Just Gaming*. Minneapolis: University of Minnesota Press, 1985.

Portoghesi, Paolo. *After Modern Architecture*. New York: Rizzoli International, 1982.

Rorty, Richard, "Habermas and Lyotard on Postmodernity," in *Habermas on Modernity*, ed. R. Bernstein, 161–176. Cambridge, Massachusetts: MIT Press, 1985.

Wellmer, Albrecht. "On the Dialectic of Modernism and Postmodernism," *Praxis International* 4 (1985), 337–362.

The Postmodern Condition

Jean-François Lyotard

The object of this study is the condition of knowledge in the most highly developed societies. I have decided to use the word *postmodern* to describe that condition. The word is in current use on the American continent among sociologists and critics; it designates the state of our culture following the transformations that, since the end of the nineteenth century, have altered the game rules for science, literature, and the arts. The present study will place these transformations in the context of the crisis of narratives.

Science has always been in conflict with narratives. Judged by the yardstick of science, the majority of them prove to be fables. But to the extent that science does not restrict itself to stating useful regularities and seeks the truth, it is obliged to legitimate the rules of its own game. It then produces a discourse of legitimation with respect to its own status, a discourse called philosophy. I will use the term *modern* to designate any science that legitimates itself with reference to a metadiscourse of this kind making an explicit appeal to some grand narrative, such as the dialectics of Spirit, the hermeneutics of meaning, the emancipation of the rational or working subject, or the creation of wealth. For example, the rule of consensus between the sender and addressee of a statement with truth value is deemed acceptable if it is cast in terms of a possible unanimity between rational minds: this is the Enlightenment narrative, in which the hero of knowledge works toward a good ethico-political end — universal peace. As can be seen from this example, if a metanarrative implying a philosophy of history is used to legitimate knowledge, questions are raised concerning the validity of the institutions governing the social bond: these must be legitimated as well. Thus justice is consigned to the grand narrative in the same way as truth.

Simplifying to the extreme, I define *postmodern* as incredulity toward metanarratives. This incredulity is undoubtedly a product of progress in the sciences: but that progress in turn presupposes it. To the obsolescence of the metanarrative apparatus of legitimation corresponds, most notably, the crisis of metaphysical philosophy and of the university institution that in the past relied on it. The narrative function is losing its functors, its great hero, its great dangers, its great voyages, its great goal. It is being dispersed in clouds of narrative language elements — narrative, but also denotative, prescriptive, descriptive, and so on. Conveyed within each cloud are pragmatic valencies specific to its kind. Each of us lives at the intersection of many of these. However, we do not necessarily establish stable language combinations, and the properties of the ones we do establish are not necessarily communicable.

Thus the society of the future falls less within the province of a Newtonian anthropology (such as structuralism or systems theory) than a pragmatics of language particles. There are many different language games — a heterogeneity of elements. They only give rise to institutions in patches — local determinism.

The decision makers, however, attempt to manage these clouds of sociality according to input/output matrices, following a logic that implies that their elements are commensurable and that the whole is determinable. They allocate our lives for the growth of power. In matters of social justice and of scientific truth alike, the legitimation of that power is based on its optimizing the system's performance — efficiency. The application of this criterion to all our games necessarily entails a certain level of terror, whether soft or hard: be operational (that is, commensurable) or disappear.

The logic of maximum performance is no doubt inconsistent in many ways, particularly with respect to contradiction in the socioeconomic field: it demands both less work (to lower production costs) and more (to lessen the social burden of the idle population). But our incredulity is now such that we no longer expect salvation to rise from these inconsistencies, as did Marx.

Still, the postmodern condition is as much a stranger to disenchantment as it is to the blind positivity of delegitimation. Where, after the metanarratives, can legitimacy reside? The operativity criterion is technological; it has no relevance for judging what is true or just. Is legitimacy to be found in consensus obtained through discussion, as Jürgen Habermas thinks? Such consensus does violence to the heterogeneity of language games. And invention is always born of dissension. Postmodern knowledge is not simply a tool of the authorities; it refines our sensitivity to differences and reinforces our ability to tolerate the incommensurable. Its principle is not the expert's homology, but the inventor's paralogy.

. . . In a society whose communication component is becoming more prominent day by day, both as a reality and as an issue,[1] it is clear that language assumes a new importance. It would be superficial to reduce its significance to the traditional alternative between manipulatory speech and the unilateral transmission of messages on the one hand, and free expression and dialogue on the other.

A word on this last point. If the problem is described simply in terms of communication theory, two things are overlooked: first, messages have quite different forms and effects depending on whether they are, for example, denotatives, prescriptives, evaluatives, performatives, etc. It is clear that what is important is not simply the fact that they communicate information. Reducing them to this function is to adopt an outlook that unduly privileges the system's own interests and point of view. A cybernetic machine does indeed run on information, but the goals programmed into it, for example, originate in prescriptive and evaluative statements it has no way to correct in the course of its functioning — for example, maximizing its own performance. How can one guarantee that performance maximization is the best goal for the social system in every case? In any case the "atoms" forming its matter are competent to handle statements such as these — and this question in particular.

Second, the trivial cybernetic version of information theory misses something of decisive importance: the agonistic aspect of society. The atoms are placed at the crossroads of pragmatic relationships, but they are also displaced by the messages that traverse them, in perpetual motion. Each language partner, when a "move" pertaining to him is made, undergoes a "displacement," an alteration of some kind that affects him not only in his capacity as addressee and referent, but also as sender. These "moves" necessarily provoke "countermoves" — and everyone knows that a countermove that is merely reactional is not a "good" move. Reactional countermoves are no more than programmed effects in the opponent's strategy; they play into his hands and thus have no effect on the balance of power. That is why it is important to increase displacement in the games, and even to disorient it, in such a way as to make an unexpected "move" (a new statement).

What is needed if we are to understand social relations in this manner, on whatever scale we choose, is not only a theory of communication but a theory of games that accepts agonistics as a founding principle. In this context, it is easy to see that the essential element of newness is not simply "innovation." Support for this approach can be found in the work of a number of contemporary sociologists,[2] in addition to linguists and philosophers of language.

This "atomization" of the social into flexible networks of language games may seem far removed from the modern reality, which is depicted, on the contrary, as afflicted with bureaucratic paralysis.[3] The objection will be made, at least, that the weight of certain institutions imposes limits on the games, and thus restricts the inventiveness of the players in making their moves. But I think this can be taken into account without causing any particular difficulty.

In the ordinary use of discourse — for example, in a discussion between two friends — the interlocutors use any available ammunition, changing games from one utterance to the next: questions, requests, assertions, and narratives are launched pell-mell into battle. The war is not without rules,[4] but the rules allow and encourage the greatest possible flexibility of utterance.

From this point of view, an institution differs from a conversation in that it always requires supplementary constraints for statements to be declared admissible within its bounds. The constraints function to filter discursive potentials, interrupting possible connections in the communication networks: there are things that should not be said. They also privilege certain classes of statements (sometimes only one) whose predominance characterizes the discourse of the particular institution: there are things that should be said, and there are ways of saying them. Thus: orders in the army, prayer in church, denotation in the schools, narration in families, questions in philosophy, performativity in businesses. Bureaucratization is the outer limit of this tendency.

However, this hypothesis about the institution is still too "unwieldy": its point of departure is an overly "reifying" view of what is institutionalized. We know today that the limits the institution imposes on potential language "moves" are never established once and for all (even if they have been formally defined).[5] Rather, the limits are themselves the stakes and provisional results of language strategies, within the institution and without. Examples: Does the university have a place for language experiments (poetics)? Can you tell stories in a cabinet meeting? Advocate a cause in the barracks? The answers are clear: yes, if the university opens creative workshops; yes, if the cabinet works with prospective scenarios; yes, if the limits of the old institution are displaced.[6] Reciprocally, it can be said that the boundaries only stabilize when they cease to be stakes in the game.

This, I think, is the appropriate approach to contemporary institutions of knowledge.

. . . I have leveled two objections against the unquestioning acceptance of an instrumental conception of knowledge in the most highly developed societies. Knowledge is not the same as science, especially in its contemporary form; and science, far from successfully obscuring the problem of its legitimacy, cannot avoid raising it with all of its implications, which are no less sociopolitical than epistemological. Let us begin with an analysis of the nature of "narrative" knowledge; by providing a point of comparison, our examination will clarify at least some of the characteristics of the form assumed by scientific knowledge in contemporary society. In addition, it will aid us in understanding how the question of legitimacy is raised or fails to be raised today.

Knowledge [*savoir*] in general cannot be reduced to science, nor even to learning [*connaissance*]. Learning is the set of statements that, to the exclusion of all other statements, denote or describe objects and may be declared true or false.[7] Science is a subset of learning. It is also composed of denotative statements, but imposes two supplementary conditions on their acceptability: the objects to which they refer must be available for repeated access, in other words, they must be accessible in explicit conditions of observation; and it must be possible to decide whether or not a given statement pertains to the language judged relevant by the experts.[8]

But what is meant by the term *knowledge* is not only a set of denotative statements; far from it. It also includes notions of "know-how," "knowing how to live," "how to listen" [*savoir-faire, savoir-vivre, savoir-écouter*], etc. Knowledge, then, is a question of competence that goes beyond the simple determination and application of the criterion of truth, extending to the determination and application of criteria of efficiency (technical qualification), of justice and/or happiness (ethical wisdom), of the beauty of a sound or color (auditory and visual sensibility), etc. Understood in this way, knowledge is what makes someone capable of forming "good" denotative utterances, but also "good" prescriptive and "good" evaluative utterances . . . . It is not a competence relative to a particular class of statements (for example, cognitive ones) to the exclusion of all others. On the contrary, it makes "good" performances in relation to a variety of objects of discourse possible: objects to be known, decided on, evaluated, transformed . . . . From this derives one of the principal features of knowledge: it coincides with an extensive array of competence-building measures and is the only form embodied in a subject constituted by the various areas of competence composing it.

Another characteristic meriting special attention is the relation between this kind of knowledge and custom. What is a
"good" prescriptive or evaluative utterance, a "good" performance in denotative or technical matters? They are all judged
to be "good" because they conform to the relevant criteria (of
justice, beauty, truth, and efficiency respectively) accepted in
the social circle of the "knower's" interlocutors. The early philosophers called this mode of legitimating statements opinion.[9]
The consensus that permits such knowledge to be circumscribed and makes it possible to distinguish one who knows
from one who doesn't (the foreigner, the child) is what constitutes the culture of a people.[10]

This brief reminder of what knowledge can be in the way of
training and culture draws on ethnological description for its
justification.[11] But anthropological studies and literature that
take rapidly developing societies as their object can attest to
the survival of this type of knowledge within them, at least in
some of their sectors.[12] The very idea of development presupposes a horizon of nondevelopment where, it is assumed, the
various areas of competence remain enveloped in the unity of
a tradition and are not differentiated according to separate
qualifications subject to specific innovations, debates, and inquiries. This opposition does not necessarily imply a difference
in nature between "primitive" and "civilized" man,[13] but is
compatible with the premise of a formal identity between "the
savage mind" and scientific thought;[14] it is even compatible
with the (apparently contrary) premise of the superiority of
customary knowledge over the contemporary dispersion of
competence.[15]

It is fair to say that there is one point on which all of the
investigations agree, regardless of which scenario they propose
to dramatize and understand the distance separating the customary state of knowledge from its state in the scientific age:
the preeminence of the narrative form in the formulation of
traditional knowledge. Some study this form for its own sake;[16]
others see it as the diachronic costume of the structural operators that, according to them, properly constitute the knowledge in question;[17] still others bring to it an "economic"
interpretation in the Freudian sense of the term.[18] All that is

important here is the fact that its form is narrative. Narration is the quintessential form of customary knowledge, in more ways than one.

It is therefore impossible to judge the existence of validity of narrative knowledge on the basis of scientific knowledge and vice versa: the relevant criteria are different. All we can do is gaze in wonderment at the diversity of discursive species, just as we do at the diversity of plant or animal species. Lamenting the "loss of meaning" in postmodernity boils down to mourning the fact that knowledge is no longer principally narrative. Such a reaction does not necessarily follow. Neither does an attempt to derive or engender (using operators like development) scientific knowledge from narrative knowledge, as if the former contained the latter in an embryonic state.

Nevertheless, language species, like living species, are interrelated, and their relations are far from harmonious. The second point justifying this quick reminder on the properties of the language game of science concerns, precisely, its relation to narrative knowledge. I have said that narrative knowledge does not give priority to the question of its own legitimation and that it certifies itself in the pragmatics of its own transmission without having recourse to argumentation and proof. This is why its incomprehension of the problems of scientific discourse is accompanied by a certain tolerance: it approaches such discourse primarily as a variant in the family of narrative cultures.[19] The opposite is not true. The scientist questions the validity of narrative statements and concludes that they are never subject to argumentation or proof.[20] He classifies them as belonging to a different mentality: savage, primitive, underdeveloped, backward, alienated, composed of opinions, customs, authority, prejudice, ignorance, ideology. Narratives are fables, myths, legends, fit only for women and children. At best, attempts are made to throw some rays of light into this obscurantism, to civilize, educate, develop.

This unequal relationship is an intrinsic effect of the rules specific to each game. We all know its symptoms. It is the entire history of cultural imperialism from the dawn of Western civilization. It is important to recognize its special tenor, which sets it apart from all other forms of imperialism: it is governed by the demand for legitimation.

. . . The explicit appeal to narrative in the problematic of knowledge is concomitant with the liberation of the bourgeois classes from the traditional authorities. Narrative knowledge makes a resurgence in the West as a way of solving the problem of legitimating the new authorities. It is natural in a narrative problematic for such a question to solicit the name of a hero as its response: *Who* has the right to decide for society? Who is the subject whose prescriptions are norms for those they obligate?

This way of inquiring into sociopolitical legitimacy combines with the new scientific attitude: the name of the hero is the people, the sign of legitimacy is the people's consensus, and their mode of creating norms is deliberation. The notion of progress is a necessary outgrowth of this. It represents nothing other than the movement by which knowledge is presumed to accumulate — but this movement is extended to the new sociopolitical subject. The people debate among themselves about what is just or unjust in the same way that the scientific community debates about what is true or false; they accumulate civil laws just as scientists accumulate scientific laws; they perfect their rules of consensus just as the scientists produce new "paradigms" to revise their rules in light of what they have learned.[21]

It is clear that what is meant here by "the people" is entirely different from what is implied by traditional narrative knowledge, which, as we have seen, requires no instituting deliberation, no cumulative progression, no pretension to universality; these are the operators of scientific knowledge. It is therefore not at all surprising that the representatives of the new process of legitimation by "the people" should be at the same time actively involved in destroying the traditional knowledge of peoples, perceived from that point forward as minorities or potential separatist movements destined only to spread obscurantism.[22]

We can see too that the real existence of this necessarily abstract subject (it is abstract because it is uniquely modeled on the paradigm of the subject of knowledge — that is, one who sends-receives denotative statements with truth value to the exclusion of other language games) depends on the institutions within which that subject is supposed to deliberate and decide, and which comprise all or part of the State. The question of the State becomes intimately entwined with that of scientific knowledge.

But it is also clear that this interlocking is many sided. The "people" (the nation, or even humanity), and especially their political institutions, are not content to know — they legislate. That is, they formulate prescriptions that have the status of norms.[23] They therefore exercise their competence not only with respect to denotative utterances concerning what is true, but also prescriptive utterances with pretentions to justice. As already said, what characterizes narrative knowledge, what forms the basis of our conception of it, is precisely that it combines both of these kinds of competence, not to mention all the others.

The mode of legitimation we are discussing, which reintroduces narrative as the validity of knowledge, can thus take two routes, depending on whether it represents the subject of the narrative as cognitive or practical, as a hero of knowledge or a hero of liberty. Because of this alternative, not only does the meaning of legitimation vary, but it is already apparent that narrative itself is incapable of describing that meaning adequately.

In contemporary society and culture — postindustrial society, postmodern culture[24] — the question of the legitimation of knowledge is formulated in different terms. The grand narrative has lost its credibility, regardless of what mode of unification it uses, regardless of whether it is a speculative narrative or a narrative of emancipation.

The decline of a narrative can be seen as an effect of the blossoming of techniques and technologies since the Second World War, which has shifted emphasis from the ends of action to its means; it can also be seen as an effect of the redeployment of advanced liberal capitalism after its retreat under the protection of Keynesianism during the period 1930–1960, a renewal that has eliminated the communist alternative and valorized the individual enjoyment of goods and services.

Any time we go searching for causes in this way we are bound to be disappointed. Even if we adopted one or the other of these hypotheses, we would still have to detail the correlation between the tendencies mentioned and the decline of the unifying and legitimating power of the grand narratives of speculation and emancipation.

It is, of course, understandable that both capitalist renewal and prosperity and the disorienting upsurge of technology would have an impact on the status of knowledge. But in order to understand how contemporary science could have been susceptible to those effects long before they took place, we must first locate the seeds of "delegitimation"[25] and nihilism that were inherent in the grand narratives of the nineteenth century.

First of all, the speculative apparatus maintains an ambiguous relation to knowledge. It shows that knowledge is only worthy of that name to the extent that it reduplicates itself ("lifts itself up," *hebt sich auf*; is sublated) by citing its own statements in a second-level discourse (autonymy) that functions to legitimate them. This is as much as to say that, in its immediacy, denotative discourse bearing on a certain referent (a living organism, a chemical property, a physical phenomenon, etc.) does not really know what it thinks it knows. Positive science is not a form of knowledge. And speculation feeds on its suppression. The Hegelian speculative narrative thus harbors a certain skepticism toward positive learning, as Hegel himself admits.[26]

A science that has not legitimated itself is not a true science; if the discourse that was meant to legitimate it seems to belong to a prescientific form of knowledge, like a "vulgar" narrative, it is demoted to the lowest rank, that of an ideology or instrument of power. And this always happens if the rules of the science game that discourse denounces as empirical are applied to science itself.

Take for example the speculative statement "A scientific statement is knowledge if and only if it can take its place in a universal process of engendering." The question is, Is this statement knowledge as it itself defines it? Only if it can take its place in a universal process of engendering. Which it can. All it has to do is to presuppose that such a process exists (the Life of spirit) and that it is itself an expression of that process. This presupposition, in fact, is indispensable to the speculative language game. Without it, the language of legitimation would not be legitimate; it would accompany science in a nosedive into nonsense, at least if we take idealism's word for it.

But this presupposition can also be understood in a totally different sense, one that take us in the direction of postmodern culture: we could say, in keeping with the perspective we adopted earlier, that this presupposition defines the set of rules one must accept in order to play the speculative game.[27] Such an appraisal assumes, first, that we accept that the "positive" sciences represent the general mode of knowledge and, second, that we understand this language to imply certain formal and axiomatic presuppositions that it must always make explicit. This is exactly what Nietzsche is doing, though with a different terminology, when he shows that "European nihilism" resulted from the truth requirement of science being turned back against itself.[28]

There thus arises an idea of perspective that is not far removed, at least in this respect, from the idea of language games. What we have here is a process of delegitimation fueled by the demand for legitimation itself. The "crisis" of scientific knowledge, signs of which have been accumulating since the end of the nineteenth century, is not born of a chance proliferation of sciences, itself an effect of progress in technology and the expansion of capitalism. It represents, rather, an internal erosion of the legitimacy principle of knowledge. There is erosion at work inside the speculative game, and by loosening the weave of the encyclopedic net in which each science was to find its place, it eventually sets them free.

The classical dividing lines between the various fields of science are thus called into question — disciplines disappear, overlappings occur at the borders between sciences, and from these new territories are born. The speculative hierarchy of learning gives way to an immanent and, as it were, "flat" network of areas of inquiry, the respective frontiers of which are in constant flux. The old "faculties" splinter into institutes and foundations of all kinds, and the universities lose their function of speculative legitimation. Stripped of the responsibility for research (which was stifled by the speculative narrative), they limit themselves to the transmission of what is judged to be established knowledge, and through didactics they guarantee the replication of teachers rather than the production of researchers. This is the state in which Nietzsche finds and condemns them.[29]

The potential for erosion intrinsic to the other legitimation procedure, the emancipation apparatus flowing from the *Aufklärung*, is no less extensive than the one at work within speculative discourse. But it touches a different aspect. Its distinguishing characteristic is that it grounds the legitimation of science and truth in the autonomy of interlocutors involved in ethical, social, and political praxis. As we have seen, there are immediate problems with this form of legitimation: the difference between a denotative statement with cognitive value and a prescriptive statement with practical value is one of relevance, therefore of competence. There is nothing to prove that if a statement describing a real situation is true, it follows that a prescriptive statement based upon it (the effect of which will necessarily be a modification of that reality) will be just.

Take, for example, a closed door. Between "The door is closed" and "Open the door" there is no relation of consequence as defined in propositional logic. The two statements belong to two autonomous sets of rules defining different kinds of relevance, and therefore of competence. Here, the effect of dividing reason into cognitive or theoretical reason on the one hand, and practical reason on the other, is to attack the legitimacy of the discourse of science. Not directly, but indirectly, by revealing that it is a language game with its own rules (of which the a priori conditions of knowledge in Kant provide a first glimpse) and that it has no special calling to supervise the game of praxis (nor the game of aesthetics, for that matter). The game of science is thus put on a par with the others.

If this "delegitimation" is pursued in the slightest and if its scope is widened (as Wittgenstein does in his own way, and thinkers such as Martin Buber and Emmanuel Lévinas in theirs),[30] the road is then open for an important current of postmodernity: science plays its own game; it is incapable of legitimating the other language games. The game of prescription, for example, escapes it. But above all, it is incapable of legitimating itself, as speculation assumed it could.

The social subject itself seems to dissolve in this dissemination of language games. The social bond is linguistic, but is not woven with a single thread. It is a fabric formed by the intersection of at least two (and in reality an indeterminate number) of language games, obeying different rules. Wittgenstein writes, "Our language can be seen as an ancient city: a maze of little streets and squares, of old and new houses, and of houses with additions from various periods; and this surrounded by a multitude of new boroughs with straight regular streets and uniform houses."[31] And to drive home that the principle of unitotality — or synthesis under the authority of a metadiscourse of knowledge — is inapplicable, he subjects the "town" of language to the old sorites paradox by asking, "How many houses or streets does it take before a town begins to be a town?"[32]

New languages are added to the old ones, forming suburbs of the old town: "the symbolism of chemistry and the notation of the infinitesimal calculus."[33] Thirty-five years later we can add to the list: machine languages, the matrices of game theory, new systems of musical notation, systems of notation for non-denotative forms of logic (temporal logics, deontic logics, modal logics), the language of the genetic code, graphs of phonological structures, and so on.

We may form a pessimistic impression of this splintering: nobody speaks all of those languages, they have no universal metalanguage, the project of the system-subject is a failure, the goal of emancipation has nothing to do with science, we are all stuck in the positivism of this or that discipline of learning, the learned scholars have turned into scientists, the diminished tasks of research have become compartmentalized and no one can master them all.[34] Speculative or humanistic philosophy is forced to relinquish its legitimation duties,[35] which explains why philosophy is facing a crisis wherever it persists in arrogating such functions and is reduced to the study of systems of logic or the history of ideas where it has been realistic enough to surrender them.[36]

Turn-of-the-century Vienna was weaned on this pessimism: not just artists such as Musil, Kraus, Hofmannsthal, Loos, Schönberg, and Broch, but also the philosophers Mach and Wittgenstein.[37] They carried awareness of and theoretical and artistic responsibility for delegitimation as far as it could be taken. We can say today that the mourning process has been completed. There is no need to start all over again. Wittgenstein's strength is that he did not opt for the positivism that was being developed by the Vienna Circle,[38] but outlined in his investigation of language games a kind of legitimation not based on performativity. That is what the postmodern world is all about. Most people have lost the nostalgia for the lost narrative. It in no way follows that they are reduced to barbarity. What saves them from it is their knowledge that legitimation can only spring from their own linguistic practice and communicational interaction. Science "smiling into its beard" at every other belief has taught them the harsh austerity of realism.[39]

From the beginning of this study, I have emphasized the differences (not only formal but also pragmatic) between the various language games, especially between denotative, or knowledge, games and prescriptive, or action, games. The pragmatics of science is centered on denotative utterances, which are the foundation upon which it builds institutions of learning (institutes, centers, universities, etc.). But its postmodern development brings a decisive "fact" to the fore: even discussions of denotative statements need to have rules. Rules are not denotative but prescriptive utterances, which we are better off calling metaprescriptive utterances to avoid confusion (they prescribe what the moves of language games must be in order to be admissible). The function of the differential or imaginative or paralogical activity of the current pragmatics of science is to point out these metaprescriptives (science's "presuppositions")[40] and to petition the players to accept different ones. The only legitimation that can make this kind of request admissible is that it will generate ideas, in other words, new statements.

Social pragmatics does not have the "simplicity" of scientific pragmatics. It is a monster formed by the interweaving of various networks of heteromorphous classes of utterances (denotative, prescriptive, performative, technical, evaluative, etc.). There is no reason to think that it would be possible to determine metaprescriptives common to all of these language games or that a revisable consensus like the one in force at a given moment in the scientific community could embrace the totality of metaprescriptions regulating the totality of statements circulating in the social collectivity. As a matter of fact, the contemporary decline of narratives of legitimation — be they traditional or "modern" (the emancipation of humanity, the realization of the Idea) — is tied to the abandonment of this belief. It is its absence for which the ideology of the "system," with its pretensions to totality, tries to compensate and which it expresses in the cynicism of its criterion of performance.

For this reason it seems neither possible nor even prudent to follow Habermas in orienting our treatment of the problem of legitimation in the direction of a search for universal consensus[41]; through what he calls *Diskurs*, in other words, a dialogue of argumentation.[42]

This would be to make two assumptions. The first is that it is possible for all speakers to come to agreement on which rules or metaprescriptions are universally valid for language games, when it is clear that language games are heteromorphous, subject to heterogeneous sets of pragmatic rules.

The second assumption is that the goal of dialogue is consensus. But as I have shown in the analysis of the pragmatics of science, consensus is only a particular state of discussion, not its end. Its end, on the contrary, is paralogy. This double observation (the heterogeneity of the rules and the search for dissent) destroys a belief that still underlies Habermas's research, namely, that humanity as a collective (universal) subject seeks its common emancipation through the regularization of the "moves" permitted in all language games and that the legitimacy of any statement resides in its contributing to that emancipation.[43]

It is easy to see what function this recourse plays in Habermas's argument against Luhmann. *Diskurs* is his ultimate weapon against the theory of the stable system. The cause is good, but the argument is not.[44] Consensus has become an outmoded and suspect value. But justice as a value is neither outmoded nor suspect. We must thus arrive at an idea and practice of justice that is not linked to that of consensus.

A recognition of the heteromorphous nature of language games is a first step in that direction. This obviously implies a renunciation of terror, which assumes that they are isomorphic and tries to make them so. The second step is the principle that any consensus on the rules defining a game and the "moves" playable within it *must* be local, in other words, agreed on by its present players and subject to eventual cancellation. The orientation then favors a multiplicity of finite meta-arguments, by which I mean argumentation that concerns meta-prescriptives and is limited in space and time.

This orientation corresponds to the course that the evolution of social interaction is currently taking; the temporary contract is in practice supplanting permanent institutions in the professional, emotional, sexual, cultural, family, and international domains, as well as in political affairs. This evolution is of course ambiguous: the temporary contract is favored by the system due to its greater flexibility, lower cost, and the creative turmoil of its accompanying motivations — all of these factors contribute to increased operativity. In any case, there is no question here of proposing a "pure" alternative to the system: we all know that an attempt at an alternative of that kind would end up resembling the system it was meant to replace. We should be happy that the tendency toward the temporary contract is ambiguous: it is not totally subordinated to the goal of the system, yet the system tolerates it. This bears witness to the existence of another goal within the system: knowledge of language games as such and the decision to assume responsibility for their rules and effects. Their most significant effect is precisely what validates the adoption of rules — the quest for paralogy.

We are finally in a position to understand how the computerization of society affects this problematic. It could become the "dream" instrument for controlling and regulating the market system, extended to include knowledge itself and governed exclusively by the performativity principle. In that case it would inevitably involve the use of terror. But it could also aid groups discussing metaprescriptives by supplying them with the information they usually lack for making knowledgeable decisions. The line to follow for computerization to take the second of these two paths is, in principle, quite simple: give the public free access to the memory and data banks.[45] Language games would then be games of perfect information at any given moment. But they would also be non-zero-sum games, and by virtue of that fact discussion would never risk fixating in a position of minimax equilibrium because it had exhausted its stakes. For the stakes would be knowledge (or information, if you will), and the reserve of knowledge — language's reserve of possible utterances — is inexhaustible. This sketches the outline of a politics that would respect both the desire for justice and the desire for the unknown.

Notes

1. See the work of Michel Serres, especially *Hermès I–IV* (Paris: Editions de Minuit, 1969–1977).

2. For example, Erving Goffman, *The Presentation of Self in Everyday Life* (Garden City, New York: Doubleday, 1959); Gouldner, *The Coming Crisis* (New York: Basic Books, 1970), chap. 10; Alain Touraine et al., *Lutte étudiante* (Paris: Seuil, 1978); M. Callon, "Sociologie des techniques?" *Pandore* 2 (February 1979): 28–32; Watzlawick et al., *Pragmatics of Human Communication* (New York: Norton, 1967).

3. John Kenneth Galbraith, *The New Industrial State* (Boston: Houghton-Mifflin, 1967); Raymond Aron, *Eighteen Lectures on Industrial Society* (London: Weidenfeld and Nicholson, 1967). The theme of general bureaucratization as the future of modern societies was first developed by B. Rizzi, *La Bureaucratisation du monde* (Paris: B. Rizzi, 1939).

4. See H. P. Grice, "Logic and Conservation," in Peter Cole and Jeremy Morgan, eds., *Speech Acts III, Syntax and Semantics* (New York: Academic Press, 1975), pp. 59–82.

5. For a phenomenological approach to the problem, see Maurice Merleau-Ponty, *Résumés de cours*, ed. Claude Lefort (Paris: Gallimard, 1968), the course for 1954–55. For a psychosociological approach, see R. Loureau, *L'Analyse institutionnelle* (Paris: Editions de Minuit, 1970).

6. M. Callon, "Sociologie des techniques?" p. 30: "Sociologics is the movement by which actors constitute and institute differences, or frontiers, between what is social and what

is not, what is technical and what is not, what is imaginary and what is real: the outline of these frontiers is open to dispute, and no consensus can be achieved except in cases of total domination." Compare this with what Alain Touraine calls permanent sociology in *La Voix et le regard*.

7. The object of knowledge in Aristotle is strictly circumscribed by what he defines as apophantics: "While every sentence has meaning (*semantikos*) . . . not all can be called propositions (*apophantikos*). We call propositions those only that have truth or falsity in them. A prayer is, for instance, a sentence, but neither has truth nor has falsity." "De Interpretatione," 4, 17a, *The Organon*, vol. 1, trans. Harold Cooke and Hugh Tredennick (Cambridge, Massachusetts: Harvard, 1938), 121. [TRANS: The translation of *connaissance* as "learning" is not uniform. It was sometimes necessary to translate it as "knowledge" (especially where it occurs in the plural); it should be clear from the context whether it is a question of *connaissance* (in Lyotard's usage, a body of established denotative statements) or *savoir* (knowledge in the more general sense). *Savoir* has been uniformly translated as "knowledge."]

8. See Karl Popper, *Logik der Forschung* (Wien: Springer, 1935) [Eng. trans. Popper et al., *The Logic of Scientific Discovery* (New York: Basic Books, 1949)], and "Normal Science and Its Dangers," in Imre Lakatos and Alan Musgrave, eds., *Criticism and the Growth of Knowledge* (Cambridge: Cambridge University Press, 1970).

9. See Jean Beaufret, *Le Poème de Parménide* (Paris: Presses Universitaires de France, 1955).

10. Again in the sense of *Bildung* (or, in English, "culture"), as accredited by culturalism. The term is preromantic and romantic; cf. Hegel's *Volksgeist*.

11. See the American culturalist school: Cora DuBois, Abram Kardiner, Ralph Linton, Margaret Mead.

12. See studies of the institution of European folklore traditions from the end of the eighteenth century in their relation to romanticism, for example, the brothers Grimm and Vuk Karadic (Serbian folktales).

13. This was, briefly stated, Lucien Lévy-Bruhl's thesis in *La Mentalité primitive* (Paris: Alcan, 1922) [Eng. trans. Lillian Clare, *Primitive Mentality* (New York: Macmillan, 1923)].

14. Claude Lévi-Strauss, *La Pensée sauvage* (Paris: Plon, 1962) [Eng. trans. *The Savage Mind* (Chicago: University of Chicago, 1966)].

15. Robert Jaulin, *La Paix blanche* (Paris: Seuil, 1970).

16. Vladimir Propp, *Morphology of the Folktale*, trans. Laurence Scott with intro. by Suatana Pirkora-Jakobson [Publications of the American Folklore Society, Bibliographical and Special Series, no. 9 (Bloomington, Indiana, 1958); 2d ed. rev. (Austin, Texas: University of Texas Press, 1968).

17. Claude Lévi-Strauss, "La Structure des mythes" (1955), in *Anthropologie structurale* (Paris: Plon, 1958) [Eng. trans. Claire Jacobson and Brooke Grundfest Schoepf, *Structural Anthropology* (New York: Basic Books, 1963)], and "La Structure et la forme: "Réflexions sur un ouvrage de Vladimir Propp, *Cahiers de l'Institut de Science Economique Appliquée*, 99, series M, 7 (1960) [in Claude Lævi-Strauss, *Structural Anthropology II*, trans. Monique Layton (New York: Basic Books, 1976). The essay will also be included in Vladimir Propp, *Theory and History of Folklore*, trans. Ariadna and Richard Martin,

intro. by Anatoly Liberman, Theory and History of Literature, vol. 5 (Minneapolis: University of Minnesota Press, 1985)].

18. Geza Róheim, *Psychoanalysis and Anthropology* (New York: International Universities Press, 1959).

19. Cf. children's attitude toward their first science lessons, or the way natives interpret the ethnologist's explanations (see Lévi-Strauss, *The Savage Mind* [note 14], chap. 1).

20. That is why Métraux commented to Clastres, "To be able to study a primitive society, it already has to be a little decayed." In effect, the native informant must be able to see his own society through the eyes of the ethnologist; he must be able to question the functioning of its institutions and therefore their legitimacy. Reflecting on his failure with the Achè tribe, Clastres concludes, "And so the Achè accepted presents they had not asked for while at the same time refusing attempts at a dialogue, because they were strong enough not to need it: we would start talking when they were sick" [quoted by M. Cartry in "Pierre Clastres," *Libre* 4 (1978)].

21. Pierre Duhem, *Essai sur la notion de théorie physique de Platon à Galilée* (Paris: Hermann, 1908) [Eng. trans. Edmund Doland and Chaninah Maschler, *To Save the Phenomena: An Essay in the Idea of Physical Theory from Plato to Galileo* (Chicago: University of Chicago Press, 1969)]; Alexandre Koyré, *Études Galiléennes* (1940; Paris: Hermann, 1966) [Eng. trans. John Mephan, *Galileo Studies* (Hassocks, England: Harvester Press, 1978)]; Thomas Kuhn, *Structure of Scientific Revolutions*.

22. Michel de Certeau, Dominique Julia, Jacques Revel, *Une Politique de la langue: La Révolution Française et les patois* (Paris: Gallimard, 1975).

23. On the distinction between prescriptions and norms, see G. Kalinowski, "Du Métalanguage en logique. Réflexions sur la logique déontique et son rapport avec la logique des normes," *Documents de travail* 48 (Università di Urbino, 1975).

24. Alain Touraine, *La Société postindustrielle* (Paris: Denoël, 1969) [Eng. trans. Leonard Mayhew, *The Post-Industrial Society* (London: Wildwood House, 1974)]; Daniel Bell, *The Coming of Post-Industrial Society* (New York: Basic Books, 1973); Ihab Hassan, *The Dismemberment of Orpheus: Toward a Post Modern Literature* (New York: Oxford University Press, 1971); Michel Benamou and Charles Caramello, eds., *Performance in Postmodern Culture* (Wisconsin: Center for Twentieth Century Studies & Coda Press, 1977); M. Köhler, "Postmodernismus: ein begriffgeschichtlicher Überblick," *Amerikastudien* 22. 1 (1977). Certain scientific aspects of postmodernism are inventoried by Ihab Hassan in "Culture, Indeterminacy, and Immanence: Margins of the (Postmodern) Age," *Humanities in Society* 1 (1978): 51–85.

25. Claus Mueller uses the expression "a process of delegitimation" in *The Politics of Communication* (New York: Oxford University Press, 1973), p. 164.

26. "Road of doubt . . . road of despair . . . skepticism," writes Hegel in the preface to the *Phenomenology of Spirit* to describe the effect of the speculative drive on natural knowledge.

27. For fear of encumbering this account, I have postponed until a later study the exposition of this group of rules. [See "Analyzing Speculative Discourse as Language-Game," *The Oxford Literary Review*, 4, no. 3 (1981): 59–67.]

28. Nietzsche, "Der europäische Nihilismus" (MS. N VII 3); "der Nihilism, ein normaler Zustand" (MS. W II 1); "Kritik der Nihilism" (MS. W VII 3); "Zum Plane" (MS.

W II 1), in *Nietzsches Werke kritische Gesamtausgabe*, vol. 7, pts. 1 and 2 (1887–89) (Berlin: De. Gruyter, 1970). These texts have been the object of a commentary by K. Ryjik, *Nietzsche, le manuscrit de Lenzer Heide* (typescript, Département de philosophie, Université de Paris VIII [Vincennes]).

29. "On the future of our educational institutions," in *Complete Works*, vol. 3 (New York: Gordon Press, 1974).

30. Martin Buber, *Ich und Du* (Berlin: Schocken, 1922) [Eng. trans. Ronald G. Smith, *I and Thou* (New York: Charles Scribner's Sons, 1937)], and *Dialogisches Leben* (Zürich: Müller, 1947); Emmanuel Lévinas, *Totalité et infinité* (La Haye: Nijhoff, 1961) [Eng. trans. Alphonso Lingis, *Totality and Infinity: An Essay on Exteriority* (Pittsburgh: Duquesne University Press, 1969)], and "Martin Buber und die Erkenntnistheorie" (1958), in *Philosophen des 20. Jahrhunderts* (Stuttgart: Kohlhammer, 1963) [Fr. trans. "Martin Buber et la théorie de la connaissance," in *Noms propres* (Montpellier: Fata Morgana, 1976)].

31. *Philosophical Investigations*, sec. 18, p. 8.

32. *Philosophical Investigations*, sec. 18, p. 8.

33. *Philosophical Investigations*, sec. 18, p. 8.

34. See, for example, "La taylorisation de la recherche," in *(Auto)critique de la science* (Paris: Seuil, 1973), pp. 291–293. And especially D. J. de Solla Price, *Little Science, Big Science* (New York: Columbia University Press, 1963), who emphasizes the split between a small number of highly productive researchers (evaluated in terms of publication) and a large mass of researchers with low productivity. The number of the latter grows as the square of the former, so that the number of high-productivity researchers only really increases every twenty years. Price concludes that science considered as a social entity is "undemocratic" (p. 59) and that "the eminent scientist" is a hundred years ahead of "the minimal one" (p. 56).

35. See T. J. Desanti, "Sur le rapport traditionnel des sciences et de la philosophie," in *La Philosophie silencieuse, ou critique des philosophies de la science* (Paris: Seuil, 1975).

36. The reclassification of academic philosophy as one of the human sciences in this respect has a significance far beyond simply professional concerns. I do not think that philosophy as legitimation is condemned to disappear, but it is possible that it will not be able to carry out this work, or at least advance it, without revising its ties to the university institution. See on this matter the preamble to the *Projet d'un institut polytechnique de philosophie* (typescript, Département de philosophie, Université de Paris VIII [Vincennes], 1979).

37. See Allan Janik and Stephen Toulmin, *Wittgenstein's Vienna* (New York: Simon & Schuster, 1973), and J. Picl, ed., "Vienne début d'un siècle," *Critique*, 339–340 (1975).

38. See Jürgen Habermas, "Dogmatismus, Vernunft unt Entscheidung — Zur Theorie und Praxis in der verwissenschaftlichen Zivilisation" (1963), in *Theorie und Praxis* [*Theory and Practice*, abr. ed. of 4th German ed., trans. John Viertel (Boston: Beacon Press, 1971)].

39. "Science Smiling into its Beard" is the title of chap. 72, vol. 1, of Musil's *The Man without Qualities*. Cited and discussed by J. Bouveresse, "La Problématique du sujet" *Noroît* 234 and 235 (December 1978 and January 1979).

40. This is at least one way of understanding this term, which comes from Ducrot's problematic, *Dire* (Paris: Hermann, 1972).

41. *Legitimationsprobleme* (Frankfurt: Suhrkamp, 1973) [*Legitimation Crisis*, trans. T. McCarthy (Boston: Beacon Press, 1975), p. 10], passim, especially pp. 21–22: "Language functions in the manner of a transformer . . . changing cognitions into propositions, needs and feelings into normative expectations (commands, values). This transformation produces the far-reaching distinction between the subjectivity of intention, willing, of pleasure and unpleasure on the one hand, and expressions and norms with a *pretension to universality* on the other. Universality signifies the objectivity of knowledge and the legitimacy of prevailing norms; both assure the community [*Gemeinsamkeit*] constitutive of lived social experience." We see that by formulating the problematic in this way, the question of legitimacy is fixated on one type of reply, universality. This on the one hand presupposes that the legitimation of the subject of knowledge is identical to that of the subject of action (in opposition to Kant's critique, which dissociates conceptual universality, appropriate to the former, and ideal universality, or "suprasensible nature," which forms the horizon of the latter), and on the other hand it maintains that consensus (*Gemeinschaft*) is the only possible horizon for the life of humanity.

42. Habermas, *Legitimationsprobleme*, p. 20. The subordination of the metaprescriptives of prescription (i.e., the normalization of laws) to *Diskurs* is explicit, for example, on p. 144: "The normative pretension to validity is itself cognitive in the sense that it always assumes it could be accepted in a rational discussion."

43. Garbis Kortian, *Métacritique* (Paris: Editions de Minuit, 1979) [Eng. trans. John Raffan, *Metacritique: The Philosophical Argument of Jürgen Habermas* (Cambridge: Cambridge University Press, 1980)], pt. 5, examines this enlightenment aspect of Habermas's thought. See by the same author, "Le Discours philosophique et son objet," *Critique* 384 (1979): 407–419.

44. See J. Poulain, "Vers une pragmatique nucléaire" (typescript, Université de Montréal, 1977), and for a more general discussion of the pragmatics of Searle and Gehlen, see J. Poulain, "Pragmatique de la parole et pragmatique de la vie," *Phi zéro* 7, no. 1 (Université de Montréal, September 1978): 5–50.

45. See Tricot et al., *Informatique et libertés*, government report (La Documentation francaise, 1975); L. Joinet, "Les 'pièges liberaticides' de l'informatique," *Le Monde diplomatique* 300 (March 1979): these traps (*pièges*) are "the application of the technique of 'social profiles' to the management of the mass of the population; the logic of security produced by the automatization of society." See too the documents and analysis in *Interférences* 1 and 2 (Winter 1974–Spring 1975), the theme of which is the establishment of popular networks of multimedia communication. Topics treated include amateur radios (especially their role in Quebec during the FLQ affair of October 1970 and that of the "Front commun" in May 1972); community radios in the United States and Canada; the impact of computers on editorial work in the press; pirate radios (before their development in Italy); administrative files; the IBM monopoly; computer sabotage. The municipality of Yverdon (Canton of Vaud), having voted to buy a computer (operational in 1981), enacted a certain number of rules: exclusive authority of the municipal council to decide which data are collected, to whom and under what conditions they are communicated; access for all citizens to all data (on payment); the right of every citizen to see the entries on his file (about 50), to correct them and address a complaint about them to the municipal council and if need be to the Council of State; the right of all citizens to know (on request) which data concerning them is communicated and to whom (*La Semaine media* 18, 1 March 1979, 9).

3

Michel Foucault

Introduction

More consistently than any other contemporary thinker, Michel Foucault has developed the implications of Nietzsche's rejection of the Platonic idea of truth. In its place he proposes what may be called, in Deleuze's phrase, a "counterphilosophy" (1984, 149), which traces the lowly origins of truth in struggle and conflict, in arbitrariness and contingency, in a will to truth that is essentially intricated with desire and power. He confronts modern rationalism once again with Nietzsche's question: "But what if this equation [of the divine and the true] becomes less and less credible, if the only things that may still be viewed as divine are error, blindness, and lies, if God himself [the truth] turns out to be our *longest* lie?" (1958, 258).

In *The Order of Things*, Foucault joined the chorus in France who, along with Lévi-Strauss, announced "the end of man," that is, of the sovereign Kantian subject, and with it the collapse of the moral foundations of Enlightenment humanism and the epistemological foundations of the human sciences. Although Foucault eventually moved beyond the more or less structuralist program advanced in that work, he has maintained his opposition to the Kantian subject and the edifice erected upon it. But the "archeological" task of analyzing the internal logics of autonomous discourse formations — in abstraction from the social practices and institutions in which they are embedded — has been absorbed into the "genealogical" project sketched in the following interview. Genealogy, the successor discipline to philosophy, remains a kind of philosophical history. Its aim, as Foucault says, is to construct a "history of the objectification of objectivities" — a "nominalist critique," by way of historical analysis, of the fundamental ideas in terms of which we have constituted ourselves as subjects and objects of knowledge. It seeks to "break down, to disassemble, the unity of the apparently self-evident concepts from which philosophers and social scientists generally begin," to disrupt the unity of the "apparently given" and "immediate" objects of our experience and to show that they are "products that have within themselves a certain heterogeneity" (Flynn, 331). But unlike the mainstream of modern philosophy, and like Nietzsche, Foucault does not construct this heterogeneity in terms of more or less invariant structures of subjectivity, but with reference to historically variable relations of power.

Power, as he conceives it, is not something possessed by subjects; it is a "network," "grid," or "field" of relations in which subjects are first constituted as both the products and the agents of power. The modern modalities of power are misconceived if they are taken to be essentially negative, prohibitive instances at the top or the center of the social order, interdicting and repressing the actions of those below or at the margins. Power, Foucault insists, is also and essentially positive, productive and "capillary" — it circulates throughout the cells and the extremities of the social body; it is an aspect of every social practice, social relation, and social institution. The general function of the modern "disciplinary" and "confessional" technologies of power can be characterized as "normalization," the production of docile and useful bodies to staff our offices and factories, schools and armies. What makes these technologies more insidious than the classical ones is that they do not appear openly as power but mask themselves as its opposite — as the human sciences, say, or as individual self-knowledge. It is such configurations of power/knowledge that are the domain of Foucault's analysis. "Truth isn't outside power, or lacking in power . . . [or] the reward of free spirits. . . . Truth is a thing of this world: it is produced only by virtue of multiple forms of constraint. And it induces regular effects of power. Each

society has its regime of truth, its 'general politics' of truth"
(*Power/Knowledge*, 131).

In the following interview Foucault gives a particularly clear
statement of how he approaches this domain in order to determine the ways in which historically specific practices of separating, dividing, distinguishing the true from the false came
to be established. Genealogy seeks to demonstrate the interweaving of what is said with what is done, of reasons with
prescriptions, of "effects of veridiction" with "effects of jurisdiction"; to understand how we "govern ourselves and others
by the production of truth." And it treats the constitution of
domains of objects about which true or false statements can be
made as historical events, constructing an indefinite number
of internal and external relations of intelligibility, decomposing
apparent unities in a "polymorphism" of elements, relations,
and domains. The "theoretical-political" point of this "analytic
decomposition" is to "show that things weren't as necessary as
all that," to replace the unitary, necessary, and invariant with
the multiple, contingent, and arbitrary, and thereby to "contribute to changing people's ways of perceiving and doing
things, to participate in this difficult displacement of forms of
sensibility and thresholds of tolerance" — in more traditional
terms, to make us critical of the presumed rationality of our
discourses and practices. In particular, Foucault wants to break
the hold on our minds of the modern "sciences of man," behind
whose facade of universality and objectivity are concealed the
ever-spreading operations of modern techniques of domination and of the self, of which the modern self-examining, self-
policing, self-disciplining — in short, "normal" — individual is
a product.

This project is not conceived to be in the service of Truth
or Freedom; it does not reveal the secret operations of power
in the constitution of truth for the sake of liberating subjects
from its effects. With his rejection of the traditional philosophical notion of truth and his generalization of the concept of
power, Foucault calls into question the very idea of unmasking
that informs the work of two thinkers whom he superficially
resembles: Marx and Freud. He considers their projects as
having come to an end, for now we realize that we cannot
altogether escape from regimes of power/knowledge into some

transcendental realm of freedom and truth, but can only move from one regime to another.

Critics of Foucault, such as Fraser, Taylor, and Habermas, have raised the familiar questions of self-referential contradiction: What status does Foucault's own theory have? In what regime of truth is it enmeshed? In response, Foucault has maintained that he is not interested in a "theory" of truth/ power but in a practical "history of the present." Genealogy is practiced by the "specific," as opposed to the "universal," intellectual. The specific intellectual is not the voice of Reason and Truth; he or she does not stand outside of every system of power. Rather, the specific intellectual takes up local struggles and seeks to "detach the power of truth from the forms of hegemony — social, economic, and cultural — within which it operates at the present time" (*Power/Knowledge*, 133). Criticism is then an instrument of struggle, with which the critic seeks to change, if only for the moment, the balance of power in the present regime of truth.

Suggested Readings

Clarke, Michael. *Michel Foucault: An Annotated Bibliography*. New York: Garland Press, 1983.

Cousins, Mark, and Athar Hussain. *Michel Foucault*. New York: St. Martin's, 1984.

Deleuze, Gilles. "Nomad Thought," in *The New Nietzsche*, ed. D. Allison, 141–149. Cambridge, Massachusetts: MIT Press, 1984.

Dreyfus, Hubert, and Paul Rabinow. *Michel Foucault: Beyond Structuralism and Hermeneutics*. Chicago: University of Chicago Press, 1982.

Flynn, Bernard. "Sexuality, Knowledge and Power in the Thought of Michel Foucault," *Philosophy and Social Criticism* 8 (1981), 329–348.

Foucault, Michel. *Archaeology of Knowledge*. New York: Harper and Row, 1972.

Foucault, Michel. *Madness and Civilization*. New York: Vintage Books, 1973.

Foucault, Michel. *The Order of Things*. New York: Vintage Books, 1973.

Foucault, Michel. *Birth of the Clinic*. New York: Pantheon Books, 1975.

Foucault, Michel. *Michel Foucault: Language, Counter-Memory, Practice. Selected Essays and Interviews*. Ed. D. F. Bouchard. Ithaca: Cornell University Press, 1977.

Foucault, Michel. *Discipline and Punish*. New York: Vintage Books, 1979.

Foucault, Michel. *Power/Knowledge: Selected Interviews and Other Writings*. Ed. Colin Gordon. New York: Pantheon Books, 1980.

Foucault, Michel. *History of Sexuality*. Vol. 1. New York: Pantheon Books, 1980.

Foucault, Michel. *This Is Not a Pipe*. Berkeley: University of California Press, 1983.

Fraser, Nancy. "Foucault on Modern Power: Empirical Insights and Normative Confusions," *Praxis International* 1 (1981), 272–287.

Fraser, Nancy. "Michel Foucault: A 'Young Conservative'?" *Ethics* 96 (1985), 165–184.

Habermas, Jürgen. *Der philosophische Diskurs der Moderne*. Frankfurt: Suhrkamp, 1985. English translation forthcoming, MIT Press.

Hacking, Ian. Review of *History of Sexuality*, Vol. 1. *New York Review of Books* (May 14, 1981), 32–37.

Honneth, Axel. *Kritik der Macht. Reflexionsstufen einer kritischen Gesellschaftstheorie*, 121–224. Frankfurt: Suhrkamp, 1985. English translation forthcoming, MIT Press.

Hoy, David, ed. *Foucault: A Critical Reader*. London: Basil Blackwell, 1986.

Lemert, Charles, and Garth Gillian. *Michel Foucault: Social Theory and Transgression*. New York: Columbia University Press, 1982.

Nietzsche, Friedrich. *Genealogy of Morals*. New York: Anchor Books, 1958.

Philip, Mark. "Foucault on Power: A Problem of Radical Translation?" *Political Theory* 11 (1983), 29–53.

Poster, Mark. *Foucault, Marxism and History* Cambridge: Polity Press, 1984.

Rabinow, P., ed. *The Foucault Reader*. New York: Pantheon Books 1984. With introduction.

Rajchman, John. *Michel Foucault: The Freedom of Philosophy*. New York: Columbia University Press, 1985.

Roth, Michael. "Foucault's History of the Present," *History and Theory* 20 (1981), 32–46.

Taylor, Charles. "Foucault on Freedom and Truth," *Political Theory* 12 (1984), 152–183.

Taylor, Charles, and William Connolly. "Michel Foucault: An Exchange," *Political Theory* 13 (1985), 365–386.

Sheridan, Alan. *Michel Foucault: The Will to Truth*. New York: Tavistock, 1980.

Veyne, Paul. *Writing History*. Middletown: Wesleyan University Press, 1984.

Walzer, Michael. "The Politics of Michel Foucault," *Dissent* (1983), 481–490.

Wartenberg, Thomas. "Foucault's Archaeological Method," *Philosophical Forum* 15 (1984), 345–364.

Questions of Method:
An Interview with
Michel Foucault

The discussion translated here was published in a volume edited by Michelle Perrot, entitled *L'impossible prison: Recherches sur le système pénitentiaire au XIXe siècle (Paris: Editions du Seuil, 1980)*. This book is an enlarged version of a set of essays in *Annales historiques de la Révolution française*, 1977:2, in which a group of historians reflect on Michel Foucault's *Discipline and Punish* and explore a number of complementary aspects of nineteenth-century penal history.

This interview is based on a round-table debate involving Michel Foucault and Maurice Agulhon, Nicole Castan, Catherine Duprat, François Ewald, Arlette Farge, Allesandro Fontana, Carlo Ginzburg, Remi Gossez, Jacques Léonard, Pasquale Pasquino, Michelle Perrot, and Jacques Revel. In *L'impossible prison* it is preceded by two preliminary texts, "L'historien et le philosophe," an essay on *Discipline and Punish* by Jacques Léonard, and "La poussière et le nuage," a reply by Michel Foucault. As Michelle Perrot explains, the transcript of the discussion is extensively recast in its published form, Michel Foucault having revised his own contributions and the other historians' interventions having been rearranged into a series of questions by "a collective Historian."

Why the Prison?

Question: Why do you see the birth of the prison, and in particular this process you call "hurried substitution" which in the early years of the nineteenth century establishes the prison at the center of the new penal system, as being so important?

Aren't you inclined to overstate the importance of the prison in penal history, given that other quite distinct modes of punishment (the death penalty, the penal colonies, deportation) remained in effect too? At the level of historical method, you seem to scorn explanations in terms of causality or structure, and sometimes to prioritize a description of a process that is purely one of events. No doubt it's true that the preoccupation with "social history" has invaded historians' work in an uncontrolled manner, but, even if one does not accept the "social" as the only valid level of historical explanation, is it right for you to throw out social history altogether from your "interpretative diagram"?

Michel Foucault: I wouldn't want what I may have said or written to be seen as laying any claims to totality. I don't try to universalize what I say; conversely, what I don't say isn't meant to be thereby disqualified as being of no importance. My work takes place between unfinished abutments and lines of dots. I like to open up a space of research, try it out, and then if it doesn't work, try again somewhere else. On many points — I am thinking especially of the relations between dialectics, genealogy, and strategy — I am still working and don't yet know whether I am going to get anywhere. What I say ought to be taken as "propositions," "game openings" where those who may be interested are invited to join in; they are not meant as dogmatic assertions that have to be taken or left en bloc. My books aren't treatises in philosophy or studies of history: at most, they are philosophical fragments put to work in a historical field of problems.

I will attempt to answer the questions that have been posed. First, about the prison. You wonder whether it was as important as I have claimed, or whether it acted as the real focus of the penal system. I don't mean to suggest that the prison was the essential core of the entire penal system; nor am I saying that it would be impossible to approach the problems of penal history — not to speak of the history of crime in general — by other routes than the history of the prison. But it seemed to me legitimate to take the prison as my object, for two reasons. First, because it had been rather neglected in previous analyses; when people had set out to study the problems of "the penal order" [*pénalité*] — a confused enough term in any case — they usually opted to prioritize one of two directions: either the sociological problem of the criminal population or the juridical problem of the penal system and its basis. The actual practice of punishment was scarcely studied except, in the line of the Frankfurt School, by Rusche and Kirchheimer. There have indeed been studies of prisons as institutions, but very few of imprisonment as a general punitive practice in our societies.

My second reason for wanting to study the prison was the idea of reactivating the project of a "genealogy of morals," one that worked by tracing the lines of transformation of what one might call "moral technologies." In order to get a better understanding of what is punished and why, I wanted to ask the question, How does one punish? This was the same procedure as I had used when dealing with madness: rather than asking *what,* in a given period, is regarded as sanity or insanity, as mental illness or normal behavior, I wanted to ask *how* these divisions are operated. It's a method that seems to me to yield, I wouldn't say the maximum of possible illumination, but at least a fairly fruitful kind of intelligibility.

There was also, while I was writing this book, a contemporary issue relating to the prison and, more generally, to the numerous aspects of penal practice that were being brought into question. This development was noticeable not only in France but also in the United States, Britain, and Italy. It would be interesting incidentally to consider why all these problems about confinement, internment, the penal dressage of individuals and their distribution, classification, and objectification through forms of knowledge, came to be posed so urgently at this time, well in advance of May 1968: the themes of antipsychiatry were formulated around 1958 to 1960. The connection with the matter of the concentration camps is evident — look at Bettelheim. But one would need to analyze more closely what took place around 1960.

In this piece of research on the prisons, as in my other earlier work, the target of analysis wasn't "institutions," "theories," or "ideology," but *practices* — with the aim of grasping the conditions that make these acceptable at a given moment; the hypothesis being that these types of practice are not just governed by institutions, prescribed by ideologies, guided by pragmatic circumstances — whatever role these elements may actually play — but possess up to a point their own specific regularities, logic, strategy, self-evidence, and "reason." It is a question of analyzing a "regime of practices" — practices being understood here as places where what is said and what is done, rules imposed and reasons given, the planned and the taken for granted meet and interconnect.

To analyze "regimes of practices" means to analyze programs of conduct that have both prescriptive effects regarding what is to be done (effects of "jurisdiction") and codifying effects regarding what is to be known (effects of "veridiction").

So I was aiming to write a history, not of the prison as an institution, but of the *practice of imprisonment*. To show its origin, or, more exactly, to show how this way of doing things — ancient enough in itself — was capable of being accepted at a certain moment as a principal component of the penal system, thus coming to seem an altogether natural, self-evident, and indispensable part of it.

It's a matter of shaking this false self-evidence, of demonstrating its precariousness, of making visible, not its arbitrariness but its complex interconnection with a multiplicity of historical processes, many of them of recent date. From this point of view I can say that the history of penal imprisonment exceeded my wildest hopes. All the early-nineteenth-century texts and discussions testify to the astonishment at finding the prison being used as a general means of punishment — something that had not at all been what the eighteenth-century reformers had had in mind. I did not at all take this sudden change — which was what its contemporaries recognized it as being — as marking a result at which one's analysis could stop. I took this discontinuity, this in a sense "phenomenal" set of mutations, as my starting point and tried, without eradicating it, to account for it. It was a matter not of digging down to a buried stratum of continuity but of identifying the transformation that made this hasty passage possible.

As you know, no one is more of a continuist than I am: to recognize a discontinuity is never anything more than to register a problem that needs to be solved.

Eventalization

Question: What you have just said clears up a number of things. All the same, historians have been troubled by a sort of equivocation in your analyses, a sort of oscillation between "hyper-rationalism" and "infra-rationality."

Michel Foucault: I am trying to work in the direction of what one might call "eventalization." Even though the "event" has been for some while now a category little esteemed by historians, I wonder whether, understood in a certain sense, "eventalization" may not be a useful procedure of analysis. What do I mean by this term? First of all, a breach of self-evidence. It means making visible a *singularity* at places where there is a temptation to invoke a historical constant, an immediate anthropological trait, or an obviousness that imposes itself uniformly on all. To show that things "weren't as necessary as all that"; it wasn't as a matter of course that mad people came to be regarded as mentally ill; it wasn't self-evident that the only thing to be done with a criminal was to lock him up, it wasn't self-evident that the causes of illness were to be sought through the individual examination of bodies; and so on. A breach of self-evidence, of those self-evidences on which our knowledges, acquiescences, and practices rest. This is the first theoretico-political function of "eventalization."

Secondly, eventalization means rediscovering the connections, encounters, supports, blockages, plays of forces, strategies, and so on that at a given moment establish what subsequently counts as being self-evident, universal, and necessary. In this sense one is indeed effecting a sort of multiplication or pluralization of causes.

Does this mean that one regards the singularity one is analyzing simply as a fact to be registered, a reasonless break in an inert continuum? Clearly not, since that would amount to treating continuity as a self-sufficient reality that carries its own *raison d'être* within itself.

Causal multiplication consists in analyzing an event according to the multiple processes that constitute it. So to analyze the practice of penal incarceration as an "event" (not as an institutional fact or ideological effect) means to determine the processes of "penalization" (that is, progressive insertion into the forms of legal punishment) of already existing practices of internment; the processes of "carceralization" of practices of penal justice (that is, the movement by which imprisonment as a form of punishment and technique of correction becomes a central component of the penal order); and these vast processes need themselves to be further broken down: the penalization of internment comprises a multiplicity of processes such as the formation of closed pedagogical spaces functioning through rewards and punishments, etc.

As a procedure for lightening the weight of causality, "eventalization" thus works by constructing around the singular event analyzed as process a "polygon" or rather a "polyhedron" of intelligibility, the number of whose faces is not given in advance and can never properly be taken as finite. One has to proceed by progressive, necessarily incomplete saturation. And one has to bear in mind that the further one decomposes the processes under analysis, the more one is enabled and indeed obliged to construct their external relations of intelligibility. (In concrete terms: the more one analyzes the process of "carceralization" of penal practice down to its smallest details, the more one is led to relate them to such practices as schooling, military discipline, etc.). The internal analysis of processes goes hand in hand with a multiplication of analytical "salients."

This operation thus leads to an increasing polymorphism as the analysis progresses:

• A polymorphism of the elements that are brought into relation: starting from the prison, one introduces the history of pedagogical practices, the formation of professional armies, British empirical philosophy, techniques of use of firearms, new methods of division of labor.

• A polymorphism of relations described: these may concern the transposition of technical models (such as architectures of surveillance), tactics calculated in response to a particular situation (such as the growth of banditry, the disorder provoked by public tortures and executions, the defects of the practice of penal banishment), or the application of theoretical schemas (such as those representing the genesis of ideas and the formation of signs, the Utilitarian conception of behavior, etc.).

• A polymorphism of domains of reference (varying in their nature, generality, etc.), ranging from technical mutations in matters of detail to the attempted emplacement in a capitalist economy of new techniques of power designed in response to the exigencies of that economy.

Forgive this long detour, but it enables me better to reply to your question about hyper- and hypo-rationalisms, one that is often put to me.

It is some time since historians lost their love of events, and made "de-eventalization" their principle of historical intelligibility. The way they work is by ascribing the object they analyze to the most unitary, necessary, inevitable, and (ultimately) extrahistorical mechanism or structure available. An economic mechanism, an anthropological structure, or a demographic process that figures as the climactic stage in the investigation — these are the goals of de-eventalized history. (Of course, these remarks are only intended as a crude specification of a certain board tendency.)

Clearly, viewed from the standpoint of this style of analysis, what I am proposing is at once too much and too little. There are too many diverse kinds of relations, too many lines of analysis, yet at the same time there is too little necessary unity. A plethora of intelligibilities, a deficit of necessities.

But for me this is precisely the point at issue, both in historical analysis and in political critique. We aren't, nor do we have to put ourselves, under the sign of a unitary necessity.

The Problem of Rationalities

Question: I would like to pause for a moment on this question of eventalization, because it lies at the center of a certain number of misunderstandings about your work. (I am not talking about the misguided portrayal of you as a "thinker of discontinuity.") Behind the identifying of breaks and the careful, detailed charting of these networks of relations that engender a reality and a history, there persists from one book to the next something amounting to one of those historical constants or anthropologico-cultural traits you were objecting to just now: this version of a general history of rationalization spanning three or four centuries, or at any rate of a history of one particular kind of rationalization as it progressively takes effect in our society. It's not by chance that your first book was a history of reason as well as of madness, and I believe that the themes of all your other books, the analysis of different techniques of isolation, the social taxonomies, etc., all this boils down to one and the same meta-anthropological or metahistorical process of rationalization. In this sense, the "eventalization" that you define here as central to your work seems to me to constitute only one of its extremes.

Michel Foucault: If one calls "Weberians" those who set out to take on board the Marxist analyses of the contradictions of capital, treating these contradictions as part and parcel of the irrational rationality of capitalist society, then I don't think I am a Weberian, since my basic preoccupation isn't rationality considered as an anthropological invariant. I don't believe one can speak of an intrinsic notion of "rationalization" without on the one hand positing an absolute value inherent in reason, and on the other taking the risk of applying the term empirically in a completely arbitrary way. I think one must restrict one's use of this word to an instrumental and relative meaning. The ceremony of public torture isn't in itself more irrational than imprisonment in a cell; but it's irrational in terms of a type of penal practice that involves new ways of envisaging the effects to be produced by the penalty imposed, new ways of calculating its utility, justifying it, graduating it, etc. One isn't assessing things in terms of an absolute against which they could be evaluated as constituting more or less perfect forms of rationality, but rather examining how forms of rationality inscribe themselves in practices or systems of practices, and what role they play within them. Because it's true that "practices" don't exist without a certain regime of rationality. But, rather than measuring this regime against a value-of-reason, I would prefer to analyze it according to two axes: on the one hand, that of codification/prescription (how it forms an ensemble of rules, procedures, means to an end, etc.), and on the other, that of true or false formulation (how it determines a domain of objects about which it is possible to articulate true or false propositions).

If I have studied "practices" like those of the sequestration of the insane, or clinical medicine, or the organization of the empirical sciences, or legal punishment, it was in order to study this interplay between a "code" that rules ways of doing things (how people are to be graded and examined, things and signs classified, individuals trained, etc.) and a production of true discourses that serve to found, justify, and provide reasons and principles for these ways of doing things. To put the matter clearly: my problem is to see how men govern (themselves and others) by the production of truth (I repeat once again that by production of truth I mean not the production of true utterances but the establishment of domains in which the practice of true and false can be made at once ordered and pertinent).

Eventalizing singular ensembles of practices, so as to make them graspable as different regimes of "jurisdiction" and "veridiction." That, to put it in exceedingly barbarous terms, is what I would like to do. You see that this is neither a history of knowledge contents (*connaissances*) nor an analysis of the advancing rationalities that rule our society, nor an anthropology of the codifications that, without our knowledge, rule our behavior. I would like in short to resituate the production of true and false at the heart of historical analysis and political critique.

Question: It's not an accident that you speak of Max Weber. There is in your work, no doubt in a sense you wouldn't want to accept, a sort of "ideal type" that paralyzes and mutes analysis when one tries to account for reality. Isn't this what led you to abstain from all commentary when you published the memoir of Pierre Rivière?

Michel Foucault: I don't think your comparison with Max Weber is exact. Schematically one can say that the "ideal type" is a category of historical interpretation; it's a structure of understanding for the historian who seeks to integrate, after the fact, a certain set of data: it allows him to recapture an "essence" (Calvinism, the State, the capitalist enterprise), working from general principles that are not at all present in the thoughts of the individuals whose concrete behavior is nevertheles to be understood on their basis.

When I try to analyze the rationalities proper to penal imprisonment, the psychiatrization of madness, or the organization of the domain of sexuality, and when I lay stress on the fact that the real functioning of institutions isn't confined to the unfolding of this rational schema in its pure form, is this an analysis in terms of "ideal types"? I don't think so, for a number of reasons.

The rational schemas of the prison, the hospital, or the asylum are not general principles that can be rediscovered only through the historian's retrospective interpretation. They are explicit *programs;* we are dealing with sets of calculated, reasoned prescriptions in terms of which institutions are meant to be reorganized, spaces arranged, behaviors regulated. If they have an ideality, it is that of a programming left in abeyance, not that of a general but hidden meaning.

Of course this programming depends on forms of rationality much more general than those that they directly implement. I tried to show that the rationality envisaged in penal imprisonment wasn't the outcome of a straightforward calculation of immediate interest (internment turning out to be, in the last analysis, the simplest and cheapest solution), but that it arose out of a whole technology of human training, surveillance of behavior, individualization of the elements of a social body. "Discipline" isn't the expression of an "ideal type" (that of "disciplined man"); it's the generalization and interconnection of different techniques themselves designed in response to localized requirements (schooling; training troops to handle rifles).

These programs don't take effect in the institutions in an integral manner; they are simplified, or some are chosen and not others; and things never work out as planned. But what I wanted to show is that this difference is not one between the purity of ideal and the disorderly impurity of the real, but that in fact there are different strategies that are mutually opposed, composed, and superposed so as to produce permanent and solid effects that can perfectly well be understood in terms of their rationality, even though they don't conform to the initial programming: this is what gives the resulting apparatus *(dispositif)* its solidity and suppleness.

Programs, technologies, apparatuses — none of these is an "ideal type." I try to study the play and development of a set of diverse realities articulated onto each other; a program, the connection that explains it, the law that gives it its coercive power, etc., are all just as much realities — albeit in a different mode — as the institutions that embody them or the behaviors that more or less faithfully conform to them.

You say to me: Nothing happens as laid down in these "programs", they are no more than dreams, utopias, a sort of imaginary production that you aren't entitled to substitute for reality. Bentham's *Panopticon* isn't a very good description of "real life" in nineteenth-century prisons.

To this I would reply: If I had wanted to describe "real life" in the prisons, I wouldn't indeed have gone to Bentham. But the fact that this real life isn't the same thing as the theoreticians' schemas doesn't entail that these schemas are therefore utopian, imaginary, etc. That would be to have a very impoverished notion of the real. For one thing, the elaboration of these schemas corresponds to a whole series of diverse practices and strategies: the search for effective, measured, unified penal mechanisms is unquestionably a response to the inadequation of the institutions of judicial power to the new economic forms, urbanization, etc.; again, there is the attempt, very noticeable in a country like France, to reduce the autonomy and insularity of judicial practice and personnel within the overall workings of the State; there is the wish to respond to emerging new forms of criminality; and so on. For another thing, these programs induce a whole series of effects in the real (which isn't of course the same as saying that they take the place of the real): they crystallize into institutions, they inform individual behavior, they act as grids for the perception and evaluation of things. It is absolutely true that criminals stubbornly resisted the new disciplinary mechanism in the prison; it is absolutely correct that the actual functioning of the prisons, in the inherited buildings where they were established and with the governors and guards who administered them, was a witches' brew compared to the beautiful Benthamite machine. But if the prisons were seen to have failed, if criminals were perceived as incorrigible, and a whole new criminal "race" emerged into the field of vision of public opinion and "Justice," if the resistance of the prisoners and the pattern of recidivism took the forms we know they did, it's precisely because this type of programming didn't just remain a utopia in the heads of a few projectors.

These programmings of behavior, these regimes of jurisdiction and veridiction aren't abortive schemas for the creation of a reality. They are fragments of reality that induce such particular effects in the real as the distinction between true and false implicit in the ways men "direct," "govern," and "conduct" themselves and others. To grasp these effects as historical events — with what this implies for the question of truth (which is the question of philosophy itself) — this is more or less my theme. You see that this has nothing to do with the project — an admirable one in itself — of grasping a "whole society" in its "living reality."

The question that I won't succeed in answering here but have been asking myself from the beginning is roughly the following: What is history, given there is continually being produced within it a separation of true and false? By that I mean four things. First, in what sense is the production and transformation of the true/false division characteristic and decisive for our historicity? Second, in what specific ways has this relation operated in "Western" societies that produce scientific knowledge whose forms are perpetually changing and whose values are posited as universal? Third, what historical knowledge is possible of a history that itself produces the true/false distinction on which such knowledge depends? Fourth, isn't the most general of political problems the problem of truth? How can one analyze the connection between ways of distinguishing true and false and ways of governing oneself and others? The search for a new foundation for each of these practices, in itself and relative to the other, the will to discover a different way of governing oneself through a different way of dividing up true and false — this is what I would call "political *spiritualité.*"

The Anaesthetic Effect

Question: There is a question here about the way your analyses have been transmitted and received. For instance, if one talks to social workers in the prisons, one finds that the arrival of *Discipline and Punish* had an absolutely sterilizing, or rather anaesthetizing effect on them, because they felt your critique had an implacable logic that left them no possible room for initiative. You said just now, talking about eventalization, that you want to work toward breaking up existing self-evident-nesses, to show both how they are produced and how they are nevertheless always unstable. It seems to me that the second half of the picture — the aspect of instability — isn't clear.

Michel Foucault: You're quite right to pose this problem of anaesthesis, one that is of capital importance. It's quite true that I don't feel myself capable of effecting the "subversion of all codes," "dislocation of all orders of knowledge," "revolutionary affirmation of violence," "overturning of all contemporary culture," these hopes and prospectuses that currently underpin all those brilliant intellectual ventures that I admire all the more because the worth and previous achievements of those who undertake them guarantee an appropriate outcome. My project is far from being of comparable scope. To give some assistance in wearing away certain self-evidentnesses and commonplaces about madness, normality, illness, crime, and punishment; to bring it about, together with many others, that certain phrases can no longer be spoken so lightly, certain acts no longer, or at least no longer so unhesitatingly, performed, to contribute to changing certain things in people's ways of perceiving and doing things, to participate in this difficult displacement of forms of sensibility and thresholds of tolerance — I hardly feel capable of attempting much more than that. If only what I have tried to say might somehow, to some degree, not remain altogether foreign to some such real effects. . . . And yet I realize how much all this can remain precarious, how easily it can all lapse back into somnolence.

But you are right, one has to be more suspicious. Perhaps what I have written has had an anaesthetic effect. But one still needs to distinguish on whom.

To judge by what the psychiatric authorities have had to say, the cohorts on the Right who charge me with being against any form of power, those on the Left who call me the "last bulwark of the bourgeoisie" (this isn't a "Kanapa phrase"; on the contrary), the worthy psychoanalyst who likened me to the Hitler of *Mein Kampf,* the number of times I've been "autopsied" and "buried" during the past fifteen years — well, I have the impression of having had an irritant rather than anaesthetic effect on a good many people. The epidermi bristle with a constancy I find encouraging. A journal recently warned its readers in deliciously Pétainist style against accepting as a credo what I had had to say about sexuality ("the importance of the subject," "the personality of the author" rendered my enterprise "dangerous"). No risk of anaesthetic in that direction. But I agree with you, these are trifles, amusing to note but tedious to collect. The only important problem is what happens on the ground.

We have known at least since the nineteenth century the difference between anaesthesis and paralysis. Let's talk about paralysis first. Who has been paralyzed? Do you think what I wrote on the history of psychiatry paralyzed those people who had already been concerned for some time about what was happening in psychiatric institutions? And, seeing what has been happening in and around the prisons, I don't think the effect of paralysis is very evident there either. As far as the people in prison are concerned, things aren't doing too badly. On the other hand, it's true that certain people, such as those who work in the institutional setting of the prison — which is not quite the same as being in prison — are not likely to find advice or instructions in my books that tell them "what is to be done." But my project is precisely to bring it about that they "no longer know what do do," so that the acts, gestures, discourses that up until then had seemed to go without saying become problematic, difficult, dangerous. This effect is intentional. And then I have some news for you: for me the problem of the prisons isn't one for the "social workers" but one for the prisoners. And on that side, I'm not so sure that what's been said over the last fifteen years has been quite so — how shall I put it? — demobilizing.

But paralysis isn't the same thing as anaesthesis — on the contrary. It's insofar as there's been an awakening to a whole series of problems that the difficulty of doing anything comes to be felt. Not that this effect is an end in itself. But it seems to me that "what is to be done" ought not to be determined from above by reformers, be they prophetic or legislative, but by a long work of comings and goings, of exchanges, reflections, trials, different analyses. If the social workers you are talking about don't know which way to turn, this just goes to show that they're looking, and hence not anaesthetized or sterilized at all — on the contrary. And it's because of the need not to tie them down or immobilize them that there can be no question for me of trying to tell them "what is to be done." If the questions posed by the social workers you spoke of are going to assume their full amplitude, the most important thing is not to bury them under the weight of prescriptive, prophetic discourse. The necessity of reform mustn't be allowed to become a form of blackmail serving to limit, reduce, or halt the exercise of criticism. Under no circumstances should one pay attention to those who tell you, "Don't criticize, since you're not capable of carrying out a reform." That's ministerial cabinet talk. Critique doesn't have to be the premise of a deduction that concludes: This then is what needs to be done. It should be an instrument for those who fight, those who resist and refuse what is. Its use should be in processes of conflict and confrontation, essays in refusal. It doesn't have to lay down the law for the law. It isn't a stage in a programming. It is a challenge directed to what is.

The problem, you see, is one for the subject who acts — the subject of action through which the real is transformed. If prisons and punitive mechanisms are transformed, it won't be because a plan of reform has found its way into the heads of the social workers; it will be when those who have to do with that penal reality, all those people, have come into collision with each other and with themselves, run into dead ends, problems, and impossibilities, been through conflicts and confrontations; when critique has been played out in the real, not when reformers have realized their ideas.

Question: This anaesthetic effect has operated on the historians. If they haven't responded to your work it's because for them the "Foucauldian schema" was becoming as much of an encumbrance as the Marxist one. I don't know if the "effect" you produce interests you. But the explanations you have given here weren't so clear in *Discipline and Punish*.

Michel Foucault: I really wonder whether we are using this word "anaesthetize" in the same sense. These historians seemed to me more to be "aesthetized," "irritated" (in Broussais's sense of the term, of course). Irritated by what? By a schema? I don't believe so, because there is no schema. If there is an "irritation" (and I seem to recall that in a certain journal a few signs of this irritation may have been discreetly manifested), it's more because of the absence of a schema. No infra or superstructure, no Malthusian cycle, no opposition between State and civil society: none of these schemas that have bolstered historians' operations, explicitly or implicitly, for the past hundred or hundred and fifty years.

Hence no doubt the sense of malaise and the questions enjoining me to situate myself within some such schema: "What do you do with the State? What theory do you offer of the State?" Some say I neglect its role, others that I see it everywhere, imagining it capable of minutely controlling individuals' everyday lives. Or that my descriptions leave out all reference to an infrastructure — while others say that I make an infrastructure out of sexuality. The totally contradictory nature of these objections proves that what I am doing doesn't correspond to any of these schemas.

Perhaps the reason why my work irritates people is precisely the fact that I'm not interested in constructing a new schema, nor in validating one that already exists. Perhaps it's because my objective isn't to propose a global principle for analyzing society. And it's here that my project has differed since the outset from that of the historians. They — rightly or wrongly, that's another question — take "society" as the general horizon of their analysis, the instance relative to which they set out to situate this or that particular object ("society, economy, civilization," as the *Annales* have it). My general theme isn't society but the discourse of true and false, by which I mean the correlative formation of domains and objects and the verifiable, falsifiable discourses that bear on them; and it's not just their formation that interests me, but the effects in the real to which they are linked.

I realize I'm not being clear. I'll take an example. It's perfectly legitimate for the historian to ask whether sexual behaviors in a given period were supervised and controlled, and to ask which among them were heavily disapproved of. (It would of course be frivolous to suppose that one has explained a certain intensity of "repression" by the delaying of the age of marriage; here one has scarcely even begun to outline a problem: why is it that the delay in the age of marriage takes effect thus and not otherwise?) But the problem I pose myself is a quite different one; it's a matter of how the rendering of sexual behavior into discourse comes to be transformed, what types of jurisdiction and "veridiction" it's subject to; and how the constitutive elements are formed of this domain that comes — and only at a very late stage — to be termed "sexuality." Among the numerous effects the organization of this domain has undoubtedly had, one is that of having provided historians with a category so "self-evident" that they believe they can write a history of sexuality and its repression.

The history of the "objectification" of those elements that historians consider as objectively given (if I dare put it thus: of the objectification of objectivities), this is the sort of circle I want to try and investigate. It's a difficult tangle to sort out: this, not the presence of some easily reproducible schema, is what doubtless troubles and irritates people. Of course this is a problem of philosophy to which the historian is entitled to remain indifferent. But if I am posing it as a problem within historical analysis, I'm not demanding that history answer it. I would just like to find out what effects the question produces within historical knowledge. Paul Veyne saw this very clearly:[1] it's a matter of the effect on historical knowledge of a nominalist critique formulated elsewhere but by way of a historical analysis.

Note

1. Cf. "Foucault révolutionne l'histoire," in Paul Veyne, *Comment on écrit l'histoire,* (Paris: Editions du Seuil, 1978) [Ed.].

4

Jacques Derrida

Introduction

In 1967 Jacques Derrida moved quickly to the center of the French philosophical scene with the publication of three books: *Of Grammatology, Speech and Phenomena,* and *Writing and Difference.* Together these works inaugurated a project of deconstructing Western metaphysics or "logocentrism," with its characteristic hierarchizing oppositions: *logos/mythos,* logic/rhetoric, intelligible/sensible, speech/writing, literal/figurative, nature/culture, intuition/signification. Derrida's claim is that these conceptual orderings are not in the nature of things, but reflect strategies of exclusion and repression that philosophical systems have been able to maintain only at the cost of internal contradictions and suppressed paradoxes. The task of "deconstruction" is to bring these contradictions and paradoxes to light, to undo, rather than to reverse, these hierarchies, and thereby to call into question the notions of Being as presence that give rise to them — such notions, for instance, as "presence of the thing to sight as *eidos,* presence as substance/essence/existence (*ousia*), temporal presence as point (*stigme*) of the now or of the moment (*nun*), the self-presence of the cogito, consciousness, subjectivity, the co-presence of the other and the self, intersubjectivity as the intentional phenomenon of the ego, and so forth" (1974, 12).

This mode of reading and interpreting philosophical texts does not assume an external vantage point; it is rather a form of internal criticism of a philosopher's own concepts and claims (even if this is frequently achieved only on "the margins of philosophy," that is, with reference to more obscure texts or to footnotes). To use a metaphor Derrida borrows from Lévi-Strauss, the deconstructor is a *bricoleur,* a handyman, who makes critical use of the tools, materials, and strategies of others, but without attempting to construct his or her own edifice. A deconstructive reading looks for the "tension between gesture and statement" in a text — that is, for the ways in which the text implicitly undercuts its own stated views — and it shows how this tension contains a basic insight into the matter at hand. What is excluded by the manifest content of the text as inessential, what is separated off by it as a mere superaddition to what is central, will turn out to be essential, central after all. This is the "logic of the supplement": the marginal and inessential (rhetoric, writing, the sensible, absence) reveal something basic to the nature of the central and essential (reason, speech, the intelligible, presence) and thus place it in a different light (Culler, 102ff.). According to Derrida, this type of paradox cannot be entirely avoided, for we are never complete masters of the language we use; its effects always go beyond what we control. Thus deconstruction is not understood as a kind of dialectical process of purification that finally results in a pure reason; nor is it conceived as a hermeneutic strategy that will eventually lead us to the "true meaning" of a philosophical text or to the "truth of the matter" it discusses. Its intent is dissemination rather than integration, a proliferation of readings made possible by the indeterminacy or undecidability of meanings. It does not aim to produce a unified theory, but only to actively and repeatedly undercut the domination of inherited metaphysical concepts in our discourse. Like Adorno's negative dialectics and Foucault's genealogy, it can aid us in questioning the status of our own discourse and in expanding our awareness of alternatives, but it can never take us completely beyond or outside of the metaphysics of presence. Bringing philosophy to an end can only mean, then, continuing to read philosophical texts in a certain way, repeatedly deconstructing philosophical attempts to attain to full presence or self-sufficient intelligibility, and thus un-doing again and again, but never once and for all, the influence in our discourse of the basic categories of Western intellectual life.

These general observations on deconstruction can be made more specific in relation to Derrida's critique of a major variant of logocentrism: "phonocentrism," or the priority accorded to speech over writing. The Western tradition has typically de-valued writing — the twice-removed "sign of a sign" — in favor of living speech, which seems to stand in a more immediate relation to being, the spoken word in which thought seems to be made immediately and transparently present. Thus, Plato called writing a bastard, while he considered speech to be the legitimate child of *logos;* Rousseau viewed it as a dangerous, if necessary, supplement to speech; and Saussure systematically excluded it from the general study of linguistics, because it usurped the "natural bond" between the phonic signifier and the signified (concept or sense). Drawing upon Saussure's own thesis of the purely relational identity of the sign, Derrida argues that the characteristics associated with writing (the sup-plement), as opposed to speech (the essential), are essential marks of speech as well. Meaning is not a matter of immediate presence or self-presence (compare Husserl's notion of evi-dence, the intuitive fulfillment of meaning-intentions); under-lying it is always the differential structure of a language that goes beyond anything present, a system of contrasts and dif-ferences that are not themselves present (compare Saussure). Signs, spoken no less than written, are essentially relational units. Moreover, the "dangers" of the written form that derive from the detachability of the text from its context — from its author and audience, from its object and occasion — are pres-ent in spoken language as well, since it is inherently repeatable, quotable, utterable in the absence of a specific context. Thus Derrida's stress on writing is not meant to reverse the usual speech/writing hierarchy but to undercut it altogether: the writ-ing of which he speaks is an "archewriting" underlying both speech and writing in the narrower senses.

Derrida marks his radicalization of Saussure by introducing the neologism *différance*. Like archewriting, *différance* refers to the play of differences that accounts for the signifying capacity of language. Moreover, *différance* is both active and passive, cause and effect; it is not the product of a constituting subject, nor does it refer to a "transcendental signified" that is somehow made fully present within it. Beyond the text there are only more texts and traces of texts: external reference can only be a matter of intertextuality.

"The Ends of Man" explores the possibility of a kind of philosophy without a center, without a transcendental or constituting subject, and without a *telos* or ends in light of which our projects and practices acquire their significance. The leading question of the essay is why humanistic readings of Hegel, Husserl, and Heidegger dominated the intellectual scene in postwar France, despite the fact that each of these authors understood his own project in opposition to "anthropologism" and "metaphysical humanism." Employing his method of deconstruction, Derrida suggests that these "misreadings" are instructive for assessing the earlier projects. The "we" of Hegel's *Phenomenology*, the reduction to self-present meaning in Husserl, and even Heidegger's approach to the meaning of Being through an analysis of *Dasein* indicate the pervasive hold of logocentrism on Western thought. They show that we (and Derrida asks, "who, we?") have not yet abandoned the quest for an ultimate signified, that we have not yet understood the call of Nietzsche's Zarathustra for one who would dance with joy outside the house of Being. Heidegger, in particular, is a favored point of departure (in both senses) for Derrida; whether he succeeds in getting beyond Heidegger's destruction of metaphysics and critique of humanism (or even in getting them right) is an oft-debated issue (Silverman and Ihde, part 6). It is clear, however, that he sees no need for any transcendental signified that comes to presence in language and grounds it, that he is opposed to the idea of a still-concealed "truth of Being" and any chiliastic hopes that might be associated with it, and that he rejects the whole metaphorics of the "proximity of Being" (Hoy, 1982).

Suggested Readings

Bloom, Harold, *et al. Deconstruction and Criticism.* New York: Seabury Press, 1979.

Casey, Edward. "Origin(S) In (Of) Heidegger/Derrida," *Journal of Philosophy* 81 (1984), 601–610.

Culler, Jonathan. *On Deconstruction: Theory and Criticism after Structuralism.* Ithaca, New York: Cornell University Press, 1982.

Cumming, Robert. "The Odd Couple: Heidegger and Derrida," *Review of Metaphysics* 34 (1981), 487–521.

Derrida, Jacques. *Speech and Phenomena.* Evanston: Northwestern University Press, 1973.

Derrida, Jacques. *Of Grammatology.* Baltimore: Johns Hopkins University Press, 1974.

Derrida, Jacques. "Limited Inc.," *Glyph* 2 (1977), 162–254.

Derrida, Jacques. "The Retrait of Metaphor," *Enclitic* 2 (1978), 5–33.

Derrida, Jacques. *Writing and Difference.* Chicago: University of Chicago Press, 1978.

Derrida, Jacques. *Spurs: Nietzsche's Styles.* Chicago: University of Chicago Press, 1979.

Derrida, Jacques. *Dissemination.* Chicago: University of Chicago Press, 1981.

Derrida, Jacques. *Positions.* Chicago: University of Chicago Press, 1981.

Derrida, Jacques. "The Conflict of Faculties," in *Language of Knowledge and of Inquiry,* ed. Michael Riffaterre. New York: Columbia University Press, 1982.

Derrida, Jacques. *Margins of Philosophy.* Chicago: University of Chicago Press, 1982.

Derrida, Jacques. "Sending: On Representation," *Social Research* 49 (1982), 294–326.

Derrida, Jacques. "The Time of a Thesis: Punctuations," in *Philosophy in France Today,* ed. Alan Montefiore, 34–50. New York: Cambridge University Press, 1983.

Derrida, Jacques. *Signeponge=Signsponge.* New York: Columbia University Press, 1984.

Descombes, Vincent. *Modern French Philosophy.* New York: Cambridge University Press, 1980.

Fraser, Nancy. "The French Derrideans: Politicizing Deconstruction or Deconstructing the Political?" *New German Critique* 33 (1984), 127–154.

Gasché, Rodolphe. "Deconstruction as Criticism," *Glyph* 6 (1979), 177–216.

Gasché, Rodolphe. "Joining the Text: From Heidegger to Derrida," in *The Yale Critics: Deconstruction in America,* ed. Jonathan Arac, Wlad Godzich, and Wallace Martin, 156–175. Minneapolis: University of Minnesota Press, 1983.

Habermas, Jürgen. *Der Philosophische Diskurs der Moderne.* Frankfurt: Suhrkamp, 1985. English translation forthcoming, MIT Press.

Harari, Josué, ed. *Textual Strategies: Perspectives in Post-Structuralist Criticism.* New York: Methuen, 1979.

Hartman, Geoffrey. *Saving the Text: Literature/Derrida/Philosophy.* Baltimore: Johns Hopkins University Press, 1981.

Hoy, David. "Forgetting the Text: Derrida's Critique of Heidegger," in *The Question of Textuality,* ed. William V. Spanos, Paul A. Bove, and Daniel O'Hara, 223–236. Bloomington: Indiana University Press, 1982.

Hoy, David. "Jacques Derrida," in *The Return of Grand Theory in the Human Sciences,* 43–64. Cambridge: Cambridge University Press, 1985.

Krapnick, M., ed. *Displacement, Derrida and After.* Bloomington: Indiana University Press, 1983.

Magliola, Robert. *Derrida on the Mend.* Lafayette: Purdue University Press, 1984.

Nancy, Jean-Luc, and Philippe Lacoue-Labarthe, eds. *Les fins de l'homme: A partir du travail de Jacques Derrida.* Paris: Galilee, 1981.

Norris, Christopher. *Deconstruction: Theory and Practice.* London: Methuen, 1982.

Rorty, Richard. "Philosophy as a Kind of Writing," in *Consequences of Pragmatism,* 90–109. Minneapolis: University of Minnesota Press, 1983.

Ryan, Michael. *Marxism and Deconstruction: A Critical Articulation.* Baltimore: Johns Hopkins University Press, 1982.

Searle, John. "Reiterating the Differences: A Reply to Derrida," *Glyph* 1 (1977), 198–208.

Silverman, Hugh, and Don Ihde, eds. *Hermeneutics and Deconstruction.* Albany: SUNY Press, 1985.

The Ends of Man

Jacques Derrida

"Now, I say, man and, in general, every rational being exists as an end in himself and not merely as a means to be arbitrarily used by this or that will. In all his actions, whether they are directed to himself or to other rational beings, he must always be regarded at the same time as an end. . . ."
Kant, *Foundations of the Metaphysics of Morals*[1]

"Ontology . . . has merely enabled us to determine the ultimate ends of human reality, its fundamental possibilities, and the value which haunts it."
Jean-Paul Sartre, *Being and Nothingness*[2]

"As the archeology of our thought easily shows, man is an invention of recent date. And one perhaps nearing its end."
Michel Foucault, *The Order of Things*[3]

Every philosophical colloquium necessarily has a political significance.* And not only due to that which has always linked the essence of the philosophical to the essence of the political. Essential and general, this political import nevertheless burdens the a priori link between philosophy and politics, aggravates it in a way, and also determines it when the philosophical colloquium is announced as an international colloquium. Such is the case here.

*Given first as a paper to a colloquium on the topic "Philosophy and Anthropology," in New York, October 1968.

The possibility of an international philosophical colloquium can be examined infinitely, along many pathways, and at multiple levels of generality. In its greatest extension, to which I will return in a moment, such a possibility implies that contrary to the essence of philosophy — such as it has always represented itself at least — philosophical nationalities have been formed. At a given moment, in a given historical, political, and economic context, these national groups have judged it possible and necessary to organize international encounters, to present themselves, or to be represented in such encounters by their national identity (such, at least, as it is assumed by the organizers of the colloquium), and to determine in such encounters their proper difference, or to establish relations between their respective differences. Such an establishment of relations can be practiced, if at all, only in the extent to which national philosophical identities are assumed, whether they are defined in the order of doctrinal content, the order of a certain philosophical "style," or quite simply the order of language, that is, the unity of the academic institution, along with everything implied by language and institution. But the establishing of relations between differences is also the promised complicity of a common element: the colloquium can take place only in a medium, or rather in the representation that all the participants must make of a certain transparent ether, which here would be none other than what is called the universality of philosophical discourse. With these words I am designating less a fact than a project, which is linked by its essence (and we should say by essence itself, by the thought of Being and of truth) to a certain group of languages and "cultures." For something must happen or must have happened to the diaphanous purity of this element.

How else are we to understand that international colloquia — which aim to repair, to surmount, to erase, or simply to relate national philosophical differences one to another — seem possible and necessary? Conversely, and above all, how are we to understand that something like an international philosophical encounter is an extremely rare thing in the world? The philosopher knows, and today can say to himself, that this extremely recent and unexpected thing, which was unimaginable a century ago, becomes a frequent phenomenon — of a disconcerting facility, I even would say — in certain societies, but is of a no less remarkable rarity in the greater part of the world. On the one hand, as far as thought — which perhaps is repulsed by this haste and volubility — is concerned, what is disquieting has to do more with the fever for colloquia and the multiplication of organized or improvised exchanges. On the other hand, it remains no less the case that the societies, languages, cultures, and political or national organizations with which no exchange in the form of an international philosophical colloquium is possible are of considerable number and extent. Nor must we hasten to interpret this impossibility. Essentially, it does not have to do with a prohibition overtly deriving from politico-ideological jurisdiction. For when this prohibition exists, there is every chance that this issue already has become meaningful within the occidental orb of metaphysics or philosophy, that it already has been formulated in political concepts drawn from the metaphysical reserve, and that the *possibility* of such a colloquium henceforth is apparent. Without this no overt prohibition could be articulated. Also, speaking of the noncolloquium, I was not alluding to some ideologico-political barrier that would sector, with borders or curtains, an already philosophical field. I was thinking, first of all, of all those places — cultural, linguistic, political, etc. — where the organization of philosophical colloquium simply would have no meaning, where it would be no more meaningful to instigate it than to prohibit it. If I permit myself to recall this obvious fact, it is because a colloquium that has chosen *anthropos*, the discourse on anthropos, philosphical anthropology, as its theme must feel bearing down on its borders the insistent weight of this difference, which is of an entirely other order than that of the internal or intraphilosophical differences of opinion that could be freely exchanged here. Beyond these borders, what I will call the philosophical *mirage* would consist as much in perceiving philosophy — a more or less constituted and adult philosophy — as in perceiving the desert. For this other space is neither philosophical nor desertlike, that is, barren. If I recall this obvious fact, it is also for another reason: the anxious and busy multiplication of colloquia in the West is doubtless an effect of that difference which I just said bears down, with a mute, growing, and menacing pressure, on the enclosure of Western collocution. The latter doubtless makes an effort to interiorize this difference, to master it, if we may put it thus, by affecting itself with it. The interest in the universality of the anthropos is doubtless a sign of this effort.

Now I would like to specify, still as a preamble, but in another direction, what appears to be one of the general political implications of our colloquium. While refraining from any precipitous appreciation of this fact, simply rendering it for all to reflect upon, I will indicate here what links the possibility of an international philosophical colloquium with the form of democracy. I am indeed saying with the *form,* and with the form of *democracy.*

Here, *democracy* must be the *form* of the political organization of society. This means at least that

1. The national philosophical identity accommodates a nonidentity, does not exclude a relative diversity and the coming into language of this diversity, eventually as a minority. It goes without saying that the philosophers present here no more identify with each other in their thought (why else would they be several?) than they are mandated by some unanimous national discourse. As for the fact that the totality of this diversity might be exhaustively represented — this can only remain problematical, and in part depends upon the discourses to be proffered here.

2. No more than they identify with each other, the philosophers present here do not assume the official policies of their countries. Let me be permitted to speak in my own name here. Moreover, I will do so only insofar as the problem before me refers in truth to an essential generality; and it is in the form of this generality that I wish to state it. When I was invited to this meeting, my hesitation could end only when I was assured that I could bear witness here, now, to my agreement and to a certain point my solidarity with those in this country who were fighting against what was then their country's official policy in certain parts of the world, notably in Vietnam. It is evident

that such a gesture — and the fact that I am authorized to make it — signifies that those who are welcoming my discourse do not identify with the policies of their country any more than I do, and do not feel justified in assuming those policies, at least insofar as they are participating in this colloquium.

And yet it would be naive or purposely blind to let oneself be reassured by the image or appearance of such a freedom. It would be illusory to believe that political innocence has been restored and evil complicities undone when opposition to them can be expressed in the country itself, not only through the voices of its own citizens but also through those of foreign citizens, and that henceforth diversities, i.e. oppositions, may freely and discursively relate to one another. That a declaration of opposition to some official policy is authorized, and authorized by the authorities, also means, precisely to that extent, that the declaration does not upset the given order, is not *bothersome*. This last expression, "bothersome," may be taken in all its senses. This is what I wished to recall, in order to begin, by speaking of the *form of democracy* as the political milieu of every international philosophical colloquium. And this is also why I proposed to place the accent on *form* no less than on *democracy*. Such, in its most general and schematic principle, is the question that put itself to me during the preparations for this encounter, from the invitation and the deliberations that followed, up to acceptance, and then to the writing of this text, which I date quite precisely from the month of April 1968: it will be recalled that these were the weeks of the opening of the Vietnam peace talks and of the assassination of Martin Luther King. A bit later, when I was typing this text, the universities of Paris were invaded by the forces of order — and for the first time at the demand of a rector — and then reoccupied by the students in the upheaval you are familiar with. This historical and political horizon would call for a long analysis. I have simply found it necessary to mark, date, and make known to you the historical circumstances in which I prepared this communication. These circumstances appear to me to belong, by all rights, to the field and the problematic of our colloquium.

Humanism or Metaphysics

Thus the transition will be made quite naturally between the preamble and the theme of this communication, as it was imposed upon me, rather than as I chose it.

Where is France, as concerns man?

The question "of man" is being asked in very current fashion in France, along highly significant lines, and in an original historico-philosophical structure. What I will call "France," then, on the basis of several indices and for the time of this exposition, will be the nonempirical site of a movement, a structure and an articulation of the question "of man." Following this it would be possible, and doubtless necessary — but then only — rigorously to relate this site with every other instance defining something like "France."

Where then is France, as concerns man?

After the war, under the name of Christian or atheist existentialism, and in conjunction with a fundamentally Christian personalism, the thought that dominated France presented itself essentially as humanist. Even if one does not wish to summarize Sartre's thought under the slogan "existentialism is a humanism," it must be recognized that in *Being and Nothingness, The Sketch of a Theory of the Emotions,* etc., the major concept, the theme of the last analysis, the irreducible horizon and origin is what was then called "human-reality." As is well known, this is a translation of Heideggerian *Dasein.* A monstrous translation in many respects, but so much the more significant. That this translation proposed by Corbin was adopted at the time, and that by means of Sartre's authority it reigned, gives us much to think about the reading or the nonreading of Heidegger during this period, and about what was at stake in reading or not reading him in this way.

Certainly the notion of "human-reality" translated the project of thinking the meaning of man, the humanity of man, on a new basis, if you will. If the neutral and undetermined notion of "human reality" was substituted for the notion of man, with all its metaphysical heritage and the substantialist motif or temptation inscribed in it, it was also in order to suspend all the presuppositions that had always constituted the concept of the unity of man. Thus, it was also a reaction against a certain intellectualist or spiritualist humanism that had dominated French philosophy (Brunschvig, Alain, Bergson, etc.). And this neutralization of every metaphysical or speculative thesis as concerns the unity of the anthropos could be considered in some respects as the faithful inheritance of Husserl's transcendental phenomenology and of the fundamental ontology in *Sein und Zeit* (the only partially known work of Heidegger's at the time, along with *What Is Metaphysics?* and *Kant and the Problem of Metaphysics*). And yet, despite this alleged neutralization of metaphysical presuppositions,[4] it must be recognized that the unity of man is never examined in and of itself. Not only is existentialism a humanism, but the ground and horizon of what Sartre then called his "phenomenological ontology" (the subtitle of *Being and Nothingness*) remains the unity of human-reality. To the extent that it describes the structures of human-reality, phenomenological ontology, is a philosophical anthropology. Whatever the breaks marked by this Hegelian-Husserlian-Heideggerian anthropology as concerns the classical anthropologies, there is an uninterrupted metaphysical familiarity with that which, so naturally, links the *we* of the philosopher to "we men," to the *we* in the horizon of humanity. Although the theme of history is quite present in the discourse of the period, there is little practice of the history of concepts. For example, the history of the concept of man is never examined. Everything occurs as if the sign "man" has no origin, no historical, cultural, or linguistic limit. At the end of *Being and Nothingness*, when Sartre in programmatic fashion asks the question of the unity of Being (which in this context means the totality of beings), and when he confers upon this question the rubric "metaphysical" in order to distinguish it from phenomenological ontology, which described the essential specificity of regions, it goes without saying that this metaphysical unity of Being, as the totality of the in-itself and the for-itself, is precisely the unity of human-reality in it project. Being in-itself and Being for-itself were *of Being;* and this totality of beings, in which they were effected, itself was linked up to itself, relating and appearing to itself, by means of the essential project of human-reality.[5] What was named in this way, in an allegedly neutral and undetermined way, was nothing other than the metaphysical unity of man and God, the relation of man to God, the project of becoming God as the project constituting human-reality. Atheism changes nothing in this fundamental structure. The example of the Sartrean project remarkably verifies Heidegger's proposition according to which "every humanism remains metaphysical," metaphysics being the other name of ontotheology.

Thus defined, humanism or anthropologism, during this period, was the common ground of Christian or atheist existentialisms, of the philosophy of values (spiritualist or not), of personalisms of the right or the left, of Marxism in the classical style. And if one takes one's bearings from the terrain of political ideologies, anthropologism was the unperceived and uncontested common ground of Marxism and of Social-Democratic or Christian-Democratic discourse. This profound concordance was authorized, in its philosophical expression, by the *anthropologistic* readings of Hegel (interest in the *Phenomenology of Spirit* as it was read by Kojève), of Marx (the privilege accorded the *Manuscripts of 1844*), of Husserl (whose descriptive and regional work is emphasized, but whose transcendental questions are ignored), and of Heidegger, whose projects for a philosophical anthropology or an existential analytic only were known or retained (*Sein und Zeit*). Of course, here I am picking out the dominant traits. Nor can one say in absolutely rigorous fashion that this period started after the war, and even less that it is over today. Nevertheless, I believe that the empiricism of this cross-section is justifiable here only insofar as it permits the reading of a *dominant* motif and insofar as it takes its authority from indices that are unarguable for anyone approaching such a period. Further, the cross-section is provisional, and in an instant we will reinscribe this sequence in the time and space of a larger totality.

In order to mark in boldface the traits that opposed this period to the following one, the one in which we are, and which too is probably undergoing a mutation, we must recall that during the decade that followed the war we did not yet see the reign of the all-powerful motif of what we call today, more and more, and even exclusively, the "so-called *human* sciences," the expression itself marking a certain distance, but a still respectful distance. On the contrary, the current questioning of humanism is contemporary with the dominating and spellbinding extension of the "human sciences" within the philosophical field.

The *Relève* of Humanism

The anthropologistic reading of Hegel, Husserl, and Heidegger was a mistake in one entire respect, perhaps the most serious mistake. And it is this reading that furnished the best conceptual resources to postwar French thought.

First of all, the *Phenomenology of Spirit,* which had only been read for a short time in France, does not have to do with something one might simply call man. As the science of the experience of consciousness, the science of the structures of the phenomenality of the spirit itself relating to itself, it is rigorously distinguished from anthropology. In the *Encyclopedia* the section entitled *Phenomenology of Spirit* comes after the *Anthropology* and quite explicitly exceeds its limits. What is true of the *Phenomenology* is a fortiori true of the system of the *Logic.*

Similarly, in the second place, the critique of anthropologism was one of the inaugural motifs of Husserl's transcendental phenomenology. This is an explicit critique, and it calls anthropologism by its name from the *Prolegomena to Pure Logic* on.[6] Later this critique will have as its target not only empirical anthropologism but also transcendental anthropologism.[7] The transcendental structures described after the phenomenological reduction are not those of the intraworldly being called "man." Nor are they essentially linked to man's society, culture, language, or even to his "soul" or "psyche." Just as, according to Husserl, one may imagine a consciousness without soul (*seelenlos*),[8] similarly — and a fortiori — one may imagine a consciousness without man.

Therefore it is astonishing and highly significant that at the moment when the authority of Husserlian thought was asserted and then established in postwar France, even becoming a kind of philosophical mode, the critique of anthropologism remained totally unnoticed, or in any event without effect. One

of the most paradoxical pathways of this motivated miscon-
struing passes through a reductive reading of Heidegger. Because one has interpreted the analytic of Dasein in strictly
anthropological terms, occasionally one limits or criticizes Husserl on the basis of Heidegger, dropping all the aspects of
phenomenology that do not serve anthropological description.
This pathway is quite paradoxical because it follows the itin-
erary of a reading of Heidegger that was also Husserl's. In
effect, Husserl precipitously interpreted *Sein und Zeit* as an
anthropologistic deviation from transcendental phenomenology.[9]

In the third place, immediately following the war and after
the appearance of *Being and Nothingness,* Heidegger, in his *Letter
on Humanism,* recalled — for all those who did not yet know,
and who had not even taken into account the very first sections
of *Sein und Zeit* — that anthropology and humanism were not
the milieu of his thought and the horizon of his questions. The
"destruction" of metaphysics or of classical ontology was even
directed against humanism.[10] After the tide of humanism and
anthropologism that had covered French philosophy, one
might have thought that the antihumanist and antianthropol-
ogist ebb that followed, and in which we are now, would redis-
cover the heritage of the systems of thought that had been
disfigured, or in which rather, the figure of man too quickly
had been discerned.

Nothing of the sort has happened, and it is the significance
of such a phenomenon that I now wish to examine. The critique of humanism and anthropologism, which is one of the
dominant and guiding motifs of current French thought, far
from seeking its sources or warranties in the Hegelian, Husserlian, or Heideggerian critiques of the same humanism or
the same anthropologism, on the contrary seem, by means of
a gesture sometimes more implicit than systematically articulated, to *amalgamate* Hegel, Husserl, and — in a more diffuse
and ambiguous fashion — Heidegger with the old metaphysical
humanism. I am purposely using the word "amalgam," which
in its usage unites references to alchemy, which is the primary
one here, with a strategic or tactical reference to the domain
of political ideology.

Before attempting to interpret this phenomenon of paradoxical demeanor, we must take several precautions. First of
all, this amalgam does not exclude that some progress has been
made in France in the reading of Hegel, Husserl, or Heidegger,
nor that this progress has led to requestioning the humanist
insistence. But this progress and requestioning do not occupy
center stage, and this must be significant. Conversely and sym-
metrically, among those who do practice the amalgamation, the
schemas of the anthropologistic misinterpretation from Sartre's
time are still at work, and occasionally it is these very schemas
that govern the rejection of Hegel, Husserl, and Heidegger
into the shadows of humanist metaphysics. Very often, *in fact*,
those who denounce humanism at the same time as metaphysics
have remained at the stage of this "first reading" of Hegel,
Husserl, and Heidegger, and one could locate more than one
sign of this in numerous recent texts. Which leads us to think
that in certain respects, and at least to this extent, we are still
on the same shore.

But no matter, as concerns the question I would like to ask,
that such and such an author has read such and such a text
poorly, or simply not at all, or that he remains, as concerns
systems of thought he believes he has surpassed or overturned,
in a state of great ingenuousness. This is why we shall not
concern ourselves here with any given author's name or with
the title of any given work. What must hold our interest, beyond the justifications that, as a matter of fact, are most often
insufficient, is the kind of profound justification, whose necessity is subterranean, that makes the Hegelian, Husserlian, and
Heideggerian critiques or *de-limitations* of metaphysical humanism appear to belong to the very sphere of that which they
criticize or de-limit. In a word, whether this has been made
explicit or not, and whether it has been articulated or not (and
more than one index leads us to believe that it has not), what
authorizes us today to consider as essentially *anthropic* or an-
thropocentric everything in metaphysics, or at the limits of
metaphysics, that believed itself to be a critique or delimitation
of anthropologism? What is the *relève* of man in the thought
of Hegel, Husserl, and Heidegger?

The Near End of Man

Let us reconsider, first of all, within the order of Hegelian discourse, which still holds together the language of our era by so many threads, the relations between anthropology on the one hand and phenomenology and logic on the other.[11] Once the confusion of a purely anthropological reading of the *Phenomenology of Spirit* has been rigorously avoided, it must be recognized that according to Hegel the relations between anthropology and phenomenology are not simply external ones. The Hegelian concepts of truth, negativity, and *Aufhebung*, with all their results, prevent this from being so. In the third part of the *Encyclopedia,* which treats the "Philosophy of Spirit," the first section ("Philosophy of Spirit") inscribes the *Phenomenology of Spirit* between the "Anthropology" and the "Psychology." The *Phenomenology of Spirit* succeeds the Anthropology and precedes the Psychology. The Anthropology treats the spirit — which is the "truth of nature" — as soul or as natural-spirit (*Seele* or *Naturgeist*). The development of the soul, such as it is retraced by the anthropology, passes through the natural soul (*natürliche Seele*), through the sensible soul (*fühlende Seele*), and through the real or effective soul (*wirkliche Seele*). This development accomplishes and completes itself, and then opens onto consciousness. The last section of the Anthropology[12] defines the general form of consciousness, the very one from which the *Phenomenology of Spirit* will depart, in the first chapter on "Sensuous Certitude."[13] Consciousness, i.e. the phenomenological, therefore, is the *truth* of the soul, that is, precisely the truth of that which was the object of the Anthropology. Consciousness is the truth of man, phenomenology is the truth of anthropology. "Truth," here, must be understood in a rigorously Hegelian sense. In this Hegelian sense, the metaphysical essence of truth, the truth of the truth, is achieved. Truth is here the presence or presentation of essence as *Gewesenheit*, of *Wesen* as having-been. Consciousness is the truth of man to the extent that man appears to himself in consciousness in his Being-past, in his to-have-been, in his past surpassed and conserved, retained, interiorized (*erinnert*) and *relevé*. *Aufheben* is *relever*, in the sense in which *relever* can com-

bine to relieve, to displace, to elevate, to replace, and to promote, in one and the same movement.[14] Consciousness is the
Aufhebung of the soul or of man, phenomenology is the *relève*
of anthropology. It is *no longer,* but it is *still* a science of man.
In this sense, all the structures described by the phenomenology of spirit — like everything that articulates them with the
Logic — are the structures of that which has *relevé* man. In
them, man remains in relief. His essence rests in *Phenomenology*.
This equivocal relationship of *relief* doubtless marks the end of
man, man past, but by the same token it also marks the achievement of man, the appropriation of his essence. *It is the end of
finite man* [*C'est la fin de l'homme fini*]. The end of the finitude
of man, the unity of the finite and the infinite, the finite as the
surpassing of the self — these essential themes of Hegel's are
to be recognized at the end of the Anthropology when consciousness is finally designated as the "infinite relationship to
self." The *relève* or *relevance* of man is his *telos* or *eskhaton.* The
unity of these two *ends* of man, the unity of his death, his
completion, his accomplishment, is enveloped in the Greek
thinking of *telos,* in the discourse on *telos,* which is also a discourse on *eidos,* on *ousia,* and on *alētheia.* Such a discourse, in
Hegel as in the entirety of metaphysics, indissociably coordi-
nates teleology with an eschatology, a theology, and an ontology. *The thinking of the end of man, therefore, is always already
prescribed in metaphysics, in the thinking of the truth of man.* What
is difficult to think today is an end of man that would not be
organized by a dialectics of truth and negativity, an end of man
that would not be a teleology in the first person plural. The
we, which articulates natural and philosophical consciousness
with each other in the *Phenomenology of Spirit,* assures the proximity to itself of the fixed and central being for which this
circular reappropriation is produced. The *we* is the unity of
absolute knowledge and anthropology, of God and man, of
onto-theo-teleology and humanism. "*Being*" and language —
the group of languages — that the *we* governs or opens: such
is the name of that which assures the transition between metaphysics and humanism via the *we.*[15]

   We have just perceived the necessity that links the thinking
of the *phainesthai* to the thinking of the *telos.* The teleology that

governs Husserl's transcendental phenomenology can be read in the same opening. Despite the critique of anthropologism, "humanity," here, is still the name of the being to which the transcendental *telos* — determined as Idea (in the Kantian sense) or even as Reason — is announced. It is man as *animal rationale* who, in his most classical metaphysical determination, designates the site of teleological reason's unfolding, that is, history. For Husserl as for Hegel, reason is history, and there is no history but of reason. The latter "functions in every man, the *animal rationale,* no matter how primitive he is . . ." Every kind of humanity and human sociality has "a root in the essential structure of what is generally human, through which a teleological reason running throughout all historicity announces itself. With this is revealed a set of problems in its own right related to the totality of history and to the full meaning which ultimately gives it its unity."[16] Transcendental phenomenology is in this sense the ultimate achievement of the teleology of reason that traverses humanity.[17] Thus, under the jurisdiction of the founding concepts of metaphysics, which Husserl revives and restores (if necessary affecting them with phenomenological brackets or indices), the critique of empirical anthropologism is only the affirmation of a transcendental humanism. And, among these metaphysical concepts that form the essential resource of Husserl's discourse, the concept of *end* and of *telos* plays a decisive role. It could be shown that at each stage of phenomenology, and notably each time that a recourse to the "Idea in the Kantian sense" is necessary, the infinity of the *telos*, the infinity of the end regulates phenomenology's capabilities. The end of man (as a factual anthropological limit) is announced to thought from the vantage of the end of man (as a determined opening or the infinity of a *telos*). Man is that which is in relation to his end, in the fundamentally equivocal sense of the word. Since always. The transcendental end can appear to itself and be unfolded only on the condition of mortality, of a relation to finitude as the origin of ideality. The name of man has always been inscribed in metaphysics between these two ends. It has meaning only in this eschato-teleological situation.

Reading Us

The "we," which in one way or another always has had to refer
to itself in the language of metaphysics and in philosophical
discourse, arises out of this situation. To conclude, what about
this *we* in the text which better than any other has given us to
read the essential, historical complicity of metaphysics and humanism in all their forms? What about this *we,* then, in Heidegger's text?

This is the most difficult question, and we will only begin to
consider it. We are not going to imprison all of Heidegger's
text in a closure that this text has delimited better than any
other. That which links humanism and metaphysics as ontotheology became legible as such in *Sein und Zeit,* the *Letter on
Humanism,* and the later texts. Referring to this acquisition,
attempting to take it into account, I would like to begin to
sketch out the forms of the hold that the "humanity" of man
and the thinking of Being, a certain humanism and the truth
of Being, maintain on one another. Naturally, it will not be a
question of the falsification that, in opposition to Heidegger's
most explicit warnings, consists in making this hold into a
mastery or an ontic relationship in general. What will preoc-
cupy us here will concern, rather, a more subtle, hidden, stub-
born privilege, which, as in the case of Hegel or Husserl, leads
us back to the position of the *we* in discourse. Once one has
given up positing the *we* in the metaphysical dimension of "*we
men,*" once one has given up charging the *we men* with the
metaphysical determinations of the proper of man (*zōon logon
ekhon,* etc.), it remains that man — and I would even say, in a
sense that will become clear in a moment, the *proper of man* —
the thinking of the proper of man is inseparable from the
question or the truth of Being. This occurs along the Heideggerian pathways by means of what we may call a kind of magnetic attraction.

Here, I can only indicate the general rubric and several
effects of this magnetization. In the effort to disclose it at the
continuous depth at which it operates, the distinction between
given periods of Heidegger's thought, between the texts before
and after the so-called *Kehre,* has less pertinence than ever. For,

on the one hand, the existential analytic had already over-
flowed the horizon of a philosophical anthropology: *Dasein* is
not simply the man of metaphysics. On the other hand, conversely, in the *Letter on Humanism* and beyond, the attraction
of the "proper of man" will not cease to direct all the itineraries
of thought. At least this is what I would like to suggest, and I
will regroup the effects or indices of this magnetic attraction
beneath the general concept of *proximity*. It is in the play of a
certain proximity, proximity to oneself and proximity to Being,
that we will see constituted, against metaphysical humanism
and anthropologism, another insistence of man, one that re-
lays, relieves, supplements that which it destroys, along pathways on which we are, from which we have hardly emerged —
perhaps — and which remain to be examined.

What about this proximity? First, let us open *Sein und Zeit* at
the point at which the question of Being is asked in its "formal
structure" (sec. 2). Our "vague average" understanding of the
words "Being" or "is" finds itself acknowledged as a Fact (*Fak-
tum*): "Inquiry (*Suchen*), as a kind of seeking, must be guided
beforehand by what is sought. So the meaning of Being must
already be available to *us* in some way. As we have intimated,
we always already conduct our activities in an understanding of
Being. Out of this understanding arise both the explicit question of the meaning of Being and the tendency that leads us
toward its conception. We do not *know* what 'Being' means. But
even if we ask, 'What is "Being"?,' *we* keep within an understanding of the 'is,' though *we* are unable to fix conceptually
what that 'is' signifies. We do not even know the horizon in
terms of which that meaning is to be grasped and fixed. *But
this vague average understanding of Being is still a Fact.*"[18] I have
italicized the *we* (*us*) and the *always already*. They are determined, then, in correspondence with this understanding of
"Being" or of the "is." In the absence of every other determination or presupposition, the "we" at *least* is what is open to
such an understanding, what is always already accessible to it,
and the means by which such a factum can be recognized as
such. It automatically follows, then, that this *we* — however
simple, discreet, and erased it might be — inscribes the so-
called formal structure of the question of Being within the

horizon of metaphysics, and more widely within the Indo-European linguistic milieu, to the possibility of which the origin of metaphysics is essentially linked. It is within these limits that the factum can be understood and accredited; and it is within these determined, and therefore material, limits that the factum can uphold the so-called formality of the question. It remains that the meaning of these "limits" is given to us only on the basis of the question of the meaning of Being. Let us not pretend, for example, to know what "Indo-European linguistic milieu" means.

This "formal structure of the question of Being" having been asked by Heidegger, the issue then, as is well known, is to acknowledge the exemplary being (*exemplarische Seiende*) that will constitute the privileged text for a reading of the meaning of Being. And I recall that according to Heidegger the formal structure of the question, of any question, must be composed of three instances: the *Gefragte,* that which is asked about, here the meaning of Being; the *Erfragte,* that which is to be found out insofar as it is properly targeted by a question, the meaning of Being as what is questioned; finally the *Befragte,* that which is interrogated, the being that will be interrogated, to which will be put the question of the meaning of Being. The issue then is to choose or to recognize this exemplary *interrogated* being with one's sights set on the meaning of Being: "In *which* entities is the meaning of Being to be discerned (*abgelesen*)? From which entities is the disclosure of Being to take its departure? Is the starting point optional, or does some particular entity have priority (*Vorrang*) when we come to work out the question of Being? Which entity shall we take for our example, and in what sense does it have priority?"[19]

What will dictate the answer to this question? In what milieu of evidentiality, of certitude, or at least of understanding must it be unfolded? Even before claiming the phenomenological method (sec. 7), at least in a "provisional concept," as the method for the elaboration of the question of Being, the determination of the exemplary being is in principle "phenomenological." It is governed by phenomenology's principle of principles, the principle of presence and of presence in self-presence, such as it is manifested to the being and in the being that *we* are. It is this self-presence, this absolute proximity of the (questioning) being to itself, this familiarity with itself of the being ready to understand Being, that intervenes in the determination of the *factum,* and that motivates the choice of the exemplary being, of the text, the good text for the hermeneutic of the meaning of Being. It is the proximity to itself of the questioning being that leads it to be chosen as the privileged interrogated being. The proximity to itself of the inquirer authorizes the identity of the inquirer and the interrogated. We who are close to ourselves, *we* interrogate *ourselves* about the meaning of Being. Let us read this protocol of reading: "If the question about Being is to be explicitly formulated and carried through in such a manner as to be completely transparent to itself, then any treatment of it in line with the elucidations we have given requires us to explain how Being is to be looked at, how its meaning is to be understood and conceptually grasped; it requires us to prepare the way for choosing the right entity for our example, and to work out the genuine way of access to it. Looking at something, understanding and conceiving it, choosing access to it — all these ways of behaving are constitutive of our inquiry, and therefore are modes of Being for those particular entities which we, the inquirers, are ourselves (*eines bestimmten Seienden, des Seienden, das wir, die Fragenden, je selbst sind*). Thus to work out the question of Being adequately, we must make an entity — the inquirer — transparent in his own Being. The very asking of this question (*das Fragen dieser Frage*) is an entity's mode of *Being;* and as such it gets its essential character from what is inquired about (*gefragt*) — namely, Being. *This entity which each of us is himself* and which includes inquiring as one of the possibilities of its Being, we shall denote by the term '*Dasein*' (*fassen wir terminologisch als Dasein*). If we are to formulate our question explicitly and transparently, we must first give a proper explication of an entity (Dasein) with regard to its Being."[20]

Doubtless this proximity, this identity or self-presence of the "entity that we are" — of the inquirer and of the interrogated — does not have the form of subjective consciousness, as in transcendental phenomenology. Doubtless too, this proximity is still prior to what the metaphysical predicate "human" might name. The *Da*-of *Dasein* can be determined as a coming presence only on the basis of a rereading of the question of Being that summons it up. Nevertheless, the process of disengaging or of elaborating the question of Being, as a question of the *meaning* of Being, is defined as a *making explicit* or as an interpretation that makes explicit. The reading of the text *Dasein* is a hermeneutics of unveiling or of development (see sec. 7). If one looks closely, it is the phenomenological opposition "implicit/explicit" that permits Heidegger to reject the objection of the vicious circle, the circle that consists of first determining a being in its Being, and then of posing the question of Being on the basis of this ontological predetermination (p. 27). This style of a reading that makes explicit, practices a continual bringing to light, something that resembles, at least, a coming into consciousness, without break, displacement, or change of terrain. Moreover, just as Dasein — the being that *we ourselves are* — serves as an exemplary text, a good "lesson" for making explicit the meaning of Being, so the name of man remains the link or the paleonymic guiding thread that ties the analytic of Dasein to the totality of metaphysics' traditional discourse. Whence the strange status of such sentences or parentheses as, "As ways in which man behaves, sciences have the manner of Being which this entity — man himself — possesses. This entity we denote by the term '*Dasein*' (*Dieses Seiende fassen wir terminologisch als Dasein*)" (p. 32). Or again: "The problematic of Greek ontology, like that of any other, must take its clues from Dasein itself. In both ordinary and philosophical usage, Dasein, man's Being (*das Dasein, d.h. das Sein des Menschen*), is 'defined' (*umgrenzt*) as the *zōon logon ekhon* — as that living thing whose Being is essentially determined by the potentiality for discourse (*Redenkonnen*)" (p. 47). Similarly, a "complete ontology of Dasein" is posited as the prerequisite condition for a "'philosophical' anthropology" (p. 38). We can see then that Dasein, though *not* man, is nevertheless *nothing other* than man. It is, as we shall see, a repetition of the essence of man permitting a return to what is before the metaphysical concepts of *humanitas*. The subtlety and equivocality of this gesture, then, are what appear to have authorized all the anthropologistic deformations in the reading of *Sein und Zeit,* notably in France.

The value of proximity, that is, of presence in general, therefore decides the essential orientation of this analytic of Dasein. The motif of proximity surely finds itself caught in an opposition that henceforth will unceasingly regulate Heidegger's discourse. The fifth section of *Sein und Zeit* in effect seems not to contradict but to limit and contain what was already gained, to wit that the Dasein "which we are" constitutes the exemplary being for the hermeneutic of the meaning of Being by virtue of it proximity to itself, of our proximity to ourselves, our proximity to the being that we are. At this point Heidegger marks that this proximity is *ontic.* Ontologically, that is, as concerns the Being of that being which we are, the distance, on the contrary, is as great as possible. "Ontically, of course, Dasein is not only close to us — even that which is closest: we *are* it, each of us, we ourselves. In spite of this, or rather for just this reason, it is ontologically that which is farthest."[21]

The analytic of *Dasein,* as well as the thinking that, beyond the *Kehre,* will pursue the question of Being, will maintain itself in the space that separates and relates to one another such a proximity and such a distance. The *Da* of *Dasein* and the *Da* of *Sein* will signify as much the near as the far. Beyond the common closure of humanism and metaphysics, Heidegger's thought will be guided by the motif of Being as presence — understood in a more originary sense than it is in the metaphysical and ontic determinations of presence or of presence as the present — and by the motif of the proximity of Being to the essence of man. Everything transpires as if one had to reduce the ontological distance acknowledged in *Sein und Zeit* and to state the proximity of Being to the essence of man.

To support this last proposition, several indicative references to the *Letter on Humanism.* I will not insist upon the major and well-known theme of this text: the unity of metaphysics and humanism.[22] Any questioning of humanism that does not first catch up with the archeological radicalness of the questions sketched by Heidegger, and does not make use of the information he provides concerning the genesis of the concept and the value man (the reedition of the Greek *paideia* in Roman culture, the Christianizing of the Latin *humanitas,* the rebirth of Hellenism in the fourteenth and eighteenth centuries, etc.), any metahumanist position that does not place itself within the opening of these questions remains historically regional, periodic, and peripheral, juridically secondary and dependent, whatever interest and necessity it might retain as such.

It remains that the thinking of Being, the thinking of the truth of Being, in the name of which Heidegger de-limits humanism and metaphysics, remains as thinking *of* man. Man and the name of man are not displaced in the question of Being such as it is put to metaphysics. Even less do they disappear. On the contrary, at issue is a kind of reevaluation or revalorization of the essence and dignity of man. What is threatened in the extension of metaphysics and technology — and we know the essential necessity that leads Heidegger to associate them one to another — is the essence of man, which here would have to be thought before and beyond its metaphysical determinations. "The widely and rapidly spreading devastation of language not only undermines aesthetic and moral responsibility in every use of language; it arises from a threat to the essence of humanity (*Gefährdung des Wesens des Menschen*).[23] Only thus does the overcoming of homelessness (*Überwindung der Heimatlosigkeit*) begin from Being, a homelessness in which not only man but the essence of man (*das Wesen der Menschen*) stumbles aimlessly about."[24] Therefore, this essence will have to be reinstated. "But if man is to find his way once again into the nearness of Being (*in die Nähe des Seins*) he must first learn to exist in the nameless (*im Namenlosen*). In the same way he must first recognize the seductions of the public realm as well as the impotence of the private. Before he speaks (*bevor er spricht*) man must first let himself be claimed again (*wieder ansprechen*) by Being, taking the risk that under this claim (*Anspruch*) he will seldom have much to say. Only thus will the preciousness of its essence be once more bestowed upon the word (*dem Wort*), and upon man a home (*Behausung*) for dwelling in the truth of Being. But in the claim (*Anspruch*) upon man, in the attempt to make man ready for this claim, is there not implied a concern about man? Where else does 'care' tend but in the direction of bringing man back to his essence (*den Menschen wieder in sein Wesen zurückzubringen*)? What else does that in turn betoken but that man (*homo*) becomes human (*humanus*)? Thus *humanitas* really does remain the concern of such thinking. For this is humanism: meditating and caring (*Sinnen und Sorgen*) that man be human and not inhumane (*unmenschlich*), 'inhuman,' that is, outside his essence. But in what does the humanity of man consist? It lies in his essence."[25]

Once the thinking of essence is removed from the opposition *essentia/existentia,* the proposition according to which "'man eksists' is not an answer to the question of whether man actually is or not; rather, it responds to the question concerning man's 'essence' (*Wesen*)."[26]

The restoration of the essence is also the restoration of a dignity and a proximity: the co-responding dignity of Being and man, the proximity of Being and man. "What still today remains to be said could perhaps become an impetus (*Anstoss*) for guiding the essence of man to the point where it thoughtfully (*denkend*) attends to that dimension of the truth of Being which thoroughly governs it. But even this could take place only to the honor of Being and for the benefit of Dasein which man eksistingly sustains (*nur dem Sein zur Würde und dem Dasein zugunsten geschehen, das der Mensch eksistierend aussteht*); not, however, for the sake of man so that civilization and culture through man's doings might be vindicated."[27]

The ontological distance from *Dasein* to what *Dasein* is as eksistence and to the *Da* of *Sein,* the distance that first was given as ontic proximity, must be reduced by the thinking of the truth of Being. Whence, in Heidegger's discourse, the dominance of an entire metaphorics of proximity, of simple and immediate presence, a metaphorics associating the proximity of Being with the values of neighboring, shelter, house, service, guard, voice, and listening. As goes without saying, this is not an insignificant rhetoric; on the basis of both this metaphorics and the thinking of the ontico-ontological difference, one could even make explicit an entire theory of metaphoricity in general.[28] Several examples of this language, so surely connoted by its inscription in a certain landscape: "But if man is to find his way once again into the nearness of Being (*in die Nähe des*

Seins), he must first learn to exist in the nameless." "The statement 'The "substance" of man is eksistence' says nothing else but that the way that man in his proper essence (*in seinem eigenen Wesen*) becomes present to Being (*zum Sein anwest*) is ecstatic inherence in the truth of Being. Through this determination of the essence of man the humanistic interpretations of man as *animal rationale,* as 'person,' as spiritual-ensouled-bodily being, are not declared false and thrust aside. Rather, the sole implication is that the highest determinations of the essence of man in humanism still do not realize the proper dignity of man (*die eigentliche Würde des Menschen*). To that extent the thinking in *Being and Time* is against humanism. But this opposition does not mean that such thinking aligns itself against the humane and advocates the inhuman, that it promotes the inhumane and deprecates the dignity of man. Humanism is opposed because it does not set the *humanitas* of man high enough."[29] "'Being' — that is not God and not a cosmic ground. Being is farther than all beings and is yet nearer (*näher*) to man than every being, be it a rock, a beast, a work of art, a machine, be it angel or God. Being is the nearest (*Das Sein ist das Nächste*). Yet the near remains farthest from man. Man at first clings always and only to beings."[30] "Because man as the one who ek-sists comes to stand in this relation that Being destines (*schickt*) for itself, in that he ecstatically sustains it, that is, in care takes it upon himself, he at first fails to recognize the nearest (*das Nächste*) and attaches himself to the next nearest (*das Übernächste*). He even thinks that this is the nearest. But nearer than the nearest and at the same time for ordinary thinking farther than the farthest is *nearness* itself: the truth of Being."[31] "The one thing (*das Einzige*) thinking would like to attain and for the first time tries to articulate in *Being and Time* is something simple (*etwas Einfaches*). As such, Being remains mysterious, the simple (*schlicht*) nearness of an unobtrusive governance. The nearness occurs essentially as language itself."[32] "But man is not only a living creature who possesses language along with other capacities. Rather, language is the house of Being in which man ek-sists by dwelling, in that he belongs to the truth of Being, guarding it (*hütend gehört*).[33]

This proximity is not ontic proximity, and one must take into account the properly ontological repetition of this thinking of the near and the far.[34] It remains that Being, which is nothing, is not a being, cannot be said, cannot say itself, except in the ontic metaphor. And the choice of one or another group of metaphors is necessarily significant. It is within a metaphorical insistence, then, that the interpretation of the meaning of Being is produced. And if Heidegger has radically deconstructed the domination of metaphysics by the *present*, he has done so in order to lead us to think the presence of the present. But the thinking of this presence can only metaphorize, by means of a profound necessity from which one cannot simply decide to escape, the language that it deconstructs.[35]

Thus, the prevalence granted to the *phenomenological* metaphor, to all the varieties of *phainesthai*, of shining, lighting, clearing, *Lichtung*, etc., opens onto the space of presence and the presence of space, understood within the opposition of the near and the far — just as the acknowledged privilege not only of language, but of spoken language (voice, listening, etc.), is in consonance with the motif of presence as self-presence.[36] The near and the far are thought here, consequently, before the opposition of space and time, according to the opening of a spacing that *belongs* neither to time nor to space, and that dislocates, while producing it, any presence of the present.

Therefore, if "Being is farther than all beings and is yet nearer to man than every being," if "Being is the nearest," then one must be able to say that Being is *what is near* to man, and that man is *what is near* to Being. The near is the proper; the proper is the nearest (*prope, proprius*). Man is the proper of Being, which right near to him whispers in his ear; Being is the proper of man, such is the truth that speaks, such is the proposition that gives the *there* of the truth of Being and the truth of man. This proposition of the *proper*, certainly, is not to be taken in a metaphysical sense: the proper of man, here, is not an essential attribute, the predicate of a substance, a characteristic among others, however fundamental, of a being, object or subject, called man. No more can one speak in this sense of man as the proper of Being. Propriety, the co-propriety of Being and man, is proximity as inseparability. But it is indeed as inseparability that the relations between being (substance, or *res*) and its essential predicate were thought in metaphysics *afterward*. Since this co-propriety of man and of Being, such as it is thought in Heidegger's discourse, is not ontic, does not relate two "beings" one to the other but rather, within language, relates the *meaning* of Being and the *meaning* of man. The proper of man, his *Eigenheit*, his "authenticity," is to be related to the meaning of Being; he is to hear and to question (*fragen*) it in ek-sistence, to stand straight in the proximity of its light: "Das Stehen in der Lichtung des Seins nenne ich die Ek-sistenz des Menschen. Nur dem Menschen eignet diese Art zu sein" ("Such standing in the lighting of Being I call the ek-sistence of man. This way of Being is proper only to man").[37]

Is not this security of the near what is trembling today, that is the co-belonging and co-propriety of the name of man and the name of Being, such as this co-propriety inhabits, and is inhabited by, the language of the West, such as it is buried in its *oikonomia*, such as it is inscribed and forgotten according to the history of metaphysics, and such as it is awakened also by the destruction of ontotheology? But this trembling — which can only come from a certain outside — was already requisite within the very structure that it solicits.[38] Its margin was marked in its own (*propre*) body. In the thinking and the language of Being, the end of man has been prescribed since always, and this prescription has never done anything but modulate the equivocality of the *end,* in the play of *telos* and death. In the reading of this play, one may take the following sequence in all its senses: the end of man is the thinking of Being, man is the end of the thinking of Being. Man, since always, is his proper end, that is, the end of his proper. Being, since always, is its proper end, that is, the end of its proper.

To conclude, I would like to reassemble, under several very general rubrics, the signs that appear, in accordance with the anonymous necessity that interests me here, to mark the effects of the total trembling as concerns what I have called, for convenience, and with the necessary quotation marks or precautions, "France" or French thought.

1. *The reduction of meaning.* The attention given to system and structure, in its most original and strongest aspects, that is, those aspects that do not immediately fall back into cultural or journalistic gossip, or, in the best of cases, into the purest "structuralist" tradition of metaphysics — such an attention, which is rare, consists neither (*a*) in restoring the classical motif of the system, which can always be shown to be ordered by *telos, alētheia,* and *ousia,* all of which are values reassembled in the concepts of essence or of *meaning;* nor (*b*) in erasing or destroying meaning. Rather, it is a question of determining the possibility of *meaning* on the basis of a "formal" organization that in itself has no meaning, which does not mean that it is either the non-sense or the anguishing absurdity that haunts metaphysical humanism. Now, if one considers that the critique of anthropologism in the last great metaphysical systems (Hegel and Husserl, notably) was executed in the name of truth and meaning, if one considers that these "phenomenologies" — which were metaphysical systems — had as their essential motif a *reduction to meaning* (which is *literally* a Husserlian proposition), then one can conceive that the reduction *of* meaning — that is, of the signified — first takes the form of a critique of phenomenology. Moreover, if one considers that the Heideggerian destruction of metaphysical humanism is produced initially on the basis of a *hermeneutical* question on the *meaning* or the *truth* of Being, then one also conceives that the reduction of meaning operates by means of a kind of break with a thinking of Being that has all the characteristics of a *relève (Aufhebung)* of humanism.

2. *The strategic bet.* A radical trembling can only come from the *outside.* Therefore, the trembling of which I speak derives no more than any other from some spontaneous decision or philosophical thought after some internal maturation of its history. This trembling is played out in the violent relationship of the whole of the West to its other, whether a "linguistic" relationship (where very quickly the question of the limits of everything leading back to the question of the meaning of Being arises), or ethnological, economic, political, military, relationships, etc. Which does not mean, moreover, that military or economic violence is not in structural solidarity with "linguistic" violence. But the "logic" of every relation to the outside

is very complex and surprising. It is precisely the force and the efficiency of the system that regularly change transgressions into "false exits." Taking into account these effects of the system, one has nothing, from the inside where "we are," but the choice between two strategies:

a. To attempt an exit and a deconstruction without changing terrain, by repeating what is implicit in the founding concepts and the original problematic, by using against the edifice the instruments or stones available in the house, that is, equally, in language. Here, one risks ceaselessly confirming, consolidating, *relifting (relever)*, at an always more certain depth, that which one allegedly deconstructs. The continuous process of making explicit, moving toward an opening, risks sinking into the autism of the closure.

b. To decide to change terrain, in a discontinuous and irruptive fashion, by brutally placing oneself outside, and by affirming an absolute break and difference. Without mentioning all the other forms of *trompe-l'oeil* perspective in which such a displacement can be caught, thereby inhabiting more naively and more strictly than ever the inside one declares one has deserted, the simple practice of language ceaselessly reinstates the new terrain of the oldest ground. The effects of such a reinstatement or of such a blindness could be shown in numerous precise instances.

It goes without saying that these effects do not suffice to annul the necessity for a "change of terrain." It also goes without saying that the choice between these two forms of deconstruction cannot be simple and unique. A new writing must weave and interlace these two motifs of deconstruction. Which amounts to saying that one must speak several languages and produce several texts at once. I would like to point out especially that the style of the first deconstruction is mostly that of the Heideggerian questions, and the other is mostly the one that dominates France today. I am purposely speaking in terms of a dominant style: because there are also breaks and changes of terrain in texts of the Heideggerian type; because the "change of terrain" is far from upsetting the entire French landscape to which I am referring; because what we need, perhaps, as Nietzsche said, is a change of "style"; and if there is style, Nietzsche reminded us, it must be *plural.*

3. *The difference between the superior man and the superman.*
Beneath this rubric is signaled both the increasingly insistent
and increasingly rigorous recourse to Nietzsche in France, and
the division that is announced, perhaps, between two *relèves* of
man. We know how, at the end of *Zarathustra*, at the moment
of the "sign," when *das Zeichen kommt,* Nietzsche distinguishes,
in the greatest proximity, in a strange resemblance and an
ultimate complicity, at the eve of the last separation, of the
great Noontime, between the superior man (*höhere Mensch*) and
the superman (*Übermensch*). The first is abandoned to his dis-
tress in a last movement of pity. The latter — who is not the
last man — awakens and leaves, without turning back to what
he leaves behind him. He burns his text and erases the traces
of his steps. His laughter then will burst out, directed toward
a return that no longer will have the form of the metaphysical
repetition of humanism, nor doubtless, "beyond" metaphysics,
the form of a memorial or a guarding of the meaning of Being,
the form of the house and of the truth of Being. He will dance,
outside the house, the *aktive Vergesslichkeit,* the "active forgetting" and the cruel (*grausam*) feast of which the *Genealogy of
Morals* speaks. No doubt that Nietzsche called for an active
forgetting of Being: it would not have the metaphysical form
imputed to it by Heidegger.

Must one read Nietzsche, with Heidegger, as the last of the
great metaphysicians? Or, on the contrary, are we to take the
question of the truth of Being as the last sleeping shudder of
the superior man? Are we to understand the eve as the guard
mounted around the house or as the awakening to the day that
is coming, at whose eve we are? Is there an economy of the
eve?

Perhaps we are between these two eves, which are also two
ends of man. But who, we?

Notes

1. In *The Critique of Practical Reason and Other Writings on Moral Philosophy,* trans. Lewis
White Beck (Chicago: University of Chicago Press, 1949), p. 86. Further references
are to this edition.

2. Trans. Hazel Barnes (New York: Pocket Books, 1966), p. 784.

3. (*Les mots et les choses*) (London: Tavistock Publications, 1970), p. 387.

4. The humanism that marks Sartre's philosophical discourse in its depths, however, is very surely and very ironically taken apart in *Nausea:* in the caricature of the Autodidact, for example, the same figure reassembles the theological project of absolute knowledge and the humanist ethic, in the form of the encyclopedic epistemophilia that leads the Autodidact to undertake the reading of the world library (which is really the Western library, and definitely the municipal library) in alphabetical order by author's name, and in areas where he is able to love Man ("There is an aim, sir, there is an aim . . . there are men . . . one must love them, one must love them") in the representation of men, preferably young men. It is in the dialogue with the Autodidact that Roquentin levels the worst charges against humanism, against all humanist styles; and at the moment when nausea is slowly rising in him, he says to himself, for example, "I don't want to be integrated, I don't want my good red blood to go and fatten this lymphatic beast: I will not be fool enough to call myself 'antihumanist.' I *am not* a humanist, that's all there is to it." *Nausea,* trans. Lloyd Alexander (New York: New Directions, 1959), p. 160.

5. "Each human reality is at the same time a direct project to metamorphose its own For-itself in an In-itself-For-itself and a project of the appropriation of the world as a totality of being-in-itself, in the form of a fundamental quality. Every human reality is a passion in that it projects losing itself so as to found being and by the same stroke to constitute the In-itself which escapes contingency by being its own foundation, the *Ens causa sui,* which religions call God. Thus the passion of man is the reverse of that of Christ, for man loses himself as man in order that God may be born. But the idea of God is contradictory and we lose ourselves in vain. Man is a useless passion." *Being and Nothingness,* trans. Hazel Barnes (New York: Pocket Books, 1966), p. 784. This synthetic unity is determined as *lack:* lack of totality in beings, lack *of* God that is soon transformed into a lack *in* god. Human-reality is a *failed* God: "Also the *ens causa sui* remains as the *lacked* . . ." (p.789); ". . . the for-itself determines its being as a *lack* . . ." (p.795). As concerns the meaning of the Being of this totality of beings, as concerns the history of this concept of negativity as a relationship to God, the meaning and origin of the concept of (human) reality, and the reality of the real, no questions are asked. In this respect, what is true of *Being and Nothingness* is even more so of the *Critique of Dialectical Reason.* The concept of *lack,* linked to the non-self identity of the subject (as consciousness) and to the desire and agency of the Other in the dialectic of the master and the slave, was then beginning to dominate the French ideological scene.

6. Chapter 7, "Psychologism as Sceptical Relativism," sec. 39, "Anthropologism in Sigwart's Logic," sec. 40, "Anthropologism in Erdmann's Logic."

7. *Ideas I,* see e.g. secs. 49 and 54.

8. *Ideas I,* secs. 49 and 54.

9. See the Afterword to *Ideas,* and the marginal notes in the copy of *Sein und Zeit* (Husserl Archives, Louvain).

10. "Every humanism is either grounded in a metaphysics or is itself made to be the ground of one. Every determination of the essence of man that already presupposes an interpretation of being without asking about the truth of Being, whether knowingly or not, is metaphysical. The result is that what is peculiar to all metaphysics, specifically with respect to the way the essence of man is determined, is that it is 'humanistic.'

Accordingly, every humanism remains metaphysical." "Letter on Humanism," in *Basic Writings*, ed. David Farrell Krell (New York: Harper and Row, 1977), p. 202.

11. Without neglecting the complexity of the relations between the *Logic* and the *Phenomenology of Spirit*, the question we are asking authorizes us to consider them *together* at the point of opening where Absolute Knowledge articulates them one with the other.

12. "The actual soul with its sensation and its concrete self-feeling turned into habit, has implicitly realised the 'ideality' of its qualities; in this externality it has recollected and inwardized (*erinnert*) itself, and is infinite self-relation. This free universality thus made explicit shows the soul awaking to the higher stage of the ego, or abstract universality, in so far as it is *for* the abstract universality. In this way it gains the position of thinker and subject — especially a subject of the judgment in which the ego excludes from itself the sum total of its merely natural features as an object, a world external to it — but with such respect to that object that in it it is immediately reflected into itself. Thus soul rises to become *Consciousness*. (Die wirkliche Seele in der *Gewohnheit* des Empfindens und ihres *konkreten* Selbst gefühlt ist an sich die für sich seiende *Idealität* ihrer Bestimmtheiten, in ihrer Äusserlichkeit *erinnert* in sich und unendliche Beziehung an sich. Die Fürsichsein der freien Allgemeinheit ist das höhere Erwachen der Seele zum *Ich*, der abstrakten Allgemeinheit, insofern sie für die abstrakte Allgemeinheit ist, welche so *Denken* und *Subjekt* für sich und zwar bestimmt Subjekt seines Urteils ist, in welchem es die natürliche Totalität seiner Bestimmungen als ein Objekt, eine ihm *äussere* Welt, von sich ausschliesst und sich darauf bezieht, so dass es in derselben unmittelbar in sich reflektiert ist, das *Bewusstsein*.)" *Philosophy of Mind*, trans. William Wallace (Oxford: Oxford University Press, 1971), sec. 412, p. 151.

13. That is, objectivity in general, the relation of an "I" in general with a being-object in general.

14. TN. This passage should be read in conjunction with the discussion of *relève* in "La différance," "Ousia and Grammē," and "The Pit and the Pyramid," all in *Margins of Philosophy*.

15. We could verify the necessity of the framework of this ambiguity or *relevance*, which is accomplished in Hegelian metaphysics and persists wherever metaphysics — that is, our language — maintains its authority, not only in our immediate vicinity, but already in all pre-Hegelian systems. In Kant, the figure of finitude organizes the capacity to know from the very emergence of the anthropological limit.
    A. *On the one hand*, it is precisely when Kant wishes to think something like the *end*, the pure *end*, the *end* in itself, that he must criticize anthropologism, in the *Metaphysics of Morals*. One cannot deduce the principles of morality on the basis of a knowledge of the nature of a particular being named *man:* "But a completely isolated metaphysics of morals, mixed with no anthropology, no theology, no physics or hyperphysics, and even less with occult qualities (which might be called hypophysical), is not only an indispensable substrate of all theoretically sound and definite knowledge of duties; it is also a desideratum of the highest importance to the actual fulfilment of its precepts" ("Foundations of the Metaphysics of Morals," in *The Critique of Practical Reason . . .*, p. 70). "Furthermore, it is evident that it is not only of the greatest necessity in a theoretical point of view when it is a question of speculation but also of the utmost practical importance to derive the concepts and laws of morals from pure reason and to present them pure and unmixed, and to determine the scope of this entire practical but pure rational knowledge (the entire faculty of pure practical reason) without making the principles depend upon the particular nature of human reason, as speculative philosophy may permit and even sometimes find necessary. But since moral laws should hold for every rational being as such, the principles must be derived from

the universal concept of a rational being generally. In this manner all morals, which need anthropology for their application to men, must be completely developed first as pure philosophy, i.e. metaphysics, independently of anthropology" (ibid., p. 71). "With a view to attaining this, it is extremely important to remember that we must not let ourselves think that the reality of this principle can be derived from the *particular constitution of human nature (aus der besondern Eigenschaft der menschlichen Natur)*. For duty is practical unconditional necessity of action; it must, therefore, hold for all rational beings (to which alone an imperative can apply), and *only for that reason* can it be a law for all human wills" (ibid., p. 83). We see in these three passages that what is always of the "greatest importance" (*von der höchsten Wichtigkeit . . . von der grössten praktischen Wichtigkeit . . . von der äussersten Wichtigkeit*) is to determine the end in itself (as an unconditioned principle of morality), independently of any anthropological givens. One cannot think the purity of the end of the basis of man.

B. But, *on the other hand*, and inversely, man's specificity, man's essence as a rational being, as the rational animal (*zōon logon ekhon*), announces itself to itself only on the basis of thinking the end in itself; it announces itself to itself *as* the end in itself; that is, equally, as an infinite end, since the thinking of the unconditioned is also the thinking that raises itself above experience, that is, above finitude. Thus is explained the fact that despite the critique of anthropologism, of which we have just given a few indices, man is the *only example*, the only case of a rational being that can ever be cited at the very moment when by all rights one distinguishes the universal concept of a rational being from the concept of the human being. It is through the offices of this *fact* that anthropology regains all its contested authority. This is the point at which the philosopher says "we," and at which in Kant's discourse "rational being" and "humanity" are always associated by the conjunction "and" or *vel*. For example, "Now, I say, man *and in general (und überhaupt)* every rational being, *exists* as an end in himself, and not merely as a means" (*Foundations . . .* , p. 86). [Note that this phrase is from the passage that serves as the first epigraph to this text. The deconstruction of the end and of man takes place on the *margins* of philosophy: in titles and footnotes.] "This principle of humanity and of every rational creature as an end in itself" (ibid., pp. 88–89).

16. "The Origin of Geometry," in *The Crisis of European Sciences and Transcendental Phenomenology*, trans. David Carr (Evanston: Northwestern University Press, 1970), p. 378.

17. In a brief fragment from 1934 (*Stufen der Geschichtlichkeit. Erste Geschichtlichkeit*, Beilage XXVI, in *Die Krisis der europäischen Wissenschaften und die transzendentale Phänomenologic* [The Hague: Martinus Nijhoff, 1954], pp. 502–503) Husserl distinguishes between three levels and three stages of historicity: culture and tradition as human sociality in general; European culture and the theoretical project (science and philosophy); "the conversion of philosophy into phenomenology."

18. TN. *Being and Time*, trans. John Macquarrie and Edward Robinson (New York: Harper and Row, 1962), p. 25.

19. TN. *Being and Time*, p. 26. Note that Macquarrie and Robinson translate *Seiend* (which we give as "being," as do most of the recent Heidegger translations) as "entity."

20. TN. *Being and Time*, pp. 26–27. Further references are to this edition.

21. "In demonstrating that Dasein is ontico-ontologically prior, we may have misled the reader into supposing that this entity must also be what is given as ontico-ontologically primary (*primär*), not only in the sense that it can itself be grasped 'immediately,' but also in that the kind of Being which it possesses is presented just as 'immediately.' Ontically, of course, Dasein is not only close to us — even that which is closest: we *are*

it, each of us, we ourselves. In spite of this, or rather for just this reason, it is ontologically that which is farthest. . . . Dasein is ontically 'closest' (*am nächsten*) to itself and ontologically farthest; but pre-ontologically it is surely not a stranger (*nicht fremd*)" (pp. 36–37).

22. "Every humanism is either grounded in a metaphysics or is itself made to be the ground of one. Every determination of the essence of man that already presupposes an interpretation of being without asking about the truth of Being, whether knowingly or not, is metaphysical. The result is that what is peculiar to all metaphysics, specifically with respect to the way the essence of man is determined, is that it is 'humanistic.' Accordingly, every humanism remains metaphysical. In defining the humanity of man humanism not only does not ask about the relation of Being to the essence of man; because of its metaphysical origin humanism even impedes the question by neither recognizing nor understanding it." "Letter on Humanism," in *Basic Writings*, ed. Krell, p. 202.

23. "Letter on Humanism," p. 198.

24. "Letter on Humanism," p. 218.

25. "Letter on Humanism," pp. 199–200. In the same sense, one could cite many other passages of the "Letter." Thus, for example, "But we must be clear on this point, that when we do this we abandon man to the essential realm of *animalitas* even if we do not equate him with beasts but attribute a specific difference to him. In principle we are still thinking of *homo animalis* — even when *anima* is posited as *animus sive mens*, and this in turn is later posited as subject, person or spirit. Such positing is the manner of metaphysics. But then the essence of man is too little (*zu gering*) heeded and not thought in its origin, the essential provenance that is always the essential future for historical mankind (*geschichtliche Menschentum*). Metaphysics thinks of man on the basis of *animalitas* and does not think in the direction of his *humanitas*.

"Metaphysics closes itself to the simple essential fact that man essentially occurs only in his essence (*in seinem Wesen west*) where he is claimed (*angesprochen*) by Being. Only from that claim 'has' he found that wherein his essence dwells. Only from this dwelling 'has' he 'language' as the home that preserves the ecstatic for his essence. Such standing in the lighting of Being (*Lichtung des Seins*) I call the ek-sistence of man. This way of Being is proper (*eignet*) only to man. Ek-sistence so understood is not only the ground of the possibility of reason, *ratio,* but is also that in which the essence of man preserves (*wahrt*) the source that determines him.

"Ek-sistence can be said only of the essence of man, that is, only of the human 'to be.' For as far as our experience shows, only man is admitted to the destiny of ek-sistence (*in das Geschick der Eksistence*)." "Letter," pp. 203–204.

The motif of the *proper (eigen, eigentlich)* and the several modes of *to propriate* (particularly *Ereignen* and *Ereignis*), both of which thematically dominate the question of the truth of Being in *Zeit und Sein,* has long been at work in Heidegger's thought. In the "Letter on Humanism" in particular. The themes of the *house* and of the *proper* are regularly brought together: as we will attempt to show later, the value of *oikos* (and of *oikēsis*) plays a decisive, if hidden, role in the semantic chain that interests us here. [See "La différance," note 2, on *Oikos* and *Oikēsis,* in *Margins of Philosophy.*]

26. "Letter," p. 207.

27. "Letter," p. 209.

28. See "White Mythology," in *Margins of Philosophy.*

29. "Letter," pp. 209–210.

30. "Letter," pp. 210–211.

31. "Letter," pp. 211–212.

32. "Letter," p. 212.

33. "Letter," p. 213.

34. "The 'Introduction' to *Being and Time* says simply and clearly, even in italics, 'Being is the *transcendens* pure and simple (*das Transcendens schlechthin*).' Just as the openness of spatial nearness seen from the perspective of a particular thing exceeds all things near and far, so is Being essentially broader than all beings, because it is the lighting (*Lichtung*) itself. For all that, Being is thought on the basis of beings, a consequence of the approach — at first unavoidable — within a metaphysics that is still dominant." "Letter," p. 216.

35. Several examples of the predominance granted to the value of ontological proximity: "This destiny comes to pass as the lighting of Being (*Lichtung des Seins*), as which it is. The lighting grants nearness to Being. In this nearness, in the lighting of the *Da*, man dwells as the ek-sisting one without yet being able properly to experience and take over this dwelling. In the lecture on Hölderlin's elegy 'Homecoming' (1943) this nearness 'of' Being, which the *Da* of Dasein is, is thought on the basis of *Being and Time* . . . it is called the 'homeland' (ibid., p. 217). "The homeland of this historical dwelling is nearness to Being" (ibid., p. 218). "In his essential unfolding within the history of Being, man is the being whose Being as ek-sistence consists in his dwelling in the nearness of Being (*in der Nähe des Seins wohnt*). Man is the neighbor of Being (*Nachbar des Seins*)" (ibid., p. 222). "'Ek-sistence,' in fundamental contrast to every *existentia* and '*existence*,' is ecstatic dwelling in the nearness of Being" (ibid.). "Or should thinking, by means of open resistance to 'humanism,' risk a shock that could for the first time cause perplexity concerning the *humanitas* of *homo humanus* and its basis? In this way it could awaken a reflection (*Besinnung*) — if the world-historical moment did not itself already compel such a reflection — that thinks not only about man but also about the 'nature' of man, not only about his nature but even more primordially about the dimension in which the essence of man, determined by Being itself is at home" (ibid., p. 225). "Thinking does not overcome metaphysics by climbing still higher, surmounting it, transcending it somehow or other, thinking overcomes metaphysics by climbing back down into the nearness of nearest (*in die Nähe des Nächsten*)" (ibid., p. 231).

    To destroy the privilege of the present-now (*Gegenwart*) always leads back, on the Heideggerian pathway, to a presence (*Anwesen, Anwesenheit*) that none of the three modes of the present (present-present, past-present, future-present) can exhaust or terminate, but which, on the contrary, provides their playing space, on the basis of a fourfold whose thinking entirely informs what is at stake in our question. The fourfold can be maintained or lost, risked or reappropriated — an alternative always suspended over its "own proper" abysm — never winning except by losing (itself). It is the text of dissemination.

    Now this presence of the fourfold, in turn, is thought, in *On Time and Being* notably, according to the opening of propriation as the nearness of the near, proximation, approximation. Here we will refer to the analysis of the four-dimensionality of time and of its play. "True time is four-dimensional. . . . For this reason we call the first, original, literally incipient extending (*Reichen*) in which the unity of true (*eigentlichen*) time consists 'nearing nearness,' 'nearhood' (*Nahheit*), an early word still used by Kant. But it brings future, past and present near to one another by distancing them." *On Time and Being*, trans. Joan Stambaugh (New York: Harper and Row, 1972), p. 15. "In the sending of the destiny of Being (*Im Schicken des Geschickes von Sein*), in the extending (*Reichen*) of time, there becomes manifest a dedication (*Zueignen*), a delivering over

(*Übereignen*) into what is their own (*in ihr Eigenes*), namely of Being as presence (*Anwesenheit*) and of time as the realm of the open. What determines both, time and Being, in their own, that is in their belonging together, we shall call: *Ereignis*, or event of Appropriation" (ibid., p. 19). "What the name 'event of Appropriation' (*Ereignis*) names can no longer be represented by means of the current meaning of the word; for in that meaning 'event of Appropriation' is understood in the sense of occurrence and happening — not in terms of Appropriating (*Eignen*) as the extending and sending which opens and preserves" (ibid., p. 20).

The facility, and also the necessity, of the transition from the near to the proper will have been noticed. The Latin medium of this transition (*prope, proprius*) is lost in other languages, for example in German.

36. On the topic of what unites the values of self-presence and spoken language, I permit myself to refer to *Of Grammatology* and *Speech and Phenomena*. Implicitly or explicitly, the valorization of spoken language is constant and massive in Heidegger. I will study it elsewhere in and of itself. Having reached a certain point in the analysis, it is necessary to measure the extent of this valorization rigorously: if it covers almost the entirety of Heidegger's text (in that it leads all the metaphysical determinations of the *present* or of *being* back to the matrix of Being as presence, *Anwesenheit*), it is also erased at the point at which is announced the question of a *Wesen* that would not even be an *Anwesen*. (On this subject, see "Ousia and Grammē," above.) Thus is explained, for example, the disqualification of literature, which is opposed to thinking and to *Dichtung*, and also to an artisan- and "peasant" -like practice of the letter: "In written form thinking easily loses its flexibility. . . . On the other hand, written composition exerts a wholesome pressure toward deliberate linguistic formulation" ("Letter," p. 195). "The truth of Being . . . would thus be more easily weaned from mere supposing and opining and directed to the now rare handicraft of writing" (ibid., p. 223). "What is needed in the present world crisis is less philosophy, but more attentiveness in thinking; less literature, but more cultivation of the letter" (ibid., p. 242). "We must liberate *Dichtung* from literature" (text published in *Revue de poésie*, Paris, 1967).

37. Elsewhere ("La parole soufflée," in *Writing and Difference*, and in *Of Grammatology*) I have attempted to indicate the passage between the near, the "proper" and the *erection* of the "standing upright."

38. TN. Derrida is using "to solicit" in its etymological sense here, as he often does elsewhere. "To solicit" derives from the Latin *sollus*, whole, and *ciere*, to move, and thus has the sense of "to make the whole move." The reference to *oikonomia* and burial in the preceding sentence is explained in "La différance," note 2, in *Margins of Philosophy*.

II

The Transformation of Philosophy: Systematic Proposals

5

Donald Davidson

Introduction

The turn to language in the twentieth century has transformed the way in which philosophers treat what were traditionally called "metaphysical" issues. In the "heyday of meanings," to borrow Ian Hacking's phrase, verificationists like A. J. Ayer used an empirical criterion of significance to settle questions about what could and could not be true of the world. More recently, Davidson's teacher, Quine, forged other links between science, language, and ontology: the formal structures of accepted theoretical sentences entail ontological commitments. In this essay Donald Davidson gives a new twist to the semantic transformation of metaphysics: to share a language is to share a picture of the world that must in its large features be true; it follows that to make manifest these features is to make manifest the general features of reality. Thus, metaphysical questions are to be approached not by analyzing the meaning of words or concepts but by studying the semantic structures of natural languages.

As he first presented it in his article "Truth and Meaning" (1966; reprinted 1983), Davidson's theory of meaning is an application to natural languages of the theory of truth Tarski developed for formal languages. Like so many other philosophers of language from the early Wittgenstein onward, Davidson is here advancing an interpretation of Frege's fundamental insight that the meaning of a sentence is to be found in its truth conditions. The debate that has continued since Frege centers around how to specify, in a general enough way, the truth conditions for all types of sentences. Tarski viewed his formal definition of truth ("'Snow is white' is true if and only if snow is white") as a way of eliminating semantic terms through presupposing *translation* as a purely "syntactic" notion. Davidson, however, assumes a "partial understanding" of *truth* in order to define the notions of translation, interpretation, and meaning in purely extensional terms. Through what he calls Convention T ("'S' is T if and only if p"), the predicate "is true" can be applied recursively to all sentences of a natural language, so as to give a "theory of truth" and thus a theory of meaning for that language. "What we require of a theory of meaning for that language L is that without appeal to any (further) semantic notions it places enough restrictions on 'is T' to entail all sentences got from schema T when 'S' is replaced by a structural description of a sentence of L and p by that sentence" (1983, 23). By applying this definition recursively to the sentences of a language, we account for the truth values and thus for the meanings of a potential infinity of sentences in terms of a finite stock of "atoms" (axioms) and the "complex molecules" (theorems) built from them. It is this placing of the truth conditions of sentences in the context of a comprehensive (recursive) theory of truth that yields metaphysical insight. "What a theory of truth does for a natural language is reveal structure."

But before we can go from these humble origins to a powerful and austere method for resolving metaphysical questions, we require some assurances: formal semantics will be metaphysically useful only if it is indeed the case that most of our beliefs are true; and it can be generalized to natural languages only if there are no deep philosophical problems with translation. Davidson resolves both of these problems at once in "The Very Idea of a Conceptual Scheme" with what Hacking, Rorty, and he himself call "a transcendental argument." The argument takes the form of an attempt to demonstrate the incoherence of conceptual relativism. Davidson summarizes its conclusion at the beginning of this essay: "In order to communicate, most of our beliefs must be true." Conceptual relativism of the usual varieties, from Kuhn's paradigm shifts to

Quine's ontological relativity, presupposes that we can make epistemological sense of the idea of experiential input as a theory-free basis about which there can be radically different theories. Davidson denies this emphatically. There is, he allows, a connection between belief and experience, but it is purely causal and hence not of particular epistemological significance. Davidson bases "translation (and thus also the meaning) of a sentence not on stimulus patterns or sense perceptions or experience (whatever that may be) but on the familiar macroscopic events and objects through which the sentence is interpreted. This brings objective truth and meaning in close relation . . . since it is impossible to be generally in error" (Interview, 1983, 19–20). Error can be found only in the setting of largely true beliefs. Massive error about the world is simply unintelligible.

If this "transcendental" argument works, it follows that there is a correspondence between general aspects of our language and general aspects of reality. These aspects can be identified through formal semantic analysis, thus yielding a "metaphysics of logical grammar," the appropriate contemporary form of Kant's "metaphysics of experience." In this enterprise Davidson sees himself as continuing the central tradition of analytic philosophy extending from Plato and Aristotle, through Hume and Kant, to Frege, Russell, and Wittgenstein, and beyond. Unlike Rorty, he does not see this tradition as having played itself out. The project of comprehending basic concepts such as truth and knowledge, of grasping the nature of explanation of the physical and the human worlds, remains; only the means are transformed by "the method of truth." This method, finally, places philosophical inquiry on an *empirical* basis: "A theory of meaning . . . is an empirical theory, and its ambition is to account for the workings of natural language. . . . Empirical power in such a theory depends on success in recovering the structure of a very sophisticated ability — the ability to speak and understand a language" ("Truth and Meaning," p. 311). In short, Davidson's "transformation of philosophy" redirects our energies (in large part) to the construction of empirical theories of meaning for natural languages (as that part of a unified theory of speech and action that enables us to interpret linguistic behavior).

Suggested Readings

Apel, K.-O. "Comments on Donald Davidson's 'Communication and Convention,'" *Synthese* 59 (1984), 19–26.

Davidson, Donald. *Essays on Action and Events.* Oxford: Clarendon Press, 1975.

Davidson, Donald. "Toward a Unified Theory of Meaning and Action," *Grazer Philosophische Studien* 2 (1980), 1–12.

Davidson, Donald. "Paradoxes of Irrationality," in *Philosophical Essays on Freud*, ed. R. Wollheim and J. Hopkins, 289–305. Cambridge: Cambridge University Press, 1982.

Davidson, Donald. *Inquiries into Truth and Interpretation.* Cambridge: Cambridge University Press, 1983.

Davidson, Donald. "Analytische Philosophie ohne empiristische Dogmen." Interview with Dirk Koppelberg in *Information Philosophie* (1983) vol. 1, pp. 18–21, and vol. 2, pp. 18–25.

Davidson, Donald, and Gilbert Harman, eds. *The Semantics of Natural Language.* Dordrecht: Reidel, 1975.

Davidson, Donald, and Jakko Hintikka, eds. *Words and Objections.* Dordrecht: Reidel, 1969.

Dummett, Michael. "What Is a Theory of Meaning? (I)," in *Mind and Language,* ed. S. Guttenplan, 97–138. Oxford: Clarendon Press, 1975.

Evans, Gareth, and John McDowell, eds. *Truth and Meaning.* Oxford: Clarendon Press, 1976.

Field, Harty. "Tarski's Theory of Truth," in *Language, Truth and Reality,* ed. M. Platts, 83–110. London: Routledge and Kegan Paul, 1980.

Hacking, Ian. *Why Does Language Matter to Philosophy?* Cambridge: Cambridge University Press, 1978.

LePore, Ernest, ed. *Truth and Interpretation: Perspectives on the Philosophy of Donald Davidson.* New York: Basil Blackwell, 1986.

LePore, Ernest, and Brian McLaughlin, eds. *Actions and Events: Perspectives on the Philosophy of Donald Davidson.* New York: Basil Blackwell, 1986.

Platts, Mark. *Ways of Meaning.* London: Routledge and Kegan Paul, 1979.

Platts, Mark, ed. *Reference, Truth and Reality.* London: Routledge and Kegan Paul, 1980.

Stich, Stephen. "Davidson's Semantic Program," *Canadian Journal of Philosophy* 6 (1976), 201–227.

Stoutland, Frederick. "Realism and Anti-Realism in Davidson's Philosophy of Language, (I) and (II)," *Critica* 14 (1982), 41, 13–53; 42, 19–43.

Strawson, P. F. *Logico-Linguistic Papers.* London: Methuen, 1971.

Tarski, Alfred. *Logic, Semantics and Metamathematics.* Oxford: Clarendon Press, 1976.

Wallace, John. "Positive, Comparative, Superlative," *Journal of Philosophy* 69 (1972), 773–782.

Wright, Crispin. "Truth Conditions and Criteria," *Proceedings of the Aristotelian Society,* supplementary volume 50 (1976), 217–245.

The Method of Truth in Metaphysics

Donald Davidson

In sharing a language, in whatever sense this is required for communication, we share a picture of the world that must, in its large features, be true. It follows that in making manifest the large features of our language, we make manifest the large features of reality. One way of pursuing metaphysics is therefore to study the general structure of our language. This is not, of course, the sole true method of metaphysics; there is no such. But it is one method, and it has been practiced by philosophers as widely separated by time or doctrine as Plato, Aristotle, Hume, Kant, Russell, Frege, Wittgenstein, Carnap, Quine, and Strawson. These philosophers have not, it goes without saying, agreed on what the large features of language are or on how they may best be studied and described; the metaphysical conclusions have in consequence been various.

The method I will describe and recommend is not new; every important feature of the method can be found in one philosopher or another, and the leading idea is implicit in much of the best work in philosophy of language. What is new is the explicit formulation of the approach, and the argument for its philosophical importance. I begin with the argument; then comes a description of the method; finally, some applications are sketched.[1]

1

Why must our language — any language — incorporate or depend upon a largely correct, shared view of how things are?

First consider why those who can understand one another's speech must share a view of the world, whether or not that view is correct. The reason is that we damage the intelligibility of our readings of the utterances of others when our method of reading puts others into what we take to be broad error. We can make sense of differences all right, but only against a background of shared belief. What is shared does not in general call for comment; it is too dull, trite, or familiar to stand notice. But without a vast common ground, there is no place for disputants to have their quarrel. Of course, we can no more agree than disagree with someone else without much mutuality; but perhaps this is obvious.

Beliefs are identified and described only within a dense pattern of beliefs. I can believe a cloud is passing before the sun, but only because I believe there is a sun, that clouds are made of water vapor, that water can exist in liquid or gaseous form; and so on, without end. No particular list of further beliefs is required to give substance to my belief that a cloud is passing before the sun; but some appropriate set of related beliefs must be there. If I suppose that you believe a cloud is passing before the sun, I suppose you have the right sort of pattern of beliefs to support that one belief, and these beliefs I assume you to have must, to do their supporting work, be enough like my beliefs to justify the description of your belief as a belief that a cloud is passing before the sun. If I am right in attributing the belief to you, then you must have a pattern of beliefs much like mine. No wonder, then, I can interpret your words correctly only by interpreting so as to put us largely in agreement.

It may seem that the argument so far shows only that good interpretation breeds concurrence, while leaving quite open the question whether what is agreed upon is true. And certainly agreement, no matter how widespread, does not guarantee truth. This observation misses the point of the argument, however. The basic claim is that much community of belief is needed to provide a basis for communication or understanding; the extended claim should then be that objective error can occur only in a setting of largely true belief. Agreement does not make for truth, but much of what is agreed must be true if some of what is agreed is false.

Just as too much attributed error risks depriving the subject of his subject matter, so too much actual error robs a person of things to go wrong about. When we want to interpret, we work on one or another assumption about the general pattern of agreement. We suppose that much of what we take to be common is true, but we cannot, of course, assume we know where the truth lies. We cannot interpret on the basis of known truths, not because we know none, but because we do not always know which they are. We do not need to be omniscient to interpret, but there is nothing absurd in the idea of an omniscient interpreter; he attributes beliefs to others and interprets their speech on the basis of his own beliefs, just as the rest of us do. Since he does this as the rest of us do, he perforce finds as much agreement as is needed to make sense of his attributions and interpretations; and in this case, of course, what is agreed is by hypothesis true. But now it is plain why massive error about the world is simply unintelligible, for to suppose it intelligible is to suppose there could be an interpreter (the omniscient one) who correctly interpreted someone else as being massively mistaken, and this we have shown to be impossible.

2

Successful communication proves the existence of a shared, and largely true, view of the world. But what led us to demand the common view was the recognition that sentences held true — the linguistic representatives of belief — determine the meanings of the words they contain. Thus the common view shapes the shared language. This is why it is plausible to hold that by studying the most general aspects of language we will be studying the most general aspects of reality. It remains to say how these aspects may be identified and described.

Language is an instrument of communication because of its semantic dimension, the potentiality for truth or falsehood of its sentences, or better, of its utterances and inscriptions. The study of what sentences are true is in general the work of the various sciences; but the study of truth conditions is the province of semantics. What we must attend to in language, if we want to bring into relief general features of the world, is what it is in general for a sentence in the language to be true. The suggestion is that if the truth conditions of sentences are placed in the context of a comprehensive theory, the linguistic structure that emerges will reflect large features of reality.

The aim is a theory of truth for a reasonably powerful and significant part of a natural language. The scope of the theory — how much of the language is captured by the theory, and how convincingly — will be one factor on which the interest of any metaphysical results depends. The theory must show us how we can view each of a potential infinity of sentences as composed from a finite stock of semantically significant atoms (roughly, words) by means of a finite number of applications of a finite number of rules of composition. It must then give the truth conditions of each sentence (relative to the circumstances of its utterance) on the basis of its composition. The theory may thus be said to explain the conditions of truth of an utterance of a sentence on the basis of the roles of the words in the sentence.

Much here is owed to Frege. Frege saw the importance of giving an account of how the truth of a sentence depends on the semantic features of its parts, and he suggested how such an account could be given for impressive stretches of natural language. His method was one now familiar: he introduced a standardized notation whose syntax directly reflected the intended interpretation, and then urged that the new notation, as interpreted, had the same expressive power as important parts of natural language. Or rather, not quite the same expressive power, since Frege believed natural language was defective in some respects, and he regarded his new language as an improvement.

Frege was concerned with the semantic structure of sentences, and with semantic relations between sentences, in so far as these generated entailments. But he cannot be said to have conceived the idea of a comprehensive formal theory of truth for language as a whole. One consequence was a lack of interest in the semantic paradoxes. Another was an apparent willingness to accept an infinity of meanings (senses) and referents for every denoting phrase in the language.

Because Frege took the application of function to argument to be the sole mode of semantic combination, he was bound to treat sentences as a kind of name — the name of a truth value. Seen simply as an artful dodge on the way to characterizing the truth conditions of sentences, this device of Frege's is unexceptionable. But since sentences do not operate in language the way names do, Frege's approach undermines confidence that the ontology he needs to work his semantics has any direct connection with the ontology implicit in natural language. It is not clear, then, what one can learn about metaphysics from Frege's method. (I certainly do not mean by this that we can't learn about metaphysics from Frege's work; but to see how, arguments different from mine must be marshaled.)

Quine provided an essential ingredient for the project at hand by showing how a holistic approach to the problem of understanding a language supplies the needed empirical foundation. If metaphysical conclusions are to be drawn from a theory of truth in the way that I propose, the approach to language must be holistic. Quine himself does not see holism as having such direct metaphysical significance, however, and for a number of reasons. First, Quine has not made the theory of truth central either as a key to the ontology of a language or as a test of logical form. Second, like Frege, he views a satisfactorily regimented language as an improvement on natural language rather than as part of a theory about it. In one important respect, Quine seems even to go beyond Frege, for where Frege thinks his notation makes for better language, Quine thinks it also makes for better science. As a consequence, Quine ties his metaphysics to his canonical notation rather than to natural language; as he puts it, "The quest of a simplest, clearest overall pattern of canonical notation is not to be distinguished from a quest of ultimate categories, a limning of the most general traits of reality."[2]

The formal languages toward which I gravitate — first-order languages with standard logic — are those preferred by Quine. But our reasons for this choice diverge somewhat. Such languages please Quine because their logic is simple and the scientifically respectable parts of natural language can be translated into them; and with this I agree. But since I am interested not in improving on natural language but in understanding it, I view formal languages or canonical notations as devices for exploring the structure of natural language. We know how to give a theory of truth for the formal language; so if we also knew how to transform the sentences of a natural language systematically into sentences of the formal language, we would have a theory of truth for the natural language. From this point of view, standard formal languages are intermediate devices to assist us in treating natural languages as more complex formal languages.

Tarski's work on truth definitions for formalized languages serves as inspiration for the kind of theory of truth that is wanted for natural languages.[3] The method works by enumerating the semantic properties of the items in a finite vocabulary, and on this basis recursively characterizes truth for each of the infinity of sentences. Truth is reached from the basis by the intervention of a subtle and powerful concept (satisfaction) that relates both sentences and nonsentential expressions to objects in the world. An important feature of Tarski's approach is that a characterization of a truth predicate "x is true in L" is accepted only if it entails, for each sentence of the language L, a theorem of the form "x is true in L if and only if . . ." with "x" replaced by a description of the sentence and the dots replaced by a translation of the sentence into the language of the theory.

It is evident that these theorems, which we may call T-sentences, require a predicate that holds of just the true sentences of L. It is also plain, from the fact that the truth conditions for a sentence translate that sentence (i.e., what appears to the right of the "if and only if" in a T-sentence translates the sentence described on the left), that the theory shows how to characterize truth for any given sentence without appeal to conceptual resources not available in that sentence.

These remarks are only roughly correct. A theory of truth for a natural language must relativize the truth of a sentence to the circumstances of utterance, and when this is done the truth conditions given by a T-sentence will no longer translate the described sentence, nor will it be possible to avoid using concepts that are, perhaps, semantical, in giving the truth conditions of sentences with indexical elements. More important, the notion of translation, which can be made precise for artificial languages on which interpretations are imposed by fiat, has no precise or even clear application to natural languages.

For these and other reasons it is important to stress that a theory of truth for a natural language (as I conceive it) differs widely in both aim and interest from Tarski's truth definitions. Sharpness of application is lost, and with it most of what concerns mathematicians and logicians: consequences for consistency, for example. Tarski could take translation as syntactically specified and go on to define truth. But in application to a natural language it makes more sense to assume a partial understanding of truth and use the theory to throw light on meaning, interpretation, and translation.[4] Satisfaction of Tarski's Convention T remains a desideratum of a theory but is no longer available as a formal test.

What a theory of truth does for a natural language is reveal a structure. In treating each sentence as composed in accountable ways out of a finite number of truth-relevant words, it articulates this structure. When we study terms and sentences directly, not in the light of comprehensive theory, we must bring metaphysics to language; we assign roles to words and sentences in accord with the categories we independently posit on epistemological or metaphysical grounds. Operating in this way, philosophers ponder such questions as whether there must be entities, perhaps universals, that correspond to predicates, or nonexistent entities to correspond to nondenoting names or descriptions; or they argue that sentences do or do not correspond to facts or propositions.

A different light is shed on these matters when we look for a comprehensive theory of truth, for such a theory makes its own unavoidable demands.

3

Now let us consider some applications. We noticed that the requirement that the truth conditions of a sentence be given using only the conceptual resources of that sentence is not entirely clear where it can be met, nor everywhere applicable. The cases that invite exception are sentences that involve demonstratives, and here the cure of the difficulty is relatively simple.[5] These cases aside, the requirement, for all its obscurity, has what seem, and I think are, important implications.

Suppose we were to admit a rule like this as part of a theory of truth: "A sentence consisting of a singular term followed by a one-place predicate is true if and only if the object named by the singular term belongs to the class determined by the predicate."[6] This rule offends the requirement, for if the rule were admitted, the T-sentence for "Socrates is wise" would be "'Socrates is wise' is true if and only if the object named by 'Socrates' belongs to the class determined by the predicate 'is wise,'" and here the statement of truth conditions involves two semantic concepts (naming and determining a class) not plausibly among the conceptual resources of "Socrates is wise."

It would be easy to get from the tendentious T-sentence just mentioned to the noncommittal and admissible "'Socrates is wise' is true if and only if Socrates is wise" if the theory also contained as postulates statements that the object named by "Socrates" is Socrates and that x belongs to the class determined by the predicate "is wise" if and only if x is wise. If enough such postulates are available to care for all proper names and primitive predicates, the results are clear. First, T-sentences free from unwanted semantic terms would be available for all the sentences involved; and the extra semantic terms would be unnecessary. For there would have to be a postulate for each name and predicate, and this there could be only if the list of names and primitive predicates were finite. But if the list were finite, there would be only a finite number of sentences consisting of a name and a one-place predicate, and nothing would stand in the way of giving the truth conditions for all such sentences straight off — the T-sentences themselves could serve as the axioms.

The example illustrates how keeping the vocabulary finite may allow the elimination of semantic concepts; it also shows how the demand for a satisfactory theory has ontological consequences. Here, the call for entities to correspond to predicates disappears when the theory is made to produce T-sentences without excess semantic baggage. Indeed in the case at hand the theory does not need to put expressions and objects into explicit correspondence at all, and so no ontology is involved; but this is because the supply of sentences whose truth conditions are to be given is finite.

Not that an infinity of sentences necessarily demands ontology. Given the finite supply of sentences with unstructured predicates that we have been imagining, it is easy to go on to infinity by adding one or more iterable devices for constructing sentences from sentences, such as negation, conjunction, or alternation. If ontology was not required to give the truth conditions for the simplest sentences, these devices will not call for more.

In general, however, semantically relevant structure is apt to demand ontology. Consider, for example, the view that quotations are to be treated as semantic atoms, on a par with proper names in lacking significant structure. Tarski says of this way of viewing quotation that it "seems to be the most natural one and completely in accordance with the customary way of using quotation marks."[7] He gives a model argument to show that quotation marks cannot be treated as an ordinary functional expression since a quotation does not name an entity that is a function of anything named by what the quotation marks enclose. About this Tarski is certainly right, but the moral of the lesson cannot be that quotations are like proper names — not, anyway, if a Tarski-style theory of truth can be given for a language containing quotation. For clearly there is an infinite number of quotations.

One idea for a possible solution can be extracted from Quine's remark that quotations may be replaced by spelling (much the same is said by Tarski). Spelling does have structure. It is a way of giving a semantically articulate description of an expression by the use — repeated if necessary — of a finite number of expressions: the concatenation sign, with associated parentheses, and (proper) names of the letters. Following this line, we should think of a quotation like "'cat'" as having a form more clearly given by "'c'⌢'a'⌢'t'," or, better still, by "(see)⌢(eh)⌢(tee)." This idea works, at least up to a point. But note the consequences. We no longer view the quotation "'cat'" as unstructured; rather we are treating it as an abbreviation of a sort for a complex description. Not, however, as an arbitrary abbreviation to be specified for the case at hand, but as a *style* of abbreviation that can be expanded mechanically into a description that shows structure more plainly. Indeed, talk of abbreviations is misleading; we may as well say this theory treats quotations as complex descriptions.

Another consequence is that in giving structure to quotations we have had to recognize in quotations repeatable and independent "words": names of the individual letters and of the concatenation sign. These "words" are, of course, finite in number — that was required — but they also reveal an ontological fact not apparent when quotations were viewed as unstructured names, a commitment to letters. We get a manageable theory when we explain molecules as made from atoms of a finite number of kinds; but we also get atoms.

A more stirring example of how postulating needed structure in language can bring ontology in its wake is provided by Frege's semantics for the oblique contexts created by sentences about propositional attitudes. In Frege's view, a sentence like "Daniel believes that there is a lion in the den" is dominated by the two-place predicate "believes" whose first place is filled by the singular term "Daniel" and whose second place is filled by a singular term that names a proposition or "sense." Taking this line requires us not only to treat sentences as singular terms but to find entities for them to name. And more is to come. For clearly an infinite number of sentences may occupy the spot after "Daniel believes that. . . ." So if we are to provide a truth definition, we must discover semantic structure in these singular terms: it must be shown how they can be treated as descriptions of propositions. To avoid the absurdities that would ensue if the singular terms in a sentence had their usual reference, Frege takes them as referring instead to intensional entities. Analogous changes must come over the semantic features of predicates, quantifiers, and sentential connectives. So far, a theory of truth of the sort we have been looking for can handle the situation, but only by treating each word of the language as ambiguous, having one interpretation in ordinary contexts and another after "believes that" and similar verbs. What is to the eye one word must, from the vantage point of this theory, be treated as two. Frege appreciated this, and held the ambiguity against natural language; Church, in the artificial languages of "A Formulation of the Logic of Sense and Denotation," eliminated the ambiguity by introducing distinct expressions, differing in subscript.[8]

Frege suggested that with each addition of a verb of propositional attitude before a referring expression that expression comes to refer to an entity of a higher semantical level. Thus every word and sentence is infinitely many-ways ambiguous; on Church's theory there will be an infinite basic vocabulary. In neither case is it possible to provide a theory of truth of the kind we want.

Frege was clear on the need, if we are to have a systematic theory, to view the truth value of each sentence as a function of the semantic roles of its parts or aspects — far clearer than anyone who went before, and clearer than most who followed. What Frege did not appreciate, as this last example brings out, was the additional restraints, in particular to a finite vocabulary, that flow from the demand for a comprehensive theory of truth. Frege brought semantics to a point where the demand was intelligible and even, perhaps, satisfiable; but it did not occur to him to formulate the demand.

Let us take a closer look at the bootstrap operation that enables us to bring latent structure to light by characterizing a truth predicate. Early steps may be illustrated by as simple a sentence as "Jack and Jill went up the hill" — under what conditions is this sentence true? The challenge lies in the presence in the sentence of an iterative device — conjunction. Clearly we can go on adding phrases like "and Mary" after the word "Jill" *ad libitum*. So any statement of truth conditions for this sentence must bear in mind the infinity of sentences, generated by the same device, that lie waiting for treatment. What is called for is a recursive clause in the truth theory that can be called into play as often as needed. The trick, as we all know, is to define truth for a basic, and finite, stock of simplest sentences, such as "Jack went up the hill" and "Jill went up the hill," and then make the truth conditions of "Jack and Jill went up the hill" a function of the truth of the two simple sentences. So we get

"Jack and Jill went up the hill" is true if and only if Jack went up the hill and Jill went up the hill.

as a consequence of a theory of truth. On the left a sentence of the vernacular, its structure transparent or not, is described; on the right of the "if and only if" a sentence of that same vernacular, but a part of the vernacular chosen for its ability to make explicit, through repeated applications of the same simple devices, the underlying semantic structure. If a theory of truth yields such a purified sentence for every sentence in the language, the portion of the total language used on the right may be considered a canonical notation. Indeed, with symbols substituted for some words, and grouping made plain by parentheses or some equivalent device, the part of the language used in stating truth conditions for all sentences may become indistinguishable from what is often called a formalized or artificial language. It would be a mistake, however, to suppose that it is essential to find such a canonical subdivision of the language. Since "and" may be written between sentences in English, we take the easy route of transforming "Jack and Jill went up the hill" into "Jack went up the hill and Jill went up the hill" and then giving the truth conditions of the latter in accord with a rule that says a conjunction of sentences is true if and only if each conjunct is. But suppose "and" never stood between sentences; its role as sentential connective would still be recognized by a rule saying that a sentence composed of a conjunctive subject ("Jack and Jill") and a predicate ("went up the hill") is true if and only if the sentence composed of the first conjoined subject and the predicate, and the sentence composed of the second conjoined subject and the predicate, are true. The rule required is less perspicuous and needs to be supplemented with others to do the work of the simple original rule. But the point remains: canonical notation is a convenience we can get along without if need be. It is good, but not necessary, to bring logical form to the surface.

Similarly, it would greatly ease the treatment of negation if we could plausibly transform all sentences containing negation into sentences, recognizably the same in truth value, in which the negating phrase always governed a sentence (as with, "it is not the case that"). But if this were not possible, negation would still be a sentential connective if the truth condition of a sentence like "Coal is not white" were given by adverting to the truth condition of "Coal is white." ("Coal is not white" is true if and only if "Coal is white" is not true.)

The issue of ontology is forced into the open only where the theory finds quantificational structure, and that is where the theory best accounts for the pattern of truth dependencies by systematically relating expressions to objects. It is striking how firmly the demand for theory puts to rest an ancient aporia: the question how to demonstrate the asymmetry, if any, of subject and predicate. As long as our attention is focused on single, simple sentences, we may wonder why an explanation of truth should involve predicates in ontology any less than singular terms. The class of wise objects, or the property of wisdom, offers itself as what might correspond to the predicate "wise" in "Socrates is wise" in much the same way Socrates corresponds to "Socrates." As pointed out above, no finite number of such sentences requires a theory of truth to bring ontology into the picture. Multiple generality, however — the admission of whatever, in natural language, is treated by theory as sentences with mixed quantification and predicates of any degree of complexity — totally changes the picture. With complex quantificational structure, the theory must match up expressions with objects. But there is no need, as long as the underlying logic is assumed to be first order, to introduce entities to correspond to predicates. Recognition of this fact will not, of course, settle the question whether there are such things as universals or classes. But it does demonstrate that there is a difference between singular term and predicate; for large stretches of language, anyway, variables, quantifiers, and singular terms must be construed as referential in function; not so for predicates.

It is not always evident what the quantificational structure of a sentence in natural language is; what appear to be singular terms sometimes melt into something less ontic in implication when their logical relations with other sentences are studied, while the requirements of theory may suggest that a sentence plays a role that can be explained only by treating it as having a quantificational structure not apparent on the surface. Here is a familiar illustration: What is the ontology of a sentence like "Jack fell down before Jack broke his crown"? Jack and his crown seem to be the only candidates for entities that must exist if this sentence is to be true. And if, in place of "before," we had "and," this answer might satisfy us for the reason already explored: namely, that we can state, in a way that will work for endless similar cases, the truth conditions of the whole sentence "Jack fell down *and* Jack broke his crown" on the basis just of the truth of the component sentences, and we can hope to give the truth conditions for the components without more ontology than Jack and his crown. But "Jack fell down before Jack broke his crown" does not yield to this treatment, because "before" cannot be viewed as a truth-functional semantical connective: to see this, reflect that for the sentence to be true, both component sentences must be true, but this is not sufficient for its truth, since interchanging the components will make it false.

Frege showed us how to cope with the case: we can formulate the truth conditions for the sentence "Jack fell down before Jack broke his crown" as follows: it is true if and only if there exists a time t and there exists a time t'' such that Jack fell down at t, Jack broke his crown at t'', and t is before t''. So apparently we are committed to the existence of times if we accept any such sentence as true. And thinking of the holistic character of a truth definition, the discovery of hidden ontology in sentences containing "before" must carry over to other sentences: thus, "Jack fell down" is true if and only if there exists a time t such that Jack fell down at t.

Now for a more disturbing example. Consider first "Jack's fall caused the breaking of his crown." Here it is natural to take "Jack's fall" and the "breaking of his crown" as singular terms describing events, and "caused" as a two-place, or relational, predicate. But then, what is the semantic relation between such general terms as "fall" in "Jack's fall" or "the fall of Jack" and such verbs as "fell" in "Jack fell"? For that matter, how does "Jack's fall caused the breaking of his crown" differ, in its truth conditions, from "Jack fell, which caused it to be the case that Jack broke his crown," where the phrase "which caused it to be the case that" is, on the face of it, a sentential connective?

The correct theory of "caused" as I have argued at more length elsewhere, is parallel to Frege's theory for "before."[9] I suggest that "Jack fell down, which caused the breaking of his crown" is true if and only if there exist events e and f such that e is a fall Jack took, f is a breaking his crown suffered, and e caused f. According to this proposal, the predicate "is a fall," true of events, becomes primary, and contexts containing the verb are derived. Thus "Jack fell" is true if and only if there is a fall such that Jack took it. "Jack took a walk" is true if and only if there is a walk that he took, and so on. On this analysis, a noun phrase like "Jack's fall" becomes a genuine description, and what it describes is the one fall that Jack took.

One consideration that may help reconcile us to an ontology of particular events is that we may then dispense with the abstract ontology of times we just now tentatively accepted, for events are as plausibly the relata of the before-relation as times. Another consideration is that by recognizing our commitment to an ontology of events we can see our way to a viable semantics of adverbs and adverbial modification. Without events there is the problem of explaining the logical relations between sentences like "Jones nicked his cheek while shaving with a razor in the bathroom on Saturday" and "Jones nicked his cheek in the bathroom" and "Jones nicked his cheek." It seems that some iterative device is at work; yet what, from a semantic point of view, can the device be? The books on logic do not say: they analyze these sentences to require relations with varying numbers of places depending on the number of adverbial modifications, but this leads to the unacceptable conclusion that there is an infinite basic vocabulary, and it fails to explain the obvious inferences. By interpreting these sentences as being about events, we can solve the problems. Then we can say that "Jones nicked his cheek in the bathroom on Saturday" is true if and only if there exists an event that is a nicking of his cheek by Jones, *and* that event took place in the bathroom, *and* it took place on Saturday. The iterative device is now obvious: it is the familiar collaboration of conjunction and quantification that enables us to deal with "Someone fell down and broke his crown."

This device works, but as we have seen, it takes an ontology to make it work: an ontology including people for "Someone fell down and broke his crown," an ontology of events (in addition) for "Jones nicked his cheek in the bathroom on Saturday." It is mildly ironic that in recent philosophy it has become a popular maneuver to try to *avoid* ontological problems by treating certain phrases as adverbial. One such suggestion is that we can abjure sense data if we render a sentence like "The mountain appears blue to Smith" as "The mountain appears bluely to Smith." Another similar idea is that we can do without an ontology of intensional objects by thinking of sentences about propositional attitudes as essentially adverbial: "Galileo said that the earth moves" would then come out, "Galileo spoke in a-that-the-earth-moves-fashion." There is little chance, I think, that such adverbial clauses can be given a systematic semantical analysis without ontological entanglements.

There is a further, rather different, way in which a theory of truth may have metaphysical repercussions. In adjusting to the presence of demonstratives, and of demonstrative elements like tense, in a natural language, a theory of truth must treat truth as an attribute of utterances that depends (perhaps among other things) on the sentence uttered, the speaker, and the time. Alternatively, it may be possible to treat truth as a relation between speakers, sentences, and times. Thus an utterance of "I am five feet tall" is true if spoken at some times in the lives of most people, and true if spoken at any time during a considerable span in the lives of a few. "Your slip is showing" may be true when uttered by a speaker at a time when he faces west, though it might not have been true if he had faced north; and "Hilary climbed Everest" was for a long time false and is now forever true. Sentences without demonstrative elements cannot do the work of sentences with demonstrative elements; but if we are to have a theory of truth, we must be able to state, without the use of demonstratives, a rule that explains under what conditions sentences with demonstratives are true. Such rules will give the truth condition of sentences like "Hilary climbed Everest" only by quantifying over utterances, speakers, and times, or, perhaps, events.

If explicit appeal must be made to speakers and their circumstances in giving a theory of truth, then on the assumption that the general features of language reflect objective features of the world, we must conclude that an intelligible metaphysics will assign a central place to the idea of people (=speakers) with a location in public space and time.

It should be clear that "the method of truth" in metaphysics does not eliminate recourse to more standard, often essentially nonlinguistic, arguments or decisions. What it is possible to do in a theory of truth, for example, depends to a large extent on the logical resources the theory itself deploys, and the theory cannot decide this for us. Nor, as we have seen, does the method suggest what truths, beyond those it counts as logical, we must accept as a condition of mutual understanding. What a theory of truth does is describe the pattern truth must make among the sentences, without telling us where the pattern falls. So, for example, I argue that a very large number of our ordinary claims about the world cannot be true unless there are events. But a theory of truth, even if it took the form I propose, would not specify what events exist, nor even that any do. However, if I am right about the logical form of sentences concerning change, then unless there are events, there are no true sentences of very common kinds about change. And if there are no true sentences about change, there are no true sentences about objects that change. A metaphysician who is willing to suppose no sentences like "Vesuvius erupted in March 1944" or "Caesar crossed the Rubicon" are true will not be forced by a theory of truth to admit the existence of events or even, perhaps, of people or mountains. But if he accepts that many such sentences are true (whichever they may be), then it is obvious that he must accept the existence of people and volcanoes; and, if I am right, the existence of events like eruptions and crossings.

The merit of the method of truth is not that it settles such matters once and for all, or even that it settles them without further metaphysical reflection. But the method does serve to sharpen our sense of viable alternatives, and gives a comprehensive idea of the consequences of a decision. Metaphysics has generality as an aim; the method of truth expresses that demand by requiring a theory that touches all the bases. Thus the problems of metaphysics, while neither solved nor replaced, come to be seen as the problems of all good theory building. We want a theory that is simple and clear, with a logical apparatus that is understood and justified, and that accounts for the facts about how our language works. What those facts are may remain somewhat in dispute, as will certainly the wisdom of various tradeoffs as between simplicity and clarity. These questions will be, I do not doubt, the old questions of metaphysics in new dress. But the new dress is in many ways an attractive one.

Notes

1. I am much indebted to Gilbert Harman, W. V. Quine, and John Wallace for comments on earlier versions of this paper.

2. W. V. Quine, *Word and Object* (Cambridge, Massachusetts, 1960), p. 161.

3. A. Tarski, "The Concept of Truth in Formalized Languages," in *Logic, Semantics, Metamathematics* (Oxford, 1956).

4. For more on this, see my "Belief and the Basis of Meaning," *Synthese* 27 (1974): 309–323, and "Radical Interpretation," *Dialectica* 27 (1973): 313–328.

5. See S. Weinstein, "Truth and Demonstratives," *Noûs* 8 (1974): 179–184.

6. Compare R. Carnap, *Meaning and Necessity* (Chicago, 1960), p. 5.

7. "The Concept of Truth in Formalized Languages," p. 160.

8. A. Church, "A Formulation of the Logic of Sense and Denotation," in *Structure, Method, and Meaning: Essays in Honor of H. M. Sheffer,* eds. Henle, Kallen, and Langer (New York, 1951).

9. D. Davidson, "Causal Relations," *The Journal of Philosophy* 64 (1967): 691–703.

6

Michael Dummett

Introduction

For Michael Dummett "analytical philosophy" is philosophy after Frege, whose epochal accomplishments have made it possible at last to give an affirmative answer to the scandalous question that troubled Kant: "Can there be progress in philosophy?" It was Frege who demonstrated that epistemological questions could be answered by advances in "logic," thus finally clarifying philosophy's proper object and approach: the analysis of "thought" through the analysis of language. In contrast to the authors represented in parts one and three of this volume, Dummett sees the Fregean revolution as warranting for philosophical analysis the strong claim to "systematic" inquiry — one with a generally accepted methodology, generally accepted criteria of success, and, consequently, a body of definitively achieved results.

In the essay reprinted here, Dummett presents the theory of meaning as a *prima philosophia,* as that part of philosophy which underlies and provides foundations for all the rest. The aim of such a theory, he tells us in another essay published in the same year, is "to give an account of how [a given] language works, that is, of how its speakers communicate by means of it: here 'communicate' has no more precise significance than 'do whatever may be done by the utterance of one or more sentences of a language.' A theory of meaning is a theory of understanding; that is, what a theory of meaning has to give is an account of what it is someone knows when he knows the language" (1975, 99). There is an evident affinity in this with Davidson's aim of "recovering the structure of a very sophisticated ability — the ability to speak and understand a language." And this extends to an agreement on the central importance of the Fregean notion of truth for such a theory. But the differences are no less important. For one thing, Dummett is opposed to taking "is true" as an unexplicated term that is somehow "already understood"; rather, it must be elucidated *within* a theory of meaning. Accordingly, he questions the adequacy of truth-conditional semantics and the objectivistic notion of truth on which it is based; "truth" must instead be related to epistemic notions like "justification" and "assertibility." That is, Dummett is opposed to regarding truth conditions as "objectively and determinately either attaching or not attaching to each sentence independently of our capacity to know whether or not a sentence is true" (1976, 129). Truth conditions of the standard sort are evidence-transcendent; they do not have the desired relation to what speakers can know. But then how could they be essentially implicated in a speaker's knowledge of his or her language? Davidson's nonepistemic notion of truth has to be replaced with an epistemic one. "Verification conditions," for instance, are recognizable by speakers and hence are a possible candidate to serve as the basis for a theory of meaning that reconstructs the practical ability of speakers to understand their language. This type of theory of meaning makes good the insight behind Wittgenstein's slogan "meaning is use" without, however, drawing his radical conclusion about the impossibility of a philosophical theory of language.

Following on this insight, Dummett requires of a systematic theory of meaning that it give an account of "force" as well as of "sense." Though we can divorce the analysis of language from the nonlinguistic activities to which the later Wittgenstein saw it inextricably tied, we cannot give an account of the ability to speak and understand a language without grasping the various, highly general types of linguistic acts effected by the utterance of different types of sentences. What we are after is an explicit account of the implicitly understood "conventional principles that govern the *practice* of speaking [a given language]." This will involve "pragmatic" as well as "semantic" considerations.

For all his differences with Davidson, Dummett agrees that the theory of meaning transforms traditional questions of metaphysics (as is suggested by the title of his William James Lectures, "The Logical Basis of Metaphysics"). The "whole point" of his unified antirealist philosophical program, he tells us, "has been to show that the theory of meaning underlies metaphysics" (1979, xl). Since "it is the essence of thought . . . to be communicable, without residue, by means of language," it is only by the analysis of language that we can analyze thought and the reality represented in thought. In this way, and against much of recent analytic philosophy since Frege, Dummett is willing to wager once again that the claims to truth of the great modern systematic thinkers can be "scientifically" adjudicated.

Suggested Readings

Baker, G. P., and P. M. S. Hacker. "Dummett's Purge: Frege without Functions," *Philosophical Quarterly* 33 (1983), 115–132.

Baker, G. P. *Language, Sense, and Nonsense: A Critical Investigation into Modern Theories of Language.* Oxford: Basil Blackwell, 1984.

Blackburn, Simon. "Truth, Realism, and the Regulation of Theory," *Midwest Studies in Philosophy* 5 (1980), 353–371.

Chomsky, Noam. *Rules and Representations.* New York: Columbia University Press, 1980.

Craig, Edward. "Meaning, Use, and Privacy," *Mind* 91 (1981), 541–564.

Devitt, Michael. *Designation.* New York: Columbia University Press, 1981.

Devitt, Michael. "Dummett's Antirealism," *Journal of Philosophy* 80 (1983), 73–99.

Dummett, Michael. *Frege: Philosophy of Language.* Cambridge, Massachusetts: Harvard University Press, 1973.

Dummett, Michael. "What Is a Theory of Meaning? (I)," in *Mind and Language,* ed. S. Guttenplan, 97–138. Oxford: Clarendon Press, 1975.

Dummett, Michael. "What Is a Theory of Meaning? (II)," in *Truth and Meaning,* ed. G. Evans and J. McDowell, 67–137. Oxford: Clarendon Press, 1976.

Dummett, Michael. *Elements of Intuitionism.* Oxford: Clarendon Press, 1977.

Dummett, Michael. *Truth and Other Enigmas.* Cambridge, Massachusetts: Harvard University Press, 1978.

Dummett, Michael. "What Does the Appeal to Use Do for a Theory of Meaning?" in *Meaning and Use,* ed. A. Margalit, 120–132. Dordrecht: Reidel, 1979.

Dummett, Michael. *The Interpretation of Frege's Philosophy.* Cambridge, Massachusetts: Harvard University Press, 1981.

Dummett, Michael. "Realism," *Synthese* 52 (1982), 55–112.

George, Alexander. "On Devitt on Dummett," *Journal of Philosophy* 81 (1984), 516–527.

McGinn, Colin. "Truth and Use," in *Reference, Truth and Reality,* ed. M. Platts, 19–40. London: Routledge and Kegan Paul, 1980.

McGinn, Colin. "Two Notions of Realism?" *Philosophical Topics* 13 (1982), 123–134.

Pragwitz, Dag. "Meaning and Proofs: On the Conflict Between Classical and Intuitionist Logic," *Theoria* 63 (1977), 2–40.

Putnam, Hilary. "Reference and Truth," in *Philosophical Papers, Vol. 3,* 69–86. Cambridge: Cambridge University Press, 1983.

Strawson, P. F. "Scruton and Wright on Antirealism," *Proceedings of the Aristotelian Society* 77 (1976–1977), 15–22.

Wright, Crispin. "Truth Conditions and Criteria," *Proceeding of the Aristotelian Society,* supplementary vol. 50 (1976), 217–245.

Wright, Crispin. "Strawson on Antirealism," *Synthese* 40 (1979), 283–299.

Wright, Crispin. "A Critical Study: Dummett and Revisionism," *Philosophical Quarterly* 31 (1981), 47–67.

Can Analytical Philosophy Be Systematic, and Ought It to Be?

Michael Dummett

The term "analytical philosophy" denotes, not a school, but a cluster of schools sharing certain basic presuppositions, but differing among themselves in every other possible way. As in all movements, its most bitter quarrels have been internal ones. When I was a student at Oxford in the late 1940s, the dominant philosophical influence was that of Ryle; and, despite the fact that Ryle had started his career as the English exponent of the philosophy of Husserl, and had in 1929 published a critical but highly respectful review of *Sein und Seit*, the enemy, at the time when I was a student, was not Heidegger; Heidegger was perceived only as a figure of fun, too absurd to be taken seriously as a threat to the kind of philosophy practiced in Oxford. The enemy was, rather, Carnap: he it was who was seen in Ryle's Oxford as the embodiment of philosophical error, above all, as the exponent of a false philosophical methodology. Of course, the Carnap whom Ryle taught us to reject was a caricature of the real Carnap; but so strong was this prejudice that it took me, for one, many years to realize that there is much worthy of study in Carnap's writings. Nothing can more vividly illustrate the contrast between the philosophical atmosphere in which my British contemporaries grew up and that in which American philosophers of the same generation developed: for in the United States Carnap was accepted as the leader of the analytical school, and the most influential American practitioners of analytical philosophy, from Quine down, are people whose philosophical formation was Carnap-ian and whose thought can be understood only as the outcome of a painful effort to scrutinize and correct certain of Carnap's fundamental doctrines.

The divergence of tradition between analytical philosophy as practiced on one side of the Atlantic and on the other bears strongly upon the question we have to examine. It would be ridiculous to address the question "Can analytical philosophy be systematic?" to the author of *Der logische Aufbau der Welt;* and, though few American philosophers have followed their mentor so closely as to produce such rivals to that work as Nelson Goodman's *Structure of Appearance,* most are unanimous in regarding philosophy, with Quine, as at least cognate with the natural sciences, as part of the same general enterprise as they. In those English philosophical circles dominated by the later Wittgenstein or by Austin, on the other hand, the answer given to this question was a resounding "No": for them, the attempt to be systematic in philosophy was the primal error, founded upon a total misconception of the character of the subject.

The reason lay in what was thought to be the fundamental discovery, enunciated in Wittgenstein's *Tractatus,* of the nature of philosophy: philosophy is not a science. Here "science" is used in the most general way, to embrace any discipline (art history, for example) whose aim is to arrive at and establish *truths.* According to Wittgenstein, both in his earlier and his later phases, this is *not* the object of philosophy. Chemistry aims to discover chemical truths, and history to discover historical truths, but the successful outcome of philosophy is not a number of true propositions whose truth was not known before. Philosophy is concerned, not to establish truths of a very general kind, not even truths that can be arrived at by ratiocination alone, but to rectify certain kinds of misunderstanding, the misunderstandings we have of our own concepts; and this means our misunderstanding of our own language, since to possess a concept is to be the master of a certain fragment of language. Human language is an instrument of enormous complexity, and our mastery of it is largely an implicit mastery: we are able to employ it in practice, but when we try to give an explicit account of that practice, we commit gross errors. Because it is in our nature to be reflective, to try to explain all that we observe, we do not rest content with being able to make practical use of our language for the ordinary transactions of life, but try to frame hypotheses about the general principles according to which that language functions; or, mistakenly regarding language as a mere external covering with which the thought is clothed, we attempt to strip off this outer clothing and penetrate to the pure thought beneath. In doing this, we are like savages gaping at a machine whose working they have not the background to comprehend: we form fantastic misconceptions of the way our language works. Like all our thoughts, these misconceptions are themselves expressed in language; but language, when it is made to serve such a purpose, is like an engine racing while disconnected — it does no work, not even the wrong work: it does not issue even in propositions that are to be denied and replaced by true ones, but merely expresses characteristic kinds of intellectual confusion the only remedy for which is extended and patient treatment, in the sense in which a doctor treats an illness. It is this treatment that is the proper work of the philosopher; and a large part of it will consist in drawing the sufferer's attention to the actual, often humdrum, facts about our employment of language, facts of which he is course already aware, but which he had overlooked in the excitement generated by the misleading picture that had gripped his mind.

If this is the nature of philosophy, then evidently it cannot be systematic. There can be no means by which every possible misunderstanding can be blocked off in advance; each must be treated as we encounter it. And even when we are concerned with the eradication of some specific misconception, we shall not accomplish it by substituting some correct theory for a mistaken one, because we are not operating in a region where theories are required at all. What we are aiming to do is to substitute a clean vision for a distorted one. What there is to be seen is not a matter for philosophy at all, but for science, for empirical observation; the philosopher has no more business saying what there is to be seen than does the oculist: what he is trying to prevent is a frame of mind in which whatever is seen is grotesquely misinterpreted. In so far as the philosopher has any business at all to state what there is to be seen, the facts that he has to recall will not be ones that the philosopher has discovered, but, rather, very familiar facts known to everybody, and he will recall them only because they fit badly into the theory, or pseudotheory, in which the conceptual confusion is embodied. But such recalling of familiar facts, particularly facts about language, will not of itself provide a sufficient treatment of the confusion, because until the confusion is removed, they will themselves be misperceived; the philosopher has to grapple with the seductive reasoning that so compulsively engendered the misunderstanding in the first place, or by which it defends itself against criticism. But the philosopher's reasoning does not issue, like the mathematician's, in theorems that he can then enunciate; when he has unpicked the tangle, and the strands lie separated from one another, he has finished his work: then we see the world aright. There is, however, nothing that we can state as the result of the philosopher's work: an undistorted vision is not itself an object of sight.

The Austinian reason for rejecting system in philosophy is less powerful than Wittgenstein's and needs less attention, partly because it no longer seems in the least attractive and partly because, to a greater extent than with other philosophers, Austin's practice failed to tally with his official methodology. His official view was this: philosophical problems are to be resolved by attention to the actual uses of words; so we may as well set about studying the uses of words without keeping our eyes on the problems, which will take care of themselves, that is, evaporate, if we do our work satisfactorily. Philosophy, on this view, is not a therapy but an empirical study: we have to describe, in detail, particular uses of particular words. But it is not a systematic study, because its subject matter is incapable of systematization; we cannot arrange our results into some aesthetically satisfying deductive theory, because they form only a collection of loosely connected *particular* facts, as particular as those entered in the dictionary.

I began by remarking that the term "analytical philosophy" covers the work of philosophers of exceedingly diverse views and approaches: but, striking as these divergences have been in the past, my remark probably applies less to the strictly contemporary scene than it does to any time in the past. There has been a very considerable rapprochement among the various branches of analytical philosophy; and this has been due to three interconnected facts. First, the ever more widespread knowledge of and attention to the work of Frege. Up to, say, 1950, the influence of Frege upon analytical philosophy had been very great, but it had been exerted largely at second hand, transmitted through a few rare, though influential, philosophers who had studied him directly — Church, Carnap, Russell, and, above all, Wittgenstein; and so, for the most part, Frege's doctrines reached others only as understood by those writers and not clearly distinguished from their own opinions. Now, a quarter-century later, and a half-century after Frege's death, every serious philosophy student in Britain or the United States acknowledges a thorough study of Frege's writings as essential to a philosophical education; and the shift in perspective — and not merely in historical perspective — brought about by the recognition of Frege as the fountainhead of analytical philosophy, rather than supposing it to have begun with Russell or with Wittgenstein or with the Vienna Circle, has had a profound and unifying effect. Second, the work of contemporary American philosophers is at the present moment far more influential in Britain than it has ever been before; for the first time since I have been at Oxford, and probably for the first time since the influence of Hegel was predominant there, work done in philosophy further away than Cambridge has come to occupy the center of the stage. Finally, as cause or consequence of the first two, the focus of interest within the subject has altered. For several decades the most vigorous branch of philosophy within Britain was philosophical psychology — the study of questions concerning motive, intention, pleasure, and the like: now it is the philosophy of language. Formerly, the most usual appellation for the type of philosophy practiced at Oxford was "linguistic philosophy": but that no more implied that its adherents worked principally upon questions concerning language than the name "logical positivism" implied that the principal contribution of the members of that school was to logic. Just as for the positivists logic was an instrument, not the field of study, so for linguistic philosophy the study of language was for the most part a means and not an end. In part this was due to the idea that no general doctrine about language was needed as a basis for the investigation, by linguistic means, of philosophically problematic concepts, in part to the idea that such a doctrine was needed but had already been attained. Neither idea would find much favor now: the philosophy of language is seen both as that part of the subject which underlies all the rest and as that which it is currently most fruitful to investigate.

This tendency within analytical philosophy is recent only so far as British philosophy is concerned: it represents an alignment of the British with the American school; and I should like to declare myself wholly in sympathy with it. In saying this, I am not wishing to endorse particular doctrines currently popular among American philosophers of language — linguistic holism, the rejection of a substantive distinction between sense and reference, the causal theory of reference, or possible-worlds semantics, all of which appear to me mistaken in whole or part — but only their general orientation. In order to give my reasons for this, I must pose the question what distinguishes analytical philosophy, in all its manifestations, from other schools.

A succinct definition would be, Analytical philosophy is post-Fregean philosophy. Frege's fundamental achievement was to alter our perspective in philosophy, to replace epistemology, as the starting point of the subject, by what he called "logic." What Frege called "logic" included, but only as a proper part, what everyone else, before and since, has called "logic": it also embraced precisely what is now called "philosophy of language". That would have sounded odd to Frege, for he almost always used the word *Sprache* to mean "natural language," and he had a strong contempt for natural language; but, even were that contempt completely justified, so that, as he believed, we have, for the purpose of serious philosophical study, to replace natural language by an artificially devised language purged of its defects, Frege's work has the interest that he claims for it only if the resulting formalized language is a more perfect instrument for doing the same thing as that which we normally do by means of natural language, and if, therefore, in studying the formalized language, we are studying the ideal that natural language strives after but fails to attain. Thus we may characterize analytical philosophy as that which follows Frege in accepting that the philosophy of language is the foundation of the rest of the subject.

For Frege, as for all subsequent analytical philosophers, the philosophy of language is the foundation of all other philosophy because it is only by the analysis of language that we can analyze thought. Thoughts differ from all else that is said to be among the contents of the mind in being wholly communicable: it is of the essence of thought that I can convey to you the very thought I have, as opposed to being able to tell you merely something about what my thought is like. It is of the essence of thought, not merely to be communicable, but to be communicable, without residue, by means of language. In order to understand thought, it is necessary, therefore, to comprehend the means by which thought is expressed. If the philosopher attempts, in the manner I mentioned earlier, to strip thought of its linguistic clothing and penetrate to its pure naked essence, he will merely succeed in confusing the thought itself with the subjective inner accompaniments of thinking. We communicate thoughts by means of language because we have an implicit understanding of the working of language, that is, of the principles governing the use of language; it is these principles which relate to what is open to view in the employment of language, unaided by any supposed contact between mind and mind other than via the medium of language that endow our sentences with the senses that they carry. In order to analyze thought, therefore, it is necessary to make explicit those principles regulating our use of language that we already implicitly grasp.

This task has both a general and a particular aspect. In its general aspect our concern is with the fundamental outlines of an account of how language functions: and that constitutes the philosophy of language, which is accordingly that philosophical theory which is the foundation of all the rest. But in its particular aspects we may be concerned with the analysis of thoughts concerning this or that particular subject matter or involving this or that cluster of concepts: and these are the branches of philosophy that spring out of the parent stem. Unless our general account of language is on the right lines, the analysis that in particular branches of philosophy, we give of special types of sentence or special forms of expression is liable to be defective, which is why the philosophy of language lies at the base of the entire structure; this, of course, does not mean that all work in other parts of philosophy ought to cease until a fully adequate philosophy of language has been attained. Frege himself did not make the claim that the only task of philosophy is the analysis of thought and hence of language — that was left for Wittgenstein to enunciate in the *Tractatus;* but by his practice in the one particular branch of philosophy in which he worked, the philosophy of mathematics, he left little doubt that that was his view; the very same grounds on which he resisted the intrusion of psychological considerations into what he called "logic," namely that thought is objective and common to all, whereas mental processes are private and subjective, are given by him for keeping them out of the philosophy of mathematics. The proper philosophical study of mathematics proceeds by analyzing the language of mathematics. Only one who persisted in confusing thoughts with inner mental processes would think that this involved diverting our attention from the *objects* of mathematics to the *experience* of mathematical activity; experience does not come into it all, and as for mathematical objects, the philosopher will need to talk about these in so far as it is necessary to do so in order to give adequate account of mathematical language. The difference between the mathematician and the philosopher of mathematics is not that the former is concerned with mathematical objects and the latter is concerned only with the inner experiences of the mathematician, but that the mathematician is concerned to establish the truth or falsity of mathematical statements, while the philosopher is concerned with the way in which they are endowed with sense. There is no reason to suppose that Frege would have adopted any different attitude to any other branch of philosophy, if he had chosen to work in it.

In the foregoing remarks I have attempted an account of certain fundamental views, expressly advocated by Frege or implicit in his philosophical method that may also be claimed, with some plausibility, to be shared by all practitioners of analytical philosophy; but even if I have succeeded, in practice the effect of these common beliefs on the work of the various analytical philosophers has been very different. Frege and the early Wittgenstein both make direct contributions to the philosophy of language: but when we reach the Vienna Circle, we have to do with philosophers whose interest in the subject was no longer much for its own sake but rather because they saw it as an armory from which they could draw weapons that would arm them for combat in other areas of philosophy. The principle of verification was for them a sword with which they could slay numberless metaphysical dragons; but now that we look back, it is difficult to see how out of that principle could be fashioned a coherent philosophy of language, or theory of meaning at all. It was not in itself even the summary of a theory of meaning, but a consequence claimed to follow from some theory even the outline of which was never once clearly formulated. And if this is to be said of the positivists, something even stronger holds for the "ordinary language" school dominant for a period at Oxford. They jettisoned the slogan "Meaning is the method verification" for the slogan, borrowed from Wittgenstein, "Meaning is use"; but while the former slogan hinted at some unitary theory of meaning, a key concept in terms of which a general model could be given for the understanding of a sentence, the latter slogan was expressly used to reject the idea that a uniform account is possible. Only particularity was acceptable; a general theory was a *fatuus ignis,* generated by the philosopher's vain hopes of finding a pattern where none existed. All that a philosopher ought to try to do was to explain the "use" of each sentence, one by one; for that was all that could be done.

Now, whatever be the right account of language, such a conception can be recognized offhand as wrong, for the obvious reason that we do not learn sentences one by one. It would fit a code of signals, the significance of each of which has to be learned separately, but not a language. It should hardly need pointing out to anyone, least of all to a school of philosophers who prided themselves on their attention to language, that we understand a sentence by understanding the words that compose it and the principles according to which they are put together. But the fact is that there is no formulation of the doctrine of total particularism advocated by this school that will fit that basic fact; for it is *sentences*, not words, that have a "use" in the intended sense, sentences by means of which, in Wittgenstein's terminology, we "make a move in the language game." Any workable account of language must, therefore, represent a mastery of language as consisting in a grasp of some principles not relating to complete individual sentences, even if these consist solely of principles relating to individual words and to modes of sentence construction. A grasp of such principles will *issue* in a knowledge of the "use" that can be made of any given sentence of the language; but it will not be *constituted* by such knowledge. The question is, what are the principles an implicit grasp of which composes an understanding of the language; and to answering this question the "ordinary language" school had virtually nothing to contribute.

The rejection of generality, the insistence on concentrating on the "use" of each individual sentence, led to the giving of accounts of "use" that were often remarkably superficial, even when subtle. They were superficial because they employed psychological and semantic concepts that a theory of meaning has no right to presuppose as already understood, since it can be expected to explain them; what else, after all, could anyone do but invoke such concepts if presented with some complex sentence and asked to describe its "use"? So they would freely employ such a notion as that of expressing an attitude or conveying a belief or rejecting a question, without the slightest consciousness that it is the business of the philosophy of language to explain what it is to do any one of these things. Nowhere is this more evident than in the constant use that was made of the concepts of truth and falsity, as needing no explanation: for these are concepts that have their home in the theory of meaning, which will have been fully elucidated only when we have understood the role that they have to play in a correct theory of meaning for a language; and yet they were employed in descriptions of "use," and disputes were conducted over whether they should be applied to this or that sentence, under given conditions, or at all, not merely as if it were perfectly clear what is the connection between truth and meaning but as if there were nothing to be known, and hence nothing capable of being said, about that connection.

Moreover, particularism led to superficiality for another reason, which can be most tersely stated by saying that it promoted a conscious disregard for the distinction between semantic and pragmatic aspects. (I do not myself care for the "semantic"/ "pragmatic" terminology; but that is because I think it obscures the differences among several distinct distinctions). Anyone not in the grip of a theory, asked to explain the meaning of a sentence like "Either he is your brother or he is not" or "I know that I am here," would be disposed to begin by distinguishing what the sentence literally said from what, in particular circumstances, someone might seek to convey by uttering it; but from the standpoint of the orthodox "ordinary-language" doctrine, only the latter notion was legitimate — *it* was what constituted the "use" of the sentence; and if no circumstances could be excogitated, however bizarre, in which it might actually be uttered for some genuine purpose, then the sentence "had no use" and was therefore meaningless. As for the former notion — that of what the sentence literally said — that was spurious, an illegitimate byproduct of the attempt to construct a theory of meaning in terms of general concepts. It was this, of course, more than anything else, that led hostile observers to form the impression of the activities of "ordinary-language" philosophers as the practice of a solemn frivolity.

Naturally, so grotesquely false a methodology could not be consistently adhered to by intelligent people. In consequence, in place of the general semantic concepts that had been expelled in the original determination to pay attention to nothing but the actual "use" of particular sentences, new ones, such as the celebrated notion of presupposition, or that of conversational implicature, or Austin's distinctions between illocutionary and perlocutionary force, and so on, were invented by the "ordinary-language" philosophers themselves; and, in the process, "ordinary-language" philosophy ceased to exist, almost without anyone noticing that it had. An era had ended, not with a bang but a whimper; and the moment was propitious for the American counterattack.

The doctrines of "ordinary-language" philosophy were a caricature, but not a gross caricature, of the views of the later Wittgenstein, from whom, as I remarked, the slogan "Meaning is use" was borrowed. No one can say about Wittgenstein that in his later phase he neglected the philosophy of language, that he used ideas about meaning only as a tool to attack problems in other areas of philosophy: large tracts of the *Philosophical Investigations* are directly devoted to the philosophy of language. The most immediately obvious difference between his conception of "use" and that of the "ordinary-language" school is that he emphatically did not envisage a description of use as making free appeal to psychological and semantic concepts: what he meant by "use" is most readily seen from the analogy that he draws in the *Investigations* with an account of the use of money. To understand the significance, that is, the conventional significance, of a coin involves understanding the *institution* of money; what would be needed to convey that significance to someone who came from a society in which money was unknown would be a description of the whole practice in which the transference of coins is embedded; such a description is therefore also needed if we wish to make explicit what it is that, in grasping the significance of a coin, we implicitly apprehend. A description of the institution of money that would serve this purpose would presuppose no economic concepts: it would give an account of what actually happens in terms of what is open to observation by someone innocent of such concepts. In the same way, what Wittgenstein conceived of as constituting an account of the use of language is illustrated by the "language games" that he described in the *Brown Book* and elsewhere. In these some very rudimentary language, or fragment of a language conceived of as existing in isolation, is displayed as being actually spoken: what is described is the complex of activities with which the utterances of sentences of the language are interwoven; and again the description does not invoke psychological or semantic concepts but is couched entirely in terms of what is open to outward view.

This conception of a language game illustrates for us what Wittgenstein would consider to be an adequate account of the functioning of an entire actual language: such an account would, again, consist of a description of the language game in which the language played a role, and would differ in principle from those described by Wittgenstein only in its immensely greater complexity. It is important to notice the difference between this idea and the conception of a theory of meaning that can be derived from Frege. Both are agreed that what is required is a description of the conventional principles that govern the *practice* of speaking the language, a description that does not invoke the notion of a sentence's expressing a thought but rather displays that which renders any given sentence the expression of a particular thought. But for Frege the institution of language is autonomous. A sentence expresses the thought it does in virtue of our being able to derive the condition for its truth in a particular way from its composition out of its constituent words; and the notion of truth can be understood only by grasping the various highly general types of linguistic practice that consist in uttering a sentence, with a given truth condition, in accordance with one or another convention that determines the linguistic act effected by the utterance — that of asserting that the condition for the truth of the sentence is fulfilled, for example, or that of asking whether it is fulfilled. Hence, on this account, it is largely irrelevant to our capacity to speak a language such as that which we have that we are able to engage in nonlinguistic activities: we could speak much the same kind of language if we were a sort of intelligent and sentient trees, who could observe the world and utter sounds but could engage in no other type of action. For Wittgenstein, on the other hand, it is essential to our language that its employment is interwoven with our nonlinguistic activities. In the language games that he describes, what confers meaning on the linguistic utterances is their immediate and direct connection with other actions; for instance, the builder asks for a certain number of stones of a certain shape, and they are passed to him. What makes it difficult for us to see that it is *use*, in this sense, that confers meaning on the sentences of our actual language, or, better, in which their meaning consists, is the remoteness of the connection between linguistic activities (for example, that on which I am now engaged) and nonlinguistic ones; it is nevertheless this connection that endows our words with the meanings they have.

Now this idea, striking as it is as a first and, if correct, fundamental insight, remains in Wittgenstein largely programmatic. Frege did not, indeed, complete the task of giving even a general sketch of a theory of meaning of the kind that he favored: notoriously, his discussions of the notion of sense supply arguments for holding that we need a theory of sense rather than merely a theory of reference, but do not provide any general model for what we should take a speaker's grasp of the sense of a word of a given logical category to consist in; nor is it clear to what extent he thought it possible to give a noncircular account of the conventions governing the various types of linguistic act such as assertion, or how, if at all, such an account is to be framed. Nevertheless, despite these lacunae, we have an outline of the general form that a Fregean theory of meaning must assume, sufficiently clear for us to be able to discuss the plausibility of the claim that by this means an adequate account of the functioning of a language can be given. But of the sort of theory of meaning favored by Wittgenstein we have no such outline: we do not know how to begin to set about constructing such a theory. The difficulty lies with those utterances that would normally be classed as assertoric. A command, after all, is aimed at eliciting a direct nonverbal response, a question at eliciting a verbal one. True enough, in the actual case, an utterance of either of these kinds may fail to elicit the response it aims at, and, at least in the case of commands, an adequate description of the linguistic institution must include a general statement of the consequences of the hearer's failure to respond in the way called for. But an assertoric utterance is not, in the general case, aimed at evoking a specific response; how the hearer responds will depend on many things, in particular upon his desires and his existing beliefs. That is not to deny that an assertion will often have effects upon behavior, and, in the long run, upon nonverbal behavior; but it does cast doubt upon the possibility of giving an account of the meanings of assertoric sentences directly in terms of their connections with nonlinguistic activities. Wittgenstein was not intending merely to make some observations about what it is that *ultimately* gives significance to our language. If that had been all that he had in mind, it could be accommodated within a Fregean framework. The connection between language and extralinguistic reality would in that case be assured by the principles that govern the conditions for the truth of our sentences; the effect that an assertion might have upon the conduct of a hearer could then be indirectly accounted for by his grasp of this connection, taken together with his wants and his capacities for action. But it is plain from several passages in the *Investigations* that Wittgenstein intended, in this respect, flatly to oppose Frege's conception of meaning. In particular, the concept of *assertion,* considered as a type of linguistic act capable of being described in a manner uniform with respect to the truth conditions of any sentence used to make an assertion, is to be rejected. Our difficulty is not merely that Wittgenstein has shown us no compelling reason why we must reject it, but that he has not given us any indication of what we are to put in its place.

The particularism that was so marked a feature of the official doctrine of the "ordinary-language" school, though it became less and less discernible in their practice, took its source from Wittgenstein. It was part of Frege's doctrine that since a sentence is the smallest unit of language by the utterance of which it is possible to *say* anything, the meaning of a word is to be explained in terms of the contribution it makes to the meaning of any sentence in which it may occur; we derive the meaning of each *particular* sentence from the meanings of the words that compose it, but the *general* notion of sentence meaning is prior to that of word meaning. This idea has not been challenged by Wittgenstein or anyone else. Now suppose that we face the task of giving a general account of the meanings of the expressions of a language. We might begin by dividing into large categories the sentences of the language, on the basis of the different kinds of linguistic act — assertion, question, command, and so on — that are effected by uttering them; for, it would be natural to think, if sentence meaning is to be taken as primary, we had better first distinguish types of sentence meaning as possessed by sentences employed for such very different purposes. Now, for any given sentence there will be two moments in the understanding of its meaning: the recognition of it as belonging to a particular category and the grasp of its individual content, whereby it is distinguished from other sentences in the same category. Thus, if one sentence serves to give a command and another to voice a wish, we must know these facts about the categories to which they belong if we are to understand them; and to know that involves knowing what it is, in general, to give a command or to express a wish. In order to understand those sentences, we must also grasp their individual contents: we must know *which* command the one conveys and *which* wish the other expresses; and this will, in each case, be determined by the composition of the sentence out of its constituent words.

The difficulty now is that if the sentences in each category possess a different type of sentence meaning from those in any other category, and if the meaning of a word consists in the contribution it makes to determining the meaning of a sentence containing it, it appears that the words in an imperative sentence must have a meaning of a quite different kind from the same words when they occur in an optative sentence; and this is absurd. The escape from such an intolerable conclusion is provided by the obvious fact that most words in any sentence serve to determine, not the category to which it belongs, but its individual content as against that of other members of the category, together with the idea that the individual content of a sentence is determined in a uniform manner, regardless of its category. Thus it seems natural to suggest that, granted that we know the category to which each sentence belongs, we know the individual content of an imperative sentence by knowing in what circumstances the command it conveys will have been obeyed, and that we know the individual content of an optative sentence by knowing in what circumstances the wish it expresses will have been fulfilled. In this way we may think of the individual content of a sentence of most of the other categories as being determined by associating with that sentence a certain range of circumstances, the *significance* of that association depending upon the category in question. We thus arrive at the distinction, originally drawn by Frege, between the *sense* (*Sinn*) of a sentence and the *force* (*Kraft*) attached to it. Those constituents of the sentence that determine its sense associate a certain state of affairs with the sentence; that feature of it which determines the force with which it is uttered fixes the conventional significance of the utterance in relation to that state of affairs (i.e., according as the speaker is asserting that the state of affairs obtains, asking whether it obtains, commanding that it should obtain, expressing a wish that it obtain, etc.).

It is difficult to see how a systematic theory of meaning for a language is possible without acknowledging the distinction between sense and force, or one closely similar. Whether the categories I have used as examples — assertoric, interrogative, imperative, and optative — are legitimate ones or ought to be replaced by some others is a secondary question; in this context even the question whether the notion of the sense of a sentence that I have just sketched is correct is secondary. What seems essential is that we should have some division of sentential utterances into a determinate range of categories, according to the type of linguistic act effected by the utterance; that there should be some notion of the sense of a sentence, considered as an ingredient in its meaning and as capable of being shared by sentences belonging to different categories; that the notion of sense be such that, once we know both the category to which a sentence belongs and the sense which it carries, then we have an essential grasp of the significance of an utterance of the sentence; and that, for each category, it should be possible to give a uniform explanation of the linguistic act effected by uttering a sentence of that category, in terms of its sense, taken as given. I do not think that we have at present any conception of what a theory of meaning for a language would look like if it did not conform to this pattern.

It is, however, just this conception that Wittgenstein attacks. He does not stop at rejecting the claim that all assertoric sentences form a single category, of which a uniform account can be given: he denies that *any* surveyable list of types of linguistic act can be arrived at. This is precisely to deny that the distinction between sense and force is available to simplify the task of explaining the meanings of sentences by distinguishing two different components of their meanings: our theory of meaning must, for each individual sentence, issue in a direct account of the conventional significance of an utterance of that sentence, rather than one derived from a general description of the use of sentences of some general category to which it belongs. Not only do we not know in the least how to set about devising a theory of meaning in conformity with this maxim, but it leads to that neglect of the difference between semantic and pragmatic considerations which I noted in the practice of the "ordinary-language" philosophers.

Wittgenstein's deliberately unsystematic philosophical method makes it difficult to be certain what his intention was. Did he have in mind some theory of meaning of a completely different kind from the proposed by Frege? Or did he reject the whole idea of a systematic theory of meaning? I should not myself attempt to answer these questions; I think it better to approach Wittgenstein's later work bearing in mind different possible interpretations, without always trying to decide which is the intended one; frequently, his ideas will be found fruitful and stimulating under all possible interpretations of them. But the fact of the matter is that, powerful and penetrating as are many of his discussions of detailed questions in philosophy, including ones relating to language, we do not know how to go about extracting from his later writings any coherent general philosophy of language. The idea — if it *is* Wittgenstein's idea — that no systematic theory of meaning is possible is not merely one that is, at the present stage of inquiry, defeatist but one that runs counter to obvious facts. The fact that anyone who has a mastery of any given language is able to understand an infinity of sentences of that language — an infinity that is, of course, principally composed of sentences he has never heard before — is one emphasized not only by the modern school of linguists, headed by Chomsky, but by Wittgenstein himself; and this fact can hardly be explained otherwise than by supposing that each speaker has an implicit grasp of a number of general principles governing the use in sentences of words of the language.

If, then, there exist such general principles of which every speaker has an implicit grasp, and that serve to confer on the words of the language their various meanings, it is hard to see how there can be any theoretical obstacle to making those principles explicit; and an explicit statement of those principles an implicit grasp of which constitutes the mastery of the language would be, precisely, a complete theory of meaning for the language. On the other hand, if what Wittgenstein intended was some theory of meaning of a wholly new kind, there is not sufficient indication in his writings for us to be able to reconstruct even the general outlines of such a new type of theory. It is undoubtedly the case that, given a sufficient background of the beliefs and desires of both speaker and hearer, the making of an assertoric utterance will frequently have an effect upon the nonlinguistic behavior of the hearer and register the speaker's commitment to some course of action: but, just because these effects and this commitment depend so heavily upon the varying background, it appears impossible to see how a theory of meaning could be constructed that explained the meanings of assertoric sentences in terms of a direct connection between the utterance of such sentences and the nonlinguistic behavior of the speaker and hearer. That is simply to say that the language games devised by Wittgenstein to give an account of some very small fragments of language do not appear a promising model for a systematic account of an entire language; and if after all they are, Wittgenstein has not himself shown us how we are to be guided by these models.

Even among the analytical school, Wittgenstein was, during his lifetime, a highly controversial figure. Some believed him to be the discoverer of the definitely correct method in philosophy; for them, he had charted the course that henceforward all must take who wished to practice the subject, if their contribution was to be of any value. To others, his work was confused, his ideas erroneous, and his influence disastrous. No one not imbued with prejudice could deny that his personal intellectual capacity was that of a genius; unfortunately, this in no way settles the value of his contribution to philosophy, since genius may as often lead men astray onto a false path as it may set them on a correct but hitherto undiscovered track. Only now have we reached a moment at which it is beginning to be possible to arrive at an evaluation of Wittgenstein's work that can be generally agreed, at least among members of the analytical school. My own opinion is that he will come to be seen as an immensely fertile source of important and often penetrating philosophical ideas, among which are some of fundamental significance for the philosophy of language; but that his work does not constitute, as he and his followers believed that it did, and as Frege's work undoubtedly did, a solid foundation for future work in philosophy. Among those ideas of Wittgenstein that are of the greatest generality and thus relate to the main outlines that a successful theory of meaning must assume, it would be impossible at present to select any that would command general assent; but we can, I believe, select some about which it would be universally agreed that any attempt to construct a theory of meaning must come to terms with them and with the powerful arguments offered by Wittgenstein in their support. One is the rejection of the conception, advanced by Frege and by Wittgenstein himself in the *Tractatus,* that the meanings of our sentences are given by the conditions that render them determinately true or false, in favor of one according to which the meaning is to be explained in terms of what is taken as *justifying* an utterance. It is this idea that underlies both his observations on the concept of following a rule and his critique of the notion of the private ostensive definition (the so-called "private language argument") and that has, as its corollary, the ineradicably social character of language. The role of language as the vehicle of thought is secondary to its role as an instrument of communication: it could not serve the former purpose unless it served the latter; and, as serving the latter purpose, it is as much of its essence to be embedded in a social practice or complex of social practices, to be the shared possession of a community, as in the institution of money.

Nevertheless, although these are ideas with which any future attempt to construct a theory of meaning must come to terms, Wittgenstein's work did not provide a foundation for any such attempt. For one thing, his example, as regards the *style* in which he practiced philosophy, is not to be imitated. This style was the outcome not only of his unique personality but also of his general doctrines about the nature of philosophy itself. As I explained earlier, these general doctrines hinge upon the contention that philosophy is not concerned with any topic about which a systematic theory is possible; it seeks to remove, not ignorance or false beliefs, but conceptual confusion, and therefore has nothing positive to set in place of what it removes. Now this conception implies that a systematic theory of meaning for a language is an impossibility; alternatively, the impossibility of such a theory can be viewed as the only premise from which Wittgenstein's thesis about the nature of philosophy could be derived. Furthermore, as was remarked earlier, some passages in the *Investigations* appear to offer specific grounds for denying the possibility of a systematic theory of meaning, those, namely, that impugn the legitimacy of any distinction corresponding to that of Frege between sense and force. It would be a mistake to conflate the rejection of the sense/force distinction with the substitution of an account of meaning in terms of what justifies an utterance for one in terms of its truth conditions: the replacement of the notion of truth by that of justification, as the central notion for the theory of meaning, is quite compatible with the retention of a distinction analogous to that between sense and force; and it is the rejection of this latter distinction that calls in question the feasibility of a systematic theory of meaning. I do not feel certain that Wittgenstein thought a systematic account of the functioning of language to be impossible. If he did, then he would, of course, repudiate the claim that any of his ideas provided guidelines for the construction of such a systematic account, but would, on the contrary, hold that they ought to deter anyone from any such enterprise. But even if he did not, it remains that, while we can extract from his work conditions that any successful theory of meaning must satisfy and warnings against trying to construct such a theory along certain lines, he does not provide us with any outline of what a correct theory of meaning will look like, any strategy or sketch of a strategy for constructing one. This is why I say that, fundamentally important as it is, Wittgenstein's work does not supply us with a *foundation* for future work in the philosophy of language or in philosophy in general. I have already given my reasons for supposing that a systematic theory of meaning must be possible; and even if it should prove in the end not to be possible, we certainly have no adequate insight at present into what makes it impossible and shall therefore learn much that is of the greatest value if we continue for the time being in our endeavors to construct such a theory.

If this analysis is correct, the most urgent task that philosophers are now called upon to carry out is to devise what I have called a "systematic theory of meaning," that is to say, a systematic account of the functioning of language that does not beg any questions by presupposing as already understood any semantic concepts, even such familiar ones as those of truth and of assertion. Such an account will necessarily take the form of a *theory*, because it is evident that the mastery of a language involves the implicit apprehension of a vast complex of interconnections and does not merely consist in a number of in principle isolable practical abilities. We are by no means as yet agreed even upon the general form that such a theory of meaning ought to take; but, thanks primarily to Frege, we understand enough both about the underlying syntactical structure of our language and about what is demanded of a theory of meaning to be able to undertake the investigation as a collective enterprise to the same extent that advance in the sciences is also the result of cooperative endeavor. These remarks apply directly only to the philosophy of language, not to other branches of philosophy; but I speak as a member of the analytical school of philosophy, of which I have already observed that the characteristic tenet is that the philosophy of language is the foundation for all the rest of philosophy. This is not to suggest that work in all other branches of philosophy must wait upon the completion of a satisfactory theory of meaning; intellectual construction is not like architecture, in that we do not in the former case need to complete the foundation before work on the upper storeys can begin. But it does mean, I think, that the correctness of any piece of analysis carried out in another part of philosophy cannot be fully determined until we know with reasonable certainty what form a

correct theory of meaning for our language must take. I am
maintaining that we have now reached a position where the
search for such a theory of meaning can take on a genuinely
scientific character; this means, in particular, that it can be
carried on in such a way, not, indeed, that disputes do not
arise, but that they can be resolved to the satisfaction of everyone, and, above all, that we may hope to bring the search within
a finite time to a successful conclusion. The history of the
subject indeed makes it very tempting to adopt the frequently
expressed view that there are never any agreed final conclusions in philosophy; but, few as they may be, there exist counterexamples to this thesis, examples, that is, of solutions to
what were once baffling problems that have now been accepted
as part of the established stock of knowledge; for such an
example we need look no further than to Frege's resolution,
by means of the quantifier-variable notation, of the logic of
generality. Whether, once we have attained an agreed theory
of meaning, the other parts of philosophy will then also take
on a similarly scientific character, or whether they will continue
to be able to be explored only in the more haphazard manner
that has been traditional in philosophy for many centuries, I
do not claim to know.

It will have been noticed that I have slipped into discussing
simultaneously whether or not, from the standpoint of the
analytical school, future work in philosophy can and ought to
be systematic in two distinct senses of "systematic." In one
sense, a philosophical investigation is systematic if it is intended
to issue in an articulated theory, such as is constituted by any
of the great philosophical "systems" advanced in the past by
philosophers like Spinoza or Kant. In the other sense, a philosophical investigation is systematic if it proceeds according to
generally agreed methods of enquiry and its results are generally accepted or rejected according to commonly agreed criteria. These two senses in which it may be asked whether or
not philosophy can and ought to be systematic are independent
of one another. Most, perhaps all, the natural sciences are
systematic in both senses; but history, for example, is systematic
only in the second sense, namely that there are agreed methods
of investigation and agreed criteria for testing what are claimed

as results of such investigation, and not in the first sense, since historical research does not issue in any articulated theory. When, in the past, philosophy has been systematic, it has generally been systematic in the first sense only, not in the second: I have been advancing the view that, at least in the philosophy of language, philosophy ought henceforward to be systematic in both senses. The subject matter of this part of philosophy demands an articulated theory; and we have reached a stage in our investigations at which that minimum has been established which makes it possible for future research to proceed according to more or less agreed methods of inquiry, and for its results to be judged in accordance with generally accepted standards.

For those who value it at all, it has always been something of a scandal that philosophy has through most of its history failed to be systematic in the second sense, to such an extent that the question "Can there be progress in philosophy?" is a perennial one. If philosophy is regarded, as most of its practitioners have regarded it, as one — perhaps the most important — sector in the quest for truth, it is then amazing that in all its long history it should not yet have established a generally accepted methodology, generally accepted criteria for success, and, therefore, a body of definitively achieved results. (On the same assumption, it is to be expected that the truths discovered by philosophical inquiry should permit themselves to be arranged into an articulated theory or system, that is, that philosophy should be systematic in the first of the two senses, since the manifold interconnections between one part of philosophy and another are a matter of common philosophical experience; but this expectation gives rise to no scandal, since, as already remarked, the work of individual philosophers has frequently resulted in the creation of just such theories or systems.) We should expect any activity that has as its goal the establishment of truths to be systematic in the *second* sense, precisely because it is of the essence of the concept of truth that truth should be an objective feature of the propositions to which it attaches; wherever commonly agreed criteria for the correctness of a proposition appear to be lacking, we naturally entertain the suspicion that that proposition cannot rightly be supposed even to be capable of possessing the property of being true. (The step from saying that there exists no agreed standard by which the correctness of a proposition may be judged to saying that there is no notion of objective truth that may be applied to that proposition is, however, far from being a certain one; it remains an as yet unresolved question within the theory of meaning — which, as already remarked, is where the concept of truth has its home — what is the exact relation between the notion of truth and our capacity for recognizing a proposition as true.) In any case, even if the apparent failure of philosophers to make their subject systematic in the second sense does not lead us to doubt whether it is the business of philosophy to arrive at truths at all, the whole enterprise seems somewhat pointless if its goal cannot be attained or at least cannot be attained to the satisfaction of most of its practitioners. What is the use of conducting any inquiry if it cannot be told when the results of that inquiry have been achieved? In this respect philosophy shows at great disadvantage when compared with mathematics; both appear to represent different sector in the quest for truth, both appear to proceed solely by means of ratiocination, but mathematics has amassed a great body of established results, while philosophy appears to engender nothing but unending disagreements. It is this scandalous situation that renders attractive such a conception of philosophy, as not being, after all, in the least concerned with establishing true propositions, as that held by Wittgenstein; on such a view, there may indeed be progress in philosophy, namely as philosophers become better at curing conceptual confusions, without there being any body of established doctrine to show for that progress.

I have contended in this essay for a more traditional view of the character of philosophy than Wittgenstein's, a view, namely, that accepts it for what it purports to be, a sector in the quest for truth. If that claim is accepted, then the fact that philosophy failed, throughout most of its long history, to achieve a systematic methodology does indeed cry out for explanation; and I shall not here attempt to give an adequate explanation of this remarkable fact. From Wittgenstein himself we have a striking analogy to illustrate how it is that we may claim that progress occurs in philosophy, even though so little remains settled. He compares philosophical activity with the task of rearranging in systematic order the books of a great library hitherto haphazardly disposed: in carrying out such a rearrangement, a vital step may be taken by placing a number of volumes together on a single shelf, even though they remain there only temporarily and, when the final arrangement is completed, none of those particular books remain on that shelf or together on any shelf. The illuminating power of this analogy does not depend upon Wittgenstein's particular conception of the nature of philosophy, and it could be applied, though with much less force, to some of the sciences; but that does not explain why the analogy is so much more apt when it is applied to philosophy than to any other intellectual discipline. Presumably, the analogy is liable to apply most fittingly to those subjects that remain in their early stages; so what needs explanation — an explanation that I have already said I am not going to attempt to offer — is how it comes about that philosophy, although as ancient as any other subject and a great deal more ancient than most, should have remained for so long "in its early stages." The "early stages" of any discipline are, presumably, to be characterized as those in which its practitioners have not yet attained a clear view of its subject matter and its goals. If the thesis for which I have contended in this essay is correct, philosophy has only just very recently struggled out of its early stage into maturity: the turning point was the work of Frege, but the widespread realization of the significance of that work has had to wait for half a century after his death and, at that, is still confined only to the analytical school. Such a claim may at first sight appear preposterous, until we remember that logic, as a subject, is almost as ancient as philosophy and that it, too, came of age only with the work of Frege. What has given philosophy its historical unity, what has characterized it over all the centuries as a single subject, is the range of questions that philosophers have attempted to answer: there has been comparatively little variation in what has been recognized as constituting a philosophical problem. What has fluctuated wildly is the way in which philosophers have in general characterized the range of problems with which they attempt to deal, and the kind of reasoning that they have accepted as providing answers to these problems. Sometimes philosophers have claimed that they were investigating, by purely rational means, the most general properties of the universe; sometimes, that they were investigating the workings of the human mind; sometimes, again, that they were providing, when these existed, justifications for our various claims to knowledge concerning different types of subject matter. Only with Frege was the proper object of philosophy finally established: namely, first, that the goal of philosophy is the analysis of the structure of *thought*; second, that the study of *thought* is to be sharply distinguished from the study of the psychological process of *thinking*; and, finally, that the only proper method for analyzing thought consists in the analysis of *language*. As I have argued, the acceptance of these three tenets is common to the entire analytical school; but during the interval between Frege's time and now, there have been within that school many somewhat wayward misinterpretations and distortions of Frege's basic teaching, and it has taken nearly a half-century since his death for us to apprehend clearly what the real task of philosophy, as conceived by him, involves.

I know that it is reasonable to greet all such claims with skepticism, since they have been made many times before in the history of philosophy. Just because the scandal caused by philosophy's lack of a systematic methodology has persisted for so long, it has been a constant preoccupation of philosophers to remedy that lack, and a repeated illusion that they had succeeded in doing so. Husserl believed passionately that he at last held the key that would unlock every philosophical door; the disciples of Kant ascribed to him the achievement of devising a correct philosophical methodology; Spinoza believed that he was doing for philosophy what Euclid had done for geometry; and, before him, Descartes supposed that he had uncovered the one and only proper philosophical method. I have mentioned only a few of many examples of this illusion; for any outsider to philosophy, by far the safest bet would be that I was suffering from a similar illusion in making the same claim for Frege. To this I can offer only the banal reply that any prophet has to make to any skeptic: Time will tell.

7

Hilary Putnam

Introduction

Whereas earlier in this century analytic philosophy tended to regard metaphysical problems as cognitively meaningless or as a confusion that results from overtaxing the concepts of ordinary language, more recent analytic philosophy tends to deal with these problems in light of developments in the field of semantics. Carnap and Wittgenstein are indicative of the earlier trend; Hilary Putnam is a leading exponent of the latter. Central to his approach are his critique of the traditional theory of meaning and his development of what is now called "referential semantics."

According to Putnam, the traditional theory of meaning holds (1) that meaning exists "in the head": that is, to know the meaning of a term is to be in a certain mental state; and (2) that meaning fixes reference: that is, the meaning of a term determines the truth conditions or conditions of satisfaction that anything must meet in order to be part of the extension of that term. Putnam argues that this theory is unacceptable because it fails to resolve the problem of intentionality, to explain how mental states can refer to (or set satisfaction conditions for) extramental entities. It also has the undesirable consequence that every change in meaning produces a change in what our theory is about. Accordingly, he proposes a new approach to reference, such that what a linguistic term refers to is not determined by mental states or intentions, but by paradigmatic examples established in a linguistic community (or a part of that community) *and* by historical (causal) connections that exist in the extralinguistic world. Thus, the term "gold" refers to the substance it does, not in virtue of certain concepts or rules in the head of the speaker, but in virtue of paradigmatic examples. These examples may change, but they are not simply stipulated by individual speakers or even by an entire linguistic community; there is also a causal chain that must, so to speak, be discovered.

In *Reason, Truth and History* Putnam uses this theory of referential semantics to criticize two prevalent philosophical perspectives: metaphysical realism and relativism. On his account, metaphysical realism is the view that "the world consists of some fixed totality of mind-independent objects" and that "there is exactly one true and complete description" of that world (1982, 49). Relativism, on the other hand, is the view that there are no standards of truth or rationality that transcend particular cultural or linguistic communities. Putnam argues that both of these positions are incoherent in the end: the former because it assumes a theory of reference based on a "God's Eye point of view" of the relation between words and the world; the latter because it undermines the distinction between a belief's being right and merely seeming to be right. Putnam's own alternative, which, with an explicit reference to Kant, he calls "internal realism," holds that the rejection of metaphysical realism need not entail the rejection of all transsubjective standards of rational justification. Epistemic notions such as "justified," "true," and "warrantedly assertible" are elements of an irreducibly normative conception of rationality, which it is "the task of the philosophers *par excellence*" to elaborate (1982, 113). As there are no "powerful generalizations about all rationally acceptable beliefs" now available to us, and as we cannot hope to start from a priori first principles, Putnam suggests that a theory of rationality might proceed in a manner similar to Rawls's method of "reflective equilibrium" in moral theory (1982, 104). Through a dialectical procedure in which individual judgments of what is acceptable and unacceptable, general maxims, and theoretical principles mutually inform and alter one another, the philosopher seeks to develop a theory that adequately represents our considered judgments.

Putnam argues that any adequate theory of reason will have to take account of both its immanence and its transcendence: on the one hand, we have no idea of standards of rationality wholly independent of historically concrete languages, cultures, and practices; on the other hand, reason serves as a regulative idea with reference to which we can criticize the traditions we inherit. Though never divorced from social practices of justification, reason can never be reduced to any such set of practices. Correspondingly, the notion of truth, while essentially related to warranted assertibility by the standards of this or that culture, cannot, *pace* Rorty, be reduced to it. Putnam conveys its transcendent normative dimension in the formula "truth is *idealized* rational acceptability, acceptability under epistemically *ideal* conditions." Our conception of truth, then, "gets its life" from our conception of rationality, and this in turn presupposes some conception of the good.

Any choice of a conceptual scheme presupposes values . . . because *no* conceptual scheme is a mere "copy" of the world. The notion of truth itself depends for its content on our standards of rational acceptability, and these in turn rest on and presuppose our values. Put schematically and too briefly, I am saying that theory of truth presupposes theory of rationality which in turn presupposes our theory of the good. "Theory of the good," however, is not only programmatic, but is itself dependent upon assumptions about human nature, about society, about the universe (including theological and metaphysical assumptions). We have to revise our theory of the good (such as it is) again and again as our knowledge has increased and our world-view has changed (1982, 215).

To pursue these theories in this way is to practice philosophy without foundations, but not without reason.

In the following selection Putnam develops this (Kantian) notion of the transcendence and immanence of reason in connection with a critique of "naturalized epistemology" — the attempt to account for our beliefs (or for what Quine calls the gap between theory and evidence) solely in terms of the "natural" processes that give rise to them. He argues that this approach either must presuppose metaphysical realism, which he has shown to be incoherent, or must abandon altogether the question of whether beliefs are justified — a position he equates with mental suicide. Thus, in a provocative interpretation of one influential attempt to naturalize epistemology, Putnam argues that Quine's positivism yields "a conception of rationality so narrow as to exclude the very activity of producing that conception," and that his "epistemology naturalized" either abandons justification or reduces it to acceptability to oneself. In an equally challenging reading of Rorty's historicism, he argues that insofar as it identifies reason exclusively with the norms or standards of a local culture, it amounts to a version of (an anthropologically) naturalized epistemology that eliminates questions of justification altogether.

Suggested Readings

Demopoulous, William. "The Rejection of Truth Conditional Semantics by Putnam and Dummett," *Philosophical Topics* 13 (1982), 135–154.

Devitt, Michael. "Realism and the Renegade Putnam: A Critical Study of *Meaning and the Moral Sciences*," *Nous* 17 (1983), 291–301.

Devitt, Michael. *Realism and Truth.* Princeton: Princeton University Press, 1984.

Donnellan, Keith. "Kripke and Putnam on Natural Kind Terms," in *Knowledge and Mind: Philosophical Essays*, ed. C. Ginet and S. Shoemaker, 84–104. New York: Oxford, 1983.

Dummett, Michael. "Comments on Putnam," in *Meaning and Use*, ed. A. Margalit, 218–225. Dordrecht: Reidel, 1979.

Field, Hartry. "Realism and Reason" (APA Symposium on Putnam's *Reason, Truth and History*), *Journal of Philosophy* 79 (1982), 553–567.

Fodor, Jerry. "Cognitive Psychology and the Twin Earth Problem," *Notre Dame Journal of Formal Logic* 23 (1982), 98–118.

Glymour, Clark. "Conceptual Scheming, Or, Confessions of a Metaphysical Realist," *Synthese* 51 (1982), 181–202.

Hanson, Philip. Review of *Meaning and the Moral Sciences*, *Canadian Journal of Philosophy* 10 (1980), 525–543.

Harman, Gilbert. "Metaphysical Realism and Moral Relativism," *Journal of Philosophy* 79 (1982), 568–575.

Margolis, Joseph. "Cognitive Issues in the Realist-Idealist Dispute," *Midwest Studies in Philosophy* 5 (1980), 373–390.

Martin, R. M. "A Memo on Method: Hilary Putnam," *Philosophy and Phenomenological Research* 42 (1982), 587–603; followed by a brief reply by Putnam.

McCullagh, C. Behan. "The Intelligibility of Cognitive Relativism," *The Monist* 67 (1984), 327–340.

Putnam, Hilary. *Mathematics, Matter and Method: Philosophical Papers, Vol. 1*. New York: Cambridge University Press: 1975.

Putnam, Hilary. *Mind, Language and Reality: Philosophical Papers, Vol. 2*. New York: Cambridge University Press, 1975.

Putnam, Hilary. *Meaning and the Moral Sciences*. London: Routledge and Kegan Paul, 1976.

Putnam, Hilary. "Reflections on Goodman's *Ways of Worldmaking*," *Journal of Philosophy* 76 (1979), 603–618.

Putnam, Hilary. *Reason, Truth and History*. New York: Cambridge University Press, 1982.

Putnam, Hilary. *Realism and Reason: Philosophical Papers, Vol. 3*. New York: Cambridge University Press, 1983.

Putnam, Hilary. "How Not to Solve Ethical Problems." *The 1983 Lindley Lecture*, University of Kansas. Marcio Press, 1983.

Putnam, Hilary. "On Truth," in *How Many Questions?*, ed. L. Cauman, 35–56. Indianapolis: Hackett, 1983.

Putnam, Hilary. "Is the Causal Structure of the Physical Itself Something Physical?" *Midwest Studies in Philosophy* 9 (1984), 3–16.

Putnam, Hilary. "After Empiricism," in *Post-Analytic Philosophy*, ed. J. Rajchman and C. West, 20–30. New York: Columbia University Press, 1985.

Putnam, Hilary. "Meaning Holism," in *The Philosophy of W. V. Quine*. The Library of Living Philosophers, ed. P. A. Schilpp. La Salle: Open Court Press, 1986.

Quine, W. V. "The Nature of Natural Knowledge," in *Mind and Language*, ed. S. Guttenplan, 93–96. Oxford: Clarendon Press, 1975.

Searle, John. *Intentionality*, chap. 7, "Are Meanings in the Head?" New York: Cambridge University Press, 1983.

Stabler, Edward. "Naturalized Epistemology and Metaphysical Realism: A Response to Rorty and Putnam," *Philosophical Topics* 13 (1982), 155–170.

Stroud, Barry. "The Significance of Naturalized Epistemology," *Midwest Studies in Philosophy* 6 (1981), 455–471.

Williams, Michael. Review of *Reason, Truth and History*, *Journal of Philosophy* 81 (1984), 257–261.

Why Reason Can't Be Naturalized

Hilary Putnam

I have elsewhere described the failure of contemporary attempts to "naturalize" metaphysics;[1] in the present essay I shall examine attempts to naturalize the fundamental notions of the theory of knowledge, for example the notion of a belief's being *justified* or *rationally acceptable*.

While the two sorts of attempts are alike in that they both seek to reduce "intentional" or mentalistic notions to materialistic ones, and thus are both manifestations of what Peter Strawson (1979) has described as a permanent tension in philosophy, in other ways they are quite different. The materialist metaphysician often uses such traditional metaphysical notions as *causal power* and *nature* quite uncritically. (I have even read papers in which one finds the locution "realist truth," as if everyone understood this notion except a few fuzzy antirealists.) The "physicalist" generally doesn't seek to *clarify* these traditional metaphysical notions, but just to show that science is progressively verifying the *true* metaphysics. That is why it seems just to describe *his* enterprise as "natural metaphysics," in strict analogy to the "natural theology" of the eighteenth and nineteenth centuries. Those who raise the slogan "epistemology naturalized," on the other hand, generally disparage the traditional enterprises of epistemology. In this respect, moreover, they do not differ from philosophers of a less reductionist kind; the criticisms they voice of traditional epistemology — that it was in the grip of a "quest for certainty," that it was unrealistic in seeking a "foundation" for knowledge as a whole, that the foundation it claimed to provide was by no means indubitable in the way it claimed, that the whole "Cartesian enterprise" was a mistake, etc., — are precisely the criticisms one hears from philosophers of all countries and types. Hegel already denounced the idea of an "Archimedean point" from which epistemology could judge all of our scientific, legal, moral, religious, etc. beliefs (and set up standards for all of the special subjects). It is true that Russell and Moore ignored these strictures of Hegel (as they ignored Kant) and revived "foundationalist epistemology"; but today that enterprise has few defenders. The fact that the naturalized epistemologist is trying to reconstruct what he can of an enterprise that few philosophers of any persuasion regard as unflawed is perhaps the explanation of the fact that the naturalistic tendency in epistemology expresses itself in so many incompatible and mutually divergent ways, while the naturalistic tendency in metaphysics appears to be, and regards itself as, a unified movement.

Evolutionary Epistemology

The simplest approach to the problem of giving a naturalistic account of reason is to appeal to Darwinian evolution. In its crudest form, the story is familiar: reason is a capacity we have for discovering truths. Such a capacity has survival value; it evolved in just the way that any of our physical organs or capacities evolved. A belief is rational if it is arrived at by the exercise of this capacity.

This approach assumes, at bottom, a metaphysically "realist" notion of truth: truth as "correspondence to the facts" or something of that kind. And this notion, as I have argued elsewhere (see the papers collected in Putnam, 1983) is incoherent. We don't have notions of the "existence" of things or of the "truth" of statements that are independent of the versions we construct and of the procedures and practices that give sense to talk of "existence" and "truth" within those versions. Do *fields* "exist" as physically real things? Yes, fields really exist: relative to one scheme for describing and explaining physical phenomena; relative to another there are particles, plus "virtual" particles, plus "ghost" particles, plus. . . . Is it true that *brown* objects exist? Yes, relative to a commonsense version of the world: although one cannot give a necessary and sufficient condition for an object to be brown[2] (one that applies to all objects, under all conditions) in the form of a finite closed formula in the language of physics. Do *dispositions* exist? Yes, in our ordinary way of talking (although disposition talk is just as recalcitrant to translation into physicalistic language as counterfactual talk, and for similar reasons). We have many irreducibly different but legitimate ways of talking, and true "existence" statements in all of them.

To postulate a set of "ultimate" objects, the furniture of the world, or what you will, whose "existence" is *absolute,* not relative to our discourse at all, and a notion of truth as "correspondence" to these ultimate objects is simply to revive the whole failed enterprise of traditional metaphysics. Truth, in the only sense in which we have a vital and working notion of it, is rational acceptability (or, rather, rational acceptability under sufficiently good epistemic conditions; and which conditions are epistemically better or worse is relative to the type of discourse in just the way rational acceptability itself is). But to substitute this characterization of truth into the formula "reason is a capacity for discovering truths" is to see the emptiness of that formula at once: "reason is a capacity for discovering what is (or would be) rationally acceptable" is not the most informative statement a philosopher might utter. The evolutionary epistemologist must either presuppose a "realist" (i.e., a metaphysical) notion of truth or see his formula collapse into vacuity.

Roderick Firth has argued that, in fact, it collapses into a kind of epistemic vacuity on *any* theory of rational acceptability (*or* truth).[3] For, he points out, whatever we take the correct epistemology (or the correct theory of truth) to be, we have no way of *identifying* truths except to posit that the statements that are currently rationally acceptable (by our lights) are true. Even if these beliefs are false, even if our rational beliefs contribute to our survival for some reason other than truth, the way "truths" are identified *guarantees* that reason will seem to be a "capacity for discovering truths." This characterization of reason has thus no real empirical content.

The evolutionary epistemologist could, I suppose, try using some notion other than the notion of discovering truths. For example, he might try saying that "reason is a capacity for arriving at beliefs that *promote our survival*" (or our "inclusive genetic fitness"). But this would be a loser! Science itself, and the methodology that we have developed since the seventeenth century for constructing and evaluating theories, has mixed effects on inclusive genetic fitness and all too uncertain effects on survival. If the human race perishes in a nuclear war, it may well be (although there will be no one alive to say it) that scientific beliefs did not, in a sufficiently long time scale, promote "survival." Yet that will not have been because our scientific theories were not rationally acceptable, but because our *use* of them was irrational. In fact, if rationality were measured by survival value, then the proto-beliefs of the cockroach, who has been around for tens of millions of years longer than we, would have a far higher claim to rationality than the sum total of human knowledge. But such a measure would be cockeyed; there is no contradiction in imagining a world in which people have utterly irrational beliefs that for some reason enable them to survive, or a world in which the most rational beliefs quickly lead to extinction.

If the notion of "truth" in the characterization of rationality as a "capacity for discovering truths" is problematic, so, almost equally, is the notion of a "capacity." In one sense of the term, *learning* is a "capacity" (even, a "capacity for discovering truths"), and all our beliefs are the product of that capacity. Yet, for better or worse, not all our beliefs are rational.

The problem here is that there are no sharp lines in the brain between one "capacity" and another (Chomskians to the contrary). Even seeing includes not just the visual organs, the eyes, but the whole brain; and what is true of seeing is certainly true of thinking and inferring. We draw lines between one "capacity" and another (or build them into the various versions we construct); but a sharp line at one level does not usually correspond to a sharp line at a lower level. The table at which I write, for example, is a natural unit at the level of everyday talk; I am aware that the little particle of food sticking to its surface (I must do something about that!) is not a "part" of the table; but at the physicist's level, the decision to consider that bit of food to be outside the boundary of the table is not natural at all. Similarly, "believing" and "seeing" are quite different at the level of ordinary language psychology (and usefully so); but the corresponding brain processes interpenetrate in complex ways that can only be separated by looking outside the brain, at the environment and at the output behavior *as structured by our interests and saliencies.* "Reason is a capacity" is what Wittgenstein called a "grammatical remark"; by which he meant (I think) not an analytic truth, but simply the sort of remark that philosophers often *take* to be informative when in fact it tells us nothing useful.

None of this is intended to deny the obvious scientific facts: that we would not be able to reason if we did not have brains, and that those brains are the product of evolution by natural selection. What is wrong with evolutionary epistemology is not that the scientific facts are wrong, but that they don't answer any of the philosophical questions.

The Reliability Theory of Rationality

A more sophisticated recent approach to these matters, proposed by Professor Alvin Goldman (1978), runs as follows: let us call a *method* (as opposed to a single belief) *reliable* if the method leads to a high frequency (say, 95 percent) of *true* beliefs in a long-run series of representative applications (or *would* lead to such a high truth frequency in such a series of applications). Then (the proposal goes) we can define a *rational* belief to be one that is *arrived at by using a reliable method.*

This proposal does not avoid the first objection we raised against evolutionary epistemology: it too presupposes a metaphysical notion of truth. Forgetting that rational acceptability does the lion's share of the work in fixing the notion of "truth," the reliability theorist only pretends to be giving an analysis of rationality in terms that do not presuppose it. The second objection we raised against evolutionary epistemology, namely that the notion of a "capacity" is hopelessly vague and general, is met, however, by replacing that notion with the notion of an arbitrary method for generating true or false statements, and then restricting the class to those methods (in this sense) whose reliability (as defined) is high. "Learning" may be a method for generating statements, but its reliability is not high enough for every statement we "learn" to count as rationally acceptable, on this theory. Finally, no hypothesis is made as to whether the reliable methods we employ are the result of biological evolution, cultural evolution, or what: this is regarded as no part of the theory of what rationality is, in this account.

This account is vulnerable to many counterexamples, however. One is the following: Suppose that Tibetan Buddhism is, in fact, true, and that the Dalai Lama is, in fact, infallible on matters of faith and morals. Anyone who believes in the Dalai Lama, and who invariably believes any statement the Dalai Lama makes on a matter of faith or morals, follows a method which is 100 percent reliable; thus, if the reliability theory of rationality were correct, such a person's beliefs on faith and morals would all be rational *even if his argument for his belief that the Dalai Lama is never wrong is "the Dalai Lama says so."*

Cultural Relativism

I have already said that, in my view, truth and rational acceptability — a claim's being right and someone's being in a position to make it — are relative to the sort of language we are using and the sort of context we are in. "That weighs one pound" may be true in a butcher shop, but the same sentence would be understood very differently (as demanding four decimal places of precision, perhaps) if the same object were being weighed in a laboratory. This does not mean that a claim is right whenever those who employ the language in question would accept it as right in its context, however. There are two points that must be balanced, both points that have been made by philosophers of many different kinds: (1) talk of what is "right" and "wrong" in any area only makes sense against the background of an inherited tradition; but (2) traditions themselves can be criticized. As Austin (1961) says, remarking on a special case of this, "superstition and error and fantasy of all kinds do become incorporated in ordinary language and even sometimes stand up to the survival test (only, when they do, why should we not detect it?)."

What I am saying is that the "standards" accepted by a culture or a subculture, either explicitly or implicitly, cannot *define* what reason is, even in context, because they *presuppose* reason (reasonableness) for their interpretation. On the one hand, there is no notion of reasonableness at all without cultures, practices, procedures; on the other hand, the cultures, practices, procedures we inherit are not an algorithm to be slavishly followed. As Mill said, commenting on his own inductive logic, there is no rule book that will not lead to terrible results "if supposed to be conjoined with universal idiocy." Reason is, in this sense, both immanent (not to be found outside of concrete language games and institutions) and transcendent (a regulative idea that we use to criticize the conduct of all activities and institutions).

Philosophers who lose sight of the immanence of reason, of the fact that reason is always relative to context and institution, become lost in characteristic philosophical fantasies. "The ideal language," "inductive logic," "the empiricist criterion of significance" — these are the fantasies of the positivist, who would replace the vast complexity of human reason with a kind of intellectual Walden II. "The absolute idea": this is the fantasy of Hegel, who, without ignoring that complexity, would have us (or, rather, "spirit") reach an endstage at which we (it) could comprehend it all. Philosophers who lose sight of the transcendence of reason become cultural (or historical) relativists.

I want to talk about cultural relativism because it is one of the most influential — perhaps the most influential — forms of naturalized epistemology extant, although not usually recognized as such.

The situation is complicated, because cultural relativists usually deny that they are cultural relativists. I shall count a philosopher as a cultural relativist for our purposes if I have not been able to find anyone who can explain to me why he *isn't* a cultural relativist. Thus I count Richard Rorty as a cultural relativist because his explicit formulations are relativist ones (he identifies truth with right assertibility by the standards of one's cultural peers, for example), and because his entire attack

on traditional philosophy is mounted on the basis that the
nature of reason and representation are nonproblems, because
the only kind of truth it makes sense to seek is to convince
one's cultural peers. Yet he himself tells us that relativism is
self-refuting (Rorty, 1980b). And I count Michel Foucault as a
relativist because his insistence on the determination of beliefs
by language is so overwhelming that it is an incoherence on
his part not to apply his doctrine to his own language and
thought. Whether Heidegger ultimately escaped something
very much like cultural, or rather historical, relativism is an
interesting question.

Cultural relativists are not, in their own eyes, scientistic or
"physicalistic." They are likely to view materialism and scien-
tism as just the hang-ups of one particular cultural epoch. If I
count them as "naturalized epistemologists" it is because their
doctrine is, none the less, a product of the same deference to
the claims of nature, the same desire for harmony with the
world version of some science, as physicalism. The difference
in style and tone is thus explained: the physicalist's paradigm
of science is a hard science, physics (as the term "physicalism"
suggests); the cultural relativist's paradigm is a soft science:
anthropology, or linguistics, or psychology, or history, as the
case may be. That reason is whatever the norms of the local
culture determine it to be is a naturalist view inspired by the
social sciences, including history.

There is something that makes cultural relativism a far more
dangerous cultural tendency than materialism. At bottom,
there is a deep irrationalism to cultural relativism, a denial of
the possibility of thinking (as opposed to making noises in
counterpoint or in chorus). An aspect of this that is of special
concern to philosophy is the suggestion, already mentioned,
that the deep questions of philosophy are not deep at all. A
corollary to this suggestion is that philosophy, as traditionally
understood, is a silly enterprise. But the questions *are* deep,
and it is the easy answers that are silly. Even seeing that relativism is inconsistent is, if the knowledge is taken seriously,
seeing something important about a deep question. Philosophers are beginning to talk about the great issues again and to
feel that something can be said about them, even if there are

no grand or ultimate solutions. There is an excitement in the air. And if I react to Professor Rorty's book (1980a) with a certain sharpness, it is because one more "deflationary" book, one more book telling us that the deep questions aren't deep and the whole enterprise was a mistake, is just what we don't need right now. Yet I am grateful to Rorty all the same, for his work has the merit of addressing profound questions head-on.

So, although we all know that cultural relativism is inconsistent (or say we do), I want to take the time to say again that it is inconsistent. I want to point out one reason that it is: not one of the quick, logic-chopping refutations (although every refutation of relativism teaches us something about reason) but a somewhat messy, somewhat "intuitive" reason.

I shall develop my argument in analogy with a well-known argument against "methodological solipsism." The "methodological solipsist" — one thinks of Carnap's *Logische Aufbau* or of Mach's *Analyse der Empfindungen* — holds that all our talk can be reduced to talk about experiences and logical constructions out of experiences. More precisely, he holds that everything he can conceive of is identical (in the ultimate logical analyses of his language) with one or another complex of his own experiences. What makes him a *methodological* solipsist as opposed to a real solipsist is that he kindly adds that *you*, dear reader, are the "I" of this construction when *you* perform it: he says *everybody* is a (methodological) solipsist.

The trouble, which should be obvious, is that his two stances are ludicrously incompatible. His solipsist stance implies an enormous asymmetry between persons: my body is a construction out of my experiences, in the system, but *your* body isn't a construction out of *your* experiences. It's a construction out of *my* experiences. And your experiences — viewed from within the system — are a construction out of your bodily behavior, which, as just said, is a construction out of *my* experiences. My experiences are different from everyone else's (within the system) in that they are what *everything* is constructed from. But his transcendental stance is that it's all symmetrical: the "you" he addresses his higher-order remark to cannot be the empirical "you" of the system. But if it's really true that the "you" of the system is the only "you" he can understand, then the transcendental remark is unintelligible. Moral: don't be a methodological solipsist unless you are a *real* solipsist!

Consider now the position of the cultural relativist who says, "When I say something is *true*, I mean that it is correct according to the norms of *my* culture." If he adds, "When a member of a different culture says that something is true, what he means (whether he knows it or not) is that it is in conformity with the norms of *his* culture," then he is in exactly the same plight as the methodological solipsist.

To spell this out, suppose R. R., a cultural relativist, says

When Karl says "Schnee ist weiss," what Karl means (whether he knows it or not) is that snow is white *as determined by* the norms of Karl's culture

(which we take to be German culture).

Now the sentence "Snow is white as determined by the norms of German culture" is itself one that R. R. has to *use*, not just mention, to say what Karl says. On his own account, what R. R. means by *this* sentence is

"Snow is white as determined by the norms of German culture" is true by the norms of R. R.'s culture

(which we take to be American culture).

Substituting this back into the first displayed utterance (and changing to indirect quotation) yields

When Karl says "Schnee ist weiss," what he means (whether he knows it or not) is that it is true as determined by the norms of American culture that it is true as determined by the norms of German culture that snow is white.

In general, if R. R. understands *every* utterance *p* that *he* uses as meaning "it is true by the norms of American culture that *p*," then he must understand his own hermeneutical utterances, the utterances he uses to interpret others, the same way, no matter how many qualifiers of the "according to the norms of German culture" type or however many footnotes, glosses, commentaries on the cultural differences, or whatever, he accompanies them by. Other cultures become, so to speak, logical constructions out of the procedures and practices of American culture. If he now attempts to add "the situation is reversed from the point of view of the *other* culture," he lands in the predicament the methodological solipsist found himself in: the transcendental claim of a symmetrical situation cannot be understood if the relativist doctrine is right. And to say, as relativists often do, that the other culture has "incommensurable" concepts is no better. This is just the transcendental claim in a special jargon.

Stanley Cavell (1979, part 4) has written that skepticism about other minds can be a significant problem because we don't, in fact, always fully acknowledge the reality of others, their equal validity, so to speak. One might say that the methodological solipsist is led to his transcendental observation that everyone is equally the "I" of the construction by his praiseworthy desire to acknowledge others in this sense. But you can't acknowledge others in this sense, which involves recognizing that the situation really is symmetrical, if you think they are really constructions out of *your* sense data. Nor can you acknowledge others in this sense if you think that the only notion of truth there is for you to understand is "truth-as-determined-by-the-norms-of-this-culture."

For simplicity, I have discussed relativism with respect to truth, but the same discussion applies to relativism about rational acceptability, justification, and so on; indeed, a relativist is unlikely to be a relativist about one of these notions and not about the others.

Cultural Imperialism

Just as the methodological solipsist can become a *real* solipsist, the cultural relativist can become a cultural imperialist. He can say, "Well then, truth — the only notion of truth I understand — is defined by the norms of *my* culture." ("After all," he can add, "which norms should I rely on? The norms of *somebody else's* culture?") Such a view is no longer relativist at all. It postulates an objective notion of truth, although one that is said to be a product of our culture and to be defined by our culture's criteria (I assume the cultural imperialist is one of *us*). In this sense, just as consistent solipsism becomes indistinguishable from realism (as Wittgenstein said in the *Tractatus*), consistent cultural relativism also becomes indistinguishable from realism. But cultural imperialist realism is a special kind of realism.

It is realist in that it accepts an objective difference between what is true and what is merely thought to be true. (Whether it can consistently *account for* this difference is another question.)

It is not a *metaphysical* or transcendental realism, in that truth cannot go beyond right assertibility, as it does in metaphysical realism. But the notion of right assertibility is fixed by "criteria," in a positivistic sense: something is rightly assertible only if the norms of the culture specify that it is; these norms are, as it were, an operational definition of right assertibility, in this view.

I don't know if any philosopher holds such a view, although several philosophers have let themselves fall into talking at certain times as if they did. (A philosopher in this mood is likely to say, "*X* is *our* notion," with a certain petulance, where *X* may be reason, truth, justification, evidence, or what have you.)

This view is, however, self-refuting, at least in our culture. I have discussed this elsewhere (Putnam, 1981); the argument turns on the fact that our culture, unlike totalitarian or theocratic cultures, does not have "norms" that decide philosophical questions. (Some philosophers have thought it does; but they had to postulate a "depth grammar" accessible only to them, and not describable by ordinary linguistic or anthropological investigation.) Thus the philosophical statement

A statement is true (rightly assertible) only if it is assertible according to the norms of modern European and American culture

is itself neither assertible nor refutable in a way that requires assent by everyone who does not deviate from the norms of modern European and American culture. So, if this statement is true, it follows that it is not true (not rightly assertible). Hence it is not true, QED. (I believe that all theories that identify truth or right assertibility with what people agree with, or with what they would agree with in the long run, or with what educated and intelligent people agree with, or with what educated and intelligent people would agree with in the long run, are contingently self-refuting in this same way.)

Cultural imperialism would not be contingently self-refuting in this way if, as a matter of contingent fact, our culture were a totalitarian culture that erected its own cultural imperialism into a required dogma, a culturally normative belief. But it would still be wrong. For every culture has norms that are vague, norms that are unreasonable, norms that dictate inconsistent beliefs. We have all become aware how many inconsistent beliefs about women were culturally normative until recently and are still strongly operative, not only in subcultures but in all of us to some extent; and examples of inconsistent but culturally normative beliefs could easily be multiplied. Our task is not to mechanically *apply* cultural norms, as if they were a computer program and we were the computer, but to interpret them, to criticize them, to bring them and the ideals that inform them into reflective equilibrium. Cavell has aptly described this as "confronting the culture with itself, along the lines in which it meets in me." And he adds (Cavell, 1979, p.125), "This seems to me a task that warrants the name of Philosophy." In this sense we are all called to be philosophers, to a greater or lesser extent.

The culturalist, relativist or imperialist, like the historicist, has been caught up in the fascination of something really fascinating; but caught up in a sophomorish way. Traditions, cultures, history, deserve to be emphasized, as they are not by those who seek Archimedian points in metaphysics or epistemology. It is true that we speak a public language, that we inherit versions, that talk of truth and falsity only make sense against the background of an "inherited tradition," as Wittgenstein says. But it is also true that we constantly remake our language, that we make new versions out of old ones, and that we have to use reason to do all this and, for that matter, even to understand and apply the norms we do not alter or criticize.

Consensus definitions of reason do not work, because consensus among grownups *presupposes* reason rather than defining it.

Quinian Positivism

The slogan "epistemology naturalized" is the title of a famous paper by Quine (1969). If I have not discussed that paper up to now, it is because Quine's views are much more subtle and much more elaborate than the disastrously simple views we have just reviewed, and it seemed desirable to get the simpler views out of the way first.

Quine's philosophy is a large continent, with mountain ranges, deserts, and even a few Okefenokee Swamps. I do not know how all of the pieces of it can be reconciled, if they can be; what I shall do is discuss two different strains that are to be discerned in Quine's epistemology. In the present section I discuss the positivist strain; the next section will discuss "epistemology naturalized."

The positivist strain, which occurs early and late, turns on the notion of an *observation sentence*. In his earliest writings Quine gave this a phenomenalistic interpretation, but since the 1950s at least, he has preferred a definition in neurological and cultural terms. First, a preliminary notion: The *stimulus meaning* of a sentence is defined to be the set of stimulations (of "surface neurons") that would "prompt assent" to the sentence. It is thus supposed to be a neurological correlate of the sentence. A sentence may be called "stimulus-true" for a speaker if the speaker is actually experiencing a pattern of stimulation of his surface neurons that lie in its stimulus meaning; but one should be careful to remember that a stimulus-true sentence is not necessarily true *simpliciter*. If you show me a lifelike replica of a duck, the sentence "That's a duck" may be stimulus-true for me, but it isn't true. A sentence is defined to be an observation sentence for a community if it is an occasioned sentence (one whose truth value is regarded as varying with time and place, although this is not the Quinian definition) and it has the same stimulus meaning for all speakers. Thus "He is a bachelor" is not an observation sentence, since different stimulations will prompt you to assent to it than will prompt me (we know different people); but "That's a duck" is (nearly enough) an observation sentence. Observe that the criterion is supposed to be entirely physicalistic. The key idea is that observation sentences are distinguished among occasioned sentences by being keyed to the same stimulations *intersubjectively*.

Mach held that talk of unobservables, including (for him) material objects, is justified only for reasons of "economy of thought." The business of science is *predicting regularities in our sensations*; we introduce "objects" other than sensations only as needed to get theories that neatly predict such regularities.

Quine (1975) comes close to a "physicalized" version of Mach's view. Discussing the question whether there is more than one correct "system of the world," he gives his criteria for such a system: (1) it must predict a certain number of stimulus-true observation sentences;[4] (2) it must be finitely axiomatized; (3) it must contain nothing unnecessary to the purpose of predicting stimulus-true observation sentences and conditionals. In the terminology Quine introduces in this paper, the theory formulation must be a "tight fit"[5] over the relevant set of stimulus-true observation conditionals. (This is a formalized version of Mach's "economy of thought.")

If this were all of Quine's doctrine, there would be no problem. It is reconciling what Quine says here with what Quine says elsewhere that is difficult and confusing. I am not claiming that it is impossible, however; a lot, if not all, of what Quine says *can* be reconciled. What I claim is that Quine's position is much more complicated than is generally realized.

For example, what is the status of Quine's ideal "systems of the world"? It is tempting to characterize the sentences in one of Quine's ideal "theory formulations" as truths (relative to that language and that choice of a formulation from among the equivalent-but-incompatible-at-face-value formulations of what Quine would regard as the *same* theory) and as *all* the truths (relative to the same choice of language and formulation), but this would conflict with bivalence, the principle that every sentence, in the ideal scientific language Quine envisages, is true or false.

To spell this out: Quine's ideal systems of the world are *finitely axiomatizable theories* and contain standard mathematics. Thus Gödel's celebrated result applies to them: there are sentences in them that are neither provable nor refutable on the basis of the system. If being true were just being a theorem in the system, such sentences would be neither true nor false, since neither they nor their negations are theorems. But Quine (1981) holds to bivalence.

If Quine were a metaphysical realist, there would again be no problem: the ideal system would contain everything that could be justified (from a very idealized point of view, assuming knowledge of all observations that could be made, and logical omniscience); but, Quine could say, the undecidable sentences are still determinately true or false — only we can't tell which. But the rejection of metaphysical realism, of the whole picture of a determinate "copying" relation between words and a noumenal world, is at the heart of Quine's philosophy. And, as we shall see in the next section, "justification" is a notion Quine is leery of. So what *is* he up to?[6]

I hazard the following interpretation: bivalence has two meanings for Quine: a "first-order" meaning, a meaning as viewed within the system of science (including its Tarskian metalanguage), and a "second-order" meaning, a meaning as viewed by the philosopher. In effect, I am claiming that Quine too allows himself a "transcendental" standpoint that is different from the "naive" standpoint that we get by just taking the system at face value. (I am not claiming that this is inconsistent, however; some philosophers feel that such a move is always an inconsistency, but taking this line would preclude using any notion in science that one would explain away as a useful fiction in one's commentary on one's first-order practice. There was an inconsistency in the case of the methodological solipsist, because he claimed his first-order system reconstructed the only way he could understand the notion of another mind; if he withdraws that claim, then his position becomes perfectly consistent; it merely loses all philosophical interest.)

From within the first-order system, "*p* is true or *p* is false" is simply true; a derivable consequence of the Tarskian truth definition, given standard propositional calculus. From outside, from the meta-metalinguistic point of view Quine occupies, there is no unique "world," no unique "intended model." Only structure matters; every model of the ideal system (I assume there is just one ideal theory, and we have fixed a formulation) is an intended model. Statements that are provable are true in all intended models; undecidable statements are true or false in each intended model, but not *stably* true or false. Their truth value varies from model to model.

If this is Quine's view, however, then there is still a problem. For Quine, what the philosopher says from the "transcendental" standpoint is subject to the same methodological rules that govern ordinary first-order scientific work. Even mathematics is subject to the same rules. Mathematical truths, too, are to be certified as such by showing they are theorems in a system that we need to predict sensations (or rather, stimulus-true observation conditionals), given the physics that we are constructing as we construct the mathematics. More precisely, the whole system of knowledge is justified *as a whole* by its utility in predicting observations. Quine emphasizes that there is no room in this view for a special status for philosophical utterances. There is no "first philosophy" above or apart from science, as he puts it.

Consider, now, the statement

A statement is *rightly assertible* (true in all models) just in case it is a theorem of the relevant "finite formulation," and that formulation is a "tight fit" over the appropriate set of stimulus-true observation conditionals.

This statement, like most philosophical statements, does not imply any observation conditionals, either by itself or in conjunction with physics, chemistry, biology, etc. Whether we say that some statements that are undecidable in the system are really rightly assertible or deny it does not have any effects (that one can foresee) on prediction. Thus, this statement cannot itself be rightly assertible. In short, this reconstruction of Quine's positivism makes it self-refuting.

The difficulty, which is faced by all versions of positivism, is that positivist exclusion principles are always self-referentially inconsistent. In short, *positivism produced a conception of rationality so narrow as to exclude the very activity of producing that conception.* (Of course, it also excluded a great many other kinds of rational activity.) The problem is especially sharp for Quine, because of his explicit rejection of the analytic/synthetic distinction, his rejection of a special status for philosophy, and so forth.

It may be, also, that I have just got Quine wrong. Quine would perhaps reject the notions of "right assertibility," "intended model," and so on. But then I just don't know what to make of this strain in Quine's thought.

"Epistemology Naturalized"

Quine's paper "Epistemology Naturalized" takes a very different tack. "Justification" has failed. (Quine considers the notion only in its strong "Cartesian" setting, which is one of the things that makes his paper puzzling.) Hume taught us that we can't justify our knowledge claims (in a foundational way). Conceptual reduction has also failed (Quine reviews the failure of phenomenalism as represented by Carnap's attempt in the *Logische Aufbau*.) So, Quine urges, let us give up epistemology and "settle for psychology."

Taken at face value, Quine's position is sheer epistemological eliminationism: we should just abandon the notions of justification, good reason, warranted assertion, and so on, and reconstrue the notion of "evidence" (so that the "evidence" becomes the sensory stimulations that cause us to have the scientific beliefs we have). In conversation, however, Quine has repeatedly said that he didn't mean to "rule out the normative"; and this is consistent with his recent interest in such notions as the notion of a "tight fit" (an economical finitely axiomatized system for predicting observations).

Moreover, the expression "naturalized epistemology" is being used today by a number of philosophers who explicitly consider themselves to *be* doing normative epistemology, or at least methodology. But the paper "Epistemology Naturalized" really does rule all that out. So it's all extremely puzzling.

One way to reconcile the conflicting impulses that one sees at work here might be to replace justification theory by reliability theory in the sense of Goldman; instead of saying that a belief is justified if it is arrived at by a reliable method, one might say that the notion of justification should be replaced by the notion of a verdict's being the product of a reliable method. This is an eliminationist line in that it does not try to reconstruct or analyze the traditional notion; that was an intuitive notion that we now perceive to have been defective from the start, such a philosopher might say. Instead, he proposes a better notion (by his lights).

While some philosophers would, perhaps, move in this direction, Quine would not for a reason already given: Quine rejects metaphysical realism, and the notion of reliability presupposes the notion of truth. Truth is, to be sure, an acceptable notion for Quine, if defined à la Tarski; but so defined, it cannot serve as the primitive notion of epistemology or of methodology. For Tarski simply defines "true" so that "p is true" will come out equivalent to "p"; so that, to cite the famous example, "*Snow is white*" *is true* will come out equivalent to "Snow is white." What the procedure does is to define "true" so that saying that a statement is true is equivalent to *assenting* to the statement; truth, as defined by Tarski, is not a *property* of statements at all, but a syncategoramatic notion that enables us to "ascend semantically," that is, to talk about sentences instead of about objects.[7]

I will assent to "p is true" whenever I assent to p; therefore, I will accept a method as reliable whenever it *yields verdicts I would accept*. I believe that, in fact, this is what the "normative" becomes for Quine: the search for methods that yield verdicts that one oneself would accept.

Why We Can't Eliminate the Normative

I shall have to leave Quine's views with these unsatisfactory remarks. But why not take a full-blown eliminationist line? Why *not* eliminate the normative from our conceptual vocabulary? Could it be a superstition that there is such a thing as reason?

If one abandons the notions of justification, rational acceptability, warranted assertibility, right assertibility, and the like, completely, then "true" goes as well, except as a mere device for "semantic ascent," that is, a mere mechanism for switching from one level of language to another. The mere introduction of a Tarskian truth predicate cannot define for a language any notion of rightness that was not already defined. To reject the notions of justification and right assertibility while keeping a metaphysical realist notion of truth would, on the other hand, be not only peculiar (what ground could there be for regarding truth, in the "correspondence" sense, as clearer than right assertibility?) but incoherent; for the notions the naturalistic metaphysician uses to explain truth and reference, for example, the notion of causality (explanation) and the notion of the *appropriate type* of causal chain, depend on notions that presuppose the notion of reasonableness.

But if all notions of rightness, both epistemic and (metaphysically) realist, are eliminated, then what are our statements but noise-makings? What are our thoughts but mere subvocalizations? The elimination of the normative is attempted mental suicide.

The notions "verdict I accept" and "method that leads to verdicts I accept" are of little help. If the only kind of rightness any statement has that I can understand is "being arrived at by a method that yields verdicts *I* accept," then I am committed to a solipsism of the present moment. To solipsism, because this *is* a methodologically solipsist substitute for assertibility ("verdicts *I* accept"), and we saw before that the methodological solipsist is only consistent if he is a real solipsist. And to solipsism of the present moment, because this is a *tensed* notion (a substitute for warranted assertibility at *a time*, not for assertibility in the best conditions); and if the only kind of rightness my present "subvocalizations" have is present assertibility (however defined), if there is no notion of a limit verdict, however fuzzy, then there is no sense in which my "subvocalizations" are about anything that goes beyond the present moment. (Even the thought "there is a future" is "right" only in the sense of being assertible at the present moment, in such a view.)

One could try to overcome this last defect by introducing the notion of "a verdict I would accept *in the long run*," but this would at once involve one with the use of counterfactuals and with such notions as "similarity of possible worlds." But it is pointless to make further efforts in this direction. Why should we expend our mental energy in convincing ourselves that we aren't thinkers, that our thoughts aren't really *about* anything, noumenal *or* phenomenal, that there is no sense in which any thought is right or wrong (including the thought that no thought is right or wrong) beyond being the verdict of the moment, and so on? This is a self-refuting enterprise if there ever was one! Let us recognize that one of our fundamental self-conceptualizations, one of our fundamental "self-descriptions," in Rorty's phrase, is that we are thinkers, and that as thinkers we are committed to there being some kind of truth, some kind of correctness that is substantial and not merely "disquotational." That means that there is no eliminating the normative.

If there is no eliminating the normative, and no possibility of reducing the normative to our favorite science, be it biology, anthropology, neurology, physics, or whatever, then where are we? We might try for a grand theory of the normative in its own terms, a formal epistemology, but that project seems decidedly overambitious. In the meantime there is a great deal of philosophical work to be done, and it will be done with fewer errors if we free ourselves of the reductionist and historicist hang-ups that have marred so much recent philosophy. If reason is both transcendent and immanent, then philosophy, as culture-bound reflection and argument about eternal questions, is both in time and in eternity. We don't have an Archimedean point; we always speak the language of a time and place; but the rightness and wrongness of what we say is not *just* for a time and a place.

Notes

1. See "Why There Isn't a Ready-Made World," in Putnam (1983).

2. I chose brown because brown is not a spectral color. But the point also applies to spectral colors: if being a color were purely a matter of reflecting light of a certain wavelength, then the objects we see would change color a number of times a day (and would all be black in total darkness). Color depends on background conditions, edge effects, reflectancy, relations to amount to light, etc. Giving a description of all of these would only define *perceived* color; to define the "real" color of an object one also needs

a notion of "standard conditions": traditional philosophers would have said that the color of a red object is a power (a disposition) to look red to normal observers under normal conditions. This, however, requires a counterfactual conditional (whenever the object is *not* in normal conditions); and I have demonstrated (in "Why There Isn't a Ready-Made World," in Putnam, 1983) that the attempt to define counterfactuals in "physical" terms has failed. What makes color terms physically undefinable is not that color is subjective but that it is *subjunctive*. The common idea that there is some one molecular structure (or whatever) common to all objects that look red "under normal conditions" has no foundation: consider the difference between the physical structure of a red star and a red book (and the difference in what we count as "normal conditions" in the two cases).

3. This argument appears in Firth's Presidential Address to the Eastern Division of the American Philosophical Association (29 December 1981), titled "Epistemic Merit, Intrinsic and Instrumental." Firth does not specifically refer to evolutionary epistemology, but rather to "epistemic utilitarianism"; however, his argument applies as well to evolutionary epistemology of the kind I describe.

4. Quine actually requires that a "system of the world" predict that certain "pegged observation sentences" be true. I have oversimplified in the text by writing "observation sentence" for "pegged observation sentence." Also the "stimulus meaning" of an observation sentence includes a specification of conditions under which the speaker *dissents*, as well as the conditions under which he assents. The details are in Quine (1975).

5. A theory is a "tight fit" if it is interpretable in *every* axiomatizable theory that implies the observation conditionals (conditions whose antecedent and consequent are pegged observation sentences) in question in a way that holds the pegged observation sentences fixed. To my knowledge, no proof exists that a "tight fit" even exists, apart from the trivial case in which the observation conditionals can be axiomatized *without* going outside of the observation vocabulary.

6. Quine rejected the interpretation I offer below (discussion at Heidelberg in 1981) and opted for saying that our situation is "asymmetrical": he is a "realist" with respect to his own language but not with respect to other languages. See pp. xii–xiii and 278–279 in Putnam (1983) for my rejoinder.

7. Quine himself puts this succinctly. "Whatever we affirm, after all, we affirm as a statement within our aggregate theory of nature as we now see it; and to call a statement true is just to reaffirm it" (Quine, 1975, p. 327).

References

Austin, J. L., 1970. "A Plea for Excuses," in *Philosophical Papers*, 2d ed., Oxford, 175–204.

Cavell, S., 1979. *The Claim of Reason*, Oxford, 86–125.

Goldman, A., 1978. "What Is Justified Belief?" in G. S. Pappas and M. Swain (eds.), *Justification and Knowledge*, Cornell.

Putnam, H., 1981. *Reason, Truth and History*, Cambridge.

Putnam, H., 1983. *Realism and Reason*, Cambridge.

Quine, W. V., 1969. *Ontological Relativity and Other Essays*, New York.

Quine, W. V., 1975. "On Empirically Equivalent Systems of the World," *Erkenntnis* 9:313–328.

Quine, W. V., 1981. "What Price Bivalence?" *Journal of Philosophy* 78:90–95. Reprinted in his *Theories and Things*, Cambridge, Massachusetts.

Rorty, R., 1980a. *Philosophy and the Mirror of Nature*, Oxford.

Rorty, R., 1980b. "Pragmatism, Relativism and Irrationalism," *Proceedings and Addresses of the American Philosophical Association*, 53.

Strawson, P. F., 1979. "Universals," *Midwest Studies in Philosophy* 4:3–10.

8

Karl-Otto Apel

Introduction

Karl-Otto Apel's "transformation of philosophy" has an ambivalent relation to its own heritage. On the one hand, by embracing the linguistic and the pragmatic turns in philosophy in this century, it makes a radical break with traditional "philosophy of consciousness," or what Apel calls the "philosophy of ultimate origins." On the other hand, in contrast to the empiricist and/or relativist interpretations often accompanying these turns, it retains an emphatic connection with the classical search for philosophical (transcendental) foundations, or justification and critique, of the sciences and our social institutions. In pursuing this project Apel develops one of the most systematic programs to integrate the achievements of analytic philosophy (from Peirce to Searle) with those of Continental philosophy.

For Apel the linguistic turn in philosophy entails that the conditions for intersubjectively valid knowledge cannot be explicated in terms of the structure of consciousness or the cognitive equipment of the knowing subject, but only through a systematic investigation of language as the medium of symbolically mediated knowledge. The pragmatic turn, initiated by Peirce and Morris and continued today in speech act theory, implies, further, that an adequate explanation of how meaningful communication is possible cannot be achieved by theories of syntax and semantics alone; they must be supplemented by a study of pragmatics, the relationship between linguistic signs and the conditions of their use by speakers. Apel's strong thesis is that his "transcendental pragmatics" yields a set of normative conditions and validity claims presupposed in any critical discussion or rational argumentation. Central among these is the presupposition that a participant in a genuine argument is at the same time a member of a counterfactual, ideal communication community that is in principle equally open to all speakers and that excludes all force except the force of the better argument. Any claim to intersubjectively valid knowledge (scientific or moral-practical) implicitly acknowledges this ideal communication community, as a "meta-institution" of rational argumentation, to be its ultimate source of justification (1980, 119).

Drawing upon the Continental tradition, Apel argues that the most important contribution of philosophical hermeneutics, Gadamer's in particular, has been to show that interpretation is not another method of investigation over against or in addition to the methods used within the "hard" sciences, but an unavoidable dimension of all understanding. Every empirical investigation of a domain of objects implies at the same time a relation to other subjects, to a community of interpreters. Thus, the attempt to study language from an exclusively objectivistic or behavioristic perspective involves an abstraction from the inquirer's own membership in a linguistic community. His or her verbal behavior must also be interpreted by the community of investigators, and this interpretive moment can never itself be displaced by objectivistic investigation. In fact, such investigation itself presupposes a communication community. But Apel's "transcendental hermeneutics" departs from Gadamer's historicism in that successive interpretations not only purport to understand differently but also raise an implicit claim to truth or correctness that can be clarified, once again, with reference to the ideal communication community. Further, like Habermas, Apel does not exclude the possibility of introducing causal or functional explanations to clarify systematic distortions to communication, so long as they are "considered to be capable of conversion into a reflexively heightened self-understanding of the communicating parties" (1980, 125).

In the essay that follows, Apel clarifies the status of transcendental pragmatics by way of a critique of the "critical rationalism" developed by Popper and his followers. He suggests that their skepticism with regard to the possibility of ultimate philosophical grounding is based on an "abstractive fallacy" in which sentences are viewed in isolation from the pragmatic contexts of argumentation. The so-called Münchhausen trilemma — i.e., that all attempts to discover ultimate foundations result in either logical circularity, infinite regress, or an arbitrary end to the process of justification — can be overcome by moving from the level of semantic analysis to the level of pragmatics and recognizing that some presuppositions are necessary for the very possibility of intersubjectively valid criticism and argumentation. Similarly, he argues, even the "principle of fallibilism" (which holds that any claim can, in principle, be doubted) is only meaningful within an "institution of argumentation" where some pragmatic rules and norms are not open to question. Thus, contrary to the claim of critical rationalism, the principle of fallibilism does not exclude the notion of philosophical foundations and, Apel argues, certainly could not replace it as the basic principle of rational discourse.

Although questions of ethics are only briefly alluded to in this essay, Apel has argued, at great length and in great detail, that transcendental pragmatics can be used to develop an "ethics of communication," or *Diskursethik*: like other cognitivist approaches, this ethics rejects the claim that moral judgments are ultimately the expressions of subjective preferences or an arbitrary will and hence beyond the reach of rational justification. By elucidating its basic principle in relation to the pragmatic presuppositions of argumentation in general, Apel seeks more secure foundations than Kant's appeal to a "fact of reason" or Rawls's "reflective equilibrium." According to the basic principle of his ethics of communication, only those norms are justified that could meet with the agreement of all concerned as participants in a practical discourse.

Suggested Readings

Apel, Karl-Otto. *Analytic Philosophy of Language and the Geisteswissenschaften*. Dordrecht: Reidel, 1967.

Apel, Karl-Otto. "The Apriori of Communication and the Foundations of the Humanities," *Man and World* 5 (1972), 3–37; reprinted in *Understanding and Social Inquiry*, ed. F. Dallmayr and T. McCarthy, 292–315. Notre Dame: University of Notre Dame Press, 1977.

Apel, Karl-Otto. "From Kant to Peirce: The Semiotic Transformation of Transcendental Logic," in *Kant's Theory of Knowledge*, ed. L. W. Beck. Dordrecht: Reidel, 1974.

Apel, Karl-Otto. "Sprechakttheorie und transzendentale Sprachpragmatik. Zur Frage ethischer Normen," in *Sprachpragmatik und Philosophie*, ed. K.-O. Apel, 10–173. Frankfurt a. M.: Suhrkamp, 1976.

Apel, Karl-Otto. "Transcendental Semiotics and the Paradigms of First Philosophy," *Philosophical Exchange* 2 (1978), 3–22.

Apel, Karl-Otto. "The Conflicts of Our Time and the Problem of Political Ethics," in *From Contract to Community: Political Theory at the Crossroads*, ed. F. Dallmayr. New York: Marcel Decker, 1978.

Apel, Karl-Otto. "The Common Presuppositions of Hermeneutics and Ethics: Types of Rationality beyond Science and Technology," in *Phenomenology and the Human Sciences*, ed. J. Sallis, 35–53. New York: Humanities Press, 1979.

Apel, Karl-Otto. "Types of Rationality Today: The Continuum of Reason between Science and Ethics," in *Rationality Today*, ed.T. Geraets, 307–339. Ottawa: Ottawa University Press, 1979.

Apel, Karl-Otto. *Towards a Transformation of Philosophy*. London: Routledge and Kegan Paul, 1980.

Apel, Karl-Otto. *Charles S. Peirce: From Pragmatism to Pragmaticism*. Amherst: University of Massachusetts Press, 1981.

Apel, Karl-Otto. "Intentions, Conventions and Reference to Things: Dimensions of Understanding Meaning in Hermeneutics and in Analytic Philosophy of Language," in *Meaning and Understanding*, ed. H. Parret and J. Bouveresse, 81–111. Berlin: De Gruyter, 1981.

Apel, Karl-Otto. "The *Erklären/Verstehen*-Controversy in the Philosophy of the Human and the Natural Sciences," in *Contemporary Philosophy: A New Survey*, ed. G. Floistad, 19–35. Boston: Reidel, 1982.

Apel, Karl-Otto. "Normative Ethics and Strategical Rationality: The Philosophical Problem of a Political Ethics," *Graduate Faculty of Philosophy Journal* 9 (1982), 81–107.

Apel, Karl-Otto. "C. S. Peirce and the Post-Tarskian Problem of an Adequate Explication of the Meaning of Truth," in *The Relevance of Charles Peirce*, ed. E. Freeman, 189–223. La Salle: The Hegeler Institute, 1983.

Apel, Karl-Otto. "The Situation of Man as a Problem of Ethical Reason," *Praxis International* 4 (1983), 250–265.

Apel, Karl-Otto. "Comments on Donald Davidson's 'Communication and Convention,'" *Synthese* 59 (1984), 19–26.

Apel, Karl-Otto. "The Question of the Rationality of Social Interaction," in *Philosophy in a Phenomenological Perspective*, ed. K. Cho. Boston: Nijhoff, 1984.

Apel, Karl-Otto. *Understanding and Explanation: A Transcendental-Pragmatic Perspective*. Cambridge, Massachusetts: MIT Press, 1984.

Apel, Karl-Otto. *Transcendental Semiotics as First Philosophy*. New Haven: Yale University Press, 1986.

Benhabib, Seyla, and Fred Dallmayr, eds. *The Communicative Ethics Controversy*. Cambridge, Massachusetts: MIT Press, forthcoming.

Bleicher, Josef. *Contemporary Hermeneutics: Hermeneutics as Method, Philosophy and Critique*. London: Routledge and Kegan Paul, 1980.

Böhler, Dietrich. *Rekonstruktive Pragmatik*. Frankfurt a. M.: Suhrkamp, 1985.

Dallmayr, Fred. *Language and Politics: Why Does Language Matter to Political Philosophy?* Notre Dame: University of Notre Dame Press, 1984.

Keuth, Herbert. "Fallibilismus versus transzendental-pragmatische Letztbegründung," *Zeitschrift für allgemeine Wissenschaft* 14 (1983), 320–337.

Kuhlmann, Wolfgang. *Reflexive Letztbegründung: Untersuchungen zur Transzendentalpragmatik*. München: Alber, 1985.

Kuhlmann, Wolfgang, and Dietrich Böhler, eds. *Kommunikation und Reflexion: Zur Diskussion der Transzendentalpragmatik. Antworten auf K.-O. Apel*. Frankfurt a. M.: Suhrkamp, 1982.

The Problem of Philosophical Foundations in Light of a Transcendental Pragmatics of Language*

Karl-Otto Apel

The Problem: Critical Rationalism Versus Foundationalism

The argument that it is impossible for philosophy to have foundations has been put forward recently by the "critical rationalism" that developed out of Karl Popper's *The Logic of Scientific Discovery,* in particular by W. W. Bartley and Hans Albert. This claim is made in opposition to both classical modern rationalism and Kant's transcendental critique of knowledge.[1] "Critical rationalism" combines this distancing from an uncritical rationalism — that is, from a rationalism that has not reflected critically on the impossibility of self-validating reasons — with the claim that the philosophical program of foundationalism might be superseded by the alternative program of unlimited rational criticism, if the latter were given a satisfactory form. Following upon Bartley's proclamation of a "pancritical rationalism" in his *Retreat from Commitment,*[2] Hans Albert has attempted to work out this alternative program in his *Treatise on Critical Reason.* Through the derivation of what he calls the Münchhausen Trilemma,[3] the criticism of any claim to philosophical foundations is given an impressive and, apparently, logically compelling form.

According to Albert, every attempt to make good the claim to provide philosophical foundations in the sense of Leibniz's principle of sufficient reason leads "to a situation with three

---

*The original German text has been revised and added to by the author for this edition.

alternatives, all of which appear unacceptable; that is, it leads to a trilemma." The trilemma forces one to choose between the following alternatives: (1) an infinite regress that appears to be required by the necessity of always going further back in the search for reasons, but that is not practically feasible and therefore yields no solid foundation; (2) a logical circle in the deduction that results from the fact that in the process of giving reasons one has to resort to statements that have already shown themselves to be in need of justification — a process that, because it is logically faulty, likewise leads to no firm foundation; (3) breaking off giving reasons at a particular point, which, while in principle feasible, would involve an arbitrary suspension of the principle of sufficient reason.[4]

Albert knows, of course, that the philosophical tradition since Aristotle — in particular the rationalism begun by Descartes, as well as its opposite number, empiricism — did not want to suspend giving reasons at an arbitrary point by suspending the principle of providing justification through reasons. Rather, that tradition sought premises that, on the basis of epistemic evidence, would be illuminating or convincing.[5] Albert argues, however, that every such premise "can be fundamentally doubted,"[6] so that any justification given by means of epistemic "evidence" merely amounts to an arbitrary breaking off of the process of giving reasons in the sense of the third alternative of the trilemma.

We can find many passages that illustrate this interpretation of Albert's position. According to Albert, the appeal to "evidence" in giving reasons is "entirely analogous to the suspension of the causal principle through the introduction of a *causa sui*." "An assertion whose truth is certain and, therefore, not in need of justification" is, according to Albert, "a dogma." Breaking off giving reasons in the sense of the third alternative is, therefore, "justification by appeal to a dogma." Likewise, "going back to extralinguistic stages of the process" changes nothing, since "it is always possible to ask for the justification of these stages themselves." "Any conception of self-validating reasons for such fundamental stages, as well as the corresponding claim that there are such propositions, must be viewed as a disguise for the decision to suspend the principle of sufficient reason in this case."[7]

Thus Albert not only rejects the Cartesian reduction of the validity of truth claims to epistemic evidence or certainty, but goes so far as to argue that the quest for certainty is entirely worthless; indeed, it is said to be irreconcilable with the search for truth: "All guarantees in knowledge are self-fabricated and thus worthless for comprehending reality. That is, we can always create certainty by turning this or that element of our convictions into a dogma and thus immunizing it from all possible criticism. Thus, it becomes impossible for it to fail."[8] Albert sees this criticism as confirmed by Hugo Dingler, who no longer finds the final "certainties" for epistemic justification in philosophy in the givenness of evidence, but rather in a "will" to certainty. Through the "exhaustion" principle he immunizes theoretical construction from possible failure to grasp reality. Here, Albert argues, the "will to certainty" triumphs over the "will to knowledge" and thus amounts to a *reductio ad absurdum* of the principle of philosophical foundations in classical rationalism. "The development of the classical doctrine has made it clear that the quest for certainty and the search for truth are mutually exclusive, if one does not want to restrict oneself to contentless truths" (in the sense of merely analytic truths).[9]

In light of this difficulty, Albert, following Popper, proposes that we give up the principle of sufficient reason, or philosophical foundations in general, and replace it by a decision that is not rationally justifiable — but in precisely the opposite sense from Dingler, that is to say, a decision for a method that does not regard any knowledge as certain and exempt from criticism. This method requires that "reality be given the opportunity to determine" whether or not our theoretical constructions can fail to grasp it. Such a decision in favor of Popper's principle of "fallibilism" must, according to Albert, "sacrifice the desire for certainty that underlies the classical doctrine and accept permanent uncertainty as to whether our opinions will be confirmed and supported in the future."[10]

Albert clearly admits that Popper's adoption of the method of critical testing, no less than Dingler's "will to certainty," involves a "moral decision": "it amounts to accepting a methodical practice for social life that has enormous consequences; it is a practice that is not only of great significance for the construction of theories, but also for their application and thus for the role played by knowledge in social life." Indeed, "the rational model of criticism is the scheme of a way of life, of a social practice, and has, therefore, ethical as well as political significance."[11] Albert draws these conclusion for ethics in section 12 ("Criticism and Ethics") of his *Treatise*. He also agrees with Popper that a rational philosophical foundation for ethical norms is impossible. He recommends instead that both existing moral systems and scientific theories be continually reexamined to see if they continue to be confirmed and stand up to alternative systems and theories.[12]

In what follows, I wish to submit "critical rationalism" to a metacritical examination — that is, an examination that, to begin with, will rely on nothing more than applying the method of critical rationalism to itself. From what has been said, it should already be apparent that my purpose cannot be to question the principle of "critical testing." (Who today, after all, would want to criticize "critical rationalism" in this sense?) Instead I would like to inquire into the conditions of the possibility of intersubjectively valid criticism — of the "critical testing" of scientific knowledge and moral norms. This approach, stemming from Kant, will enable me to call into question Albert's view that the denial of the possibility of philosophical foundations is connected to the positive program of "rational criticism." More specifically, I shall investigate whether — and if so, in what sense — the principle of foundations or justifying reasons can be replaced by the principle of criticism, or whether — and if so, in what sense — some type of philosophical foundation is not itself presupposed by the principle of intersubjectively valid criticism.

A Critical Reconstruction of the Münchhausen Trilemma

What does philosophical tradition really say about the problem of foundations? The problem has arisen repeatedly, ever since antiquity, in connection with the impossibility of a logico-mathematical (apodictic-deductive) derivation of the fundamental principles, or "axioms," of logico-mathematical thought and, thereby, of all the demonstrative sciences.[13] Put bluntly: ever since the time of Aristotle, the problem of foundations has been made a problem of philosophical significance precisely through the fact that logico-mathematical arguments can justify neither the truth of their own premises nor the validity of their rules of proof, but rather can only check "the transfer of the positive truth value, truth, from the set of premises to the conclusion and, in the opposite direction, the transfer of the negative truth value, falsehood, from the conclusion to the set of premises."[14] Since Descartes, the Aristotelian comprehension of axioms as intuited fundamental principles that are neither provable nor in need of proof[15] has been radicalized by taking evidence (or evidentness) as the requirement of philosophical foundations.[16] It is already clear that as long as the problem of philosophical foundations is conceived in traditional terms, it cannot be a matter of formal logic.

Albert at first seems to recognize this. For he does not understand Leibniz's "principle of sufficient reason" as it was understood in older logic textbooks, that is, as the most fundamental principle of thought, as an "axiom of logic." Rather, it becomes a "general postulate of the classical methodology of rational thought": it is understood as a "methodological principle" which presupposes that "the intelligibility of reality is connected with the determinateness of truth."[17] (As a matter of fact, the foundationalism of classical modern rationalism corresponds, in my opinion, to a subordination of logic — and of the ontological correspondence theory of truth — to the quest for evidence; epistemology is given the status of *prima philosophia*. This subordination of logic and ontology to evidence as the basic principle of the theory of knowledge is expressed most radically in the phenomenology of consciousness developed by Brentano and Husserl.)

In his treatment of the Münchhausen trilemma, however, Albert starts from the point of view of modern logic, invoking the authority of Popper and Carnap.[18] He gives the impression that he could explain the aporias of the rationalist postulate of philosophical foundations by a trilemma derived by formal logic alone, that is, by a trilemma that is in fact derived only on the condition that philosophical foundations be purely deductive. This condition leads to the alternatives: (1) infinite regress, (2) logical circle, and (3) ungrounded breaking off of the process of giving reasons.[19]

Now, whatever Albert's intention may have been, a critical reconstruction of his argument against classical rationalism must, in my opinion, make the following clear: no argument against the evidence postulate of classical rationalism is directly connected with the third alternative of the trilemma as derived by formal logical means. Rather, the trilemma can itself be understood as an explication of the problematic of axioms that Aristotle pointed out and that raised the problem of philosophical foundations in the first place. (If, with David Hilbert, we reduce the problem of the truth of the axioms of logic and mathematics to the problem of the absence of contradictions in "axiomatic systems," there results — corresponding to the Münchhausen trilemma — a metalogical or metamathematical aporia of the philosophical foundations of deduction itself, as Gödel, Church, and others have shown.)[20] Already this much is clear: unlike the logico-mathematical (and metalogical and metamathematical) problem of philosophical foundations, the modern principle of sufficient reason, as far as it requires an appeal to evidence, is from the start an epistemological principle — a principle that, to put it in a modern idiom, involves the pragmatic dimension of evidence for a knowing subject.

In our context this means that it would be legitimate to trace the aporia of philosophical foundations back to the third horn of the Münchhausen trilemma only if it could be proven that making evidence into a postulate is completely meaningless — that it, in effect, implies the replacement of the search for truth by an arbitrary decision. However, the required demonstration of the pointlessness of the evidence postulate cannot, in principle, be accomplished by formal logical means alone. How then can the demonstration be accomplished? Must not such a demonstration itself assume paradoxically that appeal to "evidence" is not an arbitrary decision, but rather indispensable to philosophical argumentation?

In order to avoid misunderstandings, I shall at this point make clear the strategy of my argumentation. In what follows I by no means wish to defend the position of classical rationalism that — in the sense of the Cartesian primacy of the theory of knowledge as a theory of consciousness — reduces the search for truth to the search for evidence. I do not, therefore, want to defend an empiricist or rationalist "philosophy of ultimate origins,"[21] a theory of knowledge that is supposed to be "a solution of the problem of origins and of validity all at once."[22] Such a strategy seems to me unpromising because epistemic evidence as such, however indispensable, is restricted to the evidential consciousness that has it. Traditional theory of knowledge, qua theory of consciousness, cannot show from its own conceptual resources how epistemic evidence — that is, the evidence accompanying judgments regarding conceptual syntheses of the ideas in some individual consciousness — can be carried over to the intersubjective validity of linguistically formulated statements. The goal of Popper and his followers, viz., intersubjectively valid statements, seems to me to be the proper methodological aim of the scientific-philosophical search for truth.[23] I completely agree with Popper and Albert that the "evidence" of convictions for a particular consciousness is not sufficient for the truth of statements. Beyond this, however, and quite contrary to Popper and his school, I shall argue that the fact that only the critical discourse of scientists can decide the intersubjective validity of scientific results has consequences for the theory of truth. In my opinion, the customary move in logical empiricism by which the linguistically mediated problematic of the intersubjective validity of statements is reduced to a (syntactic-semantical) logic of science, and the problems of traditional theory of knowledge are banished into psychology, just misunderstands the problem.

Albert seems to be of the same opinion, since in his discussion of the character of critical methodology he rightly rejects the reduction of the theory of science to an "application (or even a part) of formal logic, including the relevant elements of mathematics, even, in the best case, including elements of the semantics of artificial languages."[24] In light of "the contemporary distinction between syntax, semantics, and pragmatics,"

Albert calls for a consideration of "the epistemological relevance of pragmatics"[25] — of the linguistic and extralinguistic states of affairs that constitute the context of problematic statements. The pragmatic context includes, according to Albert, "those states of affairs which are the referents of the statements about them" and also "those states of affairs which make up the context of human epistemic activities — that is, not only the isolated activities of reflection and observation by single individuals, but also critical discussion as a model of social interaction and those institutions that support or weaken, encourage or discourage, critical discussion."[26] With good reason Albert draws the conclusion that his "criticism of the classical theory of knowledge" and the necessity, which he derives from this criticism, for a "choice between the principle of sufficient reason and the principle of critical examination" are matters that are to be dealt with "under the rubric of pragmatics."[27]

I would like not only to support this evaluation of the problem but moreover to take it seriously, since I understand the pragmatic conditions of the possibility of scientific knowledge, at least in part, as Kant did: as conditions of the possibility of intersubjectively valid knowledge and (scientific and philosophical) critique of knowledge — quite unlike Carnap and Hempel, who understood pragmatic conditions merely as the empirical sociological or psychological contexts irrelevant to the validity of knowledge. My assessment of pragmatics must be correct at least to the extent that the conflict, which occurs in "pragmatic realism," "between the principle of sufficient reason and the principle of critical examination" — whether or not it implies a decision between alternatives — is concerned with the conditions of the validity of scientific knowledge. I would like therefore to propose, as the philosophical extension of logical syntax and the semantics of ideal scientific languages, a transcendental pragmatics of language concerned with reflection on the subjective-intersubjective conditions of the possibility of linguistically formulated and, as such, intersubjectively valid knowledge. Here I shall attempt briefly to summarize the main lines of a transcendental semiotics — a transcendental-pragmatic reconstruction and extension of the foundations of the logic of language and science — that I have developed else-where.[28]

The possibility and necessity of a transcendental-pragmatic approach or method of inquiry is, in my opinion, demonstrable in a radical way by reflecting on the conditions of the possibility and the intersubjective validity of logical syntax and semantics themselves. As C. S. Peirce recognized, it is a logical implication of the three-dimensionality of the sign function, and thereby of sign-mediated knowledge and argumentation, that the in-tralinguistic (syntactic) sign functions and the reality-related (referential semantic) sign functions presuppose a (pragmatic) interpretation of the signs by a community of interpretation.[29] This presupposition obviously also applies to the correspond-ing semiotic disciplines; logical syntax and semantics are, as abstractive subdisciplines of semiotics, only a means of "in-direct" (that is, mediated through the construction of ideal systems of rules) elucidation of scientific-theoretical argu-mentation.[30] Hence, they are in principle dependent upon their extension and integration in a pragmatics of argumen-tation. This, however, means that pragmatics is the philosoph-ical discipline that deals with the subjective-intersubjective conditions of understanding meaning and of the formation of consensus in the ideal, unlimited, community of inquirers. Peirce already essentially conceived of such a semiotic trans-formation of the *Critique of Pure Reason,* in the sense of a "normative" semiotic logic of inquiry.[31]

On the one hand, Morris and Carnap accepted Peirce's foun-dations of semiotics, in the sense of the three-dimensionality of the sign function ("semiosis") and of the science of signs ("semiotics"); but — apparently because of the alleged impos-sibility of a noncontradictory self-reflection on the actual sub-jective conditions of sign interpretations[32] — they declared the pragmatic sign dimension to be the object of an empirical (behavioristic) discipline for which, at best, we might supply semantic conceptual explications in the form of a constructive, "pure, theoretical pragmatics." Whatever one thinks of the possibility of such a treatment of the pragmatics of language,[33] it is certain that the "conventions" that, according to Carnap, underlie the construction of formalizable syntactic-semantic systems of rules — and, to that extent, also underlie the construction of semantic explications of empirical-pragmatic concepts — cannot be thematized philosophically in this way. The normatively relevant conventions, which alone make possible the conceptual explications in a formal language necessary for a theoretical pragmatics, cannot themselves be made the object of such a pragmatics. Hence, the theoretical pragmatics that Carnap had in mind — and that he semanticized in a rather a priori fashion — cannot replace the methodological arguments that Popper and Albert find essential. In view of the contemporary demand for a semiotic transformation of transcendental philosophy, and in view of the fact that the presuppositions of modern constructive theories of language have not been rationally reflected upon, one might characterize the function of transcendental pragmatics for the philosophy of science as having to reflect on the conditions of the possibility and validity of conventions. A tacit substitute for such reflection within linguistic analysis can be found in Carnap's provisional, ordinary-language "introductions," which are — because of their use of implicitly self-referential "universally quantified propositions" — strictly speaking, expressed in an officially unlegitimizable "paralanguage." Here we find, in my opinion, the heritage of Wittgenstein's image of the ladder in the *Tractatus*. The problem for constructive semantics captured in this image cannot be overcome until we accept the transcendental pragmatics of language as an unformalizable fundamental metadiscipline.

In the framework of the present investigation, I would like to support this approach by examining the unavoidable question concerning the conditions of the possibility of intersubjectively valid criticism. I shall attempt to reconstruct and critically examine Albert's criticism of the classical postulate of sufficient reason from the point of view of transcendental pragmatics.

In this context I would first of all point out that the so-called Münchhausen trilemma facing any philosophical foundations can be logically derived only for sentences of an axiomatized system of propositions, in the sense of the syntactic-semantical construction of a so-called formal language. That is, such a logical derivation is only possible under prior abstraction from the pragmatic dimension of argumentative language use. To put it another way, only when one abstracts from the situation of the perceiving and argumentatively engaged subject, who offers his doubts and convictions for discussion in performatively explicable statements, is it possible to characterize the (deductively mediated) appeal to evidence as breaking off the process of giving reasons and to consider this presumed suspension, along with infinite regress and logical circularity, as the third horn of the trilemma. For only from the viewpoint of syntactic-semantic abstraction, which cannot anchor language and knowledge to the lifeworld through objective or subjective (personal) deixis, can the meaning of the process of giving reasons be understood as a deduction of sentences (about states of affairs) from sentences (about states of affairs) that in principle cannot be broken off. From the point of view of transcendental pragmatics, the logical process by which sentences are deduced from sentences — indeed, all "axiomatics" — can only be considered as an objectifiable means within the context of the argumentative grounding of statements through epistemic evidence. (In this sense Aristotle's "apodictic logic" is in fact an "organon" of argumentative discourse — no more, no less.) That is, the logical deduction of sentences from sentences is not itself the justification of the validity of knowledge — such an absolutization of the logical organon would in fact lead the problem of justification back to the Münchhausen trilemma — but is merely a mediating moment in the argumentative process of giving reasons, a moment that is indeed marked by a priori intersubjective evidence.

Corresponding to this is the following important distinction, which has been characteristically overlooked not only by logical empiricists but also — at least in *The Logic of Scientific Discovery* — by Popper. Only when one illegitimately abstracts, in the sense of an "abstractive fallacy," from the transcendental-pragmatic interpretative function of the subject of knowledge and argumentation, thereby reducing it to an object for empirical psychology, is it possible to maintain that sentences can only by justified by other sentences and that the so-called observation sentences or basic sentences are merely motivated by the experiential evidence of the knowing subject, in the sense of causation.[34] Against this the transcendental-pragmatic position takes the point of view of the argumentative knowing subject and attempts, not to explain (from the outside) his "behavior" in formulating sentences, but rather to understand it (from within): hence it must necessarily conceive of epistemic evidence as a reason for formulating observation sentences or basic sentences, although not as a reason from which these sentences might somehow be logically deduced.

It is by no means implied that epistemic evidence — for example, perceptions or ideal (categorical intuitions — is to be thought of as an unquestionable and sufficient, linguistically independent (that is, prelinguistic and intuitive) basis for the meaning and truth of scientific statements or systems of statements ("theories"). Such a view corresponds to the modern epistemological (empiricist or intellectualistic) philosophy of primordial origins, which I do not wish to defend, as I have already mentioned. In my opinion, by virtue of the "propositional acts" (the identifying "acts of reference and predication")[35] upon which the formation of judgments depends, epistemic evidence is interwoven from the outset with language use and the capacities of the knowing subjects — in the sense of the interweaving of knowledge, language use, and activities in quasi-institutionalized "language games" or "forms of life," as the later Wittgenstein analyzed them. If knowledge, language use, and so forth were not so interwoven, a child could not learn language or acquire modes of behavior based on an interpretation of experience; that is, one cannot imagine a functioning language game without paradigmatic experiential evidence. We could not communicate if we did not agree upon common experiential evidence, from which everything must proceed.

From this transcendental-pragmatic interweaving of possible epistemic evidence in language games, it follows, in my opinion, that the justification for the validity of knowledge can be equated neither with the logical deduction of sentences from sentences in axiomatized systems (as modern logic of language, or of science, does) nor with the appeal to nonlinguistic intuitive evidential consciousness (as Cartesian theory of knowledge urges). Rather, justification, as giving reasons for the validity of knowledge, must always rest on the possible evidential consciousness of the particular knowing subjects (as autonomous representatives of the transcendental knowing subject as such) and on the a priori intersubjective rules of an argumentative discourse in the context of which the epistemic evidence, as subjective proof or objective validity, has to be brought to the level of intersubjective validity. That this is necessary and also possible is guaranteed by the a priori transcendental-pragmatic "interweaving" of epistemic evidence, whose content is interpretable "as something," with the rules of language use that Wittgenstein elucidated and that have been concretized and made precise, especially by Austin, Strawson, and Searle, as an interweaving of judgment, reference, and predication in speech acts. According to this conception, it makes no sense to speak of "appeal to epistemic evidence" without presupposing linguistic discourse as a context for interpretation and logical coherence. Likewise, it makes no sense to speak of substantial argumentative discourse without presupposing certain epistemic evidence, which the particular participants of discourse apply as their criteria of truth in the argumentative procedure of building a consensus. This sort of interweaving of epistemic evidence in language games comprises, in my opinion, the transcendental-pragmatic explanation of the fact that all scientific discoveries are, as one says nowadays, "theory laden" and that the epistemic evidence that enters into "basic sentences" is more or less dependent upon those theories that are to be confirmed or falsified, or upon alternative theories.[36]

Now, one could perhaps take Albert's side and object that our treatment of the problem of philosophical foundations given by epistemic evidence begins with an inadequte, that is to say, already harmless explication of his concepts of "justification" and "evidence." One could say that the foundations, in the sense of evidence sought by classical rationalism, could only be absolutely certain or indubitable philosophical foundations. The methodological search for truth, in the sense of the principle of fallibilism, seems then indeed to be incompatible with the search for evidence, because it could not recognize any final or indubitable certainty. Let us examine this argument more closely, beginning with Albert's dictum that one "can fundamentally doubt everything."

Does the Principle of Fallibilism Contradict the Presupposition of Indubitable Evidence?

The principle of fallibilism, to my knowledge first put forward by C. S. Peirce, represents an indispensable presupposition in the methodology of empirical science.[37] It is this presupposition that distinguishes empirical science from the philosophical science of German Idealism, from philosophical science in the sense of Plato, or even Husserl, from a science justified by essential insight and seeking "episteme." But does not this distinction — as well as Albert's claimed insight into the difference between the search for evidence and the search for truth (or between criticism and justificatory rationalism) — presuppose in turn a certain evidential, essential insight in the sense of philosophical knowledge?

I do not want to claim that this rhetorical question contains a definitive counterargument against Bartley's pancritical rationalism; rather, I am willing to grant that the principle of fallibilism — in a sense to be explained later — is to be applied even with regard to the insights of the formal sciences (logic and mathematics) and transcendental philosophy. In compensation for this admission, I would like to claim — also in a sense to be explained later — that evidence in the sense of indubitable certainty is methodologically indispensable for the empirical sciences as well. I want to clarify the significance of my claims through a discussion of Albert's dictum that one "can fundamentally doubt everything."[38] The difficulty in this sentence, a sentence often casually pronounced by philosophers, is indicated by the historically remarkable circumstance that the founder of "fallibilism," Peirce, polemicized against Descartes with the argument that one could not doubt everything, if the doubt was not to amount to a contentless "paper doubt."[39] In empirical science a meaningful doubt presupposes, according to Peirce, that one does not doubt everything but rather proceeds from convictions that are taken as certain and assumed to be the standard both of what is to be doubted and of the new evidence considered possible in principle.

Quite similar arguments concerning the meaningfulness of doubting can be found in the later Wittgenstein.[40] We find in *On Certainty,* section 115, "Anyone who wanted to doubt everything would not get even as far as doubting. The game of doubt itself presupposes certainty." In other words, doubt — and thereby also criticism in Popper's and Albert's sense — is not explicable as a meaningful language game without in principle presupposing at the same time indubitable certainty. Wittgenstein generalized and radicalized this insight still further in section 114: "Whoever is certain about no facts, also cannot be certain of the meaning of his words."[41] In other words, every functioning language game (all agreement on meaning) presupposes that the communication partners, who must have learned the language at the same time as they acquired a well-established orientation toward the world, take numerous facts to be certain. In a real sense, convictions (be they principles or contingent facts) that are neither to be doubted nor to be changed function as "models" or "paradigms" of meaningful use.[42] Thus, the conviction that the earth is a sphere that rotates on its axis and revolves around the sun is a "paradigm" for possible meaningful questions in, say, the language game of aeronautics and meteorology. The conviction that there is a real external world, "outside" of consciousness, is a "paradigm" for the language of critically questioning whether something is real or is only based on delusion, illusion, hallucination, or something similar.

It seems to follow from this that argumentation in everyday life and science must have recourse to evidence that is presupposed in the appropriate language game. Thus, "appeal to evidence" cannot, at least in this sense, be equated with "appeal to dogma" or "appeal to an arbitrary decision," since criticism itself — as meaningful criticism in the framework of a language game — must be justified, at least virtually; that is, it too must in principle be based on "evidence." To put it differently, criticism cannot somehow — as it appeared to Bartley and Albert — be made into a self-sufficient, ultimate stage of rational argumentation; criticism presupposes a transcendental-pragmatic framework (a meaningful language game) in which various possible attempts at justification and various possible critical arguments correspond to each other, at least in principle, through common appeal to "paradigmatic" evidence. This analysis reveals the essential structure of the institution of argumentation. Wittgenstein had something like this in mind when he wrote, "All examination, all weakening and strengthening of any claim whatsoever, occurs within a system. And such a system is not a more or less arbitrary and doubtful starting point of all our arguments, rather it belongs to the very essence of what we call an argument. This system is not so much a point of departure as it is the element in which arguments live."[43]

In light of the kind of argument about the meaningfulness of doubt that Peirce and Wittgenstein advanced, numerous imprudent or exaggerated claims of Bartley's and Albert's "pancritical rationalism" prove to be untenable. The simple equation of sufficient grounding through a return to evidence with appeal to a dogma or an arbitrary decision, and the proposal to put "the idea of a critical examination in the place of the idea of justification," are two such claims. In fact, the language of the critical rationalists suggests, not infrequently, the misunderstanding of an anarchic criticism for criticism's sake, a critical reason without standards of criticism.

The discussion does not end here, since the point of critical rationalism does not yet seem to be fully grasped. It is now necessary to clarify the meaning of the principle of fallibilism, as formulated by Peirce.

In his discussion of Descartes, Peirce showed that one cannot doubt everything at once — say, the existence of a real outside world in toto;[44] rather, one can doubt virtually anything that is held to be certain — for instance, under the proper circumstances one might doubt the reality of each and every fact that is thought to pertain to the world outside of consciousness. This virtually universal doubt, for Peirce identical with the principle of fallibilism, also appears to be Albert's target when he writes, "A consistent criticism, which does not allow any dogma, necessarily involves a fallibilism with regard to every possible stage," and "There is neither a solution of the problem nor an appropriate stage for the solution of certain problems, which must necessarily and from the start elude criticism."[45]

But how is this fallibilism reconcilable with Peirce's and Wittgenstein's critical arguments about meaningfulness, according to which every doubt and every criticism must in principle (that is, as a constituent of a meaningful scientific argumentation game) be justified through what is presupposed as indubitable evidence?

Peirce himself found it difficult to reconcile his fallibilism with his notion of certainty within pragmatism, in the sense of "critical common sense"; and he did not, I think, satisfactorily resolve this problem.[46] It seems to me that the two Peircian principles can be considered consistent if and only if a distinction is made between the level of reflection of prescientific and scientific language games, on the one hand, and the level of transcendental-pragmatic reflection on the structure of language games in general, on the other. (In my opinion, this is not a question of an arbitrarily repeatable distinction between levels of reflection in the sense of psychology, or even of the formal hierarchy of metalanguages in metalogic; it is rather a distinction that should unequivocally distinguish the implicitly self-referential claim to universality of philosophical statements from the individual or empirically general claims to validity of nonphilosophical statements.)[47]

From the standpoint of philosophical reflection it may be said with regard to every language game, including the philosophical language game, that within its framework doubt and criticism are meaningful only under the presupposition that they can be sufficiently grounded by appeal to indubitable paradigmatic evidence. At the same time, it is also possible on this level of reflection to formulate a fallibilistic proviso, as a virtually universal doubt with regard to the paradigmatic evidence of all possible language games, except for the philosophical language game of doubt. Naturally, with this doubt all corresponding language games are made virtually nonfunctional (in the thought experiment to that effect). This is the case because every language game stands or falls (according to an insight of Wittgenstein later taken up by Thomas Kuhn in his analysis of "scientific revolutions") with paradigmatic evidence. Nevertheless, this virtually universal, metascientific doubt is not a "paper doubt" in Peirce's sense. This is because the fallibilistic proviso does not claim to doubt a statement of empirical science for empirical reasons, but only opens, or holds open, the possibility of doing so. Merely opening or holding open the possibility of justified doubt — that is, of justified criticism — on the level of metascientific reflection is not contentless inasmuch as it justifies the methodological postulate of the virtually universal attempt at well-justified criticism.

It may well be said that this argument covers the relevant meaning of "fallibilism" in the sense of Peirce and Popper, who made it a principle of the philosophy of science. At the same time, however, my argument is consistent with the transcendental-pragmatic insight of Peirce and Wittgenstein to the effect that doubt and criticism within the framework of the game of argumentation always presuppose justification by actually indubitable evidence (and by the expectation of possible evidence!) as the condition of their possibility. We must, however, inquire into the reason why the principle of fallibilism, in the sense of a principle of virtually universal criticism, and the principle of sufficiently grounding doubt and criticism through appeal to evidence can be consistent. It is not at all self-evident, but rather, philosophically remarkable that on the one hand, any evidence at the basis of a scientific theory must in principle be open to doubt and criticism, while on the other hand, criticism must be sufficiently justified, in the sense that all doubt and criticism must end with appeal to indubitable evidence. A satisfactory answer to this question, in my opinion, requires no more and no less than an appropriate transcendental-pragmatic distinction and mediation between the epistemological philosophy of ultimate origins and the twentieth-century philosophy of linguistic analysis.

This much seems clear to me: If the modern epistemological version of the philosophy of ultimate origins (whether in the form of empiricism or of rationalism) is correct in its claim to have reduced the intersubjective validity of knowledge to ("my") evidential consciousness, then it can hardly be understood how certain convictions may be doubted or criticized at all. If, on the other hand, the logic of science (oriented to the semantic analysis of sentences) is correct in its presupposition that sentences can only be justified by other sentences, while extralinguistic evidence of consciousness may only be considered as the source of external causal motives for the conventional formation of "basic statements," then it is inexplicable that criticism always presupposes possible justification by evidence. A resolution of this dilemma is, in my opinion, possible with the (transcendental-pragmatic) presupposition that evidential consciousness and intersubjective validity of linguistically formulated arguments are, on the one hand, irreducible aspects of the idea of truth and, on the other hand, always, as such, peculiarly interwoven with each other in language games.

This argument has two consequences. First, contrary to the view of the modern theory of knowledge from Descartes to Husserl, evidential consciousness *for me* (be it evidence in the sense of empirical perception or in the sense of ideal or categorical intuition) cannot in principle be equated with the intersubjective validity of arguments. The reason for this lies in the mediating function of language, conceived as the transcendental condition of the possibility of an intersubjectively valid interpretation of the world, a function overlooked from Descartes to Husserl. It seems to be a consequence of this mediating function that, to the extent that perceptual judgments possess a communicable objective content, in the form of an assertion that interpretively transcends the subjective sense data supporting them, they underlie any possible criticism: criticism now means nothing other than a possible reinterpretation of the perceptual evidence, which is itself indubitable. Kant postulated prelinguistic forms of connection and schemata of "consciousness in general" to account for the objectivity and intersubjectivity of "experiential judgments" that a priori transcend merely subjective perceptual evidence; and the modern "genetic epistemology" of Piaget appears to confirm this postulate by means of empirical psychology. It must be pointed out, however, that the prelinguistic conditions of consciousness postulated by Kant as conditions of the possibility of the intersubjective validity of knowledge are not, as Kant himself knew, sufficient conditions for the intersubjective validity of the empirical knowledge of science; further conditions are necessary to account for the validity of the empirical propositions of science. In addition, from the viewpoint of a transcendental pragmatics of language, it must be supposed that even synthetic a priori statements, which for Kant and Husserl were also certain a priori (for instance, the axioms of Euclidian geometry or the Husserlian statements concerning the simultaneity of color and extension), can be given the status of intersubjectively valid principles of science only insofar as such statements, on the basis of tacit conventions, function as paradigmatic evidence for argumentation in specific language games.

By means of this distinction and connection between the epistemological and the linguistic-pragmatic viewpoints, it becomes possible to explain why the so-called crisis of modern physics could question the intersubjective validity of the theoretical principles of classical physics on the basis of a reinterpretation of experience through explanatorily more powerful theories — and could do so despite the recognition of certain a priori evident connections between representations, as subjective conditions of the possibility of primary experience (for instance, conceptual connections in the sense of Kant's "forms of intuition" and "schematized categories"). In my opinion, the transcendental pragmatics of language lead here to a conclusion that is contrary to the theory of evidence: the answer to the question concerning the intersubjective validity of knowledge cannot be given by appealing to epistemic evidence for the individual consciousness (or even a priori evidence for "consciousness in general"); rather, intersubjective validity requires postulating a consensus that is to be reached through argumentative discourse in the community of inquirers (Peirce, Royce).[48]

This discussion of raising evidential consciousness to the level of paradigmatic evidence for language games shows, on the other hand, that the procedure of arriving at a consensus on the basis of argumentative discourse in the community of inquirers can in no way be understood without taking into account the appeal to epistemic evidence clarified by epistemology. Thus it is clear, for example, that the reinterpretations of our primary experience by means of explanatorily more powerful physical theories must in turn be sufficiently justified by appealing to evidence that is paradigmatic for these language games. As is the case with such scientific theories, this evidence need not have the character of direct, clear evidence of primary experience. Thus, for example, in the case of the Riemannian space presupposed by the general theory of relativity, one presupposes public paradigmatic evidence for a language game that is not evidence in the sense of ideal perceptual space. In this case, however, the empirical verification of the physical theory is carried out by means of measuring instruments, which for their part, in both their function and their manufacture, presuppose evidence in the sense of the perception of ideal space, which is paradigmatic in the "protophysical" language game of Euclidian geometry. This example, I believe, elucidates the a priori necessary connection between argumentation related to discourse and (sufficient justification by means of) appeal to epistemic evidence — a connection that is not considered in the semantically oriented logic of science. Although the evidential consciousness that is always mine does not guarantee the intersubjective validity of knowledge, still the argumentative redemption of claims to validity in a scientific language game must refer back ultimately to that evidence which can, in principle, ultimately be validated by every single member of the interpretation community in his or her (empirical or a priori) evidential consciousness.

Here, one should particularly note that the paradigmatic evidence, upon which Wittgenstein's criticism and doubt rest in the framework of a language game, is yet not identical with the originally experienced epistemic evidence, but rather, can and must directly refer back to conventions. Indeed, Wittgensteinian objections to Kant and Husserl are correct: without the mediation of such conventions, epistemic evidence could not function as paradigmatic evidence for language games. The conventions of paradigmatic evidence as such, however, can in no way be traced back to an arbitrary decision; rather, as evidence presented in argumentation, they must be justified, however indirectly — for example, in the empirical verification of theories that they support — by reference to that original (empirical or a priori) evidential consciousness, of which they attempt to give a convincing interpretation. From the point of view of a transcendental pragmatics of language, the fact that evidential consciousness achieves intersubjective validity only as publicly acknowledged language game paradigms shows that giving reasons in arguments necessarily leads back to appeals to epistemic evidence.

It is not yet clear, however, how the transcendental-pragmatic mediation between the philosophy of consciousness and analytic philosophy of language yields an argument in favor of philosophical foundations. Indeed, the metascientific grounding of the principle of fallibilism appears to have shown that all indubitable epistemic evidence must be looked upon as relative to certain language games that can in principle be transcended by means of critical reflection. Thus, it appears that at the philosophical level of a reflection upon validity, the principle of (progressive) criticism does have priority over the principle of sufficient justification through appeal to evidence. The evidence presupposed in special argumentative language games is to be considered in principle revisable, while permanent criticism, which may presuppose in every particular context an appeal to evidence, retains, it seems, the last word on the level of philosophical reflection, which transcends all particular language games.

At this point we should recall that the reason why criticism appears to retain the last word on the (metascientific) level of philosophical reflection is that there exists a philosophical language game in which the scope of all language games can from the outset be discussed, and with a claim to universal validity. (Wittgenstein sought to minimize this claim through the notion of simple family "resemblances" among [language] "games";[49] and the main line of analytic philosophy of science, including Russell, Carnap, and Tarski, objected to the implicit self-referentiality of the universal validity claim of philosophical discourse — although since Russell's theory of types these objections could themselves be articulated with universal validity only at the cost of self-contradiction.)[50] With regard to the critical rationalism of Popper, however, it is indisputable that he can justify his claim to replace the postulate of sufficient reason by means of principle of criticism only by making a universal a priori validity claim in philosophical argumentation. Here, however, we immediately face the prospect of a new problem of justification, involving an appeal to evidence that cannot be doubted and criticized — at least not in the same way as the paradigmatic evidence of those language games that could be seen by philosophy as revisable and to that extent could be transcended. Corresponding to the reasons that seemed to speak for the final priority of criticism — that is, to the fact that philosophical reflection can and must consider all paradigmatic evidence as in principle revisable — we now have the fact that the philosophical language game itself must be able to appeal to evidence that in principle is not identical with any of the empirically revisable language game paradigms. In this way we can argue for the priority of philosophical foundations over the principle of permanent criticism.

Philosophical Foundations via Transcendental-Pragmatic Reflection on the Conditions of Possibility of the Intersubjective Validity of Philosophical Argumentation

Before I make a final attempt to show the indubitability of certain paradigmatic evidence in the language game of philosophical argumentation, I would like to settle the question of whether, and to what extent, the principle of fallibilism is also to be employed in philosophical argumentation.

First, it should be noted that even logico-mathematical deductions are fallible, trivially, inasmuch as with regard to their pragmatic dimension they are the operations of finite men and thus can go wrong. In this respect I can gladly concede to critical rationalism that human reason in the psychological sense is always fallible. The philosopher too can never be certain that he isn't in error. But this does not mean that it makes sense to assume in either the enterprise of argumentation or that of criticism that one is always in error, or that the use of the concepts "argumentation" and "criticism" could be meaningful without indubitable presuppositions. More important than the empirical pragmatic concession that even logico-mathematical thought is always fallibilistic is the transcendental-pragmatic insight that the metalogical or metamathematical demonstrability of the absence of contradictions in axiomatic logico-mathematical systems remains in principle incomplete. Earlier, following Hans Lenk, I allowed this to be one aspect of the Münchhausen trilemma of deductively justified philosophical foundations. At the same time, however, I pointed out that this does not at all reduce the question of reflexive foundations to absurdity, but rather actually raises it. In the present context I want to appropriate the insight into the incompleteness of all demonstrations of an absence of contradictions as an aspect of reflexive transcendental-philosophical insight — that is, of insight into both the conditions of the possibility and the limits of the objectification of arguments in axiomatized and formalized language systems.

It is difficult to conceive how this insight from the extended critique of reason could be revised in its transcendental-philosophical core. Nevertheless, one never knows definitively what belongs to the transcendental philosophical core and what belongs to the complex of results that are revisable through advances in metamathematics or metalogic. To that extent, the transcendental-pragmatic interpretation of the results of metalogic or metamathematics can give an indication of the general problem of transcendental philosophy, whose situation is here somewhat different than in Kant. The Kantian claim of the definitive completeness of the "system of pure reason" can no longer be sustained; our task is rather that of progressively opening up transcendental horizons, which grow wider with the expansion of the human knowledge that we are questioning as to conditions of possibility. It in no way follows from this, however, that the principle of fallibilism, and the principle of virtually universal criticism derived from it, could show the absurdity of the postulate of transcendental-philosophical foundations or function as its replacement.

That this is impossible is shown by the fact that the application of the principle of fallibilism itself leads to something similar to the "liar paradox." If the principle of fallibilism is itself fallible, it is just to that extent not fallible, and vice versa. This application of the critical-rationalist principle of fallibilism to itself can hardly be rejected as meaningless by critical rationalists; for it is precisely they who absolutized the methodological principle of fallibilism beyond its original application to empirical science. In my opinion, it follows from this, with all the clarity one could wish, that pancritical rationalism represents an untenable standpoint, or at least an exaggeration. The principle of fallibilism and the principle of criticism derived from it are meaningful and valid only if they are restricted in their validity from the outset, so that at least some philosophical evidence is excluded from possible criticism — namely the evidence on which these principles themselves are based. In this way the transcendental-pragmatic dimension of the noncriticizable conditions of possibility of intersubjectively valid philosophical criticism and self-criticism is brought out in a sufficiently radical way. What are these conditions? In this question, I believe, is posed the problem of philosophical foundations.

That the principle of pancritical rationalism does not belong to the uncritical conditions of possibility of philosophical criticism can be seen in the successful self-criticism of pancritical rationalism by its founder, W. W. Bartley. Bartley found that logic manifestly does "not also belong to that totality . . . which should be subject to proof," since "the exercise of critical argumentation and logic are inseparably bound together."[51] In critical discussion with Bartley and Albert, Hans Lenk made Bartley's observation more precise. He stated that "at least some logical rules are fundamentally removed from rational revision."[52] Still more interesting to me is Lenk's remark that the stated rules of some minimal logic are removed a priori from criticism because they are analytically bound to the (idea of the) institution of criticism itself.[53] Thus, the rules of a minimal logic are seen as belonging to the paradigmatic evidence of that institution or language game, which can only be disclosed in transcendental pragmatic reflection upon the conditions of the possibility of criticism itself. I will call this institution the transcendental language game. Concerning this language game, the previously cited insight of the later Wittgenstein is emphatically valid: this language game as a "system" belongs "to the essence of what we call an argument": it is, so to speak, "the element in which arguments live."[54]

Laying bare this system of argumentation in transcendental pragmatics provides philosophical foundations in a nondeductive manner, since its paradigmatic evidence is precisely of a kind that can neither be called into question by criticism without performative self-contradiction nor be justified deductively without presupposing itself. The contemporary discussion of the problem of foundations, which is usually oriented toward axiomatic systems of logic, would certainly interpret this situation differently: it would be seen as showing that some evidence — for example, the logic of justification itself — can neither be denied without self-contradiction nor be justified without *petitio principii*. Therefore, it is said, ultimate foundations must be superseded by some ultimate decision — somewhat in the sense of the self-confidence of reason as opposed to skepticism (Stegmüller)[55] or in the sense of belonging to the institution of critical discussion as opposed to obscurantism (Popper).[56] This "solution" to the problem of philosophical foundations clearly corresponds again to the purely logically derived Münchhausen trilemma in Albert's sense, if one disregards the fact that Stegmüller understands "appeal to evidence" not as "appeal to dogma" but rather as a necessity of all philosophizing that cannot be denied without self-contradiction, but that cannot be logically demonstrated without a *petitio principii*.

In light of our transcendental-pragmatic reflection, however, the problem as presented by these philosophers is the result of absolutizing the objectivization and externalization of argumentation that is presupposed by the axiomatic method — that is, the "estrangement" of arguments into syntactic-semantically interpreted sentences and systems of sentences. The analysis of such sentences abstracts from the transcendental-pragmatic dimension of the self-reflection of the arguing subject. Under this abstractive presupposition all paradigmatic evidence of the transcendental language game (such as, for instance, the validity of a minimal logic) must, of course, have the status of unprovable presuppositions of any proof. And the attempt to justify the necessity of such presuppositions now must look like some bad sophistic attempt at a proof by begging the question; for on the abstract level of an axiomatized sentence system there is no difference between arbitrarily chosen presuppositions and presuppositions that one must presuppose in all possible proofs because one cannot deny then without actual self-contradiction. Thus philosophy seems doomed to resignation in regard to the problem of foundations. As Bar-Hillel argues, the logical semantics of sentences and sentence systems can only indirectly clarify argumentation in ordinary language, which is pragmatically integrated in principle; this sort of clarification is based on an abstraction from the pragmatic dimension that has to be overcome if the significance of axiomatic systems is to be brought to bear in the context of argumentation.[57] Therefore, the reduction of the meaning of philosophical foundations to the deduction of sentences from sentences (or to the metalogical proof of an absence of contradictions in certain sentence systems) appears to me to be an illegitimate reduction resting on an "abstractive fallacy" that pervades recent, purely syntactic-semantically oriented logic of scientific inquiry. When this logic is absolutized into a philosophy of argumentation, it commits an abstractive fallacy; it banishes to the domain of empirical psychology the pragmatic dimension of argumentation that cannot be objectivized and formalized (for instance, the self-reflection of participants in argumentation as expressed in performative acts of asserting). The discussion of the impossibility of providing philosophical foundations rests on a confusion between argumentation as originally related to the dialogic situation of assertion and refutation — which was for Socrates the basis of philosophizing — and Aristotle's apodictic science, which, however, could only be an organon of argumentation purified of all possible pragmatic intrusions.[58]

If, however, this abstractive fallacy is reversed by admitting transcendental-pragmatic reflection upon the subjective-intersubjective conditions of the possibility of intersubjectively valid argumentation, then the problem of philosophical foundations appears in a completely different light. The insight that certain evidence cannot be deductively grounded without presupposing itself (for example, the paradigmatic evidence of a minimal logic in the framework of an as yet unclarified transcendental language game) is no longer a proof of the impossibility in principle of philosophical foundations but rather a reflexive, transcendental-pragmatic insight into the uncriticizable foundation of argumentation itself. If, on the one hand, a presupposition cannot be challenged in argumentation without actual performative self-contradiction, and if, on the other hand, it cannot be deductively grounded without formal-logical *petitio principii*, then it belongs to those transcendental-pragmatic presuppositions of argumentation that one must always (already) have accepted, if the language game of argumentation is to be meaningful. One can, therefore, also call this a transcendental-pragmatic argument for foundations on the basis of critical arguments concerning the meaningfulness of certain practices.

As far as I can see, this reflexive transcendental-pragmatic argument for philosophical foundations is confirmed by a critical yet affirmative reconstruction of the argument of Cartesian doubt. In this way it can be shown, for example, that Descartes unreflectively undermines the possible significance of the language game he uses when he grants, in the course of his methodological doubt, that in the end all that is supposed to be real might be merely his dream, viz., merely in consciousness. If all that is supposed to be real is merely a dream, then precisely the critical significance of the expression "merely a dream" (or "merely in consciousness") cannot be maintained, since it presupposes as paradigmatic evidence that all is not merely a dream (or merely in consciousness). However, this pseudo-argument, which manifestly rests upon Descartes's illegitimate abstraction of the methodical-solipsistic search for evidence from the a priori of the language game of argumentation, can be revised, as it was by Peirce and Popper, into a virtually universal doubt (viz., the principle of fallibilism). If one undertakes this correction, then the proper significance of the Cartesian doubt is revealed, in that the certainty of the "dubito, cogito, ergo sum" can also not be doubted in the sense of the virtually universal doubt of all that is supposed to be real. What is the basis for the certainty of the "cogito, ergo sum"?

It cannot rest upon the fact that (in the sense of logical semantics) a syllogistic inference is made from thinking to the existence of that which thinks, as Hintikka showed in 1963, using the conceptual apparatus of Austin's speech act theory.[59] Descartes himself repeatedly denied that the cogito was based on such an inference. Hintikka, however, explicitly states the reason why such an interpretation is inadmissible: in the use of a syllogistic inference from thinking to the existence of that which thinks, the existence of the thinking being must be tacitly presupposed in order to reject the thinking of a fictitious person (say, Hamlet) as irrelevant. In other words, the certainty of the "cogito, ergo sum" cannot be logically demonstrated in any direct way. In this sense Descartes does not supply any philosophical foundations that could be affirmatively reconstructed. That the same person who thinks also exists is, from the viewpoint of formal logic, a claim that, in the sense of the Stegmüllerian dilemma, can be neither denied without self-contradiction nor demonstrated without *petitio principii*; for it cannot be made in the case of a fictitious person such as Hamlet, but rather only in the case of an existing thinker. For just that reason, however, the certainty of the "ego cogito, ergo sum" is a transcendental-pragmatic condition of the possibility of the language game of argumentation in our sense. How can this be shown? As Hintikka demonstrates, that my doubting or thinking guarantees my existence rests upon the fact that when I perform the act of doubting my existence — an act that is explicitly expressed in the sentence "I doubt herewith, now, that I exist" — I refute the sense of that very sentence for myself and, virtually, for every dialogue partner.[60] In other words, the propositional component contradicts the performative component of the speech act expressed by that self-referential sentence. The irrefutable certainty of the "cogito, ergo sum" thus rests not on an axiomatically objectifiable deductive relation between sentences, but rather on a transcendental-pragmatic reflexive insight mediated by the actual self-reflexivity of the act of thinking or speaking.

Hintikka remarks in addition that not only is the assertion "I do not exist" refuted by the thought or speech act that is its performance, but this is also true of the assertion "You do not exist." I would explain this as follows: Someone who used such an expression in, say, an exorcism aimed at a ghostly apparition would in truth not be denying existence to an object by means of an act of predication; rather, he would be canceling the expression of address, that is, he would be reflexively designating his communicative act as failed. I prefer to see in this an indication that the irrefutable certainty of the "ego cogito, ergo sum" does not rest upon the primacy of "inner experience," the "introspection" of an in principle solitary consciousness, as is assumed in the Cartesian theory of "evidence," right up to Franz Brentano; rather, it rests upon the primacy of an experience of the situation that is simultaneously communicative and reflexive, an experience in which actual self-understanding (and with it ego-consciousness) and understanding the existence of the other are equiprimordial — as is convincingly maintained by Mead and Heidegger. Confirmation of personal existence in the performatively understood "ego cogito, ergo sum" is only possible as an understanding with oneself about oneself, and that is to say, as part of a virtually public discussion — more precisely, as the deficient mode of such a discussion in which I am the other for myself. It is precisely this virtual publicity that is attested to in the fact that reflexive self-certainty can be made explicit with the help of a performative speech act.

Therefore, the certainty of the "cogito, sum" is not, as Husserl would have it in *Cartesian Meditations*, to be understood in such a way that it cannot be formulated in the "communicative plural."[61] In such an *epoche* of "methodological solipsism," in which the existence of other subjects is bracketed along with the real world, the evidence of Cartesian insight could in principle not be formulated in the sense of an intersubjectively valid philosophical judgment. Every one of us can see, with subjective evidence and with an a priori intersubjective claim to validity, that he cannot doubt the existence of his own ego without actual self-contradiction.[62] Unless Husserl could somehow formulate this statement in the "communicative plural," he could not bring to our knowledge the results of his transcendental reduction or *epoche* — that is, the insight, to which he gives the status of certainty, into the irreducibility of the sphere of the pure noetic-intentional, meaning-constitutive ego and its noematic correlates. This can be applied even more radically: Like Descartes, Husserl could not even bring to his own consciousness the indubitability of his ego-consciousness, in a form both intelligible and valid for him, unless he could formulate this insight as an argument in the framework of a transcendental language game of an ideal communication community. To sum up: Along with ego-consciousness, a language game is presupposed as the *fundamentum inconcussum* in the sense of the critically reconstructed and transformed Cartesian tradition of philosophical foundations. In this language game the existence of a real lifeworld and the existence of a communication community are presupposed along with the actual evidence of thinking myself as existing in the sense of paradigmatic language-game evidence. For it is of prime importance that the Cartesian insight (solitary as it actually is) must be capable of being reexamined and, in this case, also capable of being confirmed by a communication community that is in principle indefinite. This transcendental-pragmatic version of the Cartesian insight could be valid, in principle, in the form of an a priori certain and at the same time a priori intersubjectively valid judgment even for a man who happened to be the last representative of the communication community and thus was alone in an empirical sense. Even this man would have to presuppose (1) that there must have been a real communication community and (2) that there might be an unlimited ideal communication community, both capable in principle of confirming his certain insight.[63]

From this I conclude that the "vital element" of philosophical arguments is a transcendental language game in which, along with some rules of logic and the existence of a real world, something like the transcendental-pragmatic rules or norms of ideal communication are presupposed. The individual can secure a priori certainty in the solitary thought of his existence only by appealing to this transcendental language game and its rules. This means, however, that the individual cannot step into or out of the "institution" of this transcendental language game of critical argumentation in the same way we suppose he can in the case of empirical "language games" and "institutions" as "forms of life" (Wittgenstein).[64] Rather, as a successfully socialized *homo sapiens* with "communicative competence,"[65] he is necessarily constituted as a being who has identified himself with the ideal communication community in the indicated sense and who has also implicitly accepted the transcendental-pragmatic rules of communication as ethically relevant norms. This is not contradicted by our capacity to bring to consciousness the discrepancy between the normative ideal of the ideal communication community and real situations of discussion. It seems to me that this suggests instead the possibility of finding the presuppositions for a transcendental-pragmatic grounding of ethics in the a priori of communication presupposed by rational argumentation — more precisely, in the contradiction (which cannot be resolved by formal logical means) between the presupposition of a real communication community (including our real selves) and the situation of an ideal communication community that is necessarily "counterfactually anticipated" in that presupposition.[66] To that extent, the "institution" of the transcendental language game turns out to be rather different from the conventionally based institutions of empirically describable "language games" or "forms of life," in Wittgenstein's sense.[67] More accurately, the former institution could be characterized as the meta-institution of all possible human institutions,[68] since it involves the conditions of the possibility of transparent and rational conventions ("agreements"). Man can withdraw from this institution only at the price of losing the possibility of identifying himself as a meaningfully acting being — for instance, in suicide from existential despair or in the pathological process of paranoid-autistic loss of self.

Therefore — to draw the final conclusion — one cannot choose this rational form of life in an "irrational choice," as Popper would have it,[69] since any choice that could be understood as meaningful already presupposes the transcendental language game as its condition of possibility. Only under the rational presupposition of intersubjective rules can deciding in the presence of alternatives be understood as meaningful behavior. From this it does not follow that every decision is rational, but only that a decision in favor of the principle of rational legitimation of the criticism of behavior according to rules is rational a priori. In that respect the decision in favor of the "framework" of critical argumentation or discussion demanded by Popper can only be understood as an a priori rational and deliberate affirmation of the transcendental language-game rules that are always already implicitly accepted as valid. Such a decision — which is even to be repeated again and again, particularly in "existential boundary situations" — is indeed required in the interest of the realization of reason.[70] However, reason in no way needs to replace, through a decision, its rational justification, as is demanded by decisionism. For it can always confirm its own legitimation through reflection on the fact that it presupposes its own self-understanding of the very rules it opts for. Popper's assertion that irrationalism can be defended without self-contradiction because one can refuse to accept the argument[71] is simply false, since the defense of irrationalism actually refutes the attempt to refuse to engage in argumentation — it refutes it, that is, through the accompanying performative act. The effective refusal to engage in rational argumentation (or a corresponding self-understanding) is on the other hand a very much more serious matter than Popper seems to assume; it is an act of self-negation and, moreover, of self-destruction, as I have already indicated.[72] Even in such a case, however, the person making the decision must himself presuppose the denied principle so long as he understands his own decision as such. Otherwise, philosophical decisionism (upon which, in the final analysis, Popper's arguments for critical rationalism rest) could not treat the act of denying reason as an intelligible possibility of human choice.

With that I can summarize the issue at stake in this attempt at a metacriticism of critical rationalism. Critical rationalism cannot, it seems to me, succeed in putting the principle of criticism as such in the place of the principle of philosophical foundations, because its criticism of this principle — like every meaningful criticism — itself needs justification. Justification of the principle of criticism is, however, possible if and only if the principle is not absolute — if and only if it is restricted by the principle of the self-justification of critical reason through transcendental reflection upon the conditions of its own possibility.[73] The point of philosophical foundations lies, then, in the reflexive — transcendental-pragmatic and not deductive — argument that one can discursively or practically decide neither for nor against the rules of the transcendental language game without these rules being presupposed.

Notes

1. H. Albert, *Traktat über kritische Vernunft* (Tübingen, 1968, 1969), p. 15. English translation: *Treatise on Critical Reason* (Princeton, 1985), p. 14. All citations of Albert are according to the English translation.

2. W. W. Bartley, *The Retreat from Commitment* (Lasalle, 1984).

3. Albert, p. 18.

4. Albert, p. 18.

5. Cf. Albert, p. 12, as well as pp. 13–38.

6. Albert, p. 19.

7. Albert, p. 19.

8. Albert, p. 40.

9. Albert, pp. 44, 46–47.

10. Albert, pp. 46–47.

11. Albert, p. 49ff.

12. Cf. Albert, p. 72ff.

13. Aristotle's justification of the principle of noncontradiction can serve as an illustration of the classical problem of ultimate foundations. After Aristotle first explains the nature of the so-called axioms of the mathematicians and then presents the principle of noncontradiction as an example of an axiom, he continues:

Some indeed demand that even this shall be demonstrated, but this they do through want of education, for not to know of what things one should demand demonstration, and of what one should not, argues want of education. For it is impossible that there should be demonstration of absolutely everything (there would be an infinite regress, so that there would still be no demonstration); . . . We can, however, demonstrate negatively even that this view is impossible, if our opponent will only say something; and if he says nothing it is absurd to seek to give an account of our views to one who cannot give an account of anything, insofar as he cannot do so. For such a man, as such, is from the start no better than a vegetable. Now negative demonstration I distinguish from demonstration proper, because in a demonstration one might be thought to be begging the question, but if another person is responsible for the assumption we shall have negative proof, not demonstration.

The Transformation of Philosophy: Systematic Proposals

Aristotle, *Metaphysics*, trans. Arthur Platt, McKean ed. (New York, 1941), bk. 4, 10006a6–18.

14. Albert, p. 17.

15. Cf. Aristotle, *Anal. Post.* I, 2, 71b20ff.

16. To speak more precisely, Descartes ranks evidence (in the sense of "clara et distincta perceptio") above truth (in the sense of the ontological correspondence between thoughts and states of affairs) and in this way raises self-consciousness, as certain of its own being, to the "first principle" of his philosophy. Under the axioms that are grounded in clear and distinct ideas, Descartes first mentions the sentence, "All that is has a cause or a reason." (Cf., for example, *Principia* I, 11.52, and *Oeuvres*, Adam/Tannery ed., 7, 112, 135ff., and 164).

17. Albert, pp. 12–13ff.

18. Cf. Albert, p. 16.

19. Cf. Albert, p. 18.

20. Cf. Hans Lenk, "Philosophische Logikbegründung und rationaler Kritizismus," in *Metalogik und Sprachanalyse* (Freiburg, 1973), pp. 88–109.

21. Under this title T. W. Adorno distances himself from the same type of modern theory of knowledge that Albert rejects.

22. Albert, p. 30.

23. The absolute necessity of linguistic argumentation is correctly emphasized by Popper, for instance, in his arguments against the intuitionist grounding of mathematics in a theory of evidence. According to Popper, only argumentation can ultimately give rise to a decision concerning the validity of mathematical sentences. "As soon as the admissibility of a mathematical construction proposed by intuitionism can be called into question (and, naturally, it can be called into question), language proves to be more than a mere means of communication which would be in principle superfluous. It proves to be rather an indispensable medium of discussion." Popper, "Epistemology without a Knowing Subject," in *Proceedings of the Third International Congress for Logic, Methodology, and Philosophy of Science*, Rootselaar-Stall ed. (Amsterdam, 1968), p. 360; reprinted in *Objective Knowledge* (Oxford, 1972), pp. 106–152.

24. Albert, p. 52.

25. Albert, p. 53.

26. Albert, p. 52.

27. Albert, p. 52.

28. Cf. K.-O. Apel, "Programmatische Bemerkungen zur Idee einer transzendentalen Sprachpragmatik," in *Studia Philosophica in Honorem Sven Krohn*, ed. Timo Airaksinen et al. (Turku, 1973), pp. 11–36, and also in *Semantics and Communication*, ed. C. H. Heidrich (Amsterdam, London, New York, 1974), p. 79ff.; and cf. "Zur Idee einer transzendentalen Sprachpragmatik," in *Aspekte und Probleme der Sprachphilosophie*, ed. J. Simon (Freiburg, 1974). See also my "Sprechakttheorie und transzendentale Pragmatik: zur Frage ethischer Normen," in *Sprachpragmatik und Philosophie*, ed. K.-O. Apel (Frankfurt a.M., 1975), pp. 10–173.

29. Cf. my introduction to C.S. Peirce, *Schriften II* (Frankfurt, 1979). Eng. trans. *Charles Sanders Peirce: From Pragmatism to Pragmaticism* (Amherst, 1981).

30. Cf. Y. Bar-Hillel, "Argumentation in Pragmatic Languages," in *Aspects of Language,* ed. Y. Bar-Hillel (Jerusalem, 1970), p. 208ff.

31. Cf. my essay, "Von Kant zu Peirce: die semiotische Transformation der transzendentalen Logik," in *Transformation der Philosophie,* K.-O. Apel (Frankfurt, 1972), vol. 2, p. 157ff. Eng. trans. "From Kant to Peirce: The Semiotical Transformaton of Transcendental Logic," in *Kant's Theory of Knowledge,* ed. L. W. Beck (Dordrecht, Boston, 1974).

32. Cf., for example, C. W. Morris, *Writings on the General Theory of Signs* (The Hague, 1971), p. 46ff. and p. 56ff.

33. Cf. my critical introduction to C. Morris's *Zeichen, Sprache und Verhalten* (Düsseldorf, 1973).

34. As Popper wrote in *The Logic of Scientific Discovery* (London, 1959), p. 105, "Experiences can *motivate a decision,* and hence an acceptance or a rejection of a statement, but a basic statement cannot be justified by them — no more than by thumping on the table." Popper even speaks alternately of a motivational and a causal relation (cf. P. Bernays, "Reflections on Karl Popper's Epistemology," in *The Critical Approach to Science and Philosophy, Essays in Honor of Karl Popper* [London, 1964], p. 38). Albrecht Wellmer correctly remarks, "The method of linguistic analysis, which Popper holds in low esteem, is not necessary for demonstrating the untenability of the conception of a motivational relation between experience and its linguistic articulation. . . . Popper overlooks the fact that not only experientially based sentences but also experience itself transcends our momentary here and now." (*Methodologie als Erkenntnistheorie. Zur Wissenschaftslehre Karl R. Popper* [Frankfurt, 1967], p. 156ff.) Like the logical empiricists, Popper is unable to think of a conceptual alternative to the disjunctive logical relation between sentences and empirical-psychological (external-causal) motivational contexts, or between linguistic universals and prelinguistic evidential experiences. And under this (nominalistic) presupposition, Popper is correct in discarding as psychologism the "protocol sentences" qua "experience protocols" of the neopositivists. (Cf. *The Logic of Scientific Discovery,* p. 95ff.) He leaves himself no alternative but to trace back the validity of the "basic statement" to a "basic decision."

Suppose, however, that our evident experiences are always linguistically interpreted experiences and as such transcend the momentary here and now. Then two things follow: first, their evidence, as dependent on interpretation, can never be considered infallible; and second, such evidence can and must function as the internal justification of the meaning content of our linguistically articulated judgments of experience. One will certainly not appeal to such experiential evidence in the way that a psychologist explains the convictions of a man by means of experiential evidence qua cause. But one will appeal to it, in argumentation (and also in critical argumentation), as subjective testimony concerning objective evidence. Popper is unacquainted with this concept of evidence, which is presupposed in transcendental phenomenology. Rather, he equates (as does logical empiricism, only more consistently as regards the verdict of psychologism) "evidence" in the sense of the theory of knowledge with evidential experience or evidential feeling in the sense of empirical psychology (Popper, p. 46ff. and p. 99ff.) — as if evidence did not also belong to the necessary but not sufficient conditions of the validity of psychological knowledge. If one reduces the criterion of truth (in the sense of a never infallible indicator) or objective evidence (which, to be sure, must be capable of being had by a knowing subject) to the psychological status of a subjective evidential feeling, then it certainly becomes necessary to replace the notion of something being objectively justified with the notion of unlimited testability or criticizability. But without the presupposition of possible evidence, what meaning does the very idea of testing or criticizing really have? Reference to the fact that an infinite regress can be avoided in practice by a decision can scarcely be a satisfactory answer to the question concerning the positive meaning of criticism.

35. Cf. John Searle, *Speech Acts* (Cambridge, 1969), chap. 2.

36. I cannot here go into the consequences that, in the philosophy of science, result from the notion of the interweaving of evidence in language games. Suffice it to say that experiential evidence can no more be seen as an interpretation-free basis for the intersubjective validity of knowledge than its being interwoven in language games can be understood as clear dependence on theoretically precise language use. Such a consequence — drawn by followers of Kuhn, particularly Feyerabend — leads to a relativism of language games or of theories, which Popper has correctly characterized as the "myth of the frameworks." Not only are there "language games," but also, within all such language games, there is the transcendental language game of the unlimited communication community.

37. Cf. my edition of C. S. Peirce, *Schriften I und II* (Frankfurt, 1967 and 1970), subject index.

38. Albert, p. 14.

39. C. S. Peirce, *Collected Papers*, 5 (Cambridge, Massachusetts: Harvard University Press, 1933), §§ 265 and 376.

40. For steering me to the following Wittgenstein references, I am particularly indebted to an unpublished paper by Dieter Mans.

41. L. Wittgenstein, *On Certainty* (New York, 1969), p. 114.

42. Cf., for example, L. Wittgenstein, *Philosophical Investigations* (New York: Macmillan, 1958; trans. Anscombe), § 50:

There is *one* thing of which one can say neither that it is one meter long nor that it is not one meter long, and that is the standard meter in Paris. But this is, of course, not to ascribe any extraordinary property to it, but only to mark its peculiar role in the language game of measuring with a meter rule. Let us imagine samples of color being preserved in Paris like the standard meter. We define: "sepia" means the color of the standard sepia which is kept there hermetically sealed. . . . We can put it like this: This sample is an instrument of the language used in ascriptions of color. . . . What looks as if it *had* to exist is part of the language. It is a paradigm in our language game; something with which comparison is made.

In addition, § 300:

It is — we should like to say — not merely the picture of the behavior that plays a part in the language game with the words "he is in pain," but also the picture of the pain. Or, not merely the paradigm of the behavior, but also that of the pain.

With clear reference to a priori certain convictions, is the following in *Remarks on the Foundations of Mathematics* (Oxford, 1956, p. 30ff.; trans. Anscombe):

Whence comes the feeling that "white is lighter than black" expresses something about the *essence* of the two colors? . . . Is it not like this: the picture of a black and a white patch . . . serves us *simultaneously* as a paradigm of what we understand by "lighter" and "darker" and as a paradigm for "white" and for "black" . . . . That connection, a connection of the paradigms and the names, is set up in our language. And our proposition is nontemporal because it only expresses the connection of the words "white," "black," and "lighter" with a paradigm.

43. Wittgenstein, *On Certainty*, § 114.

44. That one cannot meaningfully doubt the real external world in toto can be shown also from the point of view of the later Wittgenstein. One cannot with Descartes meaningfully argue that all that is supposed to be real is finally merely my dream (or, merely in consciousness), since the expression "merely my dream" (or, merely in consciousness) is meaningful only within the framework of a language game in which it is presupposed as paradigmatic that not all that is supposed to be real is merely my dream or merely in consciousness.

45. Albert, p. 47.

46. On this, see my introduction to C. S. Peirce, *Schriften I* (Frankfurt, 1967), p. 123ff.

47. There can be no theory of reflection that is formalizable in the sense of the analytic logic of science (no "symbolic model" of reflection), as G. Frey has shown in opposition to the call for a total objectification of human consciousness and its corresponding cybernetic simulation. Cf. G. Frey, *Sprache — Ausdruck des Bewusstseins* (Stuttgart, 1965), p. 37ff., and "Sind bewusstseinsanaloge Maschinen Möglich?" in *Studium Generale*, vol. 19 (1966), pp. 191–200. Just this insight shows that we have transcendental-philosophical knowledge concerning the theoretical distinction between any imaginable level of the metalanguage hierarchy and the level of reflection of philosophical sentences — and this knowledge can be philosophically explicated. See Theodor Litt's explication of the "self-stratification" of mind and language in *Denken und Sein* (Stuttgart, 1948).

48. Cf. my essay, "Szientismus oder transzendentale Hermeneutik? Zur Frage nach dem Subjekt der Zeichen-Interpretation in der Semiotik des Pragmatismus," in *Hermeneutik und Dialektik, Festschrift für H. G. Gadamer*, vol. 1, ed. R. Bubner et al. (Tübingen, 1970), now also in *Transformation der Philosophie*, K.-O. Apel, vol. 2, pp. 178–219. See Habermas's explication of the "discourse" theory of truth in "Wahrheitstheorien," in *Wirklichkeit und Reflexion, Festschrift für W. Schulz* (Pfullinger, 1974), pp. 211–265. See also my "C. S. Peirce and Post-Tarskian Truth," in *The Relevance of C. S. Peirce* (Lasalle, 1983), pp. 189–223.

49. Cf. Wittgenstein, *Philosophical Investigations*, § 65ff.

50. Cf. Max Planck, "Russell's Philosophy of Language," in *The Philosophy of Bertrand Russell*, ed. P. A. Schilpp (Evanston, Illinois, 1944), pp. 227–255, as well as my remarks above concerning "paralinguistic" introductions of a philosophy understood according to the paradigm of constructive semantics.

51. Bartley, p. 146ff.

52. Lenk, p. 105ff.

53. Lenk, p. 107ff.

54. Wittgenstein, *On Certainty*, § 105.

55. W. Stegmüller, *Metaphysik, Skepsis, Wissenschaft*, 2nd ed. (Heidelberg, New York, 1969), p. 169.

56. K. Popper, *The Open Society and Its Enemies* (Princeton, 1950), p. 413ff.

57. See note 30, above.

58. An interesting example of the early anticipation of this confusion and of the modern reduction of philosophy to logical semantics is the following text ascribed by the commentator on Aristotle, Ammonius, to Theophrastus: "Since discourse (*logos*) has a twofold relation . . . one to the listener for whom it has a meaning, the other to the things concerning which the speaker wishes to produce in the listener a conviction, poetics and rhetoric exist with regard to the relation to the listener . . . however, the philosopher will be particularly concerned with the relation of discourse to things, by refuting the false and demonstrating the true." See Ammonius, *Aristotelis De Interpretatione Commentarium*, ed. Busse (Berlin, 1887), p. 365ff. The logic of language in logical empiricism has revived this division by putting empirical pragmatics in the place of poetics and rhetoric. Since, however, modern linguistic analysis was preceded by the transcendental philosophy of the knowing subject, today we should be in a position to see that this division is incomplete with regard to the interpreting subject. The completion can certainly not be undertaken by a transcendental philosophy of consciousness, which — like Kant — expels linguistic discourse in general into "anthropology from a pragmatic point of view."

59. J. Hintikka, "Cogito, Ergo Sum: Inference or Performance," *Philosophical Review* 71 (1962), pp. 3–32.

60. Analogously, Stegmüller shows, by the very performative act through which he claims validity for his thesis "that the problem of evidence is absolutely insoluble" (Stegmüller, p. 168), that the existence of evidence is a necessary condition of the possibility of meaningful argumentation. Naturally this does not contradict his observation that the existence of evidence cannot be demonstrated (that is, logically deduced) without logical circularity. But it indicates that the reduction of the problem of justification to the possibility of logical demonstration in the framework of an objectivized syntactic-semantic sentence system amounts to an "abstractive fallacy" when it comes to the problem of philosophical foundations. For Stegmüller himself, after all, cannot avoid entering the sphere of (transcendental) pragmatics. He does this when he concludes that the arguing subject, faced with the dilemma that the existence of evidence can be neither denied without self-contradiction nor demonstrated without *petitio principii*, is compelled to a "prerational decision concerning certainty." However, this way of entering into a pragmatic dimension without the aid of transcendental-pragmatic reflection leads him to miss the point that the reflective insight that the existence of evidence is a condition of the possibility of argumentation (which can be neither denied without self-contradiction nor logically demonstrated without *petitio principii*) — as an insight into the pragmatic situation of argumentation — renders a prerational decision in favor of the supposition of evidence completely superfluous. For, as an insight of transcendental-pragmatic reflection, it is not about some formal-logical dilemma but about an indispensable condition of the possibility of performing the act of arguing.

61. E. Husserl, *Cartesian Meditations*, trans. D. Cairns (The Hague, 1973), pp. 18–19.

62. One has to observe Husserl's uncertainty in the following formulation (Husserl, pp. 20–21): ". . . this 'phenomenological epoche' or 'bracketing' of the objective world . . . therefore does not leave *us* confronting nothing. On the contrary *we* gain possession of something by it; and what *we* (or, to speak more precisely, what *I*, the one who is meditating) acquire by it is my pure living with all the pure subjective processes making this up, and everything meant in them: the universe of 'phenomena' in the phenomenological sense" (italics added, K.-O. A.).

63. When Husserl declares, "By my living, by my experiencing, thinking, valuing, and acting, I can enter no world other than the one that gets its sense and acceptance or status in and from me, myself" (p. 21), he looks through the language (game) presup-

posed a priori by his thought as through a glass — no differently than did Descartes at the beginning of the epoch of philosophy justifying itself through the evidence of self-consciousness. Certainly if this whole epoch is rejected as in error because of its reflection upon the subjective conditions of the possibility of epistemic evidence — as has recently been done by Werner Becker, who provides a destruction of the history of transcendental philosophy from the perspective of "critical rationalism" (W. Becker, *Selbstbewusstsein und Spekulation. Zur Kritik der Transzendentalphilosophie* (Freiburg, 1972) — then, in my opinion, the baby is thrown out with the bath water. For it is not the will to evidence or the "reflection model" (Becker) that is to be rejected from the standpoint of critical discussion. What is to be rejected, rather, is the confusion of reflection on validity with genuine knowledge of a special sphere of being (as in both Descartes and Husserl) or with substantive knowledge in general (partially in German Idealism) and the confusion of actual evidence (for my consciousness) with the inter-subjective validity of knowledge. It seems to me, however, that these confusions can be unraveled and avoided through a transcendental pragmatics of language. For a convincing treatment of the Husserlian aporetic, cf. also H. Röttges, "Evidenz und Solipsismus in Husserls 'Cartesianischen Meditationen,'" in *Philosophische Beziehungswissenschaft, Festschrift für J. Schaaf,* eds. W. F. Niebel, D. Leisegang (Frankfurt, 1971).

64. In this regard I have not only to add to Hans Lenk's characterization of the noncriticizable rules of the "institution of rational criticism" but also to "dramatize" them in a transcendental philosophy, to use an expression of H. Albert. "The rules and the very idea (or institutions)" of rational criticism are, in my opinion, not only "bound together by linguistic convention" (Lenk, p. 108), but linguistic convention is in this case only the "conventional realization" of rules that originally make explicit conventions ("agreements") possible. More clearly, the idea and institution of rational criticism is not just a historical form of life among other possible forms of life — although in the form familiar to us it was grounded, that is, conventionally realized, for the first time by the Greek philosophers. It may be that the institution of rational discussion has contributed to the realization of *homo sapiens,* but obviously it could do this only because it made explicit fundamental conditions of meaningful interaction between men and between forms of life. In any case, today the situation is such that not only "can the notion of rational criticism not renounce itself" (Lenk, p. 109), but also we cannot renounce it without renouncing ourselves as men in a nonpathological sense. Naturally, this does not mean that all men must be philosophers (in the academic sense) or even disciples of critical rationalism.

65. Cf. J. Habermas, "Vorbereitende Bemerkungen zu einer Theorie der kommunikativen Kompetenz," in J. Habermas and N. Luhmann, *Theorie der Gesellschaft oder Sozialtechnologie* (Frankfurt, 1971), pp. 101–141.

66. For an attempt to carry out this program, cf. my essay "Das Apriori der Kommunikationsgemeinschaft und die Grundlagen der Ethik," in *Transformation der Philosophie,* vol. 2, pp. 358–435. Also see there (p. 397ff.) my objections to Albert's proposal to consider competing systems of morals as empirically falsifiable theories of science. Such a treatment already presupposes, in fact, an ethical norm.

67. Cf. my essay, "Die Kommunikationsgemeinschaft als transzendentale Voraussetzung der Sozialwissenschaften," in *Transformation der Philosophie,* vol. 2, pp. 220–263.

68. Cf. my essay, "Arnold Gehlens 'Philosophie der Institutionen' und die Metainstitution der Sprache," in *Transformation der Philosophie,* vol. 1, pp. 197–221.

69. Cf. note 6, above.

70. To that extent Popper's commitment to the voluntaristic tradition from Duns Scotus to Kant (*The Open Society and Its Enemies* [Princeton, 1950], p. 780) is justified,

but only because the engagement of the will in favor of the realization of reason is not directly synonymous with establishing its reflexive self-justification by means of a decisionistic "Sic volo, sic jubeo; stet pro ratione voluntas." This viewpoint, however, must, it seems to me, be brought to bear not only against Popper's decisionism but also against Habermas's argument in *Legitimation Crisis* (Boston, 1975), pp. 158–159. Indeed, I concur — as I scarcely need to emphasize — wholly and completely with Habermas's theory that we human beings (not only as arguing beings but also as acting beings) have always implicitly recognized the validity of norms of ideal communication through the counterfactual anticipation of an ideal communication situation. Nevertheless, it seems to me necessary that transcendental reflection on this "fact of reason" be mediated by the reflection of those arguing upon the conditions of the possibility of their practice. It is only in connection with argumentative discourse that the conditions of possibility of all meaningful action within the framework of language games can be made explicit and distinguished from mere convention. More importantly, reflection upon those ethical principles we have always necessarily recognized does not remove the necessity of a deliberate affirmation (renewed again and again) of this recognition in the sense of a commitment to the realization of reason. This demand amounts, in my opinion, not to a "residual decisionism," as Habermas asserts, but rather to the validation of the indispensable function of good will in the sense of an ethical unity of knowledge and interest.

71. Popper, *The Open Society and Its Enemies*, p. 780.

72. Decisions against realizing reason do not signify as a rule a denial in principle of the validity of transcendental-pragmatic rules of rational discourse. On the contrary, one claims only to be an exemption — the Devil lives on such things, as it were.

73. That this depends decidedly on following the path of transcendental reflection is indicated, in a very interesting way, by the dilemma of the pure constructivism of the Erlangen School. Although Paul Lorenzen would like to solve the problem of philosophical foundations by reconstructing Kantian transcendental philosophy, he thinks it necessary to grant that an "act of faith" is its starting point, since "the term 'justification' makes sense only after one has accepted . . . principles" (*Normative Logics and Ethics* [Mannheim/Zurich, 1969], p. 74). This problematic, however (which bears obvious analogies to that of Popper), occurs, in my opinion, only if one either no longer recognizes transcendental reflection (upon principles that one must necessarily have always accepted) as a legitimate move in the philosophical argumentation game, or simply overlooks this possibility. This appears to me to be a typical modern conceptual compulsion: One wants to practice Kant's Copernican revolution and, hence, begins immediately with an act of construction. However, in order to be able to present a logical construction as the reconstruction of our competences, we must first reflect on that which is not capable of being meaningfully questioned, the conditions of the possibility of valid criticism that are implicit in the transcendental language game. Only this act of transcendental-philosophical reflection saves us from a "framework" relativism grounded in decisionism, on the one hand, and from a naturalistic absolutization of the empirical critique of ideology into a self-reflection as self-unmasking (in the sense of the "nothing but" reductionism of the nineteenth century), on the other hand. On the distinction between transcendental reflection and critical self-reflection, cf. J. Habermas, "Nachwort" to the paperback edition of *Erkenntnis und Interesse* (Frankfurt, 1973), p. 411ff.

9

Jürgen Habermas

Introduction

For Marx and his generation, Hegel was the last in the grand tradition of philosophical thought, the tradition of totalizing knowledge about man and nature, history and society. Announcements of the death of philosophy began with the decline of the Hegelian cultural synthesis, as did the various attempts to "supersede" philosophy. For Jürgen Habermas our own century has not yet found a way beyond this impasse. Even the "great" philosopher as writer, as the embodiment of thought and the bearer of tradition, has now become extinct with the passing of the generation of thinkers like Heidegger, Jaspers, and Bloch (1983, 1). In this respect, Habermas agrees with the basic diagnosis of the more radical critics of the possibility of philosophy; but he does not draw the same historicist and relativist conclusions. Even in its postmetaphysical and post-Hegelian forms, he argues, philosophical thought "originates in reflection on the reason embodied in cognition, speech, and action" and retains its central role as a "guardian of reason" (1984, 1). The problem now, however, is to explain how this is possible given the core of truth in radical hermeneutics and "late" pragmatism, that is to say, given the inextricable ties of "reason" to language and action, to the web of everyday communication within culturally and historically variable forms of life.

It could be said without exaggeration that Habermas's basic theoretical endeavor, from *Knowledge and Human Interests* to

The Theory of Communicative Action, has been to develop a framework for a more modest, fallibilist, and yet universalist account of rationality and rationalization. Not only classical philosophy but modern philosophy, "the philosophy of consciousness," has proved unable to establish "ultimate foundations" or to construct a "first philosophy." But in the dusk of such conceptions, "the way is opened to a new constellation in the relationship of philosophy to the sciences" (1984, 2). As Habermas put it earlier in his essay "The Role of Philosophy in Marxism," the rational content of the philosophical tradition can now be saved only if philosophy begins with the self-reflection of the sciences. Through such self-reflection it retains some of its ancient dignity, as a "placeholder" (*Statthalter*) whose function is to hold open questions of "unity and universality" that might otherwise be closed or dropped by empirical scientific research (1976, 57).

In the following essay Habermas again takes up the idea of philosophy's role as a placemarker, or stand-in (*Platzhalter*), this time locating it more precisely in relation to concrete empirical research programs, particularly the "reconstructive sciences." Philosophy can no longer pretend to function as the highest arbiter or final judge of science and culture, as a *Platzanweiser* assigning each sphere to its proper place through the tribunal of pure reason. Rather, it now enters into a working relationship with the human sciences — a relationship that is already adumbrated in, for example, the cooperation between philosophy and history of science, between moral philosophy and moral psychology, and between philosophy of language and empirical linguistics. This view of the *Aufhebung* of philosophy in a peculiarly "philosophical" kind of human science can be found, in different versions, in such thinkers as Marx and Freud, Weber and Durkheim, Mead and Piaget — as well as, of course, in the programmatic statements of the early Frankfurt School. Habermas's version emphasizes the reconstructive sciences, whose conscious aim is to render theoretically explicit the intuitive, pretheoretical know-how underlying such basic human competences as speaking and understanding, judging and acting. Unlike classical transcendental analysis of the conditions of rationality, such sciences yield knowledge that is not necessary but hypothetical, not a priori but empirical, not certain but fallible. Nevertheless, they remain directed to universal structures and conditions, and they raise universal — though defeasible — claims to validity. Philosophical modes of analysis and justification are not so much abolished by them as absorbed within them. It is this "new paradigm" of "hybrid discourses" which insert philosophical ideas into contexts of empirical research that Habermas opposes both to traditional conceptions of philosophy as an ultimate court of appeals and to contemporary farewells to philosophy, whether therapeutic, heroic, or hermeneutic. Having entered upon "a phase of cooperation with the human sciences," philosophical reflection can function as a supplier (*Zuarbeiter*) of ideas that are treated as empirical hypotheses; it can function as a stand-in for empirical theories with strong universalist claims; but it can no longer "do things single-handedly."

In Habermas's view philosophy has a second role to play today, one closely tied to a specific feature of modern Western society: the differentiation of what Weber called the "cultural value spheres" of science and technology, art and criticism, law and morality — with their specialized "logics" for dealing with questions of truth, justice, or taste and with their rarefied "expert cultures" increasingly separated from the communicative practice of everyday life. Philosophy, Habermas suggests, can function as a mediator and interpreter to offset this compartmentalization and separation.

In everyday communication cognitive interpretations, moral expectations, expressions, and evaluations cannot help overlapping and interpenetrating. Reaching understanding in the lifeworld requires a cultural tradition that ranges across *the whole spectrum*, not just the fruits of science and technology. As far as philosophy is concerned, it might do well to refurbish its link with the totality by taking on the role of interpreter on behalf of the lifeworld. It might then be able to help set in motion the interplay between the cognitive-instrumental, moral-practical, and aesthetic-expressive dimensions that has come to a standstill today, like a tangled mobile.

As a mediating interpreter it can help to open up the encapsulated spheres of science, morality, and art and feed them into "the impoverished traditions of the lifeworld," so as to establish there a new balance among the now "separated moments of reason."

Thus, Habermas's transformation of philosophy envisions for it both a contributing role *within* certain specialized areas of inquiry and a mediating role *between* the various expert cultures and the lifeworld. In both roles it retains its relation to reason in the emphatic sense, that is, to the consideration of universal validity claims that can be redeemed only through the force of the better argument.

Suggested Readings

Benhabib, Seyla. *Critique, Norm, and Utopia.* New York: Columbia University Press, 1986.

Bernstein, Richard, ed. *Habermas and Modernity.* Cambridge, Massachusetts: MIT Press, 1985.

Cohen, Jean. "Why More Political Theory?" *Telos* 40 (1979), 70–94.

Dallmayr, Fred. *Materialien zu Habermas's Erkenntnis und Interesse.* Frankfurt: Suhrkamp, 1974.

Geuss, Raymond. *The Idea of Critical Theory.* Cambridge: Cambridge University Press, 1978.

Giddens, Anthony. "Jürgen Habermas," in *The Return of Grand Theory in the Social Sciences,* ed. Q. Skinner, 121–139. Cambridge: Cambridge University Press, 1986.

Habermas, Jürgen. *Knowledge and Human Interests.* Boston: Beacon Press, 1971.

Habermas, Jürgen. *Towards a Rational Society.* Boston: Beacon Press, 1971.

Habermas, Jürgen. *Theory and Practice.* Boston: Beacon Press, 1974.

Habermas, Jürgen. *Legitimation Crisis.* Boston: Beacon Press, 1975.

Habermas, Jürgen. *Rekonstruktion des historischen Materialismus.* Frankfurt: Suhrkamp, 1976.

Habermas, Jürgen. *Communication and the Evolution of Society.* Boston: Beacon Press, 1979.

Habermas, Jürgen. *Philosophical-Political Profiles.* Cambridge, Massachusetts: MIT Press, 1983.

Habermas, Jürgen. *The Theory of Communicative Action.* Vol. 1. *Rationality and Rationalization.* Boston: Beacon Press, 1984.

Habermas, Jürgen. *The Theory of Communicative Action.* Vol. 2. *The Critique of Functionalist Reason.* Forthcoming, Beacon Press.

Habermas, Jürgen. *Lectures on the Philosophical Discourse of Modernity.* Forthcoming, MIT Press.

Habermas, Jürgen. *Moral Consciousness and Communicative Action.* Forthcoming, MIT Press.

Held, David. *Introduction to Critical Theory.* Berkeley: University of California Press, 1980.

Honneth, Axel. *Kritik der Macht. Reflexionsstufen einer kritischen Gesellschaftstheorie,* 225–334. Frankfurt: Suhrkamp, 1985. English translation forthcoming, MIT Press.

Honneth, Axel, and Hans Joas, eds. *Kommunikatives Handeln: Beiträge zu Jürgen Habermas' Theorie des kommunikativen Handelns.* Frankfurt: Suhrkamp, 1986.

Jay, Martin. *Marxism and Totality.* Berkeley: University of California Press, 1984.

Kortian, Garbis. *Metacritique: The Philosophy of Jürgen Habermas.* Cambridge: Cambridge University Press, 1981.

McCarthy, Thomas. *The Critical Theory of Jürgen Habermas.* Cambridge, Massachusetts: MIT Press, 1978.

Misgeld, Dieter. "Ultimate Self-Responsibility, Practical Reasoning, and Practical Action: Habermas, Husserl, and Ethnomethodology on Action and Discourse," *Human Studies* 3 (1980), 8–44.

Schmidt, James. "Jürgen Habermas and the Difficulties of Enlightenment," *Social Research* 49 (1982), 181–208.

Thompson, John, and Held, David, eds. *Jürgen Habermas: Critical Debates.* Cambridge, Massachusetts: MIT Press, 1982.

Wellmer, Albrecht. *The Critical Theory of Society.* New York: Harper and Row, 1978.

Wellmer, Albrecht. *Zur Dialektik von Moderne und Postmoderne.* Frankfurt: Suhrkamp, 1985.

Wellmer, Albrecht. *Ethik und Dialog. Elemente des moralischen Urteils bei Kant und in der Diskursethik.* Frankfurt: Suhrkamp, 1986.

White, Stephen. "On the Normative Structure of Action: Gewirth and Habermas," *The Review of Politics* 44 (1982), 282–301.

Philosophy as Stand-In and Interpreter

Jürgen Habermas

Master thinkers have fallen on hard times. This has been true of Hegel ever since Popper unmasked him in the forties as an enemy of the open society. It has also been true — intermittently — of Marx. The last to denounce him as a false prophet were the New Philosophers in the seventies. Today even Kant is affected by this decline. If I am correct, he is being viewed for the first time as a *maître penseur,* that is, as the magician of a false paradigm from the intellectual constraints of which we have to escape. Whereas among a philosophical audience there may still be a majority of scholars whose image of Kant has stayed the same, in the world outside his reputation is being eclipsed, and not for the first time, by Nietzsche.

Historically, Kantian philosophy marks the birth of a new mode of justification. Kant felt that the physics of his time and the growth of knowledge brought by it were important developments to which the philosopher had to respond. For Kant, the new science represented, not some philosophically indifferent fact of life, but proof of man's capacity to know. Specifically, the challenge Newtonian physics posed for philosophy was to explain how empirical knowledge is at all possible, an explanation that could not itself be empirical but had to be transcendental. What Kant calls "transcendental" is an inquiry into the a priori conditions of what makes experience possible. The specific upshot of Kant's transcendental inquiry is that those conditions are identical with the conditions of possible objects of experience. The first job for the philosopher, then, is to analyze the concepts of objects as we "always already" intuitively use them. Transcendental analysis is a nonempirical reconstruction of the a priori achievements of the cognizing subject, achievements for which there is no alternative: No experience shall be thought possible under *different* conditions. Transcendental justification has nothing to do with deduction from first principles. Rather, the hallmark of the transcendental justification is the notion that we can prove the nonsubstitutability of certain mental operations that we always already (intuitively) perform in accordance with rules.

As a master thinker, Kant fell into disfavor because he used transcendental justification to found the new discipline of epistemology. In so doing he redefined the task, or vocation if you like, of philosophy in a more demanding way. There are two principal reasons why the Kantian view of philosophy's vocation has a dubious ring today.

The first reason has directly to do with the foundationalism of epistemology. In championing the idea of a cognition *before* cognition, Kantian philosophy sets up a domain between itself and the sciences, arrogating authority to itself. It wants to clarify the foundations of the sciences once and for all, defining the limits of what can and cannot be experienced. This is tantamount to an act of ushering the sciences to their proper place. I think philosophy cannot and should not try to play the role of usher.

The second reason lies in the fact that transcendental philosophy refuses to be confined to epistemology. Above and beyond analyzing the bases of cognition, the critique of pure reason is also supposed to enable us to criticize the abuses of this cognitive faculty, which is limited to phenomena. Kant replaces the substantive concept of reason found in traditional metaphysics with a concept of reason the moments of which have undergone differentiation, to the point where their unity is merely formal. He sets up practical reason, judgment, and theoretical cognition in isolation from each other, giving each a foundation unto itself, with the result that philosophy is cast in the role of the highest arbiter for all matters, including culture as a whole. Kantian philosophy differentiates what Weber was to call the "value spheres of culture" (science and technology, law and morality, art and art criticism), while at the same time legitimating them within their respective limits. Thus Kant's philosophy poses as the highest court of appeal vis-à-vis the sciences and culture as a whole.[1]

There is a necessary link between the Kantian foundationalism in epistemology, which nets philosophy the unenviable role of usher, and the ahistoricity of the conceptual system Kant superimposes on culture, which nets philosophy the equally undesirable role of judge, parceling out separate areas of jurisdiction to science, morality, and art.

Without the Kantian assumption that the philosopher can decide *questiones juris* concerning the rest of culture, this self-image collapses. . . . To drop the notion of the philosopher as knowing something about knowing which nobody else knows so well would be to drop the notion that his voice always has an overriding claim on the attention of the other participants in the conversation. It would also be to drop the notion that there is something called "philosophical method" or "philosophical technique" or "the philosophical point of view" which enables the professional philosopher, *ex officio,* to have interesting views about, say, the respectability of psychoanalysis, the legitimacy of certain dubious laws, the resolution of moral dilemmas, the soundness of schools of historiography or literary criticism, and the like.[2]

Richard Rorty's impressive critique of philosophy assembles compelling metaphilosophical arguments in support of the view that the roles Kant the master thinker had envisaged for philosophy, namely those of usher and judge, are too big for it. While I find myself in agreement with much of what Rorty says, I have trouble accepting his conclusion, which is that if philosophy forswears these two roles, it must also surrender the function of being the "guardian of rationality." If I understand Rorty, he is saying that the new modesty of philosophy involves the abandonment of any claim to reason — the very claim that has marked philosophical thought since its inception. Rorty not only argues for the demise of philosophy. He also unflinchingly accepts the end of the belief that ideas like truth or the unconditional with their transcending power are a necessary condition of humane forms of collective life.

Implied by Kant's conception of formal, differentiated reason is a theory of modernity. Modernity is characterized by a rejection of the substantive rationality typical of religious and metaphysical worldviews and by a belief in procedural rationality and its ability to give credence to our views in the three areas of objective knowledge, moral-practical insight, and aesthetic judgment. What I asking myself is this: Is it true that this (or a similar) concept of modernity becomes untenable when you dismiss the claims of a foundationalist theory of knowledge?

What follows is an attempt to narrate a story that might help put Rorty's criticism of philosophy in perspective. Granted, by going this route I cannot settle the controversy. What I can do is throw light on some of its presuppositions. At the outset (section 1, below) I will look at Hegel's critique of Kantian foundationalism and the substitution of a dialectical mode of justification for Kant's transcendental one. Next (section 2) I will retrace some of the lines of criticism and self-criticism that have emerged in the Kantian and Hegelian traditions. In section 3, I will dwell on a more radical form of criticism originating in pragmatist and hermeneuticist quarters, a form of attack that repudiates Kant and Hegel simultaneously. Section 4 deals with thinkers, respectable ones no less, who respond to this situation by annulling philosophy's long-standing claim to reason. In conclusion (section 5) I will argue that philosophy, while well advised to withdraw from the problematic roles of usher (*Platzanweiser*) and judge, can and ought to retain its claim to reason, provided it is content to play the more modest roles of stand-in (*Platzhalter*) and interpreter.

1. Hegel fashioned his dialectical mode of justification in deliberate opposition to the transcendental one of Kant. Hegel — and I can only hint at this here — agrees with those who charge that in the end Kant failed to justify or ground the pure concepts of the understanding, for he merely culled them from the table of forms of judgment, unaware of their historical specificity. Thus he failed, in Hegel's eyes, to prove that the a priori conditions of what makes experience possible are truly necessary. In his *Phenomenology of Spirit* Hegel proposes to correct this flaw by taking a genetic approach. What Kant regarded as a unique (Copernican) turn to transcendental

reflection becomes, in Hegel, a general mechanism for turning consciousness back upon itself. This mechanism has been switched on and off time and time again in the development of spirit. As the subject becomes conscious of itself, it destroys one form of consciousness after another. This process epitomizes the subjective experience that what initially appears to the subject as a being in itself acquires content only by virtue of the form imparted to it by the subject. The transcendental philosopher's experience is thus, according to Hegel, reenacted naively by every in-itself as it becomes a for-itself. What Hegel calls "dialectical" is the reconstruction of this recurrent experience and its assimilation by the subject, which is faced with ever more complex structures. In sum, Hegel goes beyond the particular manifestation of consciousness Kant analyzed, focusing instead on knowledge that has become autonomous — that is, absolute knowledge. This highest vantage point, absolute knowledge, enables Hegel to witness the genesis of structures of consciousness that Kant had assumed to be timeless.

Hegel, it should be noted, exposes himself to a criticism similar to the one he levels against Kant. Reconstructing successive forms of consciousness is one thing. Proving the necessity of their succession is quite another. Hegel is not unaware of this gap, and he tries to close it by logical means, thereby laying the basis for a philosophical absolutism that claims an even grander role for philosophy than did Kant. In Hegel's *Logic* philosophy's role is to effect an encyclopedic conceptual synthesis of the diffuse chunks of content thrown up by the sciences. In addition Hegel picks up Kant's latent theory of modernity, making it explicit and developing it into a critique of the diremptive, self-contradictory features of modernity. It is this peculiar twist that gave philosophy a new world-historical relevance in relation to culture as a whole. And this is the stuff of which the suspect image of Hegel as a master thinker is made.[3]

The metaphilosophical attack on the *maîtres penseurs,* whether its target be Hegel's absolutism or Kant's foundationalism, is a recent phenomenon. Antecedents of it can be found in the strands of self-criticism that have run through Kantianism and Hegelianism for quite some time. I shall comment briefly on two lines of self-criticism that I think complement each other in an interesting way.

2. In reference to Kant's transcendental philosophy there are today three distinct critical positions: the analytic one of Strawson, the constructivist one of Lorenzen, and the critical-rationalist one of Popper.

Analytic philosophy appropriates Kant by jettisoning any claim to ultimate justification (*Letztbegründung*). From the very outset it drops the objective Kant had in mind when he deduced the pure concepts of the understanding from the unity of self-consciousness. The analytic reception of Kant is confined to comprehending those concepts and rules that underlie experience, to the degree to which they can be couched in elementary propositions. The analysis focuses on general, indispensable, conceptual preconditions that make experience possible. Unable to prove the objective validity of its basic concepts and presuppositions, this analysis nevertheless makes a universalistic claim. Redeeming it involves changing Kant's transcendental strategy of justification into a testing procedure. If the hypothetically reconstructed conceptual system under lying experience as such is valid, then not a single intelligible alternative to it can possibly exist. This means any alternative proposal will be scrutinized with a view to proving its derivative character, that is, with a view to showing that the alleged alternative inevitably utilizes portions of the very hypothesis it seeks to supplant. A strategy of argumentation like this tries to prove that the concepts and presuppositions it singles out as fundamental cannot be dispensed with. Turned modest, the transcendental philosopher of the analytic variety takes on the role of the skeptic who keeps trying to find counterexamples that might invalidate his theories.[4] In short, he acts like a hypothesis-testing scientist.

The *constructivist position* tried to compensate for the justificatory shortfall that has now opened up from the perspective of transcendental philosophy in the following way. It concedes from the start that the basic conceptual organization of experience is conventional, while at the same time putting a constructivist critique of language in the service of epistemology.[5]

Those conventions are considered valid that are generated methodically and therefore transparently. It should be clear that this approach lays — rather than uncovers — the foundations of cognition.

On the face of it, the *critical-rationalist position* breaks completely with transcendentalism. It holds that the three horns of the "Münchhausen trilemma" — logical circularity, infinite regress, and recourse to absolute certitude — can only be avoided if one gives up any hope of grounding or justifying whatsoever.[6] Here the notion of justification is being dislodged in favor of the concept of critical testing, which becomes the critical rationalist's equivalent for justification. In this connection I would argue that criticism is itself a procedure whose employment is never presuppositionless. That is why I think that critical rationalism, by clinging to the idea of irrefutable rules of criticism, allows a weak version of the Kantian justificatory mode to sneak into its inner precincts through the back door.[7]

Self-criticism in the Hegelian tradition has become differentiated along similar lines as self-criticism among Kantians. Again, three distinct positions might be said to be represented by the young Lukacs and his materialist critique of epistemology, which restricts the claim to justification of dialectics to the man-made world and excludes nature; by K. Korsch's and H. Freyer's practicism, wherein the classical relation of theory and practice is stood on its head and the "interested" perspective of creating a society of the future informs the theoretical reconstruction of social development; and finally by the negativism of Adorno, who clings to a comprehensive logic of development for the sole purpose of proving that it is impossible to break the spell of instrumental reason gone mad.

I cannot examine these positions here. All I shall do is point out certain interesting parallels between the Hegelian and Kantian strands of self-criticism. The self-criticism that begins by doubting the Kantian transcendental deduction and the self-criticism that begins by doubting Hegel's passage to absolute knowledge have this in common: They reject the claim that the categorical makeup and the pattern of development of the human spirit, respectively, can be proved to be necessary. With regard to constructivism and practicism, a similar convergence occurs: Both are involved in a shift from rational reconstruction to creative praxis where theory is viewed as an afterthought of praxis. Critical rationalism and negativism, for their part, share something too, which is that they reject both transcendental and dialectical means of cognition while at the same time using them in a paradoxical way. In short, one way of viewing them is to say that they represent attempts at radical negation which show that these two modes of justification cannot be abolished except on penalty of self-contradiction.

Our comparison between parallel self-critical strategies to restrict the justificatory claims of transcendental and dialectical philosophies gives rise to the following question: Do these self-limiting tendencies merely reinforce each other, encouraging the skeptic to reject justification all the more roundly? Or does the retrenchment on either side to a position of diminished justificatory objectives and strategies represent a precondition for viewing them, not as opposites, but as supplementing each other? I think the second possibility deserves serious consideration. The genetic structuralism of Jean Piaget provides an instructive model along these lines, instructive I think for all philosophers but particularly those who want to remain philosophers. Piaget conceives "reflective abstraction" as that learning mechanism which explains the transition between cognitive stages in ontogenetic development. The end point of this development is a decentered understanding of the world. Reflective abstraction is similar to transcendental reflection in that it brings out the formal elements hidden in the cognitive content, identifies them as the schemata that underlie the knowing subject's action, differentiates them, and reconstructs them at the next highest stage of reflection. Seen from a different perspective, the same learning mechanism has a function similar to Hegel's power of negation which dialectically supersedes self-contradictory forms of consciousness.[8]

3. The aforementioned six positions in the tradition of Kant and Hegel stick to a claim to reason, however small in scope, however cautious in formulation. It is this final intention that sets off Popper and Lakatos from a Feyerabend, Horkheimer

and Adorno from a Foucault. They still say *something* about the indispensable conditions of claims to the validity of those opinions we hold to be justified, claims that transcend all restrictions of time and place. Now, any attack on the master thinkers questions this residual claim to reason, thus in essence making a plea for the abolition of philosophy. I can explain this radical turn by talking briefly about a wholly different criticism, one that has been raised against Kant *and* Hegel jointly.

Its proponents can be found in *pragmatism* and *hermeneutic philosophy*. Their doubts concerning the justificatory and self-justificatory potential of philosophy operate at a more profound level than do the self-criticisms within the Kantian and Hegelian traditions. They step resolutely outside the parameters set by the philosophy of consciousness and its cognitive paradigm, which stresses the perception and representation of objects. Pragmatism and hermeneutics oust the traditional notion of the solitary subject that confronts objects and becomes reflective only by turning itself into an object. In its place they put an idea of cognition that is mediated by language and linked to action. Moreover, they emphasize the web of everyday life and communication surrounding "our" cognitive achievements. The latter are intrinsically intersubjective and cooperative. Just how this web is conceptualized, whether as "form of life," "life world," "practice," "linguistically mediated interaction," "language game," "convention," "cultural background," "tradition," "effective history," or what have you, is unimportant. The important thing is that these commonsensical ideas, though they may function quite differently, attain a status that used to be reserved for the basic concepts of epistemology. Pragmatism and hermeneutics, then, accord a higher position to acting and speaking than to knowing. But there is more to it than that. Purposive action and linguistic communication play a qualitatively different role from that of self-reflection in the philosophy of consciousness. They have no justificatory function any more save one: to expose the need for foundational knowledge as unjustified.

Charles S. Peirce doubted that radical doubt is possible. His intentions were the same as those of Dilthey, who doubted that neutrality in interpretive understanding is possible. For Peirce, problems always arise in a specific situation. They come to us, as it were. We do not go to them, for we do not fully control the totality of our practical existence. In a similar vein, Dilthey argues that we cannot grasp a symbolic expression unless we have an intuitive preunderstanding of its context, for we do not have unlimited freedom to convert the unproblematic background knowledge of our own culture into explicit knowledge. Every instance of problem solving and every interpretation depend on a web of myriad presuppositions. Since this web is holistic and particularistic at the same time, it can never be grasped by an abstract, general analysis. It is from this standpoint that the myth of the given — that is, the distinctions between sensuality and intellect, intuition and concept, form and content — can be debunked, along with the distinctions between analytical and synthetic judgments, between a priori and a posteriori. These Kantian dualisms are all being dissolved, a fact that is vaguely reminiscent of Hegel's metacritique. Of course, a full-fledged return to Hegel is made impossible by the contextualism and historicism to which the pragmatist and hermeneutic approaches subscribe.

There is no denying that pragmatism and hermeneutics represent a gain. Instead of focusing introspectively on consciousness, these two points of view look outside: at objectifications of action and language. Gone is the fixation on the cognitive function of consciousness. Gone too is the emphasis on the representational function of language and the visual metaphor of the "mirror of nature." What takes their place is the notion of justified opinion, spanning the whole spectrum of what can be said — what Wittgenstein and Austin call illocutionary force — rather than just the contents of fact-stating discourses. "Saying things is not always saying how things are."[9]

Do these considerations strengthen Rorty's interpretation of pragmatism and hermeneutics, which argues for the abnegation, by philosophical thought, of any claim to rationality, indeed for the abnegation of philosophy per se? Or do they mark the beginning of a new paradigm that, while discarding the mentalistic language game of the philosophy of consciousness, retains the justificatory modes of that philosophy in the modest, self-critical form in which I have presented them? I cannot answer this question directly for want of compelling and simple arguments. Once again the answer I will give is a narrative one.

4. Marx wanted to supersede (*aufheben*) philosophy by realizing it — so convinced was he of the truth of Hegelian philosophy, whose only fault was that concept and reality cleaved unbearably, a fault that Hegel studiously overlooked. The corresponding, though fundamentally different, present-day attitude to philosophy is the dismissive goodbye and good riddance. These farewells take many forms, three of which are currently in vogue. For simplicity's sake I will call them the therapeutic, the heroic, and the salvaging farewell.

Wittgenstein championed the notion of a *therapeutic* philosophy, therapeutic in the specific sense of self-healing, for philosophy was sick to the core. Wittgenstein's diagnosis was that philosophy had disarrayed language games that function perfectly well in everyday life. The weakness of this particular farewell to philosophy is that it leaves the world as it is. For the standards by which philosophy is being criticized are taken straight from the self-sufficient, routinized forms of life in which philosophy happens to survive for now. And what about possible successors? Field research in cultural anthropology seems to be the strongest candidate to succeed philosophy after its demise. Surely, the history of philosophy will henceforth be interpreted as the unintelligible doings of some outlandish tribe that today is fortunately extinct. (Perhaps Rorty will one day be celebrated as the path-breaking Thucydides of this new approach, which incidentally could only get under way after Wittgenstein's medicine had proven effective.)

There is a sharp contrast between the soft-spoken farewell of the therapeutic philosopher and the noisy demolition undertaken by someone like Georges Bataille or Heidegger. Their goodbye is *heroic*. From their perspective too, the false habits of living and thinking are concentrated in elevated forms of philosophical reflection. But instead of blaming philosophy for homely category mistakes or simple disruptions of everday life, their deconstruction of metaphysics and repressive thought has a more incisive, epochal quality. This more dramatic farewell to philosophy does not promise a cure. Rather, it resembles Hölderlin's pathos-laden idea of a rescue attempt *in extremis*. The devalued and discredited philosophical tradition, rather than being replaced by something even more valueless than itself, is supposed to give way to a *different* medium that makes possible a return to the immemorial — to Bataille's sovereignty or Heidegger's being.

Least conspicuous, finally, is the *salvaging* type of farewell to philosophy. Contemporary neo-Aristotelians best exemplify this type, insofar as they do exegeses that are informed by hermeneutics. Some of their work is unquestionably significant. But all too often it departs from pure interpretation in an effort to salvage some old truth or other. At any rate, this farewell to philosophy has a disingenuous ring: While the salvager keeps invoking the need to preserve philosophy, he wants to have nothing to do with its systematic claims. He does not try to make the ancients relevant to the discussion of some subject matter. Nor does he present the classics as a cultural treasure prepared by philosophy and history. What he does is to appropriate by assimilation texts that were once thought to embody knowledge, treating them instead as sources of illumination and edification.

Let us return for a moment to the critique of Kant, the master thinker, in particular his foundationalism in epistemology. Clearly, present-day philosophies of the sort just described wisely sidestep the Kantian trap. The last thing they think they can do is usher the natural sciences to their proper seat. Contemporary poststructuralist, late-pragmatist, and neohistoricist tendencies share a narrow objectivistic conception of science. Over against scientific cognition they carve out a sphere where thought can be illuminating or awakening instead of being objective. These tendencies prefer to sever all links with general, criticizable claims to validity. They would rather make do without notions like consensus, incontrovertible results, and justified opinions. Paradoxically enough, whereas they make these (unnecessary) sacrifices, they somehow keep believing in the authority and superiority of philosophical insights: their own. In terms of their views on science, the philosophers of the definitive farewell agree with the existentialist proposal

(Jaspers, Sartre, Kolakowski) for a division of labor that puts science radically to one side and ends up equating philosophy with belief, life, existential freedom, myth, education, or what have you. All these juxtapositions are identical in structure. Where they differ is in their assessment of what Max Weber termed the cultural relevance of science, which may range from negative to neutral to positive. As is well known, Continental philosophy has a penchant for dramatizing the dangers of objectivism and instrumental reason, whereas Anglo-American philosophy takes a more relaxed view of them.

With his distinction between normal and abnormal discourse, Richard Rorty has come up with an interesting variation on the above theme. In times of widely acknowledged theoretical progress, normality takes hold of the established sciences. This means methods become available that make problem solving and dispute settling possible. What Rorty calls commensurable discourses are those discourses that operate with reliable criteria of consensus building. In contrast, discourses are incommensurable or abnormal when basic orientations are contested. Generally, abnormal conversations tend to pass over into normal ones, their ultimate purpose being to annul themselves and to bring about universal agreement. Occasionally, however, abnormal discourses stop short of taking this self-transcending step and are content with "interesting and fruitful disagreement." That is, they become *sufficient unto themselves*. It is at this point that abnormal discourses take on the quality that Rorty calls "edifying." According to him, philosophy as a whole verges on edifying conversation once it has sloughed off all pretensions to problem solving. Such philosophical edification enjoys the benefits of all three types of farewell: therapeutic relief, heroic overcoming, and hermeneutic reawakening. It combines the inconspicuously subversive force of leisure with an elitist notion of creative linguistic imagination and with the wisdom of the ages. The desire for edification, however, works to the detriment of the desire for truth: "Edifying philosophers can never end philosophy, but they can help prevent it from attaining the secure path of a science."[10]

I am partly sympathetic to Rorty's allocation of roles, for I agree that philosophy has no business playing the part of the highest arbiter in matters of science and culture. I find his argument unconvincing all the same. For even after pragmatism and hermeneutics have done their work and curtailed the scope of philosophy, the latter, though reduced to edifying conversation, can never find a niche *beyond* the sciences. Philosophical conversation cannot but gravitate toward argumentation and justificatory dispute. There is no alternative.

The existentialist or, if you like, exclusive division of labor between philosophy and science is untenable. This is borne out by the particular version of discourse theory Rorty proposes. Ultimately there is only one criterion by which opinions can be judged valid, and that is that they are based on agreement reached by argumentation. This means that *everything* whose validity is at all disputable rests on shaky foundations. It matters little if the ground underfoot shakes a bit less for those who debate problems of physics than for those who debate problems of morals and aesthetics. The difference is a matter of degree only, as the postempiricist philosophy of science has shown. Normalization of discourse is not a sufficiently trenchant criterion for distinguishing science from edifying philosophical conversation.

5. To those who advocate a cut-and-dried division of labor, research traditions representing a blend of philosophy and science have always been particularly offensive. Marxism and psychoanalysis are cases in point. They cannot, on this view, help being pseudosciences because they straddle normal and abnormal discourse, refusing to fall on either side of the dividing line. On this point Rorty speaks the same language as Jaspers. What I know about the history of the social sciences and psychology leads me to believe that hybrid discourses such as Marxism and psychoanalysis are by no means atypical. To the contrary, they may well stand for a type of approach that marks the beginning of new research traditions.

What holds for Freud applies to all seminal theories in these disciplines, for instance, those of Durkheim, Mead, Max Weber, Piaget, and Chomsky. Each inserted a genuinely philosophical idea like a detonator into a particular context of research. Symptom formation through repression; the creation of solidarity through the sacred; the identity-forming function of role taking; modernization as rationalization of society; decentration as an outgrowth of reflective abstraction from action; language acquisition as an activity of hypothesis testing — these key phrases stand for so many paradigms in which a philosophical idea is present in embryo while at the same time empirical, yet universal, questions are being posed. It is no coincidence that theoretical approaches of this kind are the favorite target of empiricist counterattacks. Such cyclical movements in the history of science, incidentally, do not point to a convergence of these disciplines in one unified science. It makes better sense to view them as stages on the road to the philosophization of the sciences of man (*Philosophischwerden der Humanwissenschaften*) than as stages in the triumphal march toward objectivist approaches, such as neurophysiology, that quaint favorite child of the analytic philosophers.

What I have said lies mainly in the realm of speculative conjecture. But unless I am completely mistaken, it makes sense to suggest that philosophy, instead of just dropping the usher role and being left with nothing, ought to exchange it for the part of stand-in (*Platzhalter*). Whose seat would philosophy be keeping, what would it be standing in for? Empirical theories with strong universalistic claims. As I have indicated, fertile minds have surfaced and will continue to surface in nonphilosophical disciplines, who will give such theories a try. The chance for their emergence is greatest in the reconstructive sciences. Starting primarily from the intuitive knowledge of competent subjects — competent in terms of judgment, action, and language — and secondarily from systematic knowledge handed down by culture, the reconstructive sciences explain the presumably universal bases of rational experience and judgment, as well as of action and linguistic communication. Marked down in price, the venerable transcendental and dialectical modes of justification may still come in handy. All they can fairly be expected to furnish, however, is reconstructive hypotheses for use in empirical settings. Telling examples of a successful cooperative integration of philosophy and science can be seen in the development of a theory of rationality. This is an area where philosophers work as suppliers of ideas with-

out raising foundationalist or absolutist claims à la Kant or
Hegel. Fallibilistic in orientation, they reject the dubious faith
in philosophy's ability to do things single-handedly, hoping
instead that the success that has for so long eluded it might
come from an auspicious matching of different theoretical
fragments. From the vantage point of my own research interests, I see such a cooperation taking shape between philosophy
of science and history of science; between speech act theory
and empirical approaches to pragmatics of language; between
a theory of informal argumentation and empirical approaches
to natural argumentation; between cognitivist ethics and a psychology of moral development; between philosophical theories
of action and the ontogenetic study of action competences.

If it is true that philosophy has entered upon a phase of
cooperation with the sciences of man, does it not run the risk
of losing its identity? There is some justification in Spaemann's
warning "that every philosophy makes a practical and a theoretical claim to totality and that not to make such a twofold
claim is to be doing something which does not qualify as philosophy."[11] In defense, one might argue that a philosophy that
contributes something important to an analysis of the rational
foundations of knowing, acting, and speaking does retain at
least a thematic connection with the whole. But is this enough?
What becomes of the theory of modernity, what of the window
on the totality of culture that Kant and Hegel opened with
their foundational and hypostatizing concepts of reason? Down
to Husserl's *Crisis of the European Sciences,* philosophy not only
usurped the part of supreme judge, it also played a directing
role. Again, what happens when it surrenders the role of judge
in matters of science as well as culture? Does this mean philosophy's relation to the totality is severed? Does this mean it can
no longer be the guardian of rationality?

The situation of culture as a whole is no different from the
situation of science as a whole. As totalities, neither needs to
be grounded or justified or given a place by philosophy. Since
the dawn of modernity in the eighteenth century, culture has
generated those structures of rationality that Max Weber and
Emil Lask conceptualized as cultural value spheres. Their ex-

istence calls for description and analysis, not philosophical justification.

Reason has split into three moments — modern science; positive law and posttraditional ethics; autonomous art and institutionalized art criticism — but philosophy had precious little to do with this disjunction. Ignorant of sophisticated critiques of reason, the sons and daughters of modernity have progressively learned to differentiate their cultural tradition in terms of these three aspects of rationality such that they deal with issues of truth, justice, and taste discretely, never simultaneously. At a different level, this shift toward differentiation produces the following phenomena: (1) The sciences disgorge more and more elements of religion, thus renouncing their former claim to being able to interpret nature and history as one whole. (2) Cognitivist moral theories disgorge issues of the good life, focusing instead strictly on deontological, generalizable aspects of ethics, so that all that remains of "the good" is the just. (3) With art it is likewise. Since the turn to autonomy, art has striven mightily to mirror one basic aesthetic experience, which is the increasing decentration of subjectivity. It occurs as the subject leaves the spatio-temporal structures of everyday life behind, freeing itself from the conventions of everyday perception, of purposive behavior, and of the imperatives of work and utility.

I repeat, these eminent trends toward compartmentalization, constituting as they do the hallmark of modernity, can do very well without philosophical justification. But they do pose problems of mediation. First, how can reason, once it has been thus sundered, go on being a unity on the level of culture? And second, how can expert cultures, which are being pushed more and more to the level of rarefied, esoteric forms, be made to stay in touch with everyday communication? To the extent to which philosophy keeps at least one eye trained on the topic of rationality, that is, to the extent to which it keeps inquiring into the conditions of the unconditional, to that extent it will not dodge the demand for these two kinds of efforts at mediation.

The first type of problem of mediation arises within the spheres of science, morals, and art. In this area we witness the rise of countermovements. For example, in human sciences nonobjective approaches bring moral and aesthetic criticism into play without undermining the primacy of issues of truth. Another example is the way in which the debate about ethics of responsibility versus ethics of ultimate ends (to the degree to which it emphasizes utilitarian motifs within moral cognitivism) assimilates notions like risk taking, need interpretation, and so on, notions that lie clearly in the field of the cognitive and expressive rather than the moral. Let us finally look at postmodern art as our third example. It is characterized by a strange simultaneity of realistic, politically committed schools, on the one hand, and authentic followers of that classical modernism to which we owe the crystallization of the specific meaning of the aesthetic, on the other. In realistic and politically committed art, elements of the cognitive and the moral-practical come into play once again, but at the level of the wealth of forms unloosed by the avant-garde. To that extent they act as agents of mediation. Counterdevelopments like these, it seems, mitigate the rigid compartmentalization of reason, pointing to reason's unity. In this regard, everyday life is a more promising medium for regaining the lost unity of reason than are today's expert cultures or yesteryear's classical philosophy of reason.

In everyday communication cognitive interpretations, moral expectations, expressions, and evaluations cannot help overlapping and interpenetrating. Reaching understanding in the lifeworld requires a cultural tradition that ranges across *the whole spectrum,* not just the fruits of science and technology. As far as philosophy is concerned, it might do well to refurbish its link with the totality by taking on the role of interpreter on behalf of the lifeworld. It might then be able to help set in motion the interplay between the cognitive-instrumental, moral-practical, and aesthetic-expressive dimensions that has come to a standstill today, like a tangled mobile.[12] This simile at least helps identify the issue philosophy will face when it stops playing the part of the arbiter who inspects culture and instead starts playing the part of a mediating interpreter. That issue is how to overcome the isolation of science, morals, and art and their respective expert cultures. How can they be joined to the impoverished traditions of the lifeworld, and how can this be done without detriment to their regional rationality? How can a new balance between the separated moments of reason be established in communicative everyday life?

The critic of the master thinkers will likely express his alarm one more time. What in the world, he will ask, gives the philosopher the right to offer his services as a translator mediating between the everyday world and cultural modernity with its autonomous sectors, when he is already more than busy trying to carve out a space for ambitious theoretical strategies within the system of the sciences? I think pragmatism and hermeneutics have joined forces to answer this question, by attributing epistemic authority to the community of all who cooperate and speak with one another. Everyday communication makes possible a kind of understanding that is based on claims to validity, thus furnishing the only real alternative to exerting influence on one another, which is always more or less coercive. The validity claims that we raise in conversation — that is, when we say something with conviction — transcend this specific conversational context, pointing to something beyond the spatio-temporal ambit of the occasion. Every agreement, whether produced for the first time or reaffirmed, is based on (controvertible) grounds or reasons. Grounds have a special property: They force us into yes or no positions. Built into the structure of action-oriented-to-reaching-understanding is therefore an element of unconditionality. And it is this unconditional element that makes the validity (*Gültigkeit*) we claim for our views different from the mere de facto acceptance (*Geltung*) of habitual practices.[13] From the perspective of first persons, what we consider justified is not a function of life styles but a question of justification or grounding. That is why philosophy is "rooted in the urge to see social practices of justification as more than just such practices."[14] The same urge is at work when people like me stubbornly cling to the notion that philosophy is the guardian of rationality.

Notes

1. "The critique . . ., arriving at all its decisions in the light of fundamental principles of its own institution, the authority of which no one can question, secures to us the peace of a legal order, in which our disputes have to be conducted solely by the recognized methods of legal action." I. Kant, *Critique of Pure Reason*, trans. N. K. Smith, p. 601.

2. Richard Rorty, *Philosophy and the Mirror of Nature* (Princeton, 1979), pp. 392ff.

3. Rorty approvingly paraphrases a dictum by Eduard Zeller: "Hegelianism produced an image of philosophy as a discipline which somehow both completed and swallowed up the other disciplines, rather than *grounding* them. It also made philosophy too popular, too interesting, too important, to be properly professional; it challenged philosophy professors to embody the World-Spirit, rather than simply getting on with their *Fach*." Rorty (1979), p. 135.

4. G. Schönrich, *Kategorien und transzendentale Argumentation* (Frankfurt, 1981), ch. 4, pp. 182ff.; R. Bittner, "Transzendental," in *Handbuch philosophischer Grundbegriffe*, vol. 5 (Munich 1974), pp. 1524ff.

5. C. F. Gethmann and R. Hegselmann, "Das Problem der Begründung zwischen Dezisionismus und Fundamentalismus," *Zeitschrift für allgemeine Wissenschaftstheorie* 8 (1977), pp. 432ff.

6. H. Albert, *Treatise on Critical Reason* (Princeton, 1985).

7. H. Lenk, "Philosophische Logikbegründung und rationaler Kritizismus," *Zeitschrift für philosophische Forschung* 24 (1970), pp. 183ff.

8. T. Kesselring, *Entwicklung und Widerspruch — Ein Vergleich zwischen Piagets genetischer Erkenntnistheorie und Hegels Dialektik* (Frankfurt, 1981).

9. Rorty (1979), p. 371.

10. Rorty (1979), p. 372.

11. R. Spaemann, "Der Streit der Philosophen," in H. Lübbe, ed., *Wozu Philosophie?* (Berlin, 1978), p. 96.

12. J. Habermas, "Modernity versus Postmodernity," *New German Critique* 22 (1981), pp. 3–14.

13. Cf. J. Habermas, *Theory of Communicative Action* (Boston, 1984), vol. 1, pp. 114ff.

14. Rorty (1979), p. 390.

III

The Transformation of Philosophy: Hermeneutics, Rhetoric, Narrative

10

Hans-Georg Gadamer

Introduction

One of the major achievements of Hans-Georg Gadamer's *Truth and Method* was the demonstration that hermeneutics — traditionally "the art of understanding" — has universal and ontological significance. Today "hermeneutics" no longer refers simply to the interpretive techniques employed within special disciplines such as theology and jurisprudence, but to the more basic question of how understanding in general is possible. With the disintegration of a commonly shared world view, the revolutions in culture, politics, and society, and the confrontation with other traditions, the modern age has experienced a crisis concerning its ability to understand the past, other cultures, and even itself. This awareness of our finitude has underscored "the universality of the hermeneutic problem."

The ontological significance of hermeneutics can be seen in the challenge it presents to philosophical perspectives in which a clear subject-object dichotomy is posited — both "idealist" perspectives in which a subject constitutes an objective world according to rules or "categories" grounded self-reflexively, and "realist" perspectives in which an (ideally) neutral subject discovers a world of mind-independent facts and objective meanings. "Understanding is never subjective behavior toward a given 'object' but belongs to the effective history of what is understood, to the history of its influence; in other words, understanding belongs to the being of that which is understood." According to Gadamer, understanding is an event, a happening, in which both interpreter and text (or text analogue), "subject" and "object," mutually determine one another. Thus, appeal to an objective meaning, in itself as it were, is as inappropriate to an account of what understanding is as recourse to a self-transparent subject in full methodological control of its object. Since he is often misunderstood on this point, it should be noted, however, that Gadamer's concern is not to call into question the validity of the empirical sciences, or even to propose a methodology appropriate for the human sciences; he is concerned rather with the "self-understanding" of science — that is, not with "what we do or what we ought to do, but with what happens to us over and above our wanting and doing."

A basic theme of Gadamer's philosophical hermeneutics is the constitutive role of prejudices or prejudgments in understanding: "Prejudices are not necessarily unjustified and erroneous, so that they inevitably distort the truth. In fact, the historicity of our existence entails that prejudices, in the literal sense of the word [i.e., prejudgments], constitute the initial directedness of our whole ability to experience. Prejudices are biases of our openness to the world." On one reading, this thesis is uncontroversial and common to all fallibilistic approaches. Gadamer's stronger claim, however, is that prejudices belong to the very possibility of understanding and hence that the Enlightenment ideal of objective knowledge — knowledge freed from all particular perspectives — is an illusion, even as a "limit concept." This stronger thesis is developed in relation to Heidegger's notion of the hermeneutic circle and Gadamer's own notion of "effective historical consciousness," and leads in the end to a reevaluation of the ontological assumptions underlying the Enlightenment prejudice against prejudice. Effective historical consciousness, Gadamer reminds us, is always more *Sein* than *Bewusstsein*.

The hermeneutic circle describes a process basic to all understanding: the to-and-fro movement between partial understandings and the "sense of the whole." We attempt to comprehend the whole on the basis of what we already understand, and partial understandings are successively transformed in response to resistances arising from the text and the subject matter itself (*die Sache selbst*). (Collingwood offered a similar account in his "dialectic of the question and answer.") For Heidegger, however, this circle was not merely a matter of procedure; it referred to a mode of being in the world that precedes any methodological and abstract distinction between subject and object. Gadamer retains this insight in the double meaning conveyed by the notion of "effective historical consciousness": It refers not only to the fact that consciousness is limited and determined by history but also to the fact that it essentially belongs to history, to what can be understood. "The true historical object is not an object at all, but the unity of the one and the other, a relationship in which exist both the reality of history and the reality of historical understanding. A proper hermeneutics would have to demonstrate the effectivity of history within understanding itself" (*Truth and Method,* 268).

"Effective historical consciousness" thus provides Gadamer with an alternative to objectivism and relativism. Both begin with the assumption that there is a gap between subject and object, between "conceptual scheme" and the world "out there"; objectivism then argues that this gap can be overcome through careful adherence to method, while relativism maintains that we are condemned to a plurality of incommensurable language games. Gadamer suggests that both positions misconstrue the common hermeneutic experience; he proposes that from a phenomenological viewpoint the event of understanding is more approximately described as a dialogue between interpreter and text (or text analogue). A dialogue always presupposes that no matter how foreign the text, there always exists some shared history or common basis — or at least that a common basis can be created — which can provide a point of departure for further understanding. However, there is nothing external to the dialogue as such — no self-grounding, no indubitable method, no objective world — by which its success could be judged. Rather, misunderstandings only come to light through *further* dialogue about the matter at hand (*die Sache*); the important thing is, as Rorty has put it, to keep the conversation going.

It is now possible to see in what sense hermeneutics is a practical philosophy and why Gadamer repeatedly returns to Aristotle's notion of *phronesis* (practical deliberation) for clarification. On Aristotle's account, *phronesis* is neither *techne* (skill) nor *episteme* (scientific knowledge, which involves subsuming the particular under the general) but a matter of realizing the universal (the Good) in a particular situation. As such it is rooted in a natural human capacity that cannot be replaced either by technical know-how or by theoretical science; but it can "be raised to the level of reflective awareness" in practical philosophy. Similarly, philosophical hermeneutics raises to the level of reflective awareness the natural human capacity for intelligent communication with one's fellow human beings, for achieving mutual understanding in language. In both practical philosophy and philosophical hermeneutics (and, Gadamer would add, in rhetoric) we have to do with a "particular kind of science," based in a natural capacity, and whose underlying theoretical interest is indissolubly bound up with a certain kind of practical action. Specifically, hermeneutics "only makes us aware reflectively of what is performatively at play in the practical experience of understanding." Every act of understanding involves relating what is to be understood to the situation of the interpreter and thus contains a moment of self-understanding. Hermeneutic openness to a text means a willingness to put one's own preconceptions and prejudgments on the line, that is, to take seriously the claims to validity raised by the text and thus to risk having one's own views challenged and the limits of one's own horizon exposed. Thus, every appropriation or making one's own of another's meaning harbors a potential for changing one's moral-practical self-understanding. In this sense hermeneutics is itself a continuation of practical philosophy.

Suggested Readings

Bernstein, Richard. *Beyond Objectivism and Relativism: Science, Hermeneutics and Praxis.* Philadelphia: University of Pennsylvania Press, 1983.

Bleicher, Josef. *Contemporary Hermeneutics: Hermeneutics as Method, Philosophy, and Critique.* London: Routledge and Kegan Paul, 1980.

Dallmayr, Fred. *Polis and Praxis*. Cambridge, Massachusetts: MIT Press, 1984.

Dallmayr, Fred, and Thomas McCarthy, eds. *Understanding and Social Inquiry*. Notre Dame: University of Notre Dame Press, 1977.

Ermarth, Michael. "The Transformation of Hermeneutics," *The Monist* 64 (1981), 175–194.

Forget, P., ed. *Text und Interpretation*. München: Fink Verlag, 1984.

Frei, Hans. *The Eclipse of Biblical Narrative*. New Haven: Yale University Press, 1974.

Gadamer, Hans-Georg. *Truth and Method*. New York: Seabury Press, 1975.

Gadamer, Hans-Georg. "Hermeneutics and Social Science," *Cultural Hermeneutics* 2 (1975), 307–316.

Gadamer, Hans-Georg. *Philosophical Hermeneutics*. Berkeley: University of California Press, 1976.

Gadamer, Hans-Georg. *Hegel's Dialectic: Five Hermeneutical Studies*. New Haven: Yale University Press, 1976.

Gadamer, Hans-Georg. "The Problem of Historical Consciousness," in *Interpretive Social Science: A Reader,* ed. P. Rabinow and W. Sullivan, 103–162. Berkeley: University of California Press, 1979.

Gadamer, Hans-Georg. *Dialogue and Dialectic*. New Haven: Yale University Press, 1980.

Gadamer, Hans-Georg. "Practical Philosophy as a Model of the Human Sciences," *Research in Phenomenology* 9 (1980), 74–85.

Gadamer, Hans-Georg. *Reason in the Age of Science*. Cambridge, Massachusetts: MIT Press, 1981.

Gadamer, Hans-Georg. "Heidegger and the History of Philosophy," *The Monist* 64 (1981), 423–433.

Gadamer, Hans-Georg. *Philosophical Apprenticeships*. Cambridge, Massachusetts: MIT Press, 1985.

Giddens, Anthony. *Studies in Social and Political Theory*. New York: Basic Books, 1970.

Habermas, Jürgen. "A Review of Gadamer's *Truth and Method*," in *Understanding and Social Inquiry,* ed. F. Dallmayr and T. McCarthy, 335–363. Notre Dame: University of Notre Dame Press, 1977.

Hirsch, E. D. *Validity in Interpretation*. New Haven: Yale University Press, 1967.

Hollinger, Robert, ed. *Hermeneutics and Praxis*. Notre Dame: University of Notre Dame Press, 1985.

Hoy, David. *The Critical Circle: Literature and History in Contemporary Hermeneutics*. Berkeley: University of California Press, 1978.

Mendelson, Jack. "The Habermas-Gadamer Debate," *New German Critique* 18 (1979), 44–73.

Misgeld, Dieter. "Critical Theory and Hermeneutics: The Debate Between Habermas and Gadamer," in *On Critical Theory,* ed. John O'Neill. New York: Seabury Press, 1976.

Palmer, Richard. *Hermeneutics: Interpretation Theory in Schleiermacher, Dilthey, Heidegger, and Gadamer.* Evanston: Northwestern University Press, 1969.

Shapiro, Gary, and Alan Sica, eds. *Hermeneutics.* Amherst: University of Massachusetts Press, 1984.

Silverman, Hugh, and Don Ihde, eds. *Hermeneutics and Deconstruction.* Albany: SUNY Press, 1985.

Wachterhauser, Bruce, ed. *Hermeneutics and Modern Philosophy.* Albany: SUNY Press, 1986.

Warnke, Georgia. *The Hermeneutics of Gadamer.* Cambridge: Polity Press, forthcoming.

Weinsheimer, Joel C. *Gadamer's Hermeneutics: A Reading of "Truth and Method."* New Haven: Yale University Press, 1985.

Hermeneutics as Practical Philosophy

Hans-Georg Gadamer

Not only the word *hermeneutics* is ancient. The reality designated by the word is as well, whether it be rendered today with such expressions as *interpretation, explication, translation,* or even only with *understanding.* At any rate, it precedes the idea of methodical science developed by modernity. Even modern linguistic usage itself reflects something of the peculiar two-sidedness and ambivalence of the theoretical and practical perspective under which the reality of hermeneutics appears. In the late eighteenth as well as in the early nineteenth centuries, the singular emergence of the term *hermeneutics* in certain authors shows that at that time the expression, coming probably from theology, penetrated the general language usage; and then it obviously denoted only the practical capacity of understanding, in the sense of the intelligent and empathetic entry into another's standpoint. It comes up as a term of praise among the pastoral types. I discovered the word in the German author Heinrich Seume (who of course had been a student with Morus in Leipzig) and in Johann Peter Hebel. But even Schleiermacher, the founder of the more recent development of hermeneutics into a general methodological doctrine of the *Geisteswissenschaften,* appeals emphatically to the idea that the art of understanding is required not only with respect to texts but also in one's intercourse with one's fellow human beings.

Thus hermeneutics is more than just a method of the sciences or the distinctive feature of a certain group of sciences. Above all it refers to a natural human capacity.

The oscillation of an expression like *hermeneutics* between a theoretical and a practical meaning is encountered elsewhere too. For example, we speak of logic or its lack in our day-to-day intercourse with our fellow human beings, and by this we are not at all referring to the special philosophical discipline of logic. The same holds true for the word *rhetoric,* by which we designate the teachable art of speaking, as well as the natural gift and its exercise. Here it is altogether clear that without any native endowment the learning of what can be learned leads only to quite modest success. If natural giftedness for speaking is lacking, it can scarcely be made up for by methodological doctrine. Now this will surely be the case as well for the art of understanding, for hermeneutics.

This sort of thing has its significance for the theory of science. What kind of science is it that presents itself more as a cultivation of a natural gift and as a theoretically heightened awareness of it? For the history of science this presents an open problem. Where does the art of understanding belong? Does hermeneutics stand closer to rhetoric? Or should one bring it more in proximity with logic and the methodology of the sciences? Recently I have tried to make some contributions to these questions for the history of science.[1] Like linguistic usage, inquiry into the history of science also indicates that the notion of method, fundamental to modern science, brought into dissolution a notion of science that was open precisely in the direction of such a natural human capacity.

So there arises the more general question as to whether there survives into our own day a sector within the systematic framework of the sciences that is more strongly tied to the earlier traditions of the concepts of science than to the notion of method proper to modern science. It may still be asked whether this is not at least the case for the clearly circumscribable domain of the so-called *Geisteswissenschaften* — and this without prejudice to the question whether a hermeneutic dimension does not play a role in every instance of the desire to know, even that of the modern sciences of nature.

Now there does exist at least one exemplar of the sort pertinent to the theory of science, which could lend a certain legitimacy to such a reorientation of the methodical heightening of awareness on the part of the *Geisteswissenschaften*. This is the practical philosophy established by Aristotle.[2]

. . . The most important delimitation that the concept of practice undergoes with Aristotle is not vis-à-vis theoretical science, which itself emerges from the enormous range of life possibilities as a type of the most noble practice. Rather it is the delimitation over against production based on knowledge, the *poiesis* that provides the economic basis for the life of the polis. In particular, if it is not a matter of the "lower servile" arts but of the kind a free man can engage in without disqualification, such a knowing and know-how pertain to his practice without being practical knowledge in the practical-political sense. And so practical philosophy is determined by the line drawn between the practical knowledge of the person who chooses freely and the acquired skill of the expert that Aristotle names *techne*. Practical philosophy, then, has to do not with the learnable crafts and skills, however essential this dimension of human ability is for the communal life of humanity. Rather it has to do with what is each individual's due as a citizen and what constitutes his *arete* or excellence. Hence practical philosophy needs to raise to the level of reflective awareness the distinctively human trait of having *prohairesis*, whether it be in the form of developing those fundamental human orientations for such preferring that have the character of *arete* or in the form of the prudence in deliberating and taking counsel that guides action. In any case, it has to be accountable with its knowledge for the viewpoint in terms of which one thing is to be preferred to another: the relationship to the good. But the knowledge that gives direction to action is essentially called for by concrete situations in which we are to choose the thing to be done; and no learned and mastered technique can spare us the task of deliberation and decision. As a result, the practical science directed toward this practical knowledge is neither theoretical science in the style of mathematics nor expert know-how in the sense of a knowledgeable mastery of operational procedures (*poiesis*) but a unique sort of science. It must arise from practice itself and, with all the typical generalizations that it brings to explicit consciousness, be related back to practice.

In fact, that constitutes the specific character of Aristotelian ethics and politics.

Not only is its object the constantly changing situations and modes of conduct that can be elevated to knowledge only in respect to their regularity and averageness. Conversely such teachable knowledge of typical structures has the character of real knowledge only by reason of the fact that (as is always the case with technique or know-how) it is repeatedly transposed into the concrete situation. Practical philosophy, then, certainly is "science": a knowledge of the universal that as such is teachable. But it is still a science that needs certain conditions to be fulfilled. It demands of the one learning it the same indissoluble relationship to practice it does of the one teaching it. To this extent, it does have a certain proximity to the expert knowledge proper to technique, but what separates it fundamentally from technical expertise is that it expressly asks the question of the good too — for example, about the best way of life or about the best constitution of the state. It does not merely master an ability, like technical expertise, whose task is set by an outside authority: by the purpose to be served by what is being produced.

All this holds true for hermeneutics as well. As the theory of interpretation or explication, it is not just a theory. From the most ancient times right down to our days, hermeneutics quite clearly has claimed that its reflection upon the possibilities, rules, and means of interpretation is immediately useful and advantageous for the practice of interpretation — whereas perhaps a fully worked out theory of logic has a more scientifically rarefied ambition than promoting the advance of logical thinking; just as number theory has a loftier aim than advancing calculative finesse. Hence, in a first approximation, hermeneutics may be understood as a teaching about a technical skill (*Kunstlehre*), in the manner of rhetoric. Like rhetoric, hermeneutics can designate a natural capacity of human beings, and then it refers to the human capacity for intelligent interchange with one's fellows.

. . . The art of understanding the tradition, whether it deals with sacred books, legal texts, or exemplary masterworks, not only presupposes the recognition of these works but goes on further to shape their productive transmission. As long as it remained confined to normative texts, the earlier hermeneutics did not pose a central issue for the conception of problems of traditional philosophy. To that degree it is quite a long way from our contemporary interest in hermeneutics. Nevertheless, when the remoteness of the lofty and the remoteness of the recondite needed to be overcome not simply in specialized domains such as religious documents, texts of the law, or the classics in their foreign languages, but when the historical tradition in its entirety up to the present moment moved into a position of similar remoteness, the problem of hermeneutics entered intrinsically into the philosophic awareness of problems. This took place in virtue of the great breach in tradition brought about by the French Revolution, as a result of which European civilization splintered into national cultures.

With the disappearance of its validity as a thing to be taken for granted, the common tradition of the Christian states of Europe, which of course lived on, began to enter explicit consciousness in a completely novel way as a freely chosen model, as the passionate aim of nostalgia, and finally as an object of historical knowledge. This was the hour of a universal hermeneutics through which the universe of the historical world was to be deciphered. The past as such had become alien.

Every renewed encounter with an older tradition now is no longer a simple matter of appropriation that un-self-consciously adds what is proper to itself even as it assimilates what is old; rather, tradition has to cross the abyss of historical consciousness. The standard slogan became to return to the original sources, and in this fashion our historically mediated image of the past was placed on an entirely new footing. This involved a profoundly hermeneutical task. As soon as one acknowledges that one's own perspective is utterly different from the viewpoints of the authors and the meanings of the texts of the past, there arises the need for a unique effort to avoid misunderstanding the meaning of old texts and yet to comprehend them in their persuasive force. The description of the inner structure and coherence of a given text and the mere repetition of what the author says are not yet real understanding. One has to bring his speaking back to life again, and for this one has to become familiar with the realities about which the text speaks. To be sure, one has to master the grammatical rules, the stylistic devices, the art of composition upon which the text is based, if one wishes to understand what the author wanted to say in his text; but the main issue in all understanding concerns the meaningful relationship that exists between the statements of the text and our understanding of the reality under discussion.

Only when our entire culture for the first time saw itself threatened by radical doubt and critique did hermeneutics become a matter of universal significance. This had to it a persuasive inner logic. One has only to think of the radicalism in doubting that is to be found especially in Friedrich Nietzsche. His slowly growing influence in every area of our culture possessed a depth that is usually not sufficiently realized. Psychoanalysis, for instance, is scarcely imaginable without Nietzsche's radical calling into doubt of the testimony of human reflective self-consciousness. Nietzsche posed the demand that one doubt more profoundly and fundamentally than had Descartes, who considered the ultimate unshakable foundation of all certitude to be explicit self-consciousness. The illusions of reflective self-consciousness, the idols of self-knowledge, constituted the novel discovery of Nietzsche, and later modernity may be dated in terms of his all-pervasive influence. As a result, the notion of interpretation attained a far more profound and general meaning.

Self-understanding can no longer be integrally related to a complete self-transparency in the sense of a full presence of ourselves to ourselves. Self-understanding is always on-the-way; it is on a path whose completion is a clear impossibility. If there is an entire dimension of unilluminated unconscious; if all our actions, wishes, drives, decisions, and modes of conduct (and so the totality of our human social existence) are based on the obscure and veiled dimension of the conations of our animality; if all our conscious representations can be masks, pretexts, under which our vital energy or our social interests pursue their own goals in an unconscious way; if all the insights we have, as obvious and evident as they may be, are threatened by such doubt; then self-understanding cannot designate any patent self-transparency of our human existence. We have to repudiate the illusion of completely illuminating the darkness of our motivations and tendencies. This is not to say, however, that we can simply ignore this new area of human experiences that looms in the unconscious. What comes in for methodical investigation here is indeed not only the field of the unconscious that concerns the psychoanalyst as a physician; it is just as much the world of the dominant social prejudices that Marxism claims to elucidate. Psychoanalysis and critique of ideology are forms of enlightenment, and both invoke the emancipatory mandate of the Enlightenment as formulated by Kant in terms of the "exodus from the condition of self-inflicted immaturity."

Nevertheless when we examine the range of these new insights, it seems to me that we need to cast a critical eye upon just what sort of untested presuppositions of a traditional kind are still at work in them. One has to ask oneself whether the dynamic law of human life can be conceived adequately in terms of progress, of a continual advance from the unknown into the known, and whether the course of human culture is actually a linear progression from mythology to enlightenment. One should entertain a completely different question: whether the movement of human existence does not issue in a relentless inner tension between illumination and concealment. Might it not be just a prejudice of modern times that the notion of progress that is in fact constitutive for the spirit of scientific research should be transferable to the whole of human living and human culture? One has to ask whether progress, while it is at home in the special field of scientific research, is at all consonant with the conditions of human existence in general. Is the notion of an ever-mounting and self-perfecting enlightenment finally ambiguous?

If one wishes to appraise the significance or the task and the limits of what we call hermeneutics today, one must bear in mind this philosophic and humane background, this fundamental doubt about the legitimacy of objective self-consciousness. In a certain way, the very word *hermeneutics* and its cognate word *interpretation* furnish a hint, for these words imply a sharp distinction between the claim of being able to explain a fact completely through deriving all its conditions; through calculating it from the givenness of all its conditions; and through learning to produce it by artificial arrangement — this is the well-known ideal of natural scientific knowledge; and on the other hand, the claim, say, of interpretation, which we always presume to be no more than an approximation: only an attempt, plausible and fruitful, but clearly never definitive.

The very idea of definitive interpretation seems to be intrinsically contradictory. Interpretation is always on the way. If, then, the word *interpretation* points to the finitude of human being and the finitude of human knowing, then the experience of interpretation implies something that was not implied by the earlier self-understanding when hermeneutics was coordinated with special fields and applied as a technique for overcoming difficulties in troublesome texts. Then hermeneutics could be understood as a teaching about a technical skill — but no longer.

Once we presuppose that there is no such thing as a fully transparent text or a completely exhaustive interest in the explaining and construing of texts, then all perspectives relative to the art and theory of interpretation are shifted. Then it becomes more important to trace the interests guiding us with respect to a given subject matter than simply to interpret the evident content of a statement. One of the more fertile insights of modern hermeneutics is that every statement has to be seen as a response to a question and that the only way to understand a statement is to get hold of the question to which the statement is an answer. This prior question has its own direction of meaning and is by no means to be gotten hold of through a network of background motivations but rather in reaching out to the broader contexts of meaning encompassed by the question and deposited in the statement.

What has to be held up as a first determination that will do justice to modern hermeneutics in contrast to the traditional kind is this notion that a philosophical hermeneutics is more interested in the questions than the answers — or better, that it interprets statements as answers to questions that it is its role to understand. That is not all. Where does our effort to understand begin? Why are we interested in understanding a text or some experience of the world, including our doubts about patent self-interpretations? Do we have a free choice about these things? Is it at all true that we follow our own free decision whenever we try to investigate or interpret certain things? Free decision? A neutral, completely objective concern? At least the theologian would surely have objections here and say, "Oh no! Our understanding of the Holy Scripture does not come from our own free choice. It takes an act of grace. And the Bible is not a totality of sentences offered willy-nilly as a sacrifice to human analysis. No, the gospel is directed to me in a personal way. It claims to contain neither an objective statement nor a totality of objective statements but a special address to me." I believe that not only theologians would have doubts about this notion that one ultimately encounters free decisions when interpreting transmitted texts. Rather there are always both conscious and unconscious interests at play determining us; it will always be the case that we have to ask ourselves why a text stirs our interest. The answer will never be that it communicates some neutral fact to us. On the contrary, we have to get behind such putative facts in order to awaken our interest in them or to make ourselves expressly aware of such interests. We encounter facts in statements. All statements are answers. But that is not all. The question to which each statement is an answer is itself motivated in turn, and so in a certain sense every question is itself an answer again. It responds to a challenge. Without an inner tension between our anticipations of meaning and the all-pervasive opinions, and without a critical interest in the generally prevailing opinions, there would be no questions at all.

This first step of hermeneutic endeavor, especially the requirement of going back to the motivating questions when understanding statements, is not a particularly artificial procedure. On the contrary, it is our normal practice. If we have to answer a question and we cannot understand the question correctly (but we do know what the other wants to know), then we obviously have to understand better the sense of the question. And so we ask in return why someone would ask us that. Only when I have first understood the motivating meaning of the question can I even begin to look for an answer. It is not artificial in the least to reflect upon the presuppositions implicit in our questions. On the contrary, it is artificial not to reflect upon these presuppositions. It is quite artificial to imagine that statements fall down from heaven and that they can be subjected to analytic labor without once bringing into consideration why they were stated and in what way they are responses to something. That is the first, basic, and infinitely far-reaching demand called for in any hermeneutical undertaking. Not only in philosophy or theology but in any research project, it is required that one elaborate an awareness of the hermeneutic situation. That has to be our initial aim when we approach what the question is. To state this in words expressing one of our more trivial experiences, we must understand what is behind a question. Making ourselves aware of hidden presuppositions, however, means not only and primarily illuminating our unconscious presuppositions in the sense of psychoanalysis; it means becoming aware of the vague presuppositions and implications involved in a question that comes up.

The elaboration of the hermeneutic situation, which is the key to methodical interpretation, has a unique element to it. The first guiding insight is to admit the endlessness of this task. To imagine that one might ever attain full illumination as to his motives or his interests in questions is to imagine something impossible. In spite of this, it remains a legitimate task to clarify what lies at the basis of our interests as far as possible. Only then are we in a position to understand the statements with which we are concerned, precisely insofar as we recognize our own questions in them.

In this connection, we must realize that the unconscious and the implicit do not simply make up the polar opposite of our conscious human existence. The task of understanding is not merely that of clarifying the deepest unconscious grounds motivating our interest but above all that of understanding and explicating them in the direction and limits indicated by our hermeneutic interest. In the rare cases in which the communicative intersubjectivity of the "community of conversation" is fundamentally disrupted so that one despairs of any intended and common meaning, this can motivate a direction of interest for which the psychoanalyst is competent.

But this is a limit situation for hermeneutics. One can sharpen any hermeneutic situation to this limit of despairing of meaning and of needing to get behind the manifest meaning. The labor of psychoanalysis would, it appears to me, be based on a false estimation of its legitimacy and its unique meaning if its task were not regarded as a task at the limit and if it were not to set out from the fundamental insight that life always discovers some kind of equilibrium and that there also pertains to this equilibrium a balance between our unconscious drives and our conscious human motivations and decisions. To be sure, there is never a complete concord between the tendencies of our unconscious and our conscious motivations. But as a rule neither is it always a matter of complete concealment and distortion. It is a sign of sickness when one has so dissimulated oneself to oneself that one can know nothing further without confiding in a doctor. Then in a common labor of analysis, one takes a couple of steps further toward clarifying the background of one's own unconscious — with the goal of regaining what one had lost: the equilibrium between one's own nature and the awareness and language shared by all of us.

In contrast to this, the unconscious, in the sense of what is implicit to our direct awareness, is the normal object of our hermeneutic concern. This means, however, that the task of understanding is restricted. It is restricted by the resistance offered by statements or texts and brought to an end by the regaining of a shared possession of meaning, just as happens in a conversation when we try to shed light upon a difference of opinion or a misunderstanding.

In this most authentic realm of hermeneutic experience, the conditions of which a hermeneutic philosophy tries to give an account, the neighborly affinity of hermeneutics with practical philosophy is confirmed. First of all, understanding, like action, always remains a risk and never leaves room for the simple application of a general knowledge of rules to the statements or texts to be understood. Furthermore, where it is successful, understanding means a growth in inner awareness, which as a new experience enters into the texture of our own mental experience. Understanding is an adventure and, like any other adventure, is dangerous. Just because it is not satisfied with simply wanting to register what is there or is said there but goes back to our guiding interests and questions, one has to concede that the hermeneutical experience has a far smaller degree of certainty than that attained by the methods of the natural sciences. But when one realizes that understanding is an adventure, this implies that it affords unique opportunities as well. It is capable of contributing in a special way to the broadening of our human experiences, our self-knowledge, and our horizon, for everything understanding mediates is mediated along with ourselves.

A further point is that the key terms of earlier hermeneutics, such as the *mens auctoris* or the intention of the text, together with all the psychological factors related to the openness of the reader or listener to the text, are not adequate to what is most essential to the process of understanding to the extent that it is a process of communication. For indeed it is a process of growing familiarity between the determinate experience, or the "text," and ourselves. The intrinsically linguistic condition of all our understanding implies that the vague representations of meaning that bear us along get brought word by word to articulation and so become communicable. The communality of all understanding as grounded in its intrinsically linguistic quality seems to me to be an essential point in hermeneutical experience. We are continually shaping a common perspective when we speak a common language and so are active partici-pants in the communality of our experience of the world. Experiences of resistance or opposition bear witness to this, for example, in discussion. Discussion bears fruit when a common language is found. Then the participants part from one an-other as changed beings. The individual perspectives with which they entered upon the discussion have been trans-formed, and so they are transformed themselves. This, then, is a kind of progress — not the progress proper to research in regard to which one cannot fall behind but a progress that always must be renewed in the effort of our living.

The miniature of a successful discussion can illustrate what I have developed in the theory of the fusion of horizons in *Truth and Method,* and it may provide a justification as to why I maintain that the situation of conversation is a fertile model even where a mute text is brought to speech first by the questions of the interpreter.

The hermeneutics that I characterize as philosophic is not introduced as a new procedure of interpretation or explication. Basically it only describes what always happens wherever an interpretation is convincing and successful. It is not at all a matter of a doctrine about a technical skill that would state how understanding ought to be. We have to acknowledge what is, and so we cannot change the fact the unacknowledged presuppositions are always at work in our understanding. Probably we should not want to change this at all, even if we could. It always harvests a broadened and deepened self-understanding. But that means hermeneutics is philosophy, and as philosophy it is practical philosophy.

The great tradition of practical philosophy lives on in a hermeneutics that becomes aware of its philosophic implications, so we have recourse to this tradition about which we have spoken. In both cases, we have the same mutual implication between theoretical interest and practical action. Aristotle thought this issue through with complete lucidity in his ethics. For one to dedicate one's life to theoretic interests presupposes the virtue of *phronesis.* This in no way restricts the primacy of theory or of an interest in the pure desire to know. The idea of theory is and remains the exclusion of every interest in mere utility, whether on the part of the individual, the group, or the society as a whole. On the other hand, the primacy of "practice" is undeniable. Aristotle was insightful enough to acknowledge the reciprocity between theory and practice.

So when I speak about hermeneutics here, it is theory. There are no practical situations of understanding that I am trying to resolve by so speaking. Hermeneutics has to do with a theoretical attitude toward the practice of interpretation, the interpretation of texts, but also in relation to the experiences interpreted in them and in our communicatively unfolded orientations in the world. This theoretic stance only makes us aware reflectively of what is performatively at play in the practical experience of understanding. And so it appears to me that the answer given by Aristotle to the question about the possibility of a moral philosophy holds true as well for our interest in hermeneutics. His answer was that ethics is only a theoretical enterprise and that anything said by way of a theoretic description of the forms of right living can be at best of little help when it comes to concrete application to the human experience of life. Any yet the universal desire to know does not break off at the point where concrete practical discernment is the decisive issue. The connection between the universal desire to know and concrete practical discernment is a reciprocal one. Hence, it appears to me that heightened theoretic awareness about the experience of understanding and the practice of understanding, like philosophical hermeneutics and one's own self-understanding, are inseparable.

Notes

1. Now in *Kleine Schriften IV: Variationen* (Tübingen: Mohr, 1977), 148–172.

2. When I was speaking on the theme of this essay in Münster in January 1978, I used the opportunity to pay tribute to the memory of my colleague, Joachim Ritter, whose works contain so much that has advanced the issues under discussion.

Foreword to the Second German Edition of Truth and Method

Hans-Georg Gadamer

Perhaps I might briefly sketch the intention and claim of *Truth and Method*. My adoption of the term *hermeneutics*, weighted as it is with a long tradition, has apparently led to misunderstandings. It was not my intention to produce a treatise on the art or technique of understanding (*Verstehen*) in the manner of the older hermeneutics. I never wanted to develop a system of technical rules that might describe, or even direct, the methodological procedures of the human sciences (*Geisteswissenschaften*). I also had no intention of investigating the theoretical foundations of work in the human sciences with the aim of turning such knowledge to practical purposes. If there is any practical implication of the studies presented here, it has to do not with any unscientific "engagement," but with the scientific "honesty" to acknowledge the engagement involved in all understanding. My real claim, however, was and is a philosophical one. The question is not what we do or what we ought to do, but what happens to us over and above our wanting and doing.

In that respect the methods of the human sciences are not at all under discussion here. My starting point is, rather, that the historical *Geisteswissenschaften*, as they emerged from German Romanticism and became imbued with the spirit of modern science, are the trustees of a humanistic heritage. This distinguishes them from all the other types of modern research and brings them into proximity with other, very different, extrascientific experiences, especially those proper to art. There is undoubtedly something for the sociologist of knowledge in this. In Germany, which has always been prerevolutionary, the tradition of aesthetic humanism continued on full of life in the midst of the development of modern scientific thought. In other countries there may be a larger element of political consciousness in what sustains the humanities or *lettres* — in short, everything formerly known as the *humaniora*.

This does not at all preclude the methods of the modern sciences of nature from being applied to the social world as well. Our epoch may well be marked more by the increasing rationalization of society and the scientific techniques employed in directing it than by the colossal progress of the modern natural sciences. The methodical spirit of science asserts itself everywhere. So it was the farthest thing from my mind to deny that methodical work within the *Geisteswissenschaften* is essential. Nor did I wish to revive the old methodological debates between the natural and human sciences. The issue is hardly one of contrasting methods. In that regard, the question that Windelband and Rickert once formulated in terms of the "limits of natural-scientific concept formation" strikes me as the wrong one. What we are concerned with here is not a difference in method but a difference in the aims of knowledge. The question I have posed seeks to uncover and bring to consciousness something that the methodological debates have covered up and misconstrued, something that does not so much limit or restrict modern science as precede it and make it possible. This does not at all detract from its own immanent laws of development. It would be futile to appeal to the human desire for knowledge and the human capacity for making and doing to be more considerate in their dealings with the natural and social orders of the world. There is something absurd about playing the role of the moral preacher while wearing the dress of a scholar, as there is about the claim of the philosopher who deduces from principles how "science" has to change in order to become philosophically legitimate.

Invoking the famous Kantian distinction between the *questio juris* and the *questio facti* in this connection strikes me as a simple misunderstanding. Kant certainly had no intention of prescribing to modern science the way it had to proceed if it was to prove itself before the judgment seat of Reason. He posed philosophical questions concerning the conditions of knowledge that make modern science possible and concerning how far that knowledge extends. *Truth and Method* also poses a philosophical question in this sense — but not only to the *Geisteswissenschaften* (among which certain classical disciplines would be given precedence). In fact, it is posed not only to science and its modes of experience but to the whole of our human experience of the world and our conduct of life. Expressed in Kantian terms, the question is, "How is understanding (*Verstehen*) possible?" This question is prior to any activity of understanding on the part of subjectivity, including the methodical activity of the *verstehenden* sciences, their norms and rules. In my view, Heidegger's temporal analysis of human *Dasein* has convincingly shown that understanding is not one among many modes of action on the part of the subject but rather *Dasein's* very mode of being. It is in this sense that the concept of hermeneutics is employed here. It designates the fundamental movement of *Dasein,* which constitutes its finitude and historicity and thus encompasses the whole of its experience of the world. To say that the movement of understanding is comprehensive and universal is neither arbitrary nor a constructive exaggeration of a single aspect; it lies rather in the very nature of things.

I cannot agree with those who think that the hermeneutic aspect finds its limits in extrahistorical modes of being, such as the mathematical or the aesthetic. It is of course true that the aesthetic quality of a work of art, for instance, rests on laws of construction and levels of form that ultimately transcend the limitations of historical origin and cultural context. I shall leave to one side the question whether the "sense of quality" in relation to a work of art represents an independent possibility of knowledge, or whether, like all taste, it is not only formally developed but cultivated and shaped. Taste, at any rate, is necessarily cultivated by things that indicate what it is cultivated for. In this regard, it includes, perhaps always, preferences for and barriers to specific types of content. In any case, it is true that one who experiences a work of art gathers this experience wholly into himself, that is to say, into the whole of his self-understanding, within which it means something to him. I would even go so far as to say that the achievement of understanding, which encompasses in this way the experience of the work of art, overcomes any historicism in the sphere of aesthetic experience. To be sure, it seems natural to distinguish between the original world configuration brought into being by a work of art and its continued existence in the altered circumstances of life in a later world. But where exactly is the dividing line between a given world and the later world? How does original significance for life pass over into the reflective experience of significance for culture (*Bildung*)? I think the concept of aesthetic nondifferentiation that I introduced in this connection stands up quite well; there are no sharp boundaries here and the movement of understanding cannot be restricted to the reflexive enjoyment prescribed by aesthetic differentiation. We should admit, for example, that an ancient image of the gods, which was not exhibited in the temple as a work of art for the aesthetic, reflexive enjoyment of viewers, but is now on display in a modern museum, contains in the way it stands before us today the world of religious experience from which it sprang. This has the important consequence that its world still belongs to ours. And it is the hermeneutic universe that encompasses both.

There are other respects in which the hermeneutic aspect cannot be arbitrarily restricted or curtailed. It was no mere artifice of composition that led me to begin with the experience of art in order to establish the proper scope for the phenomenon of understanding. The aesthetics of genius has done important preparatory work in this connection by showing that the experience of the work of art always surpasses in principle any subjective horizon of interpretation — that of the artist as well as that of the recipient. The *mens auctoris* cannot function as a measure of the significance of a work of art. Even the idea of the work in itself, divorced from its ever-renewed reality of being experienced, has something abstract about it. I think I have shown why this idea only describes an intention that cannot be made good in any dogmatic way. In any case, the point of my investigations is not to provide a general theory of interpretation and a differential account of its methods — a task that Emilio Betti has performed so well. Their aim is, rather, to find out what is common to all modes of understanding and to show that understanding is never subjective behavior toward a given "object" but belongs to the effective history (*Wirkungsgeschichte*) of what is understood, to the history of its influence; in other words, understanding belongs to the being of that which is understood.

I am not convinced by the objection that the reproduction of a musical work is interpretation in a different sense from, say, the achievement of understanding in reading a poem or in viewing a painting. All reproduction is first of all interpretation and strives as such to be correct. In this sense, it too is "understanding."

In my view, the universality of the hermeneutic standpoint also allows of no restriction in relation to the multiplicity of historical interests brought together under historiography. Of course there are many different ways of writing and researching history. And it is out of the question that every historical interest should be grounded in a conscious reflection on effective history. The history of North American Eskimos is certainly quite independent of whether and when they might have played a role in the "world history of Europe." And yet it cannot seriously be denied that effective-historical reflection will exert its influence even in connection with this historical task. If we were to read the histories of these Eskimos, as they are written today, in fifty or a hundred years, not only would we find them dated because we had learned more or interpreted the sources more correctly in the meantime; we would also be in a position to recognize that the sources were read differently in 1960 because we were motivated by other questions, by other prejudices and interests. Simply to remove historical writing and research from the competence of effective-historical reflection would be to reduce them to what is in the end a matter of indifference. It is precisely the universality of the hermeneutic problem that probes behind all kinds of interests in history because it is concerned with what lies at the basis of any given "historical question." And what is historical research without a "historical question"? In the terminology I have chosen on the basis of investigations into the history of key words, this would read: Application is a moment of understanding itself. Though in this regard I place the legal historian and the practicing jurist on a par, I do not mean thereby to deny that the former has an exclusively "contemplative" task and the latter an exclusively practical one. Yet application is involved in the work of both. How could understanding the legal meaning of a law be something different for the one than for the other? Of course, the judge has the practical task of passing judgment, and all sorts of considerations of legal politics may enter in there that are not entertained by the legal historian who has the same law in view. But does that make their legal *understanding* of the law different? The judge's decision, which "has a practical effect on life," is meant to be a correct application of the law and not an arbitrary one; thus it must rest on a "correct" interpretation, and that necessarily includes the mediation of history with the present in the process of understanding itself.

It is true that the legal historian will in addition have to make a "historical" assessment of a law that has been correctly understood in that sense. This means that he has to form an estimate of its historical significance, and since he is guided by his own historical pre-judgments and living pre-judices, he will do so "incorrectly." But this only means, once again, that we are dealing with the mediation of past and present, that is, with application. This course of history, to which the history of research belongs, has a way of teaching us this. But this obviously does not mean that the historian has done something that he "must" not or should not do, something that could or should have been prevented by a hermeneutic canon. I am not speaking of the errors in legal history but of its sound findings. The practice of the legal historian, like that of the judge, has its "methods" for avoiding error; in this respect I am fully in agreement with the deliberations of legal historians. But the hermeneutic interest of the philosopher begins precisely at the point where error has been successfully avoided. For it is just there that historians as well as dogmaticians testify to a truth that lies beyond what they know, inasmuch as their own transient present is discernible in what they are doing.

From the standpoint of philosophical hermeneutics, the opposition between historical and dogmatic methods has no absolute validity. This raises the question of the extent to which the hermeneutic point of view is itself historically or dogmatically valid. When the principle of effective history is put forward as a universal structural moment in understanding, this thesis is certainly not intended to be subject to historical conditions; it is put forward purely and simply as valid. And yet hermeneutic consciousness exists only under specific historical conditions. Tradition, to whose nature belongs an unquestioned passing on of what has been handed down, must become questionable so that an explicit consciousness of the hermeneutic task of appropriating tradition can take shape. Thus in Augustine we find this type of consciousness in relation to the Old Testament; and during the Reformation Protestant hermeneutics developed from an insistence on understanding the Holy Scriptures in themselves (*sola scriptura*) as against the Roman Church's principle of tradition. Since the rise of historical consciousness, which entails a fundamental distancing of the present from any historical tradition, understanding has generally become a task and requires methodological guidance. It is the thesis of *Truth and Method* that the moment of effective history is at work in any understanding of tradition, even where the methods of the modern historical sciences have gained ground and made an "object" of what has grown historically and has been transmitted historically — an "object" that has to be "established" like an experimental finding. As if tradition were alien and ununderstandable from the human point of view in the same sense as the object of physics!

Looked at in this way, there is a certain justified ambiguity in the concept of effective-historical consciousness as I have used it. It consists in the fact that the concept refers both to the consciousness brought about in the course of history and determined by history, and to a consciousness of this having been brought about and determined. The burden of my argument is clearly that effective-historical determination holds sway even over modern historical scientific consciousness, and that it does so beyond all possible knowledge of its sway. Effective-historical consciousness is finite in such a radical sense that our being, which is produced in the whole of our destiny, intrinsically goes beyond its knowledge of itself. This, however, is a fundamental insight that must not be restricted to a specific historical situation — an insight, to be sure, that in the face of modern historical research and the methodological ideal of scientific objectivity already encounters resistance in the self-interpretation of science.

We are certainly free to ask the further, historically reflexive question of why now, precisely at this point in history, the fundamental insight into the effective-historical moment in all understanding should have become possible. An indirect answer to this question can be found in my studies. Only after the breakdown of the naive historicism of the last century has it become clear that the oppositions between the unhistorical-dogmatic and the historical, between tradition and historical scholarship, between ancient and modern, are not absolute. The famous *querelle des anciens et des modernes* ceases to pose a real alternative. What I have maintained here to be the universality of the hermeneutic aspect, and particularly what I have said regarding linguisticality as the form in which understanding is achieved, encompasses "prehermeneutic" consciousness as well as all modes of hermeneutic consciousness. Even the naive appropriation of tradition is a "retelling," though it is of course not to be described as a "fusion of horizons."

And now to the basic question: How far does the aspect of understanding and its linguisticality itself extend? Can it support the general philosophical result formulated in the proposition "Being that can be understood is language"? Doesn't this proposition lead, in light of the universality of language, to the untenable metaphysical conclusion that "everything" is only language and the happening of language? The obvious reminder of the ineffable is not necessarily prejudicial to the universality of the linguistic. The endlessness of the dialogue in which understanding is achieved makes the establishment of what is ineffable in any given instance itself relative. But is understanding really the sole and sufficient access to the reality of history? Clearly there is a danger here that the proper reality of what happens, in particular its absurdity and contingency, will be attenuated and falsified into some form of experience of meaning.

It was my intention to show that despite the opposition of the Historical School to Hegel's spiritualism, the approach of Droysen and Dilthey to history was misled by its hermeneutic starting point into reading history as a book, that is to say, as something that made sense right down to the last letter. For all its protest against a philosophy of history in which the necessity of the Concept is at the core of everything that happens, Dilthey's historical hermeneutics did not get round having history culminate in the history of ideas. That was my criticism; but doesn't this same danger recur in *Truth and Method?* The traditional formation of concepts, in particular the hermeneutic circle of whole and part that is the starting point of my attempt to lay the foundations of hermeneutics, need not have such a consequence. The concept of the whole is itself to be understood only relatively. The totality of meaning that is to be understood in history or tradition is never the meaning of the totality of history. The danger of docetism is dispelled, it seems to me, if historical tradition is not thought of as the object of historical knowledge or philosophical conception, but as an effective moment of one's own being. The finitude of one's own understanding is the way in which reality, resistance, the absurd and ununderstandable make themselves felt. If one takes this finitude seriously, one must also take seriously the reality of history.

The same problem makes the experience of the *thou* so decisive for all self-understanding. From a systematic point of view, the chapter on "experience" occupies a key position in my investigations. Starting from the experience of the thou, I elucidate there the concept of effective-historical experience as well. For the experience of the thou also exhibits the paradox that something standing vis-à-vis me asserts its own rights and forces me to recognize it purely and simply — and precisely in this is "understood." I believe I have shown, however, that this understanding does not at all understand the thou, but the truth that it tells us. By that I mean such truth as becomes perceptible to one only through the thou, and only through letting oneself be told something by him. It is the same with historical tradition. It would not deserve the interest we take in it if it did not have something to teach us that we could not come to know on our own. The sentence "Being that can be understood is language" has to be read in this sense. It does not claim any absolute mastery over being by the one who understands but means, on the contrary, that being is not experienced where something can be made by us and is conceived by us to that extent; being is experienced, rather, where what is happening can only be understood.

At this point we come to a question of philosophical methodology that was raised by a number of critics of my book. I shall call it the "problem of phenomenological immanence." It is true that my book is phenomenological in its method. This may seem paradoxical to the extent that Heidegger's critique of the transcendental problematic and his thinking of the "turn" are basic to my development of the universal hermeneutic problem. In my view, however, the principle of phenomenological demonstration may be applied even to that turn of Heidegger's which first allowed the hermeneutic problem to come into its own. For this reason I held on to the concept of hermeneutics employed by the early Heidegger, not in the sense of a methodology but as a theory of the real experience that thinking is. I have to emphasize, then, that my analyses of play and language are intended in a purely phenomenological sense. Play goes beyond the consciousness of the player and is in this respect more than a subjective behavior. Language goes beyond the consciousness of the speaker and is in this respect more than a subjective behavior. Precisely this can be described as an experience of the subject, and it has nothing to do with "mythology" or "mystification."

Such a basic methodological stance is located this side of any genuine metaphysical conclusions. As I have stressed in writings published subsequent to *Truth and Method,* especially in "Hermeneutics and Historicism"[1] and "The Phenomenological Movement,"[2] I do indeed regard Kant's critique of pure reason as binding and consider statements that go in a purely dialectical manner from the finite to the infinite, from what is experienced by us to what exists in itself, from the temporal to the eternal, merely as limiting determinations, out of which no real knowledge can be developed by the power of philosophy. At the same time, the tradition of metaphysics, particularly in its last great form, Hegel's speculative dialectic, is always close at hand. Its task — the "infinite relation" — remains. But there has been an effort to free the way in which this is to be carried out from the clutches of the synthetic power of Hegelian dialectic, and even from the "logic" that has grown out of Plato's dialectic, and to locate it in the movement of dialogue (*Gespräch*) in which word and concept first become what they are.

This does not satisfy the demand for reflective self-grounding that can be raised from the standpoint of a transcendental philosophy carried out in a speculative manner — as in Fichte, Hegel, and Husserl. But is the dialogue with the whole of our philosophical tradition, in which we stand and which, as philosophers, we are, groundless? Does what already supports us require any grounding?

This raises one final question, which concerns less the method than the content of the hermeneutic universalism I have developed here. Does not the universality of understanding entail a substantive one-sidedness, inasmuch as it lacks a critical principle in relation to the tradition and indulges, as it were, in a universal optimism? However much it may belong to the nature of tradition to exist only through being appropriated, it clearly also belongs to the nature of man to be able to breach tradition, to criticize and disassemble it. And is not what takes place in the way of work, of adapting the real to suit our purposes, something far more primordial in our relationship to being? In this respect, does not the ontological universality of understanding lead to a certain one-sidedness? Understanding certainly does not mean merely the appropriation of transmitted views or the recognition of what has been sanctified by tradition. Heidegger, who first singled out the concept of *Verstehen* as a universal determination of *Dasein*, plainly intended by it the projective nature of understanding, that is to say, the future-directed character of *Dasein*. I do not wish to deny that within the universal nexus of the moments of understanding I have singled out the orientation toward appropriating what is past and handed down. Like many of my critics, Heidegger might also see here the lack of an ultimate radicality in drawing consequences. What does the end of metaphysics as a science mean? What does its ending in science mean? When science is expanded into a total technocracy and thereby brings on the "cosmic night" of the "forgetfulness of being," the nihilism predicted by Nietzsche, then may one not gaze into the evening sky at the last fading glimmer of a sun that has set — rather than turning round and looking for the first shimmer of its return?

It seems to me that the one-sidedness of hermeneutic universalism has the truth of a corrective. It enlightens the modern viewpoint of making, producing, and constructing in regard to the necessary presuppositions under which it stands. In particular, this limits the role of the philosopher in the modern world. However much he may be called upon to draw the radical consequences from everything, the role of prophet, monitor, preacher, or even know-it-all, ill suits him. What man needs is not only a persistent posing of ultimate questions, but also a sense for what is feasible, what is possible, what is right, here and now. In my view, one who philosophizes must be all the more aware of the tension between his own claim and the reality in which he stands.

The hermeneutic consciousness that I have sought to awaken and to keep awake admits to itself, therefore, that in an age of science the claim to supremacy on the part of philosophical thought has something chimerical and unreal about it. But it seeks to set against the will of man — which is more than ever intensifying its critique of what has hitherto existed, to the point of a utopian or eschatological consciousness — something from the truth of recollection: what is still and ever again actual (*Wirkliche*).

Notes

1. Printed as "Supplement I" to *Truth and Method* (New York: Seabury Press, 1975), pp. 460–491.

2. Printed in *Philosophical Hermeneutics*, trans. and ed. David E. Linge (Berkeley: University of California Press, 1976), pp. 130–181.

11

Paul Ricoeur

Introduction

The writings of Paul Ricoeur, from the early studies *Fallible Man* and *The Symbolism of Evil* (both 1960) through his most recent work, *Time and Narrative* (1983), can be read as an attempt to continue the modern tradition of reflective/reflexive philosophy from a different standpoint — within the horizon of an "ontology of human finitude" (see Thompson's introduction to Ricoeur, 1981). Against the appeal by some thinkers in this tradition to an unmediated intellectual intuition of the self, Ricoeur insists (1) that human existence can be viewed only in the mirror of its external manifestations — the objects and acts, symbols and signs in which it is expressed — and (2) that immediate consciousness and self-consciousness, far from being transparent, can harbor illusion (Freud) and mystification (Marx). Consequently, self-understanding must be mediated through the interpretation and critique of the scattered signs of the self in the world. It is only through appropriating the texts and text analogues of our tradition, in making them our own, that we come to understand ourselves — but never, of course, in the sense of attaining the complete transparence posited in traditional reflexive philosophy. Furthermore, reflection construed as hermeneutics is essentially bound up with all the human sciences concerned to comprehend the socio-cultural world. "Reflection must become interpretation because I cannot grasp the act of existing except in signs scattered in the world. This is why a reflective philosophy must include the results, methods, and presuppositions of all the sciences that try to decipher and interpret the signs of man." Thus, there can be no question here of separating "truth" from "method," or of philosophical reflection being carried out in isolation from the empirical results of the human sciences.

One central feature of Ricoeur's hermeneutic project is his rejection of the claim to comprehensiveness and self-sufficiency raised on behalf of discursive modes of thought. In opposition to the exclusive validity usually accorded univocal meaning, literal speech acts, and nonrhetorical forms of argumentation, he has drawn attention to the indispensable contribution of symbol and myth, metaphor and narrative, to our knowledge of the world and ourselves. His aim has been to develop a general theory of interpretation that "preserves the fullness, the diversity, and the irreducibility of the various uses of language" and the forms of human experience that give rise to them, without, at the same time, abandoning the rigor and clarity of argumentation proper to philosophy.

Ricoeur's early interest in symbols generated a need for two lengthy "detours" through psychoanalysis and structuralism, which, in turn, broadened his original conception of hermeneutics as the interpretation of symbols. From his extensive study of Freud, Ricoeur concluded that there was not one correct method of interpretation, but a "conflict of interpretations" with competing claims to adequacy. Alongside a "hermeneutics of trust" Ricoeur recognized a "hermeneutics of suspicion" (exemplified in the works of Freud, Marx, and Nietzsche), aimed not at recollecting and restoring the fullness of meaning in symbolism, but rather at reducing and "demystifying symbolism by unmasking the avowed forces that are concealed within it." The task of philosophy *qua* hermeneutics is to mediate the absolutist claims of both approaches and to clarify the legitimate role of each in a more general process of understanding.

The achievement of structuralism, according to Ricoeur, was to raise the study of language to a scientific status by freeing language from the domains of psychology and history and treating it as a self-contained "system of differences." His claim, against Gadamer, that a text has an objective meaning, accessible in part through the structuralist analysis of narrative codes and the like, reflects his indebtedness to this tradition. However, Ricoeur argues that language is not only a system of differences; it is also a discourse in which *speakers* say something *about something*. This reference beyond itself, to speakers and to an extralinguistic reality, is a feature of language that is excluded from consideration in structuralist approaches. Ricoeur has attempted to deal with this deficiency, as well as the inability of structuralism to account for the production of new meaning within a language, in the context of his work on metaphor.

In *The Rule of Metaphor* Ricoeur argues against the view that metaphor is the substitution of a figurative description for a literal description. According to this "substitution" theory, metaphor is merely a decorative or ornamental use of language, and therefore it is always possible in principle to replace it with an exhaustive, literal paraphrase. By contrast, Ricoeur sees metaphor as an act of semantic impertinence, in which a lexically odd or foreign attribute is predicated to a subject; the result of the tension or interaction between the two terms is a new semantic pertinence, the creation of new meaning. On this "interaction" view, metaphors cannot be literally paraphrased without loss of semantic content. Nor can the creation of new meaning be achieved simply by drawing upon a "system of associated commonplaces" (Black's theory); it is rather the work of a productive imagination that enables seeing something *as* something, in spite of, and yet thanks to, their initial differences. Further, Ricoeur claims, linguistic innovation has consequences for the theory of reference as well as for the theory of meaning, since in the creation of new meaning metaphors redescribe reality. More generally, poetic discourse brings to language aspects and values of reality that cannot be captured in direct description; it thus bears an "indirect reference" to the world, which it "disturbs" and "rearranges" through invention and redescription.

The result of Ricoeur's detours and studies has been the development of a general theory of interpretation relevant to a range of problems in the human sciences. Whether in reference to the structuralist/hermeneutic controversy over the objectivity of textual interpretation, the debate over the status of "reasons" and "causes" in the theory of action, or the debate about the appropriateness of the "covering law model" (versus *Verstehen* approaches) in historical explanation, Ricoeur has consistently argued against an undialectical opposition between explanation and understanding: "Understanding precedes, accompanies, closes, and thus *envelops* explanation. In return, explanation *develops* understanding analytically" (1978, 165).

Ricoeur's defense of the dialectic of understanding and explanation, and of its relevance for a hermeneutic transformation of philosophy, is continued in his recent studies on narrative. Against both the *Annales* School and nomological models of historical explanation, he argues that historical writing cannot do without the narrative form because it cannot dispense with understanding action. At the same time, the narrative acquires explanatory power by virtue of the intelligible character of its plot. "Historical explanation may be grafted onto narrative comprehension in the sense that in explaining more one recounts better." Hence, the laws that the historian borrows from other social sciences "take on a historical meaning to the extent that they are grafted onto a prior narrative organization." The present selection relates Ricoeur's recent interest in the narrative function to his work on metaphor and symbol and to the presuppositions of phenomenology and hermeneutics. Thus, it summarizes well his own attempt to continue, through transforming, the philosophical tradition to which he belongs.

Suggested Readings

Carr, David. *"Temps et récit* (Review Essay)," *History and Theory* 23 (1984), 357–370.

Dallmayr, Fred. *Language and Politics.* Notre Dame: University of Notre Dame Press, 1984.

Ihde, Don. *Hermeneutic Phenomenology: The Philosophy of Paul Ricoeur.* Evanston: Northwestern University Press, 1971.

McGuire, Steven. "Interpretive Sociology and Paul Ricoeur," *Human Studies* 4 (1981), 179–200.

Mitchel, W. J. T., ed. *On Narrative*. Chicago: University of Chicago Press, 1981; includes Ricoeur's "Narrative Time."

Ortony, Andrew, ed. *Metaphor and Thought*. Cambridge: Cambridge University Press, 1980.

Rasmussen, David M. *Mythic-Symbolic Language and Philosophical Anthropology: A Constructive Interpretation of Paul Ricoeur*. The Hague: Martinus Nijhoff, 1971.

Reagan, Charles E. "Review of *Time and Narrative*," *International Philosophical Quarterly* 25 (1985), 89–105.

Reagan, Charles E., ed. *Studies in the Philosophy of Paul Ricoeur*. Athens: Ohio University Press, 1978.

Ricoeur, Paul. *Fallible Man*. Trans. C. Kelbley. Chicago: Regnery Press, 1965.

Ricoeur, Paul. *History and Truth*. Trans. C. Kelbley. Evanston: Northwestern University Press, 1965.

Ricoeur, Paul. *Husserl: An Analysis of His Phenomenology*. Trans. E. G. Ballard and L. E. Embree. Evanston: Northwestern University Press, 1967.

Ricoeur, Paul. *The Symbolism of Evil: An Essay on Interpretation*. Trans. E. Buchanan. New York: Harper and Row, 1967.

Ricoeur, Paul. *Freud and Philosophy: An Essay on Interpretation*. Trans. D. Savage. New Haven: Yale University Press, 1970.

Ricoeur, Paul. *The Conflict of Interpretations: Essays in Hermeneutics*. Ed. D. Ihde. Evanston: Northwestern University Press, 1974.

Ricoeur, Paul. *Political And Social Essays*. Ed. D. Stewart and J. Bien. Athens: Ohio University Press, 1974.

Ricoeur, Paul. "History and Hermeneutics," *Journal of Philosophy* 73 (1976), 683–695.

Ricoeur, Paul. *Interpretation Theory: Discourse and the Surplus of Meaning*. Fort Worth: Texas Christian University Press, 1976.

Ricoeur, Paul. *The Rule of Metaphor: Multi-Disciplinary Studies of the Creation of Meaning in Language*. Trans. R. Czerny with K. McLaughlin and J. Costello. Toronto: University of Toronto Press, 1977.

Ricoeur, Paul. *The Philosophy of Paul Ricoeur: An Anthology of His Work*. Ed. C. Reagan and D. Stewart. Boston: Beacon Press, 1978.

Ricoeur, Paul. "The Function of Fiction in Shaping Reality," *Man and World* 12 (1979), 123–141.

Ricoeur, Paul. "The Human Experience of Time and Narrative," *Research in Phenomenology* 9 (1979), 17–34.

Ricoeur, Paul. *The Contribution of French Historiography to the Theory of History* (The Zaharoff Lecture, 1978–1979). Oxford: Clarendon Press, 1980.

Ricoeur, Paul. *Hermeneutics and the Human Sciences: Essays on Language, Action and Interpretation.* Trans. and ed. John Thompson. Cambridge: Cambridge University Press, 1981.

Ricoeur, Paul. "Narrative and Hermeneutics," in *Essays on Aesthetics: Perspectives on the Work of Monroe Beardsley,* ed. J. Fischer, 149–160. Philadelphia: Temple University Press, 1983.

Ricoeur, Paul. *Time and Narrative, Vol. 1, Vol. 2.* Trans. K. McLaughlin and D. Pellauer. Chicago: University of Chicago Press, 1984, 1986.

Sacks, Sheldon, ed. *On Metaphor.* Chicago: University of Chicago Press, 1979.

Thompson, John. *Critical Hermeneutics: A Study in the Thought of Paul Ricoeur and Jürgen Habermas.* Cambridge: Cambridge University Press, 1981.

On Interpretation

Paul Ricoeur

The most appropriate way of giving an idea of the problems that have occupied me over the past thirty years and of the tradition to which my way of dealing with these problems belongs is, it seems to me, to start with my current work on narrative function, going on from there to show the relationship between this study and my earlier studies of metaphor, psychoanalysis, symbolism, and other related problems, in order, finally, to work back from these partial investigations toward the presuppositions, both theoretical and methodological, upon which the whole of my research is based. This backwards movement into my own work allows me to leave until the end my discussion of the presuppositions of the phenomenological and hermeneutical tradition to which I belong, by showing in what way my analyses at one and the same time continue and correct this tradition and, on occasion, bring it into question.

1

I shall begin, then, by saying something about my work in progress on narrative function.

Three major preoccupations are apparent here. This inquiry into the act of storytelling responds first of all to a very general concern, one that I have previously discussed in the first chapter of my book *Freud and Philosophy* — that of preserving the fullness, the diversity, and the irreducibility of the various *uses* of language. It can thus be seen that from the start I have affiliated myself with those analytical philosophers who resist the sort of reductionism according to which "well-formed languages" are alone capable of evaluating the meaning claims and truth claims of all non- "logical" uses of language.

A second concern completes and, in a certain sense, tempers the first: that of *gathering together* the diverse forms and modes of the game of storytelling. Indeed, throughout the development of the cultures to which we are the heirs, the act of storytelling has never ceased to ramify into increasingly well-determined literary genres. This fragmentation presents a major problem for philosophers by virtue of the major dichotomy that divides the narrative field and that produces a thoroughgoing opposition between, on the one hand, narratives that have a truth claim comparable to that of the descriptive forms of discourse to be found in the sciences — let us say history and the related literary genres of biography and autobiography — and, on the other hand, fictional narratives such as epics, dramas, short stories, and novels, to say nothing of narrative modes that use a medium other than language: films, for example, and possibly painting and other plastic arts.

In opposition to this endless fragmentation, I acknowledge the existence of a *functional* unity among the multiple narrative modes and genres. My basic hypothesis, in this regard, is the following: the common feature of human experience, that which is marked, organized, and clarified by the fact of storytelling in all its forms, is its *temporal character*. Everything that is recounted occurs in time, takes time, unfolds temporally; and what unfolds in time can be recounted. Perhaps, indeed, every temporal process is recognized as such only to the extent that it can, in one way or another, be recounted. This reciprocity that is assumed to exist between narrativity and temporality is the theme of my present research. Limited as this problem may be compared to the vast scope of all the real and potential uses of language, it is actually immense. Under a single heading it groups together a number of problems that are usually treated under different rubrics: the epistemology of historical knowledge, literary criticism applied to works of fiction, theories of time (which are themselves scattered among cosmology, physics, biology, psychology, and sociology). By treating the temporal quality of experience as the common reference of both history and fiction, I make of fiction, history, and time one single problem.

It is here that a third concern comes in, one that offers the possibility of making the problematic of temporality and narrativity easier to work with: namely, the testing of the selective and organizational capacity of language itself when it is ordered into those units of discourse longer than the sentence that we can call *texts*. If, indeed, narrativity is to mark, organize, and clarify temporal experience — to repeat the three verbs employed above — we must seek in language use a standard of measurement that satisfies this need for delimiting, ordering, and making explicit. That the text is the linguistic unit we are looking for and that it constitutes the appropriate medium between temporal experience and the narrative act can be briefly outlined in the following manner. As a linguistic unit, a text is, on the one hand, an expansion of the first unit of present meaning, which is the sentence. On the other hand, it contributes a principle of transsentential organization that is exploited by the act of storytelling in all its forms.

We can term *poetics* — after Aristotle — that discipline which deals with the laws of composition that are added to discourse as such in order to form of it a text that can stand as a narrative, a poem, or an essay.

The question then arises of identifying the major characteristic of the act of story making. I shall once again follow Aristotle in his designation of the sort of verbal *composition* that constitutes a text as a narrative. Aristotle designates this verbal composition by use of the term *muthos,* a term that has been translated as "fable" or as "plot." He speaks of "the combination [*sunthesis,* or, on another context, *sustasis*] of incidents or the fable" (Poetics 1450 A 5 and 1 5). By this, Aristotle means more than a structure in the static sense of the word, but rather an operation (as indicated by the ending *-sis* as in *poiesis, sunthesis, sustasis*), namely the structuring that makes us speak of putting-into-the-form-of-a-plot (*emplotment*) rather than of *plot*. The emplotment consists mainly in the selection and arrangement of the events and the actions recounted, which make of the fable a story that is "complete and entire" (*Poetics* 1450 B 25) with a beginning, middle, and end. Let us understand by this that no action is a beginning except in a story that it inaugurates; that no action constitutes a middle unless it instigates a change of fortune in the story told, an "intrigue" to be sorted out, a surprising "turn of events," a series of "pitiful" or "terrifying" incidents; finally, no action, taken in itself, constitutes an end except insofar as it concludes a course of action in the story told, unravels an intrigue, explains the surprising turn of fortune, or seals the hero's fate by a final event that clarifies the whole action and produces in the listener the catharsis of pity and terror.

It is this notion of plot that I take as a guideline for my entire investigation, in the area of the history of historians (or historiography) as well as in that of fiction (from epics and folk tales to the modern novel). I shall limit myself here to stressing the feature that, to my mind, makes the notion of plot so fruitful, namely its *intelligibility*. The intelligible character of plot can be brought out in the following way: the plot is the set of combinations by which events are made *into* a story or — correlatively — a story is made *out of* events. The plot mediates between the event and the story. This means that nothing is an event unless it contributes to the progress of a story. An event is not only an occurrence, something that happens, but a narrative component. Broadening the scope of the plot even more in order to escape the opposition, associated with the aesthetics of Henry James, between plot and characters, I shall say that the plot is the intelligible unit that holds together circumstances, ends and means, initiatives and unwanted consequences. According to an expression borrowed from Louis Mink, it is the act of "taking together" — of composing — those ingredients of human action that, in ordinary experience, remain dissimilar and discordant.

From this intelligible character of the plot, it follows that the ability to follow a story constitutes a very sophisticated form of *understanding*.

I shall now say a few words about the problems posed by an extension of the Aristotelian notion of plot to historiography. I shall cite two.

The first concerns historiography. It would appear, indeed, to be arguing a lost cause to claim that modern history has preserved the narrative character to be found in earlier chronicles and which has continued up to our own days in the accounts given by political, diplomatic, or ecclesiastical history of battles, treaties, parceling, and, in general, of the changes of fortune that affect the exercise of power by given individuals. (1) It seems, in the first place, that as history moves away not only from the ancient form of the chronicle but also from the political model and becomes social, economic, cultural, and spiritual history, it no longer has as its fundamental referent individual action, as it generates datable events. It therefore no longer proposes to tie together events with a chronological and causal thread; and it ceases, thus, to tell stories. (2) Moreover, in changing its themes history changes its method. It seeks to move closer to the model of the nomological sciences, which explain the events of nature by combining general laws with the description of the initial conditions. (3) Finally, whereas narrative is assumed to be subject to the uncritical perspective of agents plunged into the confusion of their present experience, history is an inquiry independent of the immediate comprehension of events by those who make or undergo them.

My thesis is that the tie between history and narrative cannot be broken without history losing its specificity among the human sciences.

To take these three arguments in reverse order, I shall assert first of all that the basic error comes from the failure to recognize the intelligible character conferred upon the narrative by the plot, a character that Aristotle was the first to emphasize. A naive notion of narrative, considered as a disconnected series of events, is always to be found behind the critique of the narrative character of history. Its episodic character alone is seen, while its configurational character, which is the basis of its intelligibility, is forgotten. At the same time the distance introduced by narrative between itself and lived experience is overlooked. Between living and recounting, a gap — however small it may be — is opened up. Life is lived, history is recounted.

Second, in overlooking narrative's basic intelligibility, one overlooks the possibility that historical explanation may be grafted onto narrative comprehension in the sense that in explaining more one recounts better. The error of the proponents of nomological models is not so much that they are mistaken about the nature of the laws that the historian may borrow from other and more advanced social sciences — demography, economics, linguistics, sociology, etc. — but about how these laws work. They fail to see that these laws take on a historical meaning to the extent that they are grafted onto a prior narrative organization that has already characterized events as contributing to the development of a plot.

Third, in turning away from the history of events (*histoire événementielle*), and in particular from political history, historiography has moved less from narrative history than historians might claim. Even when history as social, economic, or cultural history becomes the history of long time-spans, it is still tied to time and still accounts for the changes that link a terminal to an initial situation. The rapidity of the change makes no difference here. In remaining bound to time and to change, history remains tied to human action, which, in Marx's words, makes history in circumstances it has not made. Directly or indirectly, history is always the history of men who are the bearers, the agents, and the victims of the currents, institutions, functions, and structures in which they find themselves placed. Ultimately, history cannot make a complete break with narrative because it cannot break with action, which itself implies agents, aims, circumstances, interactions, and results both intended and unintended. But the plot is the basic narrative unit that organizes these heterogeneous ingredients into an intelligible totality.

The second problem I should like to touch on concerns the reference, *common* to both history and fiction, to the temporal background of human experience.

This problem is of considerable difficulty. On the one hand, indeed, only history seems to refer to reality, even if this reality is a past one. It alone seems to claim to speak of events that have really occurred. The novelist can disregard the burden of material proof related to the constraints imposed by documents and archives. An irreducible asymmetry seems to oppose historical reality to fictional reality.

There is no question of denying this asymmetry. On the contrary, it must be recognized in order to perceive the overlap, the figure of the chiasmus formed by the criss-crossing, referential modes characteristic of fiction and history: the historian speaking of the absent past in terms of fiction, the novelist speaking of what is irreal as if it had really taken place. On the one hand, we must not say that fiction has no reference. On the other hand, we must not say that history refers to the historical past in the same way as empirical descriptions refer to present reality. To say that fiction does not lack a reference is to reject an overly narrow conception of reference, which would relegate fiction to a purely emotional role. In one way or another, all symbol systems contribute to *shaping* reality. More particularly, the plots that we invent help us to shape our confused, formless, and in the last resort mute temporal experience. "What is time?" Augustine asked. "If no one asks me, I know what it is; if someone asks me, I no longer know." The plot's referential function lies in the capacity of fiction to shape this mute temporal experience. We are here brought back to the link between *muthos* and *mimesis* in Aristotle's *Poetics:* "the fable," he says, "[is] an imitation of an action" (1450 A 2).

This is why suspending the reference can only be an intermediary moment between the preunderstanding of the world of action and the transfiguration of daily reality brought about by fiction itself. Indeed, the models *of* actions elaborated by narrative fiction are models *for* redescribing the practical field in accordance with the narrative typology resulting from the work of the productive imagination. Because it is a world, the world of the text necessarily collides with the real world in order to "remake" it, either by confirming it or by denying it. However, even the most ironic relation between art and reality would be incomprehensible if art did not both disturb and rearrange our relation to reality. If the world of the text were without any assignable relation to the real world, then language would not be "dangerous," in the sense in which Hölderlin called it so before both Nietzsche and Walter Benjamin.

So much for this brief sketch of the paradoxical problematic of "productive" reference, characteristic of narrative fiction. I confess to have drawn in here only the outlines of a problem, not those of its solution.

A parallel approach to history is called for. Just as narrative fiction does not lack reference, the reference proper to history is not unrelated to the "productive" reference of fictional narrative. Not that the past is unreal: but past reality is, in the strict sense of the word, unverifiable. Insofar as it no longer exists, the discourse of history can seek to grasp it only *indirectly*. It is here that the relationship with fiction shows itself as crucial. The reconstruction of the past, as Collingwood maintained so forcefully, is the work of the imagination. The historian, too, by virtue of the links mentioned earlier between history and narrative, shapes the plots that the documents may authorize or forbid but that they never contain in themselves. History, in this sense, combines narrative coherence with conformity to the documents. This complex tie characterizes the status of history as interpretation. The way is thus open for a positive investigation of all the interrelations between the asymmetrical, but also the indirect and mediate, referential modalities of fiction and of history. It is due to this complex interplay between the indirect reference to the past and the productive reference of fiction that human experience in its profound temporal dimension never ceases to be shaped.

I can only indicate here the threshold of this investigation, which is my current object of research.

2

I now propose to place my current investigation of narrative function within the broader framework of my earlier work, before attempting to bring to light the theoretical and epistemological presuppositions that have continued to grow stronger and more precise in the course of time.

I shall divide my remarks into two groups. The first concerns the structure or, better, the "sense" immanent in the statements themselves, whether they be narrative or metaphorical. The second concerns the extralinguistic "reference" of the statements and, hence, the truth claims of both sorts of statements.

A. Let us restrict ourselves in the first instance to the level of "sense."

(a) Between the narrative as a literary "genre" and the metaphorical "trope," the most basic link, on the level of sense, is constituted by the fact that both belong to discourse, that is to say, to uses of language involving units as long as or longer than the sentence.

One of the first results that contemporary research on metaphor seems to me to have attained is, indeed, to have shifted the focus of analysis from the sphere of the *word* to that of the *sentence*. According to the definitions of classical rhetoric, stemming from Aristotle's *Poetics,* metaphor is the transfer of the everyday name of one thing to another in virtue of their resemblance. This definition, however, says nothing about the operation that results in this "transfer" of sense. To understand the operation that generates such an extension, we must step outside the framework of the word to move up to the level of the sentence and speak of a metaphorical statement rather than of a word-metaphor. It then appears that metaphor constitutes a work on language consisting in the attribution to logical subjects of predicates that are incompossible with them. By this should be understood that before being a deviant naming, metaphor is a peculiar predication, an attribution that destroys the consistency or, as has been said, the semantic relevance of the sentence as it is established by the ordinary, that is the lexical, meanings of the terms employed.

(b) This analysis of metaphor in terms of the sentence rather than the word, or, more precisely, in terms of peculiar predicaton rather than deviant naming, prepares the way for a comparison between the theory of narrative and the theory of metaphor. Both indeed have to do with the phenomenon of *semantic innovation.* This phenomenon constitutes the most fundamental problem that metaphor and narrative have in common on the level of sense. In both cases the novel — the not-yet-said, the unheard-of — suddenly arises in language: here *living* metaphor, that is to say a *new* relevance in predication, there, wholly *invented* plot, that is to say a *new* congruence in the emplotment. On both sides, however, human creativity is to be discerned and to be circumscribed within forms that make it accessible to analysis.

(c) If we now ask about the reasons behind the privileged role played by metaphor and emplotment, we must turn toward the functioning of the *productive imagination* and of the *schematism* that constitutes its intelligible matrix. Indeed, in both cases innovation is produced in the milieu of language and reveals something about what an imagination that produces in accordance with rules might be. This rule-generated production is expressed in the construction of plots by way of a continual interchange between the invention of particular plots and the constitution by sedimentation of a narrative typology. A dialectic is at work in the production of new plots in the interplay between conformity and deviance in relation to the norms inherent in every narrative typology.

Now this dialectic has its counterpart in the birth of a new semantic relevance in new metaphors. Aristotle said that "to be happy in the use of metaphors" consists in the "discernment of resemblances" (*Poetics*, 1459 A 4–8). But what is it to discern resemblances? If the establishment of a new semantic relevance is that in virtue of which the statement "makes sense" as a whole, resemblance consists in the *rapprochement,* the bringing closer together, of terms that, previously "remote," suddenly appear "close." Resemblance thus consists in a change of distance in logical space. It is nothing other than this emergence of a new generic kinship between heterogeneous ideas.

It is here that the productive imagination comes into play as the schematization of this synthetic operation of bringing closer together. It is the "seeing" — the sudden insight — inherent to discourse itself, that brings about the change in logical distance, the bringing-closer-together itself. This productive character of insight may be called *predicative assimilation.* The imagination can justly be termed productive because, by an extension of polysemy, it makes terms, previously heterogeneous, *resemble* one another, and thus homogeneous. The imagination, consequently, is this competence, this capacity for producing new logical kinds by means of predicative assimilation and for producing them in spite of . . . and thanks to . . . the initial difference between the terms that resist assimilation.

(d) If, now, we put the stress on the *intelligible* character of semantic innovation, a new parallelism may be seen between the domain of the narrative and that of metaphor. We insisted above on the very particular mode of *understanding* involved in the activity of following a story and we spoke in this regard of narrative understanding. And we have maintained the thesis that historical *explanation* in terms of laws, regular causes, functions, and structures is grafted onto this narrative understanding.

This same relation between understanding and explanation is to be observed in the domain of poetics. The act of understanding that would correspond in this domain to the ability to follow a story consists in grasping the semantic dynamism by virtue of which, in a metaphorical statement, a new semantic relevance emerges from the ruins of the semantic nonrelevance as this appears in a literal reading of the sentence. To understand is thus to perform or to repeat the discursive operation by which the semantic innovation is conveyed. Now, upon this understanding by which the author or reader "makes" the metaphor is superimposed a scholarly explanation that, for its part, takes a completely different starting point from that of the dynamism of the sentence and will not admit the units of discourse to be irreducible to the signs belonging to the language system. Positing the principle of the structure homology of all levels of language, from the phoneme to the text, the explanation of metaphor is thus included within a general semiotics that takes the sign as its basic unit. My thesis here, just as in the case of the narrative function, is that explanation is not primary but secondary in relation to understanding. Explanation, conceived as a combinatory system of signs, hence as a semiotics, is built up on the basis of a first-order understanding bearing on discourse as an act that is both indivisible and capable of innovation. Just as the narrative structures brought out by explanation presuppose an understanding of the structuring act by which plot is produced, so the structures brought out by structural semiotics are based upon the structuring of discourse, whose dynamism and power of innovation are revealed by metaphor.

In the third part of this essay I shall say in what way this twofold approach to the relation between explanation and understanding contributes to the contemporary development of hermeneutics. I shall say beforehand how the theory of metaphor conspires with the theory of narrative in the elucidation of the problem of reference.

B. In the preceding discussion I have purposely isolated the "sense" of the metaphorical statement, that is to say its internal predicative structure, from its "reference," that is to say its claim to reach an extralinguistic reality, hence its claim to say something true.

Now, the study of the narrative function has already confronted us with the problem of poetic reference in the discussion of the relation between *muthos* and *mimesis* in Aristotle's *Poetics*. Narrative fiction, I said, "imitates" human action, not only in that, before referring to the text, if refers to our own preunderstanding of the meaningful structures of action and of its temporal dimensions, but also in that it contributes, beyond the text, to reshaping these structures and dimensions in accordance with the imaginary configuration of the plot. Fiction has the power to "remake" reality and, within the framework of narrative fiction in particular, to remake real praxis to the extent that the text intentionally aims at a horizon of new reality that we may call a world. It is this world of the text that intervenes in the world of action in order to give it a new configuration or, as we might say, in order to transfigure it.

The study of metaphor enables us to penetrate farther into the mechanism of this operation of transfiguration and to extend it to the whole set of imaginative productions that we designate by the general term of fiction. What metaphor alone permits us to perceive is the conjunction between the two constitutive moments of poetic reference.

The first of these moments is the easiest to identify. Language takes on a poetic function whenever it redirects our attention away from the reference and toward the message itself. In Roman Jakobson's terms, the poetic function stresses the message *for its own sake* at the expense of the referential function, which, on the contrary, is dominant in descriptive language. One might say that a centripetal movement of language toward itself takes the place of the centrifugal movement of the referential function. Language glorifies itself in the play of sound and sense.

However, the suspension of the referential function implied by the stress laid on the message for its own sake is only the reverse side, or the negative condition, of a more concealed referential function of discourse, one that is, as it were, set free when the descriptive value of statements is suspended. It is in this way that poetic discourse brings to language aspects, qualities, and values of reality that do not have access to directly descriptive language and that can be said only thanks to the complex play of the metaphorical utterance and of the ordered transgression of the ordinary meaning of our words. In my work *The Rule of Metaphor,* I compared this indirect functioning of metaphorical reference to that of models used in the physical sciences, when these are more than aids to discovery or teaching but are incorporated into the very meaning of theories and into their truth claims. These models then have the heuristic power of "redescribing" a reality inaccessible to direct description. In the same way one may say that poetic language redescribes the world thanks to the suspension of direct description by way of objective language.

This notion of metaphorical redescription exactly parallels the mimetic function that we earlier assigned to narrative fiction. The latter operates typically in the field of action and its temporal values, while metaphorical redescription reigns rather in the field of sensory, affective, aesthetic, and axiological values that make the world one that can be *inhabited.*

What is beginning to take shape in this way is the outline of a vast poetic sphere that includes both metaphorical statement and narrative discourse.

The philosophical implications of this theory of indirect reference are as considerable as those of the dialectic between explanation and understanding. Let us now set them within the field of philosophical hermeneutics. Let us say, provisionally, that the function of the transfiguration of reality that we have attributed to poetic fiction implies that we cease to identify reality with empirical reality or, what amounts to the same thing, that we cease to identify experience with empirical experience. Poetic language draws its prestige from its capacity for bringing to language certain aspects of what Husserl called the *Lebenswelt* and Heidegger *In-der-Welt-Sein*. By this very fact, we find ourselves forced to rework our conventional concept of truth, that is to say, to cease to limit this concept to logical coherence and empirical verification alone, so that the truth claim related to the transfiguring action of fiction can be taken into account. No more can be said about reality and truth — and no doubt about Being as well — until we have first attempted to make explicit the philosophical presuppositions of the entire enterprise.

3 A Hermeneutical Philosophy

I wish now to attempt to reply to two questions that the preceding analyses cannot have failed to provoke in the minds of readers who have been brought up in a different philosophical tradition from my own. What are the presuppositions that characterize the philosophical tradition to which I recognize myself as belonging? How do the preceding analyses fit into this tradition?

As to the first question, I should like to characterize this philosophical tradition by three features: it stands in the line of a *reflexive* philosophy;[1] it remains within the sphere of Husserlian *phenomenology*; it strives to be a *hermeneutical* variation of this phenomenology.

By reflexive philosophy I mean, broadly speaking, the mode of thought stemming from the Cartesian *cogito* and handed down by way of Kant and French post-Kantian philosophy, a philosophy that is little known abroad and that, for me at least, was most strikingly represented by Jean Nabert. A reflexive philosophy considers the most radical philosophical problems to be those that concern the possibility of *self-understanding* as the subject of the operations of knowing, willing, evaluating, and so on. Reflexion is that act of turning back upon itself by which a subject grasps, in a moment of intellectual clarity and moral responsibility, the unifying principle of the operations among which it is dispersed and forgets itself as subject. "The 'I think,'" says Kant, "must be able to accompany all my representations." All reflexive philosophers would recognize themselves in this formula.

But how can the "I think" know or recognize itself? It is here that phenomenology — and more especially hermeneutics — represents both a realization and a radical transformation of the very program of reflexive philosophy. Indeed, the idea of reflexion carries with it the desire for absolute transparence, a perfect coincidence of the self with itself, which would make consciousness of self indubitable knowledge and, as such, more fundamental than all forms of positive knowledge. It is this fundamental demand that phenomenology first of all, and then hermeneutics, continue to project onto an ever more distant horizon as philosophy goes on providing itself with the instruments of thought capable of satisfying it.

Thus Husserl, in those of his theoretical texts most evidently marked by an idealism reminiscent of Fichte, conceives of phenomenology not only as a method of description in terms of their essences of the fundamental modes of organizing experience (perceptive, imaginative, intellectual, volitional, axiological, etc.), but also as a radical self-grounding in the most complex intellectual clarity. In the reduction — or *epoche* — applied to the natural attitude, he then sees the conquest of an empire of sense from which any question concerning things-in-themselves is excluded by being put into brackets. It is this empire of sense, thus freed from any matter-of-fact question, that constitutes the privileged field of phenomenological experience, the domain of intuition *par excellence*. Returning, beyond Kant, to Descartes, he holds that every apprehension of transcendence is open to doubt but that self-immanence is indubitable. It is in virtue of this assertion that phenomenology remains a reflexive philosophy.

And yet, whatever the theory it applies to itself and to its ultimate claims, in its effective practice phenomenology already displays its distance from rather than its realization of the dream of such a radical grounding in the transparence of the subject to itself. The great discovery of phenomenology, within the limits of the phenomenological reduction itself, remains intentionality, that is to say, in its least technical sense, the priority of the consciousness *of something* over self-consciousness. This definition of intentionality, however, is still trivial. In its rigorous sense intentionality signifies that the *act* of intending something is accomplished only through the identifiable and reidentifiable unity of intended *sense* — what Husserl calls the "noema" or the "intentional correlate of the noetic intention." Moreover, upon this noema are superimposed the various layers that result from the synthetic activities that Husserl terms "constitution" (constitution of things, constitution of space, constitution of time, etc.). Now the concrete work of phenomenology, in particular in the studies devoted to the constitution of "things," reveals, by way of regression, levels, always more and more fundamental, at which the active syntheses continually refer to ever more radical passive syntheses. Phenomenology is thus caught up in an infinite movement of "backwards questioning" in which its project of radical self-grounding fades away. Even the last works devoted to the *life-world* designate by this term a horizon of immediateness that is forever out of reach. The *Lebenswelt* is never actually given but always presupposed. It is phenomenology's paradise lost. It is in this sense that phenomenology has undermined its own guiding idea in the very attempt to realize it. It is this that gives to Husserl's work its tragic grandeur.

It is with this paradoxical result in mind that we can understand how hermeneutics has been able to graft itself onto phenomenology and to maintain with respect to the latter the same twofold relation as that which phenomenology maintains with its Cartesian and Fichtean ideal. The antecedents of hermeneutics seem at first to set it apart from the reflexive tradition and from the phenomenological project. Hermeneutics, in fact, was born — or rather revived — at the time of Schleiermacher and of the fusion of biblical exegesis, classical philology, and jurisprudence. This fusion of several different disciplines was made possible thanks to a Copernican reversal that gave priority to the question of *what it is to understand* over that of the sense of this or that text or of this or that category of texts (sacred or profane, poetical or juridical). It is this investigation of *Verstehen* that, a century later, was to come across the phenomenological question *par excellence,* namely the investigation of the intentional sense of noetic acts. It is true that hermeneutics continued to embody concerns different from those of concrete phenomenology. Whereas the latter tended to raise the question of sense in the dimensions of cognition and perception, hermeneutics, since Dilthey, has raised it rather in those of history and the human sciences. But on both sides the fundamental question was the same, namely that of the relation between *sense* and *self,* between the *intelligibility* of the first and the *reflexive* nature of the second.

The phenomenological rooting of hermeneutics is not limited to this very general kinship between the understanding of texts and the intentional relation of a consciousness to a sense with which it finds itself faced. The theme of the *Lebenswelt,* a theme that phenomenology came up against in spite of itself, one might say, is adopted by post-Heideggerian hermeneutics no longer as something left over but as a prior condition. It is because we find ourselves first of all in a world to which we belong and in which we cannot help but participate, that we are then able, in a second movement, to set up objects in opposition to ourselves, objects that we claim to constitute and to master intellectually. *Verstehen* for Heidegger has an ontological signification. It is the response of a being thrown into the world who finds his way about it by projecting onto it his ownmost possibilities. Interpretation, in the technical sense of the interpretation of texts, is but the development, the making explicit of this ontological understanding, an understanding always inseparable from a being that has initially been thrown into the world. The subject-object relation — on which Husserl continues to depend — is thus subordinated to the testimony of an ontological link more basic than any relation of knowledge.

This subversion of phenomenology by hermeneutics calls for another such action: the famous "reduction" by which Husserl separates the "sense" from the background of existence in which natural consciousness is initially immersed can no longer be considered a primary philosophical move. Henceforth it takes on a derived epistemological meaning: it is a move of distantiation that comes second — and, in this sense, a move by which the primary rootedness of understanding is forgotten, a move that calls for all the objectivizing operations characteristic both of common and of scientific knowledge. This distantiation, however, presupposes the involvement as participant thanks to which we actually belong to the world before we are subjects capable of setting up objects in opposition to ourselves in order to judge them and to submit them to our intellectual and technical mastery. In this way Heideggerian and post-Heideggerian hermeneutics, though they are indeed heirs to Husserlian phenomenology, constitute in the end the reversal of this phenomenology to the very extent indeed that they also constitute its realization.

The philosophical consequences of this reversal are considerable. They are not apparent, however, if we limit ourselves to emphasizing the finite character of Being, which renders null and void the ideal of the self-transparence of a fundamental subject. The idea of the finite is in itself banal, even trivial. At best, it simply embodies in negative terms the renouncement of all *hubris* on the part of reflection, of any claim that the subject may make to found itself on itself. The discovery of the precedence of Being-in-the-world in relation to any foundational project and to any attempt at ultimate justification takes on its full force when we draw the positive conclusions of the new ontology of understanding for epistemology. It is in drawing these epistemological consequences that I shall bring my answers to the first question raised at the start of the third part of this essay to bear on the second question. I can sum up these epistemological consequences in the following way: there is no self-understanding that is not *mediated* by signs, symbols, and texts; in the last resort understanding coincides with the interpretation given to these mediating terms. In passing from one to the other, hermeneutics gradually frees itself from the idealism with which Husserl had tried to identify phenomenology. Let us now follow the stages of this emancipation.

Mediation by *signs*: that is to say that it is *language* that is the primary condition of all human experience. Perception is articulated, desire is articulated; this is something that Hegel had already shown in the *Phenomenology of Mind*. Freud drew another consequence from this, namely that there is no emotional experience so deeply buried, so concealed, or so distorted that it cannot be brought up to the clarity of language and so revealed in its own proper sense, thanks to desire's access to the sphere of language. Psychoanalysis, as a *talk-cure,* is based on this very hypothesis, that of the primary proximity between desire and speech. And since speech is heard before it is uttered, the shortest path from the self to itself lies in the speech of the other, which leads me across the open space of signs.

Mediation by *symbols*: by this term I mean those expressions carrying a double sense that traditional cultures have grafted onto the naming of the "elements" of the cosmos (fire, water, wind, earth, etc.), of its "dimensions" (height and depth, etc.). These double-sense expressions are themselves hierarchically ordered into the most universal symbols, then those that belong to one particular culture, and, finally, those that are the creation of a particular thinker, even of just one work. In this last case, the symbol merges into living metaphor. However, there is, on the other hand, perhaps no symbolic creation that is not in the final analysis rooted in the common symbolical ground of humanity. I myself once sketched out a *Symbolism of Evil* based entirely on this mediating role of certain double-sense expressions, such as stain, fall, deviation, in reflections on ill will. At that time I even went so far as to reduce hermeneutics to the interpretation of symbols, that is to say, to the making explicit of the second — and often hidden — sense of these double-sense expressions.

Today this definition of hermeneutics in terms of symbolic interpretation appears to me too narrow. And this for two reasons, which will lead us from mediation by symbols to mediation by texts. First of all I came to realize that no symbolism, whether traditional or private, can display its resources of *multiple meaning* (*multivocité*) outside appropriate contexts, that is to say, within the framework of an entire text, of a poem, for example. Next, the same symbolism can give rise to competitive — even diametrically opposed — interpretations, depending on whether the interpretation aims at reducing the symbolism to its literal basis, to its unconscious sources or its social motivations, or at amplifying it in accordance with its highest power of multiple meaning. In the one case, hermeneutics aims at demystifying a symbolism by unmasking the unavowed forces that are concealed within it; in the other case, it aims at a re-collection of meaning in its richest, its most elevated, most spiritual diversity. But this conflict of interpretations is also to be found at the level of texts.

It follows that hermeneutics can no longer be defined simply in terms of the interpretation of symbols. Nevertheless, this definition should be preserved at least as a stage separating the very general recognition of the linguistic character of experience and the more technical definition of hermeneutics in terms of textual interpretation. What is more, this intermediary definition helps to dissipate the illusion of an intuitive self-knowledge by forcing self-understanding to take the rounda-bout path of the whole treasury of symbols transmitted by the cultures within which we have come, at one and the same time, into both existence and speech.

Finally, mediation by *texts*: at first sight this mediation seems more limited than the mediation by signs and by symbols, which can be simply oral and even non-verbal. Mediation by texts seems to restrict the sphere of interpretation to writing and to literature to the detriment of oral cultures. This is true. But what the definition loses in extension, it gains in intensity. Indeed, writing opens up new and original resources for discourse. Thanks to writing, discourse acquires a threefold semantic autonomy: in relation to the speaker's intention, to its reception by its original audience, and to the economic, social, and cultural circumstances of its production. It is in this sense that writing tears itself free of the limits of face-to-face dialogue and becomes the condition for discourse itself *becoming-text*. It is to hermeneutics that falls the task of exploring the implications of this becoming-text for the work of interpretation.

The most important consequence of all this is that an end is put once and for all to the Cartesian and Fichtean — and to an extent Husserlian — ideal of the subject's transparence to itself. To understand oneself is to understand oneself as one confronts the text and to receive from it the conditions for a self other than that which first undertakes the reading. Neither of the two subjectivities, neither that of the author nor that of the reader, is thus primary in the sense of an originary presence of the self to itself.

Once it is freed from the primacy of subjectivity, what may be the first task of hermeneutics? It is, in my opinion, to seek in the text itself, on the one hand, the internal dynamic that governs the structuring of the work and, on the other hand, the power that the work possesses to project itself outside itself and to give birth to a world that would truly be the "thing" referred to by the text. This internal dynamic and external projection constitute what I call the work of the text. It is the task of hermeneutics to reconstruct this twofold work.

We can look back on the path that has led us from the first presupposition, that of philosophy as reflexivity, by way of the second, that of philosophy as phenomenology, right up to the third, that of the mediation first by signs, then by symbols, and finally by texts.

A hermeneutical philosophy is a philosophy that accepts all the demands of this long detour and that gives up the dream of a total mediation, at the end of which reflection would once again amount to intellectual intuition in the transparence to itself of an absolute subject.

I can now, in conclusion, attempt to reply to the second question raised at the start of the third part of this essay. If such are the presuppositions characteristic of the tradition to which my works belong, what, in my opinion, is their place in the development of this tradition?

In order to reply to this question, I have only to relate the last definition I have just given of the task of hermeneutics to the conclusions reached at the end of the two sections of part 2.

The task of hermeneutics, I have just said, is twofold: to reconstruct the internal dynamic of the text and to restore to the work its ability to project itself outside itself in the representation of a world that I could inhabit.

It seems to me that all of my analyses aimed at the interrelation of understanding and explanation, at the level of what I have called the "sense" of the work, are related to the first task. In my analyses of narrative as well as in those of metaphor, I am fighting on two fronts: on the one hand, I cannot accept the irrationalism of immediate understanding, conceived as an extension to the domain of texts of the empathy by which a subject puts himself in the place of a foreign consciousness in a situation of face-to-face intensity. This undue extension maintains the romantic illusion of a direct link of congeniality between the two subjectivities implied by the work, that of the author and that of the reader. However, I am equally unable to accept a rationalistic explanation that would extend to the text the structural analysis of sign systems that are characteristic not of discourse but of language as such. This equally undue extension gives rise to the positivist illusion of a textual objectivity closed in upon itself and wholly independent of the subjectivity of both author and reader. To these two one-sided attitudes I have opposed the dialectic of understanding and explanation. By understanding I mean the ability to take up again within oneself the work of structuring that is performed by the text, and by explanation the second-order operation grafted onto this understanding that consists in bringing to light the codes underlying this work of structuring that is carried through in company with the reader. This combat on two separate fronts against a reduction of understanding to empathy and a reduction of explanation to an abstract combinatory system leads me to define interpretation by this very dialectic of understanding and explanation at the level of the "sense" immanent to the text. This specific manner of responding to the first task of hermeneutics offers the signal advantage, in my opinion, of preserving the dialogue between philosophy and the human sciences, a dialogue that is interrupted by the two counterfeit forms of understanding and explanation that I reject. This would be my first contribution to the hermeneutical philosophy from out of which I am working.

In what I have written above, I have tried to set my analyses of the "sense" of metaphorical statements and of that of narrative plots against the background of the theory of *Verstehen*, limited to its epistemological usage, in the tradition of Dilthey and Max Weber. The distinction between "sense" and "reference," applied to these statements and to these plots, gives me the right to limit myself provisionally to what has thus been established by hermeneutical philosophy, which seems to me to remain unaffected by its later development in Heidegger and Gadamer, in the sense of a subordination of the epistemological to the ontological theory of *Verstehen*. I want neither to ignore the epistemological phase, which involves philosophy's dialogue with the human sciences, nor to neglect this shift in the hermeneutical problematic, which henceforth emphasizes Being-in-the-world and the participatory belonging that precedes any relation of a subject to an object that confronts him.

It is against this background of the new hermeneutical ontology that I should like to set my analyses of the "reference" of metaphorical statements and of narrative plots. I confess willingly that these analyses continually *presuppose* the conviction that discourse never exists *for its own sake,* for its own glory, but that in all of its uses it seeks to bring into language an experience, a way of living in and of Being-in-the-world that precedes it and that demands to be said. It is this conviction that there is always a *Being-demanding-to-be-said* (*un être-à-dire*) which precedes our actual saying, that explains my obstinacy in trying to discover in the poetic uses of language the referential mode appropriate to them and through which discourse continues to "say" Being even when it appears to have withdrawn into itself for the sake of self-celebration. This vehement insistence on preventing language from closing up on itself I have inherited from Heidegger's *Sein und Zeit* and from Gadamer's *Wahrheit und Methode*. In return, however, I should like to believe that the description I propose of the reference of metaphorical and of narrative statements contributes to this ontological vehemence an analytical precision that it would otherwise lack.

On the one hand, indeed, it is what I have just called ontological vehemence in the theory of language that leads me to attempt to give an ontological dimension to the referential claim of metaphorical statements: in this way I venture to say that to see something as . . . is to make manifest the *being-as* of that thing. I place the "as" in the position of the exponent of the verb "to be" and I make "being-as" the ultimate referent of the metaphorical statement. This thesis undeniably bears the imprint of post-Heideggerian ontology. But, on the other hand, the testimony to *being-as* . . . cannot, in my opinion, be separated from a detailed study of the referential modes of discourse and requires a properly analytical treatment of indirect reference, on the basis of the concept of "split reference" taken from Roman Jakobson. My thesis concerning the *mimesis* of the narrative work and my distinction between the three stages of *mimesis* — prefiguration, configuration, and transfiguration of the world of action by the poem — express one and the same concern to combine analytical precision with ontological testimony.

The concern I have just expressed brings me back to that other concern, which I mentioned above, not to oppose understanding and explanation on the level of the dynamic immanent to poetic utterances. Taken together, these two concerns mark my hope that in working for the progress of hermeneutical philosophy, I contribute, in however small a way, to arousing an interest in this philosophy on the part of analytical philosophers.

Note

1. *Translator's Note:* In French the adjective "réflexive" incorporates two meanings that are distinguished in English by *reflective* and *reflexive*. On the advice of the author we have chosen to retain the latter in order to emphasize that this philosophy is subject-oriented; it is reflexive in the subject's act of turning back upon itself. The other possible meaning should, however, also be kept in mind.

12

Alasdair MacIntyre

Introduction

In retrospect, much of Alasdair MacIntyre's philosophical writing can be seen to have been concerned with problems of relativism, that is, with problems generated by the differences between "incommensurable" conceptual schemes, alternative systems of belief, and incompatible ways of life. On his view, neither epistemological crises nor moral crises are the result of mere error or deception; they are associated, rather, with a questioning of basic cultural schemata. As with Kuhn's paradigm shifts, such crises — for all their pathos — have a positive side: through them we may become aware of the availability of "systematically different possibilities of interpretation, of the existence of rival schemata which yield mutually incompatible accounts of what is going on around [us]" (1977, 434). Shakespeare's *Hamlet* is a striking literary example of the interweaving of moral and epistemological crises; Galileo's and Newton's synthesis of the natural sciences is one of the best examples of how epistemological crises may be resolved; and our present moral situation is a clear case of an unresolved crisis that goes to the very foundations of our social existence. The outstanding task of philosophy today is to understand the sources of the epistemological and moral crisis of contemporary culture and of the incommensurable values that it involves.

On MacIntyre's view, the construction of historical narratives plays a central role in accomplishing this task. Above all, he is opposed to the consideration of arguments as "objects of investigation in abstraction from the social and historical contexts of activity and inquiry in which they are or were at home and from which they derive their particular import"; in place of decontextualized argumentation he proposes a "particular genre of historical writing." This "kind of philosophical history" is required not only for an adequate *understanding* of what a particular point of view is — making intelligible how it came to be advanced and in what type of situation — but also for an *evaluation* of its claim of rational justification. When such claims involve alternative or incompatible conceptual schemes, they can be evaluated only historically, that is, in terms of "the predecessors and rivals whom [a scheme] challenged and displaced." More specifically, the case for the rational superiority of a scientific, moral, or epistemological theory is made by showing that it is *the best so far* — that it transcends the limitations of its competitors (avoiding their defects while explaining them) and has successfully resisted all attempts similarly to transcend it (defeating all potential rivals while incorporating their strengths). Thus MacIntyre's "historicism" is not relativistic; the rational acceptability of general schemes — be they epistemological or moral — can be established, though it cannot be demonstrated by decontextualized analytic argument. Appeal to the *history of an argument* within some specific tradition is thus decisive for the resolution of issues between apparently incommensurable modes or schemes. It is just this sort of "philosophical history" that constitutes the narrative structure of *After Virtue*.

MacIntyre not only proposes a narrative account of the roots of the contemporary cultural crisis, he suggests a possible way out — one that requires, to be sure, a wholesale recasting of dominant conceptions of rationality and morality. The Cartesian solutions to epistemological crises and the Kantian solutions to moral ones are outmoded. Not only are they failures in themselves, but they are implicated in the very degeneration of our moral and intellectual traditions that is to be overcome. Thus, MacIntyre considers "the Enlightenment project" and its ideals of autonomy and universality to be part of the problem rather than the solution. As he puts it in a programmatic passage in *After Virtue,* "*Either* one must follow through the aspirations and the collapse of the different versions of the Enlightenment project until there remains only the Nietzschean diagnosis and the Nietzschean problematic; *or* one must hold that the Enlightenment project was not only mistaken, but should never have commenced in the first place. There is no third alternative" (1984, 111). To transcend this project in the dimension of morality, MacIntyre proposes to draw upon the resources of the Aristotelian moral tradition. A narrative account of the history of morals constructed from the perspective of that tradition becomes the primary framework for philosophical reflection in the age of the crisis of the "Enlightenment project."

Suggested Readings

Bernstein, Richard. "Nietzsche or Aristotle? Reflections on Alasdair MacIntyre's *After Virtue,*" *Soundings* 67 (1984), 6–29.

Clark, Stephen. "Morals, Moore and MacIntyre," *Inquiry* 26 (1984), 425–445.

Frankena, William. Review of *After Virtue. Ethics* 93 (1983), 579–587.

Gaita, Raimond. "Virtues, Human Good and the Unity of a Life," *Inquiry* 26 (1984), 407–424.

Hauerwas, Stanley, and Paul Wadell. Review of *After Virtue. The Thomist* 46 (1982).

MacIntyre, Alasdair. *Marxism: An Interpretation.* London: Humanities Press, 1953.

MacIntyre, Alasdair. *The Unconscious: A Conceptual Analysis.* New York: Routledge and Kegan Paul, 1958.

MacIntyre, Alasdair. *A Short History of Ethics.* New York: Macmillan, 1966.

MacIntyre, Alasdair. *Herbert Marcuse: An Exposition and a Polemic.* New York: Viking, 1970.

MacIntyre, Alasdair. *Against the Self-Images of the Age: Essays in Ideology and Philosophy.* Notre Dame: University of Notre Dame Press, 1971.

MacIntyre, Alasdair. "Epistemological Crises, Dramatic Narrative, and the Philosophy of Science," *The Monist* 60 (1977), 433–472.

MacIntyre, Alasdair. "Philosophy, 'Other' Disciplines and Their Histories: A Rejoinder to Richard Rorty," *Soundings* 45 (1982), 127–145.

MacIntyre, Alasdair. *After Virtue.* Notre Dame: University of Notre Dame Press, 1984. Second edition, with postscript.

MacIntyre, Alasdair. "Bernstein's Distorting Mirrors," *Soundings* 67 (1984), 30–41.

MacIntyre, Alasdair. "Moral Rationality, Tradition, and Aristotle: A Reply," *Inquiry* 26 (1984), 447–466.

MacIntyre, Alasdair. "The Relationship of Philosophy to Its Past," in *Philosophy in History,* ed. R. Rorty, J. B. Schneewind, and Q. Skinner, 31–48. New York: Cambridge University Press, 1984.

MacIntyre, Alasdair. "Rights, Practices and Marxism: Reply to Six Critics," *Analyse und Kritik* 7 (1985), 234–248.

MacIntyre, Alasdair, with Paul Ricoeur. *The Religious Significance of Atheism.* New York: Columbia University Press, 1967.

MacIntyre, Alasdair, ed. *Hegel: A Collection of Critical Essays.* Notre Dame: University of Notre Dame Press, 1976.

MacIntyre, Alasdair, and Dorothy Emmet, eds. *Sociological Theory and Philosophical Analysis.* New York: Macmillan, 1970.

MacIntyre, Alasdair, and Stanley Hauerwas, eds. *Revisions: Changing Perspectives in Moral Philosophy.* Notre Dame: University of Notre Dame Press, 1983.

O'Neill, Onora. "Kant After Virtue," *Inquiry* 26 (1984), 387–405.

Schneewind, J. B. "Moral Crisis and the History of Ethics," *Midwest Studies in Philosophy* 8 (1983), 525–539.

Schneewind, J. B. "Virtue, Narrative and Community: MacIntyre and Morality," *Journal of Philosophy* 79 (1982), 653–663.

Taylor, Charles. "Justice After Virtue," in *Kritische Methode und Zukunft der Anthropologie,* ed. M. Benedikt and R. Berger, 23–48. Vienna, 1985.

Wartofsky, Marx. "Virtue Lost or Understanding MacIntyre," *Inquiry* 27 (1984), 235–250.

Relativism, Power, and Philosophy

Alasdair MacIntyre

1

It was Anthony Collins, the friend of John Locke, who re-marked that had it not been for the Boyle Lecturers' annual demonstrations of the existence of God, few people would ever have doubted it.[1] It may have been a similar spirit of argumentative contrariness that led me to begin to appreciate fully both the strength and the importance of the case to be made out in favor of at least one version of relativism only after reading some recent philosophical root and branch dismissals of relativism as such.[2] But of course I ought not to have been such a late-comer to that appreciation. For relativism, like skepticism, is one of those doctrines that have by now been refuted a number of times too often. Nothing is perhaps a surer sign that a doctrine embodies some not-to-be-neglected truth than that in the course of the history of philosophy it should have been refuted again and again. Genuinely refutable doctrines only need to be refuted once.

Philosophical doctrines that are not susceptible of genuine refutation fall into at least two classes. There are some to which, in the light of the rational justification that can be provided for them, we owe simple assent. But there are others to which our assent is or ought to be accorded only with a recognition that what they present is a moment in the development of thought that has to be, if possible, transcended; and this even although we may as yet lack adequate grounds for believing ourselves able to transcend them. Sketpicism is one such doctrine; and relativism is another. But no doctrine can be genuinely transcended until we understand what is to be said in its favor. And a first step toward understanding this in the case of relativism must be to show that the purported refutations have largely missed its point and so been misdirected.

It is not that there is nothing to be learned from them. From them we can certainly learn how to formulate relativism in a way that does not gratuitously entangle it with error. So we can learn from Socrates' encounter with the formulations of Protagoras in the *Theatetus*[3] that relativists must be careful not to allow themselves to be trapped into making some type of universal self-referential claim. Such a claim, by denying to all doctrines whatsoever the predicates "is true" and "is false," unless these are radically reinterpreted to mean no more than "seems true to such and such persons" and "seems false to such and such persons," turns the interesting assertion that relativism is true into the uninteresting assertion that relativism seems true to relativists. And we can learn from Hegel's critique of Kant[4] that relativists must be careful to avoid framing their theses in a way that presupposes the legitimacy of some version of what has come to be called the scheme-content distinction, that is, the distinction between some concept or conceptual scheme on the one hand and on the other an entirely preconceptual world or given waiting to be rescued from in one version blindness, in another nakedness, by being conceptualized.

Yet it is important to be precise about what we have to learn from these refutations of particular formulations of relativism; and it is important therefore not to abstract for formulaic use what we take to be the essence of some refutation from the context in which such as Plato or Hegel embedded it and from which it drew its peculiar force. So we are perhaps entitled to express a certain polite surprise when a contemporary philosopher who has shown both assiduity and ingenuity in trying to make credible the view that "is true" says no more than is said by "seems true to such and such persons, namely *us*," asserts that if there were any contemporary relativists, one could use against them some variant of what he calls the "arguments

Socrates used against Protagoras."[5] The surprise derives from
our remembering that the premises from which Plato derived
Socrates' refutation of Protagoras' version of relativism also
entailed the necessary failure of any reinterpretative reduction
of "is true" to "seems true to such and such persons." From
these premises the one conclusion is not available without the
other.

The same kind of polite surprise is warranted when another
distinguished contemporary philosopher, having repeated the
substance of Hegel's demonstration of the illegitimacy of any
dualism that tears apart conceptual schemes on the one hand
and the world on the other, concludes to the necessary incoherence of the very idea of a conceptual scheme.[6] It was after
all Hegel who gave its canonical form both to the idea of a
conceptual scheme and to that of alternative and incompatible
conceptual schemes, and he did so without ever violating his
own ban on the illegitimate dualist scheme/content and scheme/
world distinctions.[7] Nor was Hegel alone in this; the same could
be said of his predecessor, Vico,[8] and of his successor,
Collingwood.[9]

We need, then, in order to capture the truth in relativism, a
formulation of that doctrine that has learned from both Plato
and Hegel: it must avoid Protagorean self-trivializing by giving
its due to the Platonic distinction between "is true" and "seems
true to such and such persons"; and in any appeal that it makes
to the idea of alternative conceptual schemes, it must be careful
to follow Hegel in leaving no opening for any scheme/content
or scheme/world distinction.

2

"Relativism," as I am going to use that expression, names one
kind of conclusion to inquiry into a particular class of problems.
Those questions arise in the first place for people who live in
certain highly specific types of social and cultural situation; but
this is not to say that they are not distinctively philosophical
questions. They are indeed examples of questions that *both* are
inescapable for certain ordinary agents and language users *and*
have the characteristic structure of philosophical problems. It

is perhaps unsurprising that they have been overlooked by those recent philosophers who want to make a sharp dichotomy between the realm of philosophical theorizing and that of everyday belief because they suppose both that it is philosophers themselves who largely generate philosophical problems by their own misconceptions and that everyday life cannot be apt to suffer from types of disorder that require specifically philosophical diagnosis. This attitude is perhaps a symptom of a certain lack of sociological imagination, of too impoverished a view of the types of social and institutional circumstance that generate philosophical problems. What then are the social and institutional circumstances that generate the cluster of problems to which some version of relativism can be a rational response?

They are the social and institutional circumstances of those who inhabit a certain type of frontier or boundary situation. Consider the predicament of someone who lives in a time and place where he or she is a full member of two linguistic communities, speaking one language, Zuni, say, or Irish, exclusively to the older members of his or her family and village and Spanish or English, say, to those from the world outside, who seek to engage him or her in a way of life in the exclusively Spanish- or English-speaking world. Economic and social circumstance may enforce on such a person a final choice between inhabiting the one linguistic community and inhabiting the other; and in some times and places this is much more than a choice between two languages, at least in any narrowly conceived sense of "language." For a language may be so used, and both Irish and Zuni have in some past periods been so used, that to share in its use is to presuppose one cosmology rather than another, one relationship of local law and custom to cosmic order rather than another, one justification of particular relationships of individual to community and of both to land and to landscape rather than another. In such a language even the use of proper names may on occasion have such presuppositions.

If, for example, I speak in Irish, even today, let alone three hundred years ago, of Doire Colmcille — of Doire in modern Irish — the presuppositons and implications of my utterance are quite other than if I speak in English of Londonderry. But, it may be asked, are these not simply two names of one and the same place? The answer is first that no proper name of place or person names any place or person *as such;* it names *in the first instance* only *for* those who are members of some particular linguistic and cultural community, by identifying places and persons in terms of the scheme of identification shared by, and perhaps partially constitutive of, that community. The relation of a proper name to its bearer cannot be elucidated without reference to such identifying functions.[10] And secondly that "Doire Colmcille" names — embodies a communal intention of naming — a place with a continuous identity ever since it became in fact St. Columba's oak grove in 546, and that "Londonderry" names a settlement made only in the seventeenth century and is a name whose use presupposes the legitimacy of that settlement and of the use of the English language to name it. Notice that the name "Doire Colmcille" is as a name untranslatable; you can translate the Gaelic expression "doire Colmcille:" by the English expression "St. Columba's oak grove"; but that cannot be the translation of a place name, for it is not itself the name of any place. And what is true of the relationship of "Doire Colmcille" in Irish to "Londonderry" in English holds equally of the relationship of the names of the Zuni villages in the sixteenth century, such as "Itwana," to the Spanish name for them as the Seven Cities of Cibola.[11]

To this the response may be that although there may as a matter of contingent historical fact be certain kinds of association attaching to the use of "Doire Colmcille" rather than "Londonderry" or vice versa, the use of the name merely *qua* name carries with it no presuppositions concerning political or social legitimacy. And it might be thought that this could be shown by appeal to the fact that some ignorant stranger might use the name "Londonderry" in order to ask the way and in identifying the place on the map at which he or she wished to arrive would have shown that one *can* use the name for purposes of identification without any such presupposition. But such a stranger is only able now to use a name that has indeed been made available to those outside its primary community of use because the members of the community use or used it as they do, and that stranger's secondary use of the name is therefore parasitic upon its uses by the primary community. Moreover, such secondary non-presupposition-laden uses do not thereby become names freed from any specific social context of use. They are very specifically names-as-used-by-strangers-or-tourists. Philosophers of logic have sometimes treated the way in which such names are used by strangers or tourists as exemplifying some essential core naming relation, a concept about which I shall have to say something later on in the argument; for the moment I note only that in so doing such philosophers have obscured the difference between the type of natural language in which the standard uses of a variety of expressions commit the user to an expression of a shared, communal belief and the type of natural language in which this is so minimally or not at all.

In the type of frontier or boundary situation that I have been describing, both languages — the Irish of, say 1700 and the English of the plantation settlements of the same date, or the Zuni Shiwi language of, say 1540 and the Spanish of the *conquistadores* — are at the former end of this spectrum of natural-languages-in-use. Thus what the bilingual speaker in both members of one of these pairs is going to have to choose between, in deciding to spend his or her life within one linguistic community rather than the other, is also to some substantial degree alternative and incompatible sets of beliefs and ways of life. Moreover, each of these sets of beliefs and ways of life will have internal to it its own specific modes of rational justification in key areas and its own correspondingly specific warrants for claims to truth.

It is not that the beliefs of each such community cannot be represented in any way at all in the language of the other; it is rather that the outcome in each case of rendering those beliefs sufficiently intelligible to be evaluated by a member of the other community involves characterizing those beliefs in such a way that they are bound to be rejected. What is from the one point of view a just act of war will be from the other theft; what is from the one point of view an original act of acquisition, of what had so far belonged to nobody and therefore of what had remained available to become only now someone's private property, will be from the other point of view the illegitimate seizure of what had so far belonged to nobody because it is what *cannot* ever be made into private property — for example, common land. The Spaniards brought alien concepts of ownership deriving from Roman, feudal, and canon law to their transactions with the Indians; the English brought concepts of individual property rights recognized by English common-law decisions to Ireland at a time when there was certainly a translation for the Latin "jus" in Irish, but none for the expression "a right" (understood as something that attaches not to status, role, or function, but to individuals as such).

It will not at this point be helpful to remark either that in both these pairs of linguistic communities a great many other beliefs were of course shared by members of both communities or that in particular no one had ever had any difficulty in translating "Snow is white" from one language to the other. There are indeed large parts of every language that are translatable into every other; and there are types of routine or routinizable social situations that are reproduced in many — some perhaps even in all — cultures. And the project of matching types of sentence-in-use to types of routinizable situation reproduced in many cultures, and of both to the habits of assenting to or dissenting from the uses of such sentences, will doubtless, if actually carried through rather than merely projected, lay bare the relationship between these facts and the type and range of translability that hold in consequence of that relationship. But the suspicion that I have gradually come to entertain about this type of project is that what can be expected from it is perhaps not so much an adequte semantics for natural languages or a theory of truth in such languages as a series of excellent Phrase Books for Travelers. For it is precisely those features of languages mastery of which *cannot* be acquired from such phrase books that generate untranslatability between languages.

What are those features? They include a power to extrapolate from uses of expressions learned in certain types of situations to the making and understanding of new and newly illuminating uses. The availability of this power to the members of a whole linguistic community of the type I have been characterizing depends in part upon their shared ability to refer and allude to a particular common stock of canonical texts, texts that define the literary and linguistic tradition that members of that community inhabit. For it is by allusion to such texts that linguistic innovation and extrapolation proceed; what those texts provide are both shared exemplars from which to extrapolate and shared exemplars of the activity of extrapolation.

It is characteristically poets and saga reciters who in such societies make and continually remake these at first oral and then written texts; only poetic narrative is memorable in the required way and, as we should have learned from Vico,[12] it is the linguistic capacities and abilities provided by poetry and saga that make later forms of prose possible. Concepts are first acquired and understood in terms of poetic images, and the movement of thought from the concreteness and particularity of the imaged to the abstractness of the conceptual never completely leaves that concreteness and particularity behind. Conceptions of courage and of justice, of authority, sovereignty, and property, of what understanding is and what failure to understand is, all these will continue to be elaborated from exemplars to be found in the socially recognized canonical texts. And this will still be the case when prose supplements poetry, when law books are added to myth and epic, and when dramatic works are added to both. The consequence is that when two such distinct linguistic communities confront one another, each with its own body of canonical texts, its own exemplary images, and its own tradition of elaborating concepts in terms of these, but each also lacking a knowledge of, let alone linguistic capacities informed by, the tradition of the other community, each will represent the beliefs of the other within its own discourse in abstraction from the relevant tradition and so in a way that ensures misunderstanding. From each point of view certain of the key concepts and beliefs of the other, just because they are presented apart from that context of inherited texts from which they draw their conceptual life, will necessarily appear contextless and lacking in justification.

Here we confront one more instance of the hermeneutic circle. The initial inability of the members of each linguistic community to translate certain parts of the language of the other community into their own is a barrier to knowledge of the tradition embodied in the uses of that language; but lack of knowledge of the tradition is itself sufficient to preclude accurate translation of those parts of the alien language. And once again the fact that certain other parts of the two languages may translate quite easily into each other provides no reason at all for skepticism about partial untranslatability. The sentences-in-use that are the untranslatable parts of this type of language-in-use are not in fact capable of being logically derived from, constructed out of, reduced to, or otherwise rendered into the sentences-in-use that comprise the translatable part of the same language-in-use. Nor should this surprise us. One of the marks of a genuinely adequate knowledge of two quite different languages by one and the same person is that person's ability to discriminate between those parts of each language that are translatable into the other and those that are not. Some degree of partial untranslatability marks the relationship of every language to every other.

Notice that this recognition of untranslatability never entails an acknowledgment of some necessary limit to understanding. Conversely, that we can understand completely what is being said in some language other than our own never entails that we can translate what we understand. And it is this ability both to understand and to recognize the partial untranslatability of what is understood that combines with the specific social, conceptual, and linguistic characteristics of the type of boundary situation that I have identified to create the predicament of the bilingual speaker who in that type of situation has to choose between membership in one or other of the two rival linguistic communities.

Remember that the contingent features of that speaker's situation make this a choice not only between languages but between two mutually incompatible conceptualizations of natural and social reality; and it is not only a choice between two mutually incompatible sets of beliefs but one between sets of beliefs so structured that each has internal to it its own standards of truth and justification. Moreover, this choice has to be made with only the limited linguistic and conceptual resources afforded by the two languages in question. What constraints do these limits impose?

They exclude the possibility of appeal to some neutral or independent standard of rational justification to justify the choice of one set of beliefs, one way of life, one linguistic community rather than the other. For the only standards of truth and justification made available within the two communities are those between which a choice has to be made. And the only resources afforded for the members of each community to represent the concepts, beliefs, and standards of the other ensure that from the point of view of each its own concepts, beliefs, and standards will be vindicated and those of its rival found wanting.

Here then two rival conceptual schemes do confront one another. For those culturally and linguistically able to inhabit only one of them no problem arises. But for our imagined person who has the abilities to understand both, but who must choose to inhabit only one, the nature of the choice is bound, if he or she is adequately reflective, to transform his or her understanding of truth and of rational justification. For he or she will not be able to find application for the concepts of truth and justification that are independent of the standards of one community or the other. There is no access to any subject matter that is not conceptualized in terms that already presuppose the truth of one set of claims rather than the other. Hegel's proscription of any appeal to an extraconceptual reality is not being infringed. Each community, using its own criteria of *sameness* and *difference*, recognizes that it is one and the same subject matter about which they are advancing their claim; incommensurability and incompatibility are not incompatible.

The only way to characterize adequately the predicament thus created for our imaginary person is in the idiom that Plato provided. For that person will now have to reinterpret the predicates "is true" and "is justified" so that to apply them will in future claim no more than would be claimed by "seems true to this particular community" or "seems justified to this particular community." Rational choice will have transformed our imaginary person into a relativist. But why call this a predicament? Because in so reinterpreting these predicates our imaginary Zuni or Irish person will have, without in the least intending to, separated him or herself effectively from both contending communities. For no sixteenth- or seventeenth-century community was able to understand itself relativistically.

To all this the reply may well be, So what? Even if it is conceded that I have provided a defensible version of relativism, and even if it is allowed that our imaginary person did in certain times and places have real counterparts, Irish or Zuni or whatever, what of it? That kind of relativism was imposed by the contingencies of their historical, social, and linguistic circumstances, contingencies that deprived our imaginary person and his or her real counterparts of the linguistic and conceptual resources necessary to avoid or refute relativism. But *we,* it may be suggested, do have those resources, so what is the relevance of your philosophical figment to *us?*

Just this is of course the question. Is it indeed the case if we were to specify the linguistic and conceptual resources that would have to be provided to enable our imaginary person to overcome the particular contingent limitations of his or her situation, we should have shown how relativism can be avoided or refuted? If we succeed in transforming this imaginary person, so that he or she becomes just like us, will the relativization of the predicates of truth and justification no longer be forced upon him or her, or indeed ourselves? To these questions I therefore turn, but before turning I want to inquire briefly what will be at stake in giving one kind of answer to them rather than another.

3

The same considerations that ensure that someone compelled to choose between the claims of two rival linguistic communities, in the type of circumstance that I have described, will be unable to appeal to any neutral, independent standard of rational justification by which to judge between their competing claims also ensure that more generally the members of any two such communities will have to conduct their relationship with members of the other community without resort to any such appeal. But where there is no resort to such standards, human relationships are perforce relationships of will and power unmediated by rationality. I do not mean that where there is no resort to such standards, each of the contending parties in such communal relationships will necessarily act unreasonably, that is, unreasonably from its own particular point of view as to what constitutes unreason. But it is just that point of view that in their transactions each community will be trying to impose upon the other. And when it becomes reasonable from the point of view of one of the contending parties to impose their will by force upon the other in the name of their own idiosyncratic conception of reasonableness, that is what they will do.

So it was with the Spanish in their relationships with the Zuni, so it has been with the English in their relationships with the Irish. And one instrument of such force is the imposition of one's own language at the expense of the other's. But can it ever by otherwise? Only if the relativism that emerged as the only rational attitude to the competing claims of two such antagonistic communities turns out not to be the last word on all relationships between rival human communities; only, that is, if linguistic and conceptual resources can indeed be supplied, so that that relativism can be avoided or circumvented. For only in cases where that relativism does not have the last word does the possibility open up of substituting, for a politics in which the exercise of power is unmediated by rationality, a politics in which the exercise of power is both mediated and tempered by appeal to standards of rational justification independent of the particularism of the contending parties.

I am not of course suggesting that the identification and formulation of such nonrelativist standards of truth and justification is ever by itself sufficient to overcome a politics of unmediated will and power, in the conflicts that occur within communities, let alone in the conflicts that occur between communities. And I am not suggesting that force may not on occasion be used to serve the purposes of genuine practical rationality as well as those of idiosyncratic and one-sided reasonableness. I *am* claiming that it is only in those forms of human relationship in which it is possible to appeal to impersonal standards of judgment, neutral between competing claims and affording the best type of rational justification both relevant and available, that the possibility opens up of unmasking and dethroning arbitrary exercises of power, tyrannical power within communities and imperialist power between communities. Plato was once again right: the argument against the tyrant and the argument against relativized predicates of truth and justification require the same premises.

This would of course be denied by our contemporary post-Nietzschean anti-Platonists. But even they on occasion inadvertently provide support for this thesis. Perhaps the most cogent, because the most systematic, exposition of the view that all attempts to appeal to would-be impersonal standards of truth and rational justification must fail to provide any effective alternative to established distributions of power, just because every such attempt and appeal itself operates according to the laws of some institutionalized distribution of power, is that of Michel Foucault in his earlier writings. So Foucault can write about the politics of truth and the political economy of truth in a way that treats all appeals to truth and to rational justification as themselves particularist forms of power inextricably associated with other forms of imposition and constraint.[13] But Foucault cannot articulate this view either generally or in his detailed institutional studies without presupposing a radical incommensurability thesis, a thesis that indeed only seems to emerge as a conclusion from his studies because it *was* presupposed from the outset. And that thesis is entitled to our assent if and only if the version of relativism that I have described does have the last word.

So it turns out that how we understand the politics of power depends in crucial part upon the answers that we give to certain philosophical questions. Janice Moulton[14] and Robert Nozick[15] have both recently suggested that philosophy has been damaged by an excessive use of adversarial and antagonistic idioms. We speak too readily, they think, of winning and losing arguments, of others being forced to acknowledge our conclusions, and so on; and insofar as such idioms obscure the need for the cooperative virtues in philosophical activity, they are certainly right. Nonetheless the language of antagonism has one important positive function. It signals to us that philosophy, like all other institutionalized human activities, is a milieu of conflict. And the conflicts of philosophy stand in a number of often complex and often indirect relationships to a variety of other conflicts. The complexity, the indirectness, and the variety all help to conceal from us that even the more abstract and technical issues of our discipline — issues concerning naming, reference, truth, and translatability — may on occasion be as crucial in their political or social implications as are theories of the social contract or of natural right. The former no less than the latter have implications for the nature and limitations of rationality in the arenas of political society. All philosophy, one way or another, is political philosophy.

Sometimes philosophy fares better by our forgetting this, at least temporarily, but we can scarcely avoid bearing it in mind in returning to the question to which the present argument has led: what other resources would our imaginary person in his or her sixteenth- or seventeenth-century boundary situation have had to possess, what resources that he or she lacked would we have to possess, if we are to be able to appeal to standards of judgment in respect of truth and rational justification that do not relativize these predicates to the conceptual scheme of one particular cultural and linguistic community.

4

A necessary first step out of the relativistic predicament would be the learning of some third language, a language of a very different kind from the two available to our imaginary person so far. Such a third language, if it was to provide the needed resources, would have to be a language with two central characteristics. First, its everyday use must be such that it does *not* presuppose allegiance to either of the two rival sets of beliefs between which our imaginary person has to choose, or indeed, so far as possible, to any other set of beliefs that might compete for allegiance with those two. And second, it must be able to provide the resources for an accurate representation of the two competing schemes of belief, including that in the tradition of each community which provides that background for its present beliefs, without which they cannot be fully intelligible nor their purported justification adequately understood. What kind of language-in-use would this be?

One central feature that it would have to possess, if it were to satisfy the first of these two conditions, can be illustrated by considering how its use of proper names, for example of place names, would contrast with that of the languages in terms of which the problem has so far been framed. For in this third language the relationship of a name to what is named will have to be specifiable, so far as possible, independently of any particular scheme of identification embodying the beliefs of some particular community. Names in consequence will have to have become detached from those descriptions that, within some given and presupposed context defined by the beliefs of some particular community, uniquely identify person or place. Particular proper names will have ceased to be equivalent to, and, in virtue of that loss of equivalence, will have ceased to have the same sense as, particular definite descriptions. Names of places will have become equally available for any user to employ, whatever his or her beliefs. Names, having been Fregean, will have become by a process of social change Kripkean.[16]

The immediate response of most philosophical logicians will once again be to say that I have in so characterizing these changes confused the essential function of naming with its merely contingent accompaniments. But it is just this notion of a single essential naming relationship or function that I reject; just as we have learned that meaning is not a unitary notion, so we ought also to have learned that there are multifarious modes of identifying, picking out, referring to, calling toward, in, or up, and the like, all of which connect a name and a named, but there is no single core relation of name to named for theories of reference to be theories of. Or rather, if there were to be such a relation, it would be what Russell said it was, and it is notorious that Russell's characterization of that relation entails that there is indeed a class of proper names, but that none of the expressions that we have hitherto called names are among them.[17]

A second feature of this type of language will be the absence of texts that are canonical for its common use. Allusion and quotation will have become specialized devices, and the literate will have been divorced from the literary. For texts, whether oral or written, embody and presuppose beliefs, and this type of language is, so far as possible, *qua* language-in-use, neutral between competing systems of beliefs. What it will provide are resources for the representation of an indefinite variety of systems of beliefs, most of them originally at home in very different types of linguistic community, by means of a variety of devices that enable those who construct such representations to do so in a way that is quite independent of their own commitments. What kind of devices are these? Where the text is in a foreign language, translation will be supplemented both by paraphrase and by scholarly gloss.[18] Words as common as *polis and dikaiosune* in fifth century Attic Greek cannot be translated in any strict sense into twentieth-century English or French or German — examples, it will have been obvious at once, of this type of language — but their use can be quite adequately elucidated. The traditions that appealed to canonical texts can now become matter for successful historical inquiry, and the relevant texts embodying those traditions can be established, edited, and translated or otherwise elucidated. The belief system of any and every culture, or of almost any and every culture, can thus be accurately represented within our own. But certain features of the resulting stock of representations need to be taken into account.

One concerns the asymmetry of this representation relation. From the fact that we in modern English or some other modern language, with our academic resources, can accurately represent the belief system or part of the belief system of another culture, it does not follow that the corresponding part of our belief system can be represented in the language-in-use of that other culture. Using modern English, Charles H. Kahn has shown how the Homeric uses of the verb *eimi* can be accurately and adequately represented.[19] But his explanation of why certain types of translation or paraphrase would be a misrepresentation — namely that, for example, the English verb "exist" has emerged from a history whose first stage was the transition to classical Greek and that was then informed successively by classical Latin poetic usage, by medieval Latin philosophical usage, and finally by some essentially modern preoccupations, so that we just cannot use "exist" to translate or to explicate the characteristic and varying features of Homeric uses of *eimi* — has as a consequence that it would not have been possible within the Homeric linguistic community to represent accurately the modern English uses of "exist." And what is true of the relationship of archaic Greek to modern English would be equally true of the relationship to modern English of seventeenth-century Irish or sixteenth-century Zuni. But from this fact we might be tempted to draw a mistaken conclusion.

Return to the condition of our imaginary person once poised between sixteenth-century Zuni and Spanish or seventeenth-century Irish and English, but now, presumably some three hundred years older, considering whether to address his other problems instead in twentieth-century English or French or whatever. Since such a person can provide him or herself with such an adequate degree of neutral representation of both systems of belief in a modern language, but cannot represent adequately or neutrally in either of his or her earlier languages either the systems of belief of the rival linguistic communities who spoke those languages or the standpoints afforded by twentieth-century English or French for the provision of such representation, it might seem that the only rational course for such a person is to conduct his or her inquiry from now on in one of the modern languages, thus escaping from some at least of the limitations imposed on his or her earlier condition, the very limitations that enforced relativist conclusions. But it is just at this point that a second feature of the representations of schemes of belief in specifically modern natural languages presents a crucial difficulty.

The only way in which our frustrated relativist can hope to transcend the limitations that imposed that relativism is by formulating in the language that he or she can now speak, one of the languages of modernity, an impersonal and neutral standard of rational justification in the light of which the claims of the competing belief systems can be evaluated. But what he or she will in fact learn from acquiring this new language is that it is a central feature of the culture whose language it is that rationally founded agreement as to the nature of the justification required is not to be obtained. Rational justification within the context of such cultures becomes an essentially contested concept, and this for a number of distinct but related types of reason.

One arises from the nature of the historical process that made the language of modernity what it is. A central feature of that process had to be, I have already argued, the detachment of the language-in-use from any particular set of canonical texts; and an early stage in that history was the gradual accumulation in the culture of so many different, heterogeneous, and conflicting bodies of canonical texts from so many diverse parts of the cultural past that every one of them had to forego any exclusive claim to canonical status and thereby, it soon became apparent, any claim to canonical status at all. So the accumulation of Greek, Hebrew, and Latin texts at the Renaissance proved only a prologue not only to the annexation of Chinese, Sanskrit, Mayan, and Old Irish texts, and to the bestowal of equal status upon texts in European vernacular languages from the thirteenth to the nineteenth centuries, but also to the discovery of a wide range of preliterate cultures, the whole finally to be assembled in that modern liberal-arts college museum of academic culture, whose introductory tour is provided by those Great Books courses that run from Gilgamesh to Saul Bellow via Confucius, Dante, Newton, *Tristram Shandy,* and Margaret Mead.

What the history that culminates in this kind of educational gallimaufry produced along the way was a large and general awareness of the wide range of varying and conflicting types of justificatory argument used to support various types of contending belief, and also of the wide range of varying and conflicting theoretical accounts of rational justification available to support their use. The consequence was a multiplication of rival standpoints concerning a wide range of subject matters, none of them able to provide the resources for their own final vindication and the overthrow of their competitors. So within philosophy foundationalists war with coherentists and both with skeptics and perspectivists; while conceptions of truth as empirical adequacy contend against a variety of mutually incompatible realisms and both against truth conceived as disclosure. Within the academic study of literature, controversies over the nature of interpretation and about the justification not only of particular interpretations of particular texts, but even of what it is that such interpretations are interpretations of, parody philosophical debate in both idiom and interminability. And psychology has happily accommodated numbers of mutually incompatible schools of thought, each with its own idiosyncratic account of justification, ever since it became an independent academic discipline.

Where the dominant institutions and modes of thought in our larger political society sanction and even encourage disagreement, as upon theological questions, it is widely accepted that in the debates between contending modes of justification there can be no rational conclusion. But even where those same institutions and modes of thought prescribe a large measure of agreement, as in the natural sciences, not only do nonscientific modes of thought such as astrology (which happens to have its own well-organized and far from unsophisticated standards of justification) continue to flourish alongside the sciences, but it remains impossible to secure agreement on why the key transitions in the past history of our culture from prescientific thought to scientific, and from one mode of scientific thought to another, were or are rationally justified. So incommensurability as a feature of the history of the natural sciences has continually been rediscovered and recharacterized from a variety of justificatory standpoints: by Gaston Bachelard in the context of the French debates of the 1920s; by Michael Polanyi in such a way as to warrant a blend of fideism and realism; by Thomas Kuhn in a way designed to undermine logical empiricism; by Paul Feyerabend in an anarchist mode; and by Ian Hacking in an historical thesis about "styles of thought."

The multiplicity of mutually irreconcilable standpoints concerning justification is one that each of us tends to recognize easily and even scornfully in other academic professions. But from within our own profession each of us characteristically views and describes the situation only from the specific point of view of his or her own commitments, judging the success and failure of other points of view from the standpoint afforded by standards of justification internal to our own; and by so doing we render our overall cultural situation invisible, at least for most of the time. That this should be the case, that we should tend to be guilty of this kind of onesidedness, is scarcely surprising. It says no more about us than that we are, sociologically at least, normal human beings. The danger of contemporary antirelativism, however, is that it suggests that what is in fact a contingent social condition whose limitations it is important for us to overcome is in fact a necessary condition of rational social existence. For antirelativism pictures us first as necessarily inhabiting our own conceptual scheme, our own *weltanschaung* ("*Whose* conceptual scheme, whose *weltanschaung* but our own could we be expected to inhabit?" is the rhetorical question that is sometimes posed) and second as necessarily acquiring whatever understanding we may possess of the conceptual schemes and *weltanschaungen* of others by a process of translation so conceived that any intelligible rendering of the concepts and beliefs of the others must represent them as in all central respects similar to our own.

What I have tried to suggest by contrast is that when we learn the languages of certain radically different cultures, it is in the course of discovering what is untranslatable in them, and why, that we learn not only how to occupy alternative viewpoints, but in terms of those viewpoints to frame questions to which under certain conditions a version of relativism is the inescapable answer. And in so doing we are also able to learn how to view our own peculiarly modern standpoint from a vantage point outside itself. For consider now the view of that modern standpoint afforded to our imaginary person who had hoped to remedy the deficiencies of his or her particular type of premodern language by learning to speak one of the languages of modernity.

Where in his or her premodern language he or she was unable to free him- or herself from the limitations of the justificatory schemes built into and presupposed by each particular language-in-use, and so was unable to discover a set of neutral and independent standards of rational justification, by appeal to which his or her choice of allegiance to the beliefs and way of life of one community rather than the other could be made, he or she now speaks a language the use of which is free from such commitments. But the culture that is able to make such a language available is so only because it is a culture offering, for the relevant kinds of controversial subject matter, all too many heterogeneous and incompatible schemes of rational justification. And every attempt to advance sufficient reasons for choosing any one such scheme over its rivals must always turn out to presuppose the prior adoption of that scheme itself or of some other. For without such a prior prerational commitment, no reason will count as a good reason.

Hence, our imaginary person, whose acquisition of one of the natural languages of modernity — twentieth-century English or French or whatever — was to rescue him or her from the relativism imposed by his or her previous condition, cannot find here any more than there, albeit for very different reasons, any genuinely neutral and independent standard of rational justification. And it remains only to recognize that if our imaginary sixteenth- or seventeenth-century person, knowing both the languages that he or she then knew and subsequently learning our own, would be unable to avoid relativistic conclusions, then we in turn by learning his or her languages, or languages like them, and so learning both to imagine and to understand ourselves from the standpoint of such an external observer, would have to reach the same conclusions. Relativism after all turns out to be so far immune to refutation, even by us.

5

It does not follow that relativism cannot be transcended. We may be tempted to think so by noticing that the version of relativism that resists refutation is itself a relativized relativism, since what my arguments show, if they succeed, is that relativism is inescapable from certain particular points of view — one of which happens to be that which most people in modern societies such as ours take to be their own. And this may seem to provide additional confirmation, if such is still needed, that there is after all no mode of thought, inquiry, or practice that is not from some particular point of view, and whose judgments do not therefore take place on the basis of what Edmund Burke called prejudices, prejudgments. But it does not follow, as we might suppose if we did concede the last word to relativism, that we are thereby condemned to or imprisoned within our own particular standpoint, able to controvert that of others only by appealing to standards that already presuppose the standpoint of our own prejudices. Why not?

Begin from a fact that at this stage can be little more than suggestive. It is that those natural languages in which philosophy became a developed form of inquiry, so later generating from itself first the natural and then the social sciences, were in the condition neither on the one hand of sixteenth- and seventeenth-century Zuni and Irish nor in that of the natural languages of modernity. The Attic Greek of the fifth and fourth centuries, the Latin of the twelfth to fourteenth centuries, the English, French, German, and Latin of the seventeenth and eighteenth centuries, were each of them neither as relatively presuppositionless in respect of key beliefs as the languages of modernity were to become, nor as closely tied in their use to the presuppositions of one single closely knit set of beliefs as some premodern languages are and have been. Consider in this respect the difference between Attic and Homeric Greek or that between mature philosophical Latin after Augustine and Jerome and the Latin that had preceded the discoveries by Lucretius and Cicero that they could only think certain Greek thoughts in Latin if they radically neologized. Such languages-in-use, we may note, have a wide enough range of canonical texts to provide to some degree alternative and rival modes of justification, but a narrow enough range so that the debate between these modes is focused and determinate. What emerges within the conceptual schemes of such languages is a developed problematic, a set of debates concerning a body of often interrelated problems, problems canonical for those inhabiting that particular scheme, by reference to work upon which rational progress, or failure to achieve such progress, is evaluated. Each such problematic is of course internal to some particular conceptual scheme embodied in some particular historical tradition with its own given starting point, its own prejudices. To become a philosopher always involved learning to inhabit such a tradition, a fact not likely to be obvious to those brought up from infancy within one, but very obvious to those brought up outside any such. It is no accident for example that for Irish speakers to become philosophers, they had first to learn Greek and Latin, like Johannes Scotus Eriugena in the ninth century.

The development of a problematic within a tradition characteristically goes through certain well marked stages — not necessarily of course the same stages in every tradition — among them periods in which progress, as judged by the standards internal to that particular tradition, falters or fails, attempt after attempt to solve or resolve certain key problems or issues proves fruitless, and the tradition appears, again by its own standards, to have degenerated. Characteristically, if not universally, at this stage contradictions appear that cannot be resolved within the particular tradition's own conceptual framework; that is to say, there can be drawn from within the tradition equally well-grounded support for incompatible positions; at the same time inquiries tend to become diverse and particularized and to lose any overall sense of direction; and debates about realism may become fashionable.[20] And what the adherents of such a tradition may have to learn in such a period is that their tradition lacks the resources to explain its own failing condition. They are all the more likely to learn that if they encounter some other standpoint, conceptually richer and more resourceful, that *is* able to provide just such an explanation.

So it was, for example, when Galilean and Newtonian natural philosophy turned out to provide a more adequate explanation by its own standards not only of nature than scholasticism had afforded, but also of why late medieval scholastic enquiries had been able to proceed only so far and no farther. Scholasticism's successes and more importantly its frustrations and limitation, judged by scholasticism's own standards of success and failure rather than by any later standards, only became intelligible in the light afforded by Galileo and Newton.

That the theoretical standpoint of Galileo or Newton may have been incommensurable with that of the scholastics is not inconsistent with this recognition of how the later physical tradition transcended the limitations of the earlier. And it is of course not only within the history of natural philosophy that this kind of claim can be identified and sometimes vindicated. Such a claim is implicit in the relationship of some of the medieval theistic Aristotelians to Aristotle in respect of theology and of Dante's *Commedia* to the *Aeneid* in respect of poetic imagination.

These examples direct our attention to a central characteristic of theoretical and practical rationality. Rationality, understood within some particular tradition with its own specific conceptual scheme and problematic, as it always has been and will be, nonetheless requires *qua* rationality a recognition that the rational inadequacies of that tradition from its own point of view — and every tradition must from the point of view of its own problematic view itself as to some degree inadequate — may at any time prove to be such that perhaps only the resources provided by some quite alien tradition — far more alien, it may be, than Newton was to the scholastics — will enable us to identify and to understand the limitations of our own tradition; and this provision may require that we transfer our allegiance to that hitherto alien tradition. It is because such rationality requires this recognition that the key concepts embodied in rational theory and practice within any tradition that has a developed problematic, including the concepts of truth and rational justification, cannot be defined exclusively in terms of or collapsed into those conceptions of them that are presently at home within the modes of theory and practice of the particular conceptual scheme of that tradition, or even some idealized version of those conceptions: the Platonic distinction between "is true" and "seems true to such and such person" turns out within such traditions to survive the recognition of the truth in relativism.

It is only from the standpoint of a rationality thus characterized, and that is to say from the standpoint of a tradition embodying such a conception of rationality, that a rejoinder can be made to those post-Nietzschean theories according to which rational argument, inquiry, and practice always express some interest of power and are indeed the masks worn by some will to power. And in this respect there is a crucial difference between rationality thus understood and the rationality characteristic of the Enlightenment and of its heirs. Ever since the Enlightenment our culture has been far too hospitable to the all too plainly self-interested belief that whenever we succeed in discovering the rationality of other and alien cultures and traditions, by making their behavior intelligible and by understanding their languges, what we will also discover is that in essentials they are just like us. Too much in recent and contemporary antirelativism continues to express this Enlightenment point of view and thereby makes more plausible than they ought to be those theories that identify every form of rationality with some form of contending power. What can liberate rationality from this identification is precisely an acknowledgment, only possible from within a certain kind of tradition, that rationality requires a readiness on our part to accept, and indeed to welcome, a possible future defeat of the forms of theory and practice in which it has up till now been taken to be embodied within our own tradition, at the hands of some alien and perhaps even as yet largely unintelligible tradition of thought and practice; and this is an acknowledgment of which the traditions that we inherit have too seldom been capable.

Notes

1. "An Answer to Mr. Clarke's Third Defence of his Letter to Mr. Dodwell," p. 883 in *The Works of Samuel Clarke, D.D.*, Vol. 3, London, 1738.

2. Most notably by Richard Rorty, "Pragmatism, Relativism, and Irrationalism," *Proceedings and Addresses of the American Philosophical Association*, 53 (1980) 719–738, reprinted in *Consequences of Pragmatism*, Minneapolis, 1982: 160–175; and by Donald Davidson in "On the Very Idea of a Conceptual Scheme," *Proceedings and Addresses of the American Philosophical Association*, 47 (1974): 5–20, reprinted in *Inquiries into Truth and Interpretation*, Oxford, 1984: 183–198, and in *Expressing Evaluations*, The 1982 Lindley Lecture at the University of Kansas.

3. *Theaetetus* 152a–179b, and especially 170e–171c.

4. See for example in the first part of the *Enzyklopädie der philosophischen Wissenschaften* (1817), translated by William Wallace as *The Logic of Hegel*, Oxford, 1873, section 44, and "Remark: The Thing-in-itself of Transcendental Idealism," appended to chapter 1, A(b) of section 2 of book 2, of Hegel's *Science of Logic*, London, 1969, which is A. V. Miller's translation of the *Wissenschaft der Logik* (1812).

5. Richard Rorty, "Pragmatism, Relativism and Irrationalism," in *Consequences of Pragmatism*, p. 167.

6. Donald Davidson argues in "On the Very Idea of a Conceptual Scheme" that the scheme-content distinction involves the notion of a relationship between a language or conceptual scheme on the one hand and on the other "something neutral and common that lies outside all schemes" (p. 190) and that the only relationships possible between a language or conceptual scheme and such a something are those of the scheme organizing, systematizing, or dividing whatever it is, or of it fitting for accounting for whatever it is. Davidson then shows that spelling out these relationships involves characterizing what was allegedly neutral and common, so that it is neither, but a subject matter that "we will have to individuate according to familiar principles," so that any language that enables us to speak of it "must be a language very like our own" (p. 192). Hegel argues conversely in the passages cited in note 4 that if we deny to such a something or other those characteristics that it must lack if it is to be genuinely prior to all categorization, as what is "neutral and common" (Davidson's expression) must be, it will turn out to be nothing at all. And in the context of a different discussion, after pointing out that what is alleged to be beyond all conceptualization by reason of its particularity *"cannot be reached* by language. . . . In the actual attempt to say it, it would therefore crumble away . . ." *(Phänomenologie des Geistes,* (1807), paragraph 110, A. V. Miller's translation in *Phenomenology of Spirit,* Oxford, 1977), he points out that in characterizing the whatever it is we find ourselves individuating according to familiar principles, anticipating Davidson very precisely. The page references to Davidson are to *Inquiries into Truth and Interpretation.*

7. One example of Hegel's treatment of rival conceptual schemes is found in the *Phänomenologie* 6, B, 2a, "Der Kampf der Aufklärung mit dem Aberglauben."

8. For Vico, who gave us the first genuinely historical treatment of conceptual schemes, see especially, book 4, sections 1–11 of the *Principi di Scienza Nuova* (1744), translated by T. G. Bergin and H. Fisch as *The New Science of Giambattista Vico* (Cornell, 1948).

9. It was of course Collingwood's antirealism, already spelled out in *Speculum Mentis* (Oxford, 1924), that committed him to rejection of any version of the scheme-context distinction. For his treatment of alternative conceptual schemes see especially the *Essay on Metaphysics* (Oxford, 1940).

10. Paul Ziff in "About Proper Names" (*Mind* 86, July 1977) draws attention to the importance of attending "to the relevant anthropological and linguistic data." An exemplary study is Robin Fox, "Structure of Personal Names on Tory Island" (*Man,* 1963), reprinted as "Personal Names" in *Encounter with Anthropology* (New York, 1973).

11. On the first encounters of the Zuni with the Spaniards see F. H. Cushing, "Outlines of Zuni Creation Myths," in *13th Annual Report of the Bureau of Ethnology* (Washington, D.C., 1896), pp. 326–333, and on the way places are located and the middle place named pp. 367–373.

12. *Principi di Scienza Nuova,* paragraphs 34–36, for example.

13. See for an introduction chapter 5 and chapter 6 (both originally in *Microfiscia del Potere,* Turin, 1977) of *Power/Knowledge* (New York, 1980). Chapter 5 is translated by Kate Soper, chapter 6 by Colin Gordon.

14. "A Paradigm of Philosophy: The Adversary Method," in *Discovering Reality* (Dordrecht, 1983), edited by S. Harding and M. B. Hintikka.

15. *Philosophical Explanations* (Cambridge, Massachusetts), 1981, pp. 4–8.

16. What has to be supplied here is an account of how one and the same proper name can be used in a variety of ways that connect it to one and the same bearer.

17. "The Philosophy of Logical Atomism," pp. 200–203 in *Logic and Knowledge,* edited by R. C. Marsh (London, 1956), originally published in *The Monist,* 1918.

18. See John Wallace, "Translation Theories and the Decipherment of Linear B," *Theory and Decision* 2 (1979).

19. *The Verb "Be" and Its Synonyms,* edited by J. W. M. Verhaar, part 6: *The Verb "Be" in Ancient Greek,* by Charles H. Kahn (Foundations of Language Supplement Series, volume 16, Dordrecht, 1973).

20. Neither realism nor antirealism should be thought of as mistakes (or truths) generated by philosophers reflecting upon the sciences from some external standpoint. They are in fact primarily moments in the self-interpretation of the sciences. And the growth of debates about realism characteristically is a symptom of the inability of scientists to give a cogent account to themselves of the status of their inquiries.

Acknowledgments

My colleagues John Compton, John Post, Charles Scott, and Harry Teloh subjected an earlier version of this address to rigorous and constructive criticism. A different kind of debt is to Brian Friel's play *Translations* (Faber & Faber, 1981) and to my former colleague Dennis Tedlock's translations of narrative poetry of the Zuni Indians, *Finding the Center* (University of Nebraska Press, 1978), which threw a very different light on problems of translation from that afforded by most recent philosophical writing.

The Relationship of Philosophy to History: Postscript to the Second Edition of *After Virtue*

Alasdair MacIntyre

"What bothers me is not distinguishing [history from philosophy]," wrote William K. Frankena,[1] "or giving the impression that a historical inquiry can establish a philosophical point, as MacIntyre seems to do." Frankena here speaks for what is still academic orthodoxy, although like other modern orthodoxies it is showing signs of strain. Philosophy is on this view one thing, history quite another. To the historian of ideas is assigned the task of recounting the rise and fall of ideas, just as to the political historian is assigned that of recounting the rise and fall of empires. The tasks reserved for the philosopher are twofold. Where subject matters other than philosophy itself are concerned, such as morality, it falls to the philosopher to determine what the appropriate criteria for rationality and truth are in that particular area. Where philosophy has become its own subject matter, it falls to the philosopher to determine by the best rational methods what is in fact true. It is this conception of the academic division of labor that Frankena seems to presuppose when he says of emotivism as a philosophical theory that "I can, if I have the right conceptual equipment, understand *what* the view is without seeing it as the result of a historical development; and, so far as I can see, I can also assess its status as true or false or rational to believe without seeing it as such an outcome. Indeed MacIntyre's own arguments against emotivism are drawn from analytical philosophy; and his claim that modern attempts to justify morality *fail* and *had to fail* is a claim that can be established only by analytical philosophy, not by some kind of history."[2]

Against this view I am committed to maintaining that although arguments of the kind favored by analytic philosophy do possess an indispensable power, it is only within the context of a particular genre of historical inquiry that such arguments can support the type of claim about truth and rationality that philosophers characteristically aspire to justify. As Frankena notices, I am not being original in so arguing; he names Hegel and Collingwood and he might have named Vico. For it was Vico who first stressed the importance of the undeniable fact, which it is becoming tedious to reiterate, that the subject matters of moral philosophy at least — the evaluative and normative concepts, maxims, arguments, and judgments about which the moral philosopher inquires — are nowhere to be found except as embodied in the historical lives of particular social groups and so possessing the distinctive characteristics of historical existence: both identity and change through time, expression in institutionalized practice as well as in discourse, interaction and interrelationship with a variety of forms of activity. Morality that is no particular society's morality is to be found nowhere. There was the-morality-of-fourth-century-Athens, there were the-moralities-of-thirteenth-century-Western-Europe, there are numerous such moralities, but where ever was or is *morality as such?*

Kant of course believed that he had successfully answered that question. And it is important that both the analytic moral philosophy that Frankena defends and the type of historicism that I defend are in key part responses to criticisms of Kant's transcendental answer. For Kant's thesis that the nature of human reason is such that there are principles and concepts necessarily assented to by any rational being, both in thinking and in willing, encountered two distinct kinds of crucial objection. One, to which Hegel and subsequent historicists gave great weight, was that what Kant presented as the universal and necessary principles of the human mind turned out in fact to be principles specific to particular times, places, and stages of human activity and inquiry. Just as what Kant took to be the principles and presuppositions of natural science as such turned out after all to be the principles and presuppositions specific to Newtonian physics, so what Kant took to be the principles and presuppositions of morality as such turned out after all to be the principles and presuppostions of one highly specific morality, a secularized version of Protestantism that furnished modern liberal individualism with one of its founding charters. Thus the claim to universality foundered.

A second set of objections were to the effect that the conceptions of necessity, of the a priori and of the relationship of concepts and categories of experience that the Kantian transcendental project required could not be sustained: and the history of successive philosophical criticisms of the original Kantian positions, of their reformulation first by neo-Kantians and later more radically by logical empiricists, and of the criticism in turn of those reformulations, is central to the history of how analytic philosophy came to be what it is. The final recent subversion of the distinctions central to the Kantian project and to its successors at the hands of Quine, Sellars, Goodman, and others has been chronicled by Richard Rorty, who has remarked upon how one effect has been to diminish to some large degree consensus in the analytic community as to what the central problems of philosophy are.[3] But this has not been the only or even the most important consequence.

For what the progress of analytic philosophy has succeeded in establishing is that there are *no* grounds for belief in universal necessary principles — outside purely formal inquiries — except relative to some set of assumptions. Cartesian first principles, Kantian a priori truths, and even the ghosts of these notions that haunted empiricism for so long have all been expelled from philosophy. The consequence is that analytic philosophy has become a discipline — or a subdiscipline? — whose competence has been restricted to the study of inferences. Rorty puts this by saying that "the ideal of philosophical ability is to see the entire universe of possible assertions in all their inferential relationships to one another, and thus to be able to construct, or criticize, any argument."[4] And David Lewis has written, "Philosophical theories are never refuted conclusively. (Or hardly ever, Gödel and Gettier may have done it.) The theory survives it refutation — at a price. . . . Our 'intuitions' are simply opinions; our philosophical theories are the same . . . a reasonable task for the philosopher is to bring them into equilibrium. Our common task is to find out what equilibria there are that can withstand examination, but it remains for each of us to come to rest in one or another of them. . . . Once the menu of well-worked-out theories is before us, philosophy is a matter of opinion."[5]

Analytic philosophy, that is to say, can very occasionally produce practically conclusive results of a negative kind. It can show in a few cases that just too much incoherence and inconsistency is involved in some position for *any* reasonable person to continue to hold it. But it can never establish the *rational acceptability* to any particular position in cases where each of the alternative rival positions available has sufficient range and scope and the adherents of each are willing to pay the price necessary to secure coherence and consistency. Hence the peculiar flavor of so much contemporary analytic writing — by writers less philosophically self-aware than Rorty or Lewis — in which passages of argument in which the most sophisticated logical and semantic techniques available are deployed in order to secure maximal rigor alternate with passages that seem to do no more than cobble together a set of loosely related arbitrary preferences; contemporary analytic philosophy exhibits a strange partnership between an idiom deeply indebted to Frege and Carnap and one deriving from the more simpleminded forms of existentialism.

What this outcome suggests to the historicist is first of all that analytic philosophers, as represented by Rorty and Lewis and indeed by Frankena, seem to be determined to go on considering arguments as object of investigation in abstraction from the social and historical contexts of activity and inquiry in which they are or were at home and from which they characteristically derive their particular import. But in so doing the analytical philosopher is liable to inherit from his Kantian forebears those misunderstandings that arose from the first of the two central objections to Kant's own version of the transcendental project. For if for example we regard the principles and categories of Newtonian mechanics as satisfying the requirements of rationality-as-such, we shall obscure precisely that about them which rendered them rationally superior to their only available rivals in the actual context of physical inquiry in the late seventeenth and early eighteenth centuries.

What rendered Newtonian physics rationally superior to its Galilean and Aristotelian predecessors and to its Cartesian rivals was that it was able to transcend their limitations by solving problems in areas in which those predecessors and rivals could by their own standards of scientific progress make no progress. So we cannot say wherein the rational superiority of Newtonian physics consisted except historically in terms of its relationship to those predecessors and rivals whom it challenged and displaced. Abstract Newtonian physics from its context, and then ask wherein the rational superiority of one to the other consists, and you will be met with insoluble incommensurability problems. Thus knowing how Newton and the Newtonians actually came to adopt and defend their views is essential to knowing why Newtonian physics is to be accounted rationally superior. The philosophy of physical science is dependent on the history of physical science. But the case is no different with morality.

Moral philosophies, however they may aspire to achieve more than this, always do articulate the morality of some particular social and cultural standpoint: Aristotle is the spokesman for one class of fourth-century Athenians; Kant, as I have already noted, provides a rational voice for the emerging social forces of liberal individualism. But even this way of putting matters is inadequate, for it still treats the morality as one thing, the moral philosophy as another. But any particular morality has as its core standards by which reasons for action are judged more or less adequate, conceptions of how qualities of character relate to qualities of actions, judgments as to how rules are to be formulated, and so on. Thus although there is always more to any particular morality than the philosophy implicit within it, there is no morality allegiance to which does not involve some philosophical stance, explicit or implicit. Moral philosophies are, before they are anything else, the explicit articulations of the claims of particular moralities to rational allegiance. And this is why the history of morality and the history of moral philosophy are a single history. It follows that when rival moralities make competing and incompatible claims, there is always an issue at the level of moral philosophy concerning the ability of either to make good a claim to rational superiority over the other.

How are these claims to be judged? As in the case of natural science, there are no general timeless standards. It is in the ability of one particular moral-philosophy-articulating-the-claims-of-a-particular-morality to identify and to transcend the limitations of its rival or rivals, limitations that can be — although they may not in fact have been — identified by the rational standards to which the protagonists of the rival morality are committed by their allegiance to it, that the rational superiority of that particular moral philosophy and that particular morality emerges. The history of morality-and-moral-philosophy is the history of successive challenges to some preexisting moral order, a history in which the question of which party defeated the other in rational argument is always to be distinguished from the question of which party retained or gained social and political hegemony. And it is only by reference to this history that questions of rational superiority can be settled. The history of morality-and-moral-philosophy written from this point of view is as integral to the enterprise of contemporary moral philosophy as the history of science is to the enterprise of contemporary philosophy of science.

It is, I hope, now clearer why Frankena and I disagree. He seems to hold that the methods of analytic philosophy are sufficient to establish what is true or false and what it is reasonable to believe in moral philosophy and that historical inquiry is irrelevant. I hold not only that historical inquiry is required in order to establish what a particular point of view is, but also that it is in its historical encounter that any given point of view establishes or fails to establish its rational superiority relative to its particular rivals in some specific contexts. In doing so, many of the skills and techniques of analytic philosophy will be deployed; and on rare occasions these techniques may be sufficient to discredit a view. So when Frankena correctly says that on occasion I employ arguments drawn from analytic philosophy to establish that a particular theory or set of theories fails, he imputes to me nothing that is inconsistent either with my historicism or with my rejection of the view that analytic philosophy can never provide sufficient grounds for the assertion of any positive standpoint in moral philosophy.

Thus when we understand emotivism as a rejoinder to a particular historical conjunction of intuitionist moral theorizing with the exercise of a particular kind of moral judgment, we are able to understand its claims not only as a thesis about the timeless meaning of sentences used in moral judgments (a thesis with little plausibility), but also and more importantly as an empirical thesis about the use and function of moral judgments that may hold in a wider or a narrower range of historical situations. Hence making it intelligible how the theory came to be advanced and in what type of situation is relevant to both the understanding and the evaluation of the theory in a way that Frankena's sharp distinction between philosophical inquiry and history obscures.

To this the following rejoinder may be made. If we are able to write the kind of philosophical history that I have envisaged — and it is just this that I attempted to write in *After Virtue* — then in chronicling the defeats of one theory or the victories of another in respect of rational superiority, we the chroniclers must be bringing to that history standards by which the rational superiority of one theory to another is to be judged. These standards will themselves require rational justification, and *this* justification cannot be provided by a history that can only be written after a justification for these standards has been provided. Hence the historicist is covertly appealing to nonhistorical standards, standards that would presumably have to be provided with either a transcendental or an analytic justification, types of justification that I have rejected.

This rejoinder fails. For our situation in respect of theories about what makes one theory rationally superior to another is no different from our situation in regard to scientific theories or to moralities-and-moral-philosophies. In the former as in the latter case what we have to aspire to is not a perfect theory, one necessarily to be assented to by any rational being, because invulnerable or almost invulnerable to objections, but rather the best theory to emerge so far in the history of this class of theories. So we ought to aspire to provide the best theory so far as to what type of theory the best theory so far must be: no more, but no less.

It follows that the writing of this kind of philosophical history can never be brought to completion. The possibility has always to be left open that in any particular field, whether the natural sciences or morality-and-moral-philosophy or the theory of theory, some new challenge to the established best theory so far will appear and will displace it. Hence this kind of historicism, unlike Hegel's, involves a form of fallibilism; it is a kind of historicism that exludes all claims to absolute knowledge. Nonetheless if some particular moral scheme has successfully transcended the limitations of its predecessors and in so doing provided the best means available for understanding those predecessors to date *and* has then confronted successive challenges from a number of rival points of view, but in each case has been able to modify itself in the ways required to incorporate the strengths of those points of view while avoiding their weaknesses and limitations *and* has provided the best explanation so far of those weaknesses and limitations, then we have the best possible reason to have confidence that future challenges will also be met successfully, that the principles that define the core of a moral scheme are enduring principles. And just this is the achievement that I ascribe to Aristotle's fundamental moral scheme in *After Virtue*.

That it was this type of historicist claim that I was and am making was not stated with adequate clarity; nor was the form of the argument that I was deploying in its favor adequately specified. For I was claiming of what I called the Enlightenment project not merely that it failed by its own standards, since its protagonists had never succeeded in specifying a uniquely justifiable set of moral principles to which any fully rational agent whatsoever could not fail to assent, or of Nietzsche's moral philosophy that it too failed by its own standards; but also that the grounds for understanding those failures could only be provided out of the resources afforded by an Aristotelian account of the virtues, which, in just the way that I have described, turns out to emerge from its specific historical encounters as the best theory so far. But note that I did not assert in *After Virtue* that I had as yet sustained that claim, nor do I claim that now. What more has to be done?

Annette Baier has chided me for not understanding the strengths of Hume's position;[6] Onora O'Neill has argued that my account of Kant is selective and simplified.[7] I have a good deal of sympathy with both complaints, for it is indeed the two very different accounts of practical reasoning advanced by Hume and Kant that present the central challenge to the Aristotelian scheme and to the account of practical reasoning embodied within it. And until the relationship of these three accounts has been clarified, the claim central to *After Virtue* will not have been established in the way that the historicist theory of knowledge presupposed by the argumentative narrative of *After Virtue* requires.

Finally, a very different type of criticism of the way in which philosophy and history are related in *After Virtue* cannot be allowed to pass unnoticed. Frankena thinks me insufficiently appreciative of analytic philosophy; Abraham Edel thinks me still far too much of an analyst and accuses me of being no more than "a heretic analyst whose heresy remains bound" by the cords of the analytic tradition.[8] The gist of his criticism is first that I focus too much attention upon the level of explicit theorizing, articulated concepts, and the stories told about their condition by various peoples, and not enough on the actual social and institutional life of those peoples; and second that my partisanship leads me to distort the actual complex history of morality in the interests of my own Aristotelian point of view. Where Frankena sees me as an inadequate analytic philosopher with an additional, not entirely relevant interest in history, Edel sees me as an inadequate social historian who keeps needlessly dragging in analytic philosophy. Thus Edel's criticism is the mirror image of Frankena's and not surprisingly.

For just as the kind of philosophical history that I wish to write breaks at certain points with the canons of analytic philosophy, so at others it violates those of academic social history and this perhaps in two ways. First, from the point of view that I am taking, theoretical and philosophical enterprises, their successes and failures, are far more influential in history than academic historians generally have taken them to be. The issues that need to be settled in this area are questions of fact concerning causal influence. They include such questions as the nature of the influence of the thinkers of the Scottish Enlightenment on British, French, and American social, moral, and political change. The answers to such questions depend upon inquiries into, for example, the social role and effectiveness of universities and colleges as bearers of ideas. And it may be that in the end historical inquiry will show my attention to explicit theorizing, articulated concepts, and story telling to be misplaced. But so far I remain unconvinced.

Second, the narratives of academic social history tend to be written in a way that presupposes just the kind of logical distinction between questions of fact and questions of value that the account of narrative given in *After Virtue* commits me to denying. And the philosophical history that constitutes the central narrative of *After Virtue* itself is written from the standpoint of the conclusion that it itself reaches and sustains — or rather would sustain if its narrative were amplified in the way that I hope to amplify it in the sequel to *After Virtue*. So that the narrative of *After Virtue* is not accidentally or by default a partisan narrative with its own deliberate one-sidedness.

Yet Edel is of course right to some substantial degree in both his charges. A good deal of social and institutional history to which *After Virtue* at best makes oblique reference is in fact essential to the kind of narrative toward which I pointed in *After Virtue*, but which I did not yet succeed in writing; and the history of the interrelationship of the Aristotelian account of the virtues with other moral schemes from Platonism onward to the present is of course vastly more complex than I allowed. Thus both Frankena and Edel have uttered salutary warnings both to me and to my readers by identifying issues to which I had at the very least paid insufficient attention. Their reviews have put me permanently in their debt.

The Transformation of Philosophy: Hermeneutics, Rhetoric, Narrative

Notes

1. *Ethics* 93 (1983), 580.

2. *Ethics* 93 (1983), 580.

3. *Consequences of Pragmatism,* Minneapolis, 1982, pp. 214–217.

4. *Consequences of Pragmatism,* p. 219.

5. *Philosophical Papers,* vol. 1, Oxford, 1983, pp. x–xi.

6. "Civilizing Practices," *Analyse und Kritik* 6 (1984), 61–77.

7. "Kant After Virtue," *Inquiry* 26 (1984), 387–405.

8. *Zygon* 18 (1983), 344.

13

Hans Blumenberg

Introduction

From its beginnings in Greece, philosophy has considered rhetoric a mortal enemy. Plato linked rhetoric with the Sophists, and hence with the relativism of values and the arbitrary exercise of power. Although his response to this challenge, a metaphysical grounding of the True and the Good, has not gone unchallenged in the history of philosophy, his enmity to rhetoric has persisted, as has his identification of it with sophistry. Even in modern philosophy rhetoric has typically been viewed as an enemy of reason and an instrument of the passions, as resting on a merely figurative use of words that philosophy is to correct, replacing it with a strictly literal use of language and a rigorously argumentative structure of discourse. Many of those who today call for an end to philosophy want to reverse the apparent victory of Plato over the Sophists. Thus, for instance, Foucault follows Nietzsche in insisting upon the intrinsic relation of truth to power. And Derrida argues that the separation of philosophy from rhetoric is itself rhetorical, that there is no fundamental distinction between philosophy and literature. In contrast to this, Gadamer allies rhetoric with hermeneutics as a *continuation* of practical philosophy: all three — ethics, rhetoric, and hermeneutics — are rooted in basic human capacities — for practical deliberation, for producing agreement through persuasive speech, for achieving mutual understanding in language — that cannot be replaced either by technical know-how or by theoretical science. But we can become reflectively aware of what is performatively at play in the practical exercise of these capacities, so that the theoretical interest underlying the resultant "sciences" remain indissolubly bound up with certain kinds of practical action.

Blumenberg's approach to rhetoric, stressing its anthropological position, does not quite follow any of these paths, though it comes closest perhaps to that of Gadamer. In the essay that follows, he does not call for a simple reversal of Platonism but attempts to undermine the model of human nature behind the hierarchical oppositions through which rhetoric has been distinguished from and made inferior to philosophy: *logos* versus *mythos,* concept versus metaphor, literal versus figurative, reason versus imagination, and so forth. He does not seek simply to eliminate these distinctions; his position is rather that philosophy itself must recognize the legitimacy of what it has hitherto proscribed. And it is to do so under the general rubric of *Unbegrifflichkeit* — an account of the nonconceptual, finitistic nature of the activities and creations that are necessary for our getting along in the world. Rhetoric then becomes a general heading for everything that might be included in such an account, including myth, metaphor, persuasion, and consensus — that is, for the subject matter of philosophy once it takes seriously the unattainability of eternal truths and final certainties and gives up the image of man as a disguised spirit.

For Blumenberg, the "axiom of all rhetoric" is the "principle of insufficient reason." Setting up "truth" in opposition to "effect" is, he argues, "superficial, because the rhetorical effect is not an alternative that one can choose instead of an insight that one could also have, but an alternative to a definitive evidence that one cannot have . . . . As long as philosophy was inclined to hold out at least the prospect of eternal truths and definitive certainties, then consensus as the ideal of rhetoric, and agreement subject to later revocation as the result attained by persuasion, had to seem contemptible to it." Once this prospect is abandoned, however, we realize that "in reasoning about the practical activities of life, it can be more rational to accept something on insufficient grounds than to insist on a procedure modeled after science," — more rational, that is, "to proceed rhetorically, aiming at an actual consensus." We realize, in other words, that rhetoric is "itself a form of rationality — a rational way of coming to terms with the provisionality of reason." We need then to recast the traditional, overinflated notion of reason to suit the *Mängelwesen,* creatures of deficiency, that we are. For the modes of reasoning capable of producing "the accords necessary for action," of substituting persuasion for force, will essentially involve figurative elements, such as metaphor, that are not simply surrogates for concepts that could in principle be supplied, and rhetorical structures that are not simply ornamental embellishments for structures of rigorous argument that are in principle available.

The same themes, our anthropological deficiencies and the need to compensate for them, figure centrally in Blumenberg's *Work on Myth.* There it is our poverty of instinct and the attendant threat of being overwhelmed by "the absolutism of reality" that serve as his starting point. In our anthropological situation, myth — and work on myth — has as indispensable a role to play in the "functional system of the elementary human accomplishment of life" as rationality. They are complementary from the start, with the mythical overcoming of *Angst* in the face of an uncontrolled reality creating a "breathing space" for extending our (always only partial) rational control over specific domains of that reality. As Robert Wallace has put it, all symbolic forms contribute simultaneously to the comprehensive endeavor of making human existence possible. Each can be interpreted in terms of its contribution to — its function within — this endeavor, that is, in terms of its "vital accomplishment" (Wallace 1985, xiff.).

The notion of "function" also figures importantly in Blumenberg's *The Legitimacy of the Modern Age,* but there it refers to historically rather than anthropologically based "positions" — positions in our mental space that emerge, are occupied and reoccupied, and (possibly) pass away. The aim of this sort of "functional analysis" is to produce a narrative account of the genesis of modern concepts and attitudes. As in Collingwood and MacIntyre, the emphasis is not on the continuity of solutions but on the certainty of questions, the idea being that one has to get at the historical context of problems in order to understand the answers given to them. This type of historical, narrative approach makes it possible to distinguish, for example, the (legitimate) modern ideas of human self-assertion and unrestricted theoretical curiosity from their (illegitimate) overgeneralization in the idea of universal progress.

What is fascinating about Blumenberg's rehabilitation of such traditionally disreputable pretenders to the throne of reason as rhetoric, metaphor, myth, and narrative is that it is carried out under the sign not of bringing an end to the Enlightenment but of rethinking it with the modesty proper to *Mängelwesen,* not of abandoning our commitments to modernity but of getting clear about what they really are. Thus Blumenberg opposes to would-be final myths such as German Idealism, which makes us responsible for the world as a whole, a "standard for final myths": they should present "the subject's responsibility to and for himself" (cf. Wallace 1985, xxxivff.); they should encourage "autonomous individuals," not in the sense of the "disguised spirits" that haunt modern philosophy, but in the sense of individuals who accept responsibility for who they are and what they do. The role of philosophy in this endeavor is to dismantle or "deconstruct" what is regarded as natural, to exhibit its "artificiality." It is a kind of "phenomenology of history," a "discipline of attentiveness" — not only to "prejudices" and "idols," "dogma" and "myths," but to "trivialities," to the entire "universe of what is taken for granted" (Blumenberg, "Einleitung" to 1981).

Suggested Readings

Blumenberg, Hans. "Paradigmen zu einer Metaphorologie," *Archiv für Begriffsgeschichte* 6 (1960), 7–142.

Blumenberg, Hans. *Die Legitimität der Neuzeit.* Frankfurt: Suhrkamp, 1966. Revised, enlarged edition in 3 volumes: *Säkularierung und Selbstbehauptung.* Frankfurt: Suhrkamp, 1974. *Prozess der theoretischen Neugierde.* Frankfurt: Suhrkamp, 1973. *Aspekte der Epochenschwelle.* Frankfurt: Suhrkamp, 1976. English translation: *The Legitimacy of the Modern Age.* Trans. R. M. Wallace. Cambridge, Massachusetts: MIT Press, 1983.

Blumenberg, Hans. *Pseudoplatonismen in der Naturwissenschaft der frühen Neuzeit.* Mainz: Verlagder Akademie, 1971.

Blumenberg, Hans. "On a Lineage of the Idea of Progress," *Social Research* 41 (1974) 5–27.

Blumenberg, Hans. *Die Genesis der kopernikanischen Welt.* Frankfurt: Suhrkamp, 1974.

Blumenberg, Hans. *Arbeit um Mythos.* Frankfurt: Suhrkamp, 1979. English translation: *Work on Myth.* Trans. R. M. Wallace. Cambridge, Massachusetts: MIT Press, 1985.

Blumenberg, Hans. *Schiffbruch mit Zuschauer.* Frankfurt: Suhrkamkp, 1979.

Bluemenberg, Hans. *Wirklichkeiten in denen wir leben.* Stuttgart: Reclam, 1981.

Blumenberg, Hans. *Die Lesbarkeit der Welt.* Frankfurt: Suhrkamp, 1981.

Blumenberg, Hans. "Über den Rand der Wirklichkeit hinaus: Drei Kurzessays," *Akzente* (1983), 16–57.

Blumenberg, Hans. "Self-Preservation and Inertia: On the Constitution of Modern Rationality," *Contemporary German Philosophy* 3 (1983), 209–256. English translation of "Selbsterhaltung und Beharrung: Zur Konstitution der neuzeitlichen Rationalität," *Subjektivität und Selbsterhaltung,* ed. Hans Ebling, 145–207. Frankfurt: Suhrkamp, 1976.

Blumenberg, Hans. "To Bring Myth to an End," *New German Critique* 32 (1984), 109–140.

Bohrer, K.-H., ed. *Mythos und Moderne.* Frankfurt: Suhrkamp, 1983.

Fellmann, Ferdinand. *Gelebte Philosophie in Deutschland. Denkformen der Lebensweltphänomenologie und der kritischen Theorie.* Freiburg/München: Alber, 1983.

Fuhrmann, Manfred, ed. *Terror und Spiel: Probleme der Mythenrezeption,* in *Poetik und Hermeneutik* 4. München: Fink, 1971.

Gadamer, Hans-Georg. Review of *Legitimacy of the Modern Age. Philosophische Rundschau* 15 (1968), 201–209.

Harries, Karsten. "Copernican Reflections," *Inquiry* 23 (1980), 253–269.

Löwith, Karl. *Meaning in History.* Chicago: University of Chicago Press, 1947.

Löwith, Karl. Review of *Legitimacy of the Modern Age. Philosophische Rundschau* 15 (1968), 195–201.

Marquard, Odo. *Abschied von Prinzipiellen.* Stuttgart: Reclam, 1981.

Pannenberg, Wolfgang. "Christianity as the Legitimacy of the Modern Age; Thoughts on a Book by Hans Blumenberg," in *Basic Questions in Theology.* London: SCM, 1973.

Rorty, Richard. Review of *Legitimacy of the Modern Age. London Review of Books,* March–April 1983.

Taubes, Jacob, ed. *Religionstheorie und Politischen Theologie.* Vols. 1 and 2. München: Fink, 1983.

Villock, Jörg. "Mythos und Rhetorik. Zum inneren Zusammenhang zwischen Mythologie und Metaphorologie in der Philosophie Hans Blumenbergs." *Philosophische Rundschau* 32 (1985), 68–91.

Wallace, Robert M. "Progress, Secularization, and Modernity: The Löwith/Blumenberg Debate," *New German Critique* 22 (1981) 63–77.

Wallace, Robert M. "Translator's Introduction" to *Legitimacy of the Modern Age*, xi–xxxi. Cambridge, Massachusetts: MIT Press, 1983.

Wallace, Robert M. "A Reconciliation of Myth and Rationality," *Humanities* 5 (1984), 6–8.

Wallace, Robert M. "Introduction to Blumenberg," *New German Critique* 32 (1984), 93–108.

Wallace, Robert M. "Translator's Introduction" to *Work on Myth*, viii–xl. Cambridge, Massachusetts: MIT Press, 1985.

An Anthropological Approach to the Contemporary Significance of Rhetoric

Hans Blumenberg

What man is has been formulated as a thesis in countless, more or less formal, attempted definitions. The varieties of what we now call philosophical anthropology can be reduced to one pair of alternatives: Man can be viewed either as a poor or as a rich creature. The fact that man is not fixed, biologically, to a specific environment can be understood either as a fundamental lack of proper equipment for self-preservation or as openness to the fullness of a world that is no longer accentuated only in terms of vital necessities. Man is made creative either by the urgency of his needs *or* by playful dealings with his surplus talents. He is the creature that is incapable of doing anything to no purpose *or* he is the only animal that is capable of an *acte gratuit*.[a] Man is defined by what he lacks *or* by the creative symbolism with which he makes himself at home in worlds of his own. He is the observer of the universe, in the center of the world, *or* he is [literally] "eccentric," exiled from Paradise on an insignificant dust speck called Earth. Man contains in himself the stored-up harvest of all of physical reality, *or* he is a creature of deficiencies,[b] left in the lurch by nature, plagued by residues of instincts that he does not understand and that have lost their functions. I need not go on enumerating the antitheses; the principle by which the list could be extended is easy to see.

As far as rhetoric is concerned, the traditional basic conceptions of it can likewise be reduced to one pair of alternatives: Rhetoric has to do either with the consequences of possessing the truth or with the difficulties that result from the impossibility of obtaining truth. Plato combatted the rhetoric of the Sophists by suggesting that it was based on the thesis of the impossibility of truth and that it deduced therefrom its right to pass off what people could be persuaded of as what was true. The most influential doctrine of rhetoric in our tradition, on the other hand — that of Cicero — starts from the premise that one can possess the truth, and gives the art of speaking the function of beautifying the communication of this truth, making it accessible and impressive — in short, dealing with it in a way that is appropriate to the object. The Christian tradition vacillates between the two possible consequences of the premise that one possesses the truth: on the one hand, that God's truth has no need of human aids of the kind represented by rhetoric and that it should present itself with as little adornment as possible (a pattern that is repeated in every rhetoric of straightforwardness), and on the other hand, that this same truth is humanized in the housing of the canons of rules of rhetoric. In modern aesthetics rhetoric's implication that it has to do, positively or negatively, with the truth celebrates its final triumph when the connection is reversed: It becomes permissible to infer truth content from rhetorical art, from style, from beauty — or beauty and truth can even become identical. The enmity that Plato postulated between philosophy and rhetoric is defined in philosophy itself, or at least in its languages, as aesthetics against philosophy. Only as aesthetics?

It is easy to see that one can coordinate the two radical pairs of alternatives, in anthropology and in rhetoric, unambiguously with one another. Man as a rich creature exercises his disposition over the truth that he possesses with the aid of the rhetorical *ornatus* [ornament]. Man as a poor creature needs rhetoric as the art of appearance, which helps him to deal with his lack of truth. The epistemological situation that Plato imputed to Sophism is radicalized, anthropologically, into the situation of the "creature of deficiencies," for whom everything becomes part of the economy of his means of survival, and who consequently cannot afford rhetoric — unless he *has* to afford it. A consequence of this anthropological intensification of the initial conditions is that the concept of a rhetoric that is associated with those conditions must also be formulated in a more elementary or fundamental way. Then the technique of speech appears as a special case of rule-governed modes of behavior that produce something to be understood, set up signs, bring about agreement, or provoke contradiction. Keeping silent, visibly omitting some action in a context of connected behavior, can become just as rhetorical as the reading aloud of an outcry of popular wrath, and the Platonic dialogue is no less rhetorically inclined than the Sophist's instructional discourse, which it opposed by literary means. Even when it is below the threshold of the spoken or the written word, rhetoric is form as means, obedience to rules as an instrument. Nietzsche may have erred in his statement that Plato's struggle against rhetoric is to be understood as a product of envy of rhetoric's influence, but he is right when he says in the same place that with rhetoric the Greeks had invented "form in itself."[1]

Plato's two great rejections, the rejection of atomism and the rejection of Sophism, probably had even more important consequences than the positive dogmas of the part of the history of his influence that is entitled "Platonism" and is thus identifiable. Philosophy's preference for language's semantic relation to reality produced a permanent sensitivity vis-à-vis rhetoric's pragmatic conception of language, a sensitivity that took a turn in favor of rhetoric only episodically, when conceptual language, in forms of Scholasticism, deprived its reference to reality of credibility. The Platonic Socrates's principle (now a commonplace that everyone learns in school) that virtue is knowledge makes what is evident, instead of what is an "institution,"[c] the norm of behavior. No one will want to deny that with this principle Socrates formulated an ideal without the pursuit of which — sometimes confident, sometimes desperate — the European tradition cannot be imagined. But it is equally true that it constituted an excessive demand, and hard on its heels came the resignations — beginning with the catastrophic reverse that the doctrine of the Ideas underwent in Plato's own school as a result of the outbreak of Academic Skepticism hardly a century after the death of the school's founder, and ending with what Nietzsche called "nihilism." The philosophy of absolute goals did not legitimate the theory of means; instead, it repressed and suffocated it. An ethics that takes the evidentness of the good as its point of departure leaves no room for rhetoric as the theory and practice of influencing behavior on the assumption that we do not have access to definitive evidence of the good. This also affects the "anthropology" that is founded and embodied in rhetoric; as a theory of man outside the realm of Ideas, forsaken by evidentness, it has lost the possibility of being "philosophical," and becomes the last, and belated, discipline of philosophy.

Rhetoric's anthropological importance stands out best against the background of the metaphysics that has been dominant since antiquity, a metaphysics that has a cosmological ground-plan: The Ideas constitute a cosmos that the phenomenal world imitates. Man, however privileged his position may be as an onlooker in the center of the whole, is nevertheless not a pure special case but rather a point of intersection of heterogeneous realities, a compound — and, as such, problematic. In the modernized model of levels, the idea lives on that in the case of man things have come together that have difficulty harmonizing with each other. In principle this metaphysics says that man's thoughts could also be those of a god and that what moves him could be what moves a celestial sphere or what moves an animal. Nature, which otherwise only presents itself in pure form and regulates itself straightforwardly, here confronts us with a complication that can most readily be explained as an accident or a mixture of heterogeneous elements; in which case the problem of conduct is to assign to one of these elements authority over the others — to establish a sort of substantial consistency. In short, the metaphysical tradition at bottom has had nothing special to say about man, with his asserted uniqueness. That is amazing, but it is closely related to philosophy's banishment of rhetoric. For rhetoric starts from, and only from, the respect in which man is unique: it is not that language is his specific characteristic but that language, in rhetoric, appears as a function of a specific difficulty of man's.

If one wants to express this difficulty in the language of the metaphysical tradition, one will have to say that man does not belong to this cosmos (if in fact it exists); and this is not because of a transcendent "surplus" that he possesses but because of an immanent deficiency, a deficiency of pre-given, prepared structures to fit into and of regulatory processes for a connected system that would deserve to be called a "cosmos" and within which something could be called part of the cosmos. In the language of modern biological anthropology, too, man is a creature who has fallen back out of the ordered arrangements that nature has accomplished, and for whom actions have to take the place of the automatic controls that he lacks or correct those that have acquired an erratic inaccuracy. Action compensates for the "indeterminateness" of the creature man, and rhetoric is the effort to produce the accords that have to take the place of the "substantial" base of regulatory processes in order to make action possible. From this point of view, language is a set of instruments not for communicating information or truths, but rather, primarily, for the production of mutual understanding, agreement, or toleration, on which the actor depends. This is the root of "consensus"[d] as a basis for the concept of what is "real": "We say that that which everyone thinks really is so," says Aristotle,[2] and always has a teleological argument for this in the background. Only a skeptical destruction of this teleological support makes the pragmatic substratum of consensus visible again.

I know that the term "skepticism" is not popular at present. Too much is once again known too precisely for that to be the case, and in such a situation one does not want to play the part of troublemaker. But in the tradition of skepticism (which is mostly below the surface and only occasionally flares up) the anthropology whose repression by metaphysics I have attempted briefly to locate has become especially urgent when the eternal truths had to be scaled down to what is most immediately reliable, and man no longer appeared as the disguised variant of a pure spirit. The first philosophical anthropology that deserved this name was, at the beginning of the modern age, Montaigne's *Apologie de Raimond Sebond*. In the hands of a skeptic who sees himself as prevented from extending his questioning beyond man, a body of material that is mainly conventional gets into a new overall state, in which the only object of study that is still possible for man forces everything to be, now, only a symptom of this object. This tradition leads, by way of the literature of moralism, to Kant's (explicitly so designated) *Anthropologie*.

The skepticism that is piled up — only for the purpose of definitively disposing of it — in the preparatory phase of theories of knowledge (but also of Husserl's phenomenology) deprives itself of a favorable opportunity to yield dividends for anthropology, dividends that turn on the question of what man is left with if he fails in his attempt to seize pure evidentness and absolute self-foundation. An illustration of this state of affairs is the way in which Descartes disposed not only of his radicalized theoretical doubt but also of the problem of a *morale par provision* [provisional ethics], which was supposed to act as a substitute, until the completion of theoretical knowledge, for the *morale définitive* [definitive ethics] that would then become possible. Descartes's illusion, which is still instructive, was not so much that the *morale définitive* would have to come soon, because physics could be completed quickly, but rather that the intervening period could be a static phase of holding fast to what had always been obligatory. Descartes took no cognizance of the retroactive effect of the process of theory on the supposed interim of the provisional ethics. It is very remarkable to reflect on the consequences of this idea of a *morale par provision* assuming that the eschatology of science doe not arrive, and to recognize in them much of what the final expectations directed at science, which are disappointed again and again, produce as shared characteristics. The fact that Descartes wanted to stage the preliminary situation as a standstill meant that he was not compelled to think through the anthropological implications of this state. Thus he could propose as an example of the provisional ethics a person who has lost his way in a forest, who only needs to go resolutely in one direction in order to get out of the forest, because all forests are finite and can be regarded, in the imagined situation, as unchanging. The recommendation of formal resoluteness in favor of the provisional ethics means a prohibition against considering all the concrete characteristics of the situation and their changes, including how man is equipped for dealing with situations in which his orientation is uncertain. The "method's" promised final accomplishment gets in the way of man's process of self-understanding in the present and also gets in the way of rhetoric as a technique for coming to terms in the provisional state prior to all definitive truths and ethics. Rhetoric creates institutions where evident truths are lacking.

One could dissolve the dualism of philosophy and rhetoric (which has again and again frustrated attempts at harmonization) in a specific conception, in the philosophy of history, that reshapes Descartes's model by skeptically modifying the implications of the *morale par provision*. What remains doubtful is not only the possibility of completing scientific knowledge, in whatever area, but also the possible profit of such completion for a *morale définitive*. We have almost forgotten that "progress" is nothing but the form of life, adjusted for the long term, of that Cartesian interim for which the provisional ethics was intended. Where Descartes is still correct is in his assumption that there is no sort of preliminary participation, granted in advance, in the success of the whole. To put it differently: Philosophy's program succeeds or fails, but it does not yield any profit in installments. Everything that remains, this side of definitive evidence, is rhetoric; rhetoric is the vehicle of the *morale par provision*. This statement means above all that that rhetoric is an aggregate of legitimate means. Rhetoric belongs to a syndrome of skeptical assumptions. We will not be deceived into overlooking this by the fact that it was only able to defend itself against the charge of being a "mere means" by presenting itself as the means employed by the truth. For even in its victories rhetoric had to proceed "rhetorically": When, in the fourth century B.C., rhetoric had in practice eliminated philosophy's claims, Isocrates, using a Sophistical device, called his Sophism "philosophy." For Jacob Burckhardt, the Greeks' feeling for effect, as opposed to reality, is the basis of rhetoric, which "only momentarily" rose to the level of "eloquence in public affairs" but had been primarily developed "as a means to success in the courts." But the Greeks themselves contrasted persuasion to subjugation by force: in the dealings of Greeks with Greeks, Isocrates says, the appropriate means is persuasion, whereas in dealings with barbarians it is the use of force.

This difference is understood as one of language and education, because persuasion presupposes that one shares a horizon, allusions to prototypical material, and the orientation provided by metaphors and similes. The antithesis of truth and effect is superficial, because the rhetorical effect is not an alternative that one can choose instead of an insight that one could *also* have, but an alternative to a definitive evidence that one *cannot* have, or cannot have yet, or at any rate cannot have here and now. Besides, rhetoric is not only the technique of producing such as effect, it is always also a means of keeping the effect transparent: it makes us conscious of effective means whose use does not need to be expressly prescribed, by making explicit what is already done in any case.

As long as philosophy was inclined to hold out at least the prospect of eternal truths and definitive certainties, then "consensus" as the ideal of rhetoric, and agreement subject to later revocation as the result attained by persuasion, had to seem contemptible to it. But when it was transformed into a theory of the scientific "method" of the modern age, philosophy too was not spared the renunciation on which all rhetoric is based. To be sure, it seemed at first as though science's hypotheses were always temporary expedients employed by cognition, instructions as to how to bring about their verification and thus their final guarantee; but the history of science showed in detail how verification, too, represents the pattern of agreement subject to later revocation, and how the publication of every theory implies a request that other people should follow the paths by which the theorist claims that it is confirmed and should give it the sanction of objectivity — without its ever being possible to exclude, by this process, the possibility that by other paths other things may be discovered and the theory contradicted. What Thomas S. Kuhn in *The Structure of Scientific Revolutions*[3] called the "paradigm" — the dominant fundamental conception, in a scientific discipline, for a long period of time, which integrates into itself all subsequent refining and extending inquiries — this paradigm is nothing but a "consensus," which is able to stabilize itself not, indeed, exclusively, but partly by means of the rhetoric of the academies and the textbooks.

Even if a deficiency of definitive evidence defines the situation both of the process of theory and of rhetoric, nevertheless science has provided itself with the invaluable advantage of being able to put up with the provisional character of its results indefinitely. That is not a matter of course: Descartes would have regarded it as intolerable. But his idea of "method" made it possible to understand science, and to organize it, as an overall process that is always "transferable" [from one person to another] and that integrates individuals and generations into itself as mere functionaries. All action that is based, as "application," on this sort of theory has to share the weakness of its provisional character: that it can have its authority revoked at any time. Theories, too, implicitly solicit "agreement," as rhetoric does explicitly. The decisive difference lies in the dimension of time; science can wait, or is subject to the convention of being able to wait, whereas rhetoric — if it can no longer be the *ornatus* of a truth — presupposes, as a constitutive element of its situation, that the "creature of deficiency" is compelled to act. Thus it is an imitation of the form of the process of science when discussion, as an instrument of public will formation, is regarded as though it were a mechanism for rationally arriving at results, whereas it cannot in fact afford precisely the endlessness (in principle) of rationality in the form that it takes in science. The restricted time allotted to speakers may be only a paltry substitute for rhetoric's rules of form, but even as a substitute it is an essential underlying arrangement for rhetoric; where it is disregarded or unknown, or indeed where its opposite is institutionalized (as in the "filibuster"), rhetoric's character as an alternative to terror becomes manifest. To see oneself in the perspective of rhetoric means to be conscious both of being compelled to act and of the lack of norms in a finite situation. Everything that is not force here goes over to the side of rhetoric, and rhetoric implies the renunciation of force.

In this connection the circumstance of being compelled to act, which determines the rhetorical situation and which demands primarily a physical reaction, can be transformed, rhetorically, in such a way that the enforced action becomes, by "consensus," once again "merely" a rhetorical one. Substituting verbal accomplishments for physical ones is an anthropological "radical";[e] rhetoric systematizes it. In his *Philosophy of Symbolic Forms*, Ernst Cassirer described man as the *animal symbolicum* [symbolical animal], whose original accomplishment is to reinterpret an external "impression" as the "expression" of something internal, and thus to set up, in place of something alien and inaccessible, something else that is sensuously tangible. Language, myth, art, and science are, according to Cassirer, regions of such "symbolic forms," which in principle only repeat that primary process of the conversion of "impression" into "expression." But this theory of Cassirer's makes no claim to explain why the "symbolic forms" are set up; the fact that they appear, as the world of culture, allows us to infer the existence of the *animal symbolicum,* which manifests its "nature" in its creations. An anthropology of man as "rich" sees the cultural housing of the "symbolic forms" as growing upward, layer upon layer, on the base of a secure, or at least unquestioned, biological existence. The enrichment of naked existence has no functional continuity with what makes that existence possible. But to the extent that philosophy is a process of dismantling things that are taken for granted, a "philosophical" anthropology has to address the question whether man's physical existence is not itself only a result that follows from the accomplishments that are ascribed to him as belonging to his "nature." The first proposition of an anthropology would then be, It cannot be taken for granted that man is able to exist.

The prototype for such a line of thought can be found in the modern social contract theory that deduces the necessity of establishing man's "civil" condition from its finding that his "natural" condition contradicts the conditions of the possibility of physical existence. For Hobbes, the state is the first artifact, which does not enrich (in the direction of a "world of culture") the environment in which man lives, but rather eliminates its lethal antagonism. What is philosophical about this theory is not primarily that it explains the appearance of an institution such as the state (still less that it explains the appearance of the *absolutist* state), but rather that it converts the supposed definition of man's *nature* as that of a *zoon politikon* ["political animal" — Aristotle] into a functional description. I see no

other scientific course for an anthropology except, in an analogous manner, to destroy[f] what is supposedly "natural" and
convict it of its "artificiality" in the functional system of the
elementary human accomplishment called "life." A first attempt of this kind was made by Paul Alsberg in 1922 in his
book — to which too little attention was paid, because of its
misleading title and language — *Das Menschheitsrätsel* [the riddle
of humanity]. Then in 1940 Arnold Gehlen — with his work
Der Mensch, which, though questionable in its intention, was
nevertheless fundamental — developed the beginning of a
theory of perception and of language, and since then has carried it further by founding a doctrine of "institutions." With
Gehlen's absolutism of "institutions," anthropology returns, in
a certain way, to its point of departure in the model of the
social contract. The discussion of this anthropology has not yet
settled the question of whether that fateful return is inevitable.[g]

Man's deficiency in specific dispositions for reactive behavior
vis-à-vis reality — that is, his poverty of instincts — is the
starting point for the central anthropological question as to
how this creature is able to exist in spite of his lack of fixed
biological dispositions. The answer can be reduced to the formula: by not dealing with this reality directly. The human
relation to reality is indirect, circumstantial, delayed, selective,
and above all "metaphorical." How man copes with the excess
of demands made on him by his relation to reality was laid out
a long time ago in the Nominalists' interpretation of judgment.
Predicates are "institutions"; a concrete thing is comprehended
by being analyzed into the relationships by which it belongs to
these institutions. When it has been absorbed in judgments, it
has disappeared as something concrete. But to comprehend
something *as* something is radically different from the procedure of comprehending something *by means of* something else.
The detour by which, in metaphor, we look away from the
object in question, at another one, which we imagine may be
instructive, takes the given as something alien and the other as
something more familiar and more easily at our disposal. If
the limiting case of judgment is identity, the limiting case of
metaphor is the symbol; here the other is entirely other, which
delivers nothing but the pure possibility of putting something

that is at our disposal in the place of something that is not. The *animal symbolicum* masters the reality that is originally lethal for him by letting it be represented; he looks away from what is uncanny or uncomfortable for him and toward what is familiar. This becomes clearest where judgment, with its claim to identity, cannot reach its goal at all, either because the demands of its object exceed what its procedure can handle (as in the case of the "the world," "life," "history," "consciousness") or because there is insufficient scope for the procedure, as in situations where one is compelled to act, and in which rapid orientation and vivid plausibility are needed. Metaphor is not only a chapter in the discussion of rhetorical means, it is a distinctive element of rhetoric, in which rhetoric's function can be displayed and expressed in terms of its relation to anthropology.

It would be entirely one-sided and incomplete to present rhetoric only as an "emergency" solution, in view of the deficiency of evidence in situations where one is compelled to act. It is not only a substitute for theoretical orientation for action; more importantly, it can be a substitute for action itself. Man can not only *present* one thing in place of another, he can also *do* one thing in place of another. If history teaches anything at all, it is this, that without this capacity to use substitutes for actions not much would be left of mankind. The ritualized replacement of a human sacrifice by an animal sacrifice, which is still visible through the story of Abraham and Isaac, may have been a beginning. Christianity, through two millennia, has regarded it as quite understandable that the death of one can compensate for the mischief for which all are responsible. Freud saw in the commemorative funeral feast the sons' agreement to put an end to the killing of the tribal father, and instead of that to do — something else. In Bremen, before their journey to America together in 1909, Freud persuaded C. G. Jung, whom he suspected of treachery to his school, to drink wine with his meal (which violated the principles of Jung's first teacher, Bleuler), instead of forcing him to perform an act of submission, the content of which would essentially have been a statement that he did not want to be the father himself. Politically, the rebuke that a verbal or demonstrative act is "pure rhetoric" is regarded as a serious one; but that is itself part of a rhetoric that does not want to admit (nor does it have any need to admit) that a policy is better, the more it can afford to restrict itself to "mere words." In foreign policy, warnings are most productive when they are pronounced at the moment in which the one who is being warned has in any case abandoned the idea of carrying out the act against which he is being warned. Everything can depend on (as we have become accustomed to saying) "not going beyond declarations," on "talking down" the compulsion to act, when the risk involved in the action is able to disqualify all possible gains from consideration. Here questions relating to the concept of reality become involved, which cannot be dealt with in this discussion.[h]

Lacking definitive evidence and being compelled to act are the prerequisites of the rhetorical situation. But not only substitutive and metaphorical procedures are rhetorical. Being compelled to act is itself not an utterly "real" circumstance, but also depends on the "role" that is ascribed to the actor or with which he seeks to define himself — self-understanding, too, makes use of metaphors, and "to cheer oneself up" is an expression that betrays that the internal use of rhetoric is not a novel discovery. The metaphors of roles that are popular again today are based on a very solid tradition of picturing life and the world as "theater," and it is not equally a matter of course for all of the historical forms of theater that its "roles" are as fixed as we nowadays assume when we use the metaphor. To allow someone, in the course of a conflict, to "save face" comes from a different realm of speech, but it coincides to a large extent with the precept, implied in the metaphors of roles, that one should not force the focal person of a transaction intended to bring about a change in that person's behavior to leave the identity of his role, but instead one should offer him the required change of behavior in the guise of a credible logical development [of his role]. There is no need to give illustrations of the extent to which the policy of great and small powers today can be described with the phraseology of "role definition" and "role expectation" (here the anthropological metaphor is again taken as a metaphor, on a second level), and what pragmatic instructions for dealing with potentially rhetorical behavior are contained in this description. Georg Simmel suggested that the metaphor of roles is so productive only because life is an "early form of the dramatic art"; but Simmel, especially, knew when he said this that these metaphors no longer have anything to do with the implication that it is a question of illusion, of a theatrical double life, with and without masks, with and without costume, so that one would only need to expose the stage and the actors in order to catch sight of the reality and put an end to the theatrical intermezzo. The "life" of which Simmel speaks is not incidentally and episodically an "early form" of the dramatic art; rather, being able to live and defining a role for oneself are identical.

Now I assert that not only is this talk of "roles" metaphorical, but the process of definition that goes with the role concept — a process upon which the consciousness of identity depends, and with which it can be damaged — is itself rooted in metaphor and is asserted and defended, both internally and externally, by metaphor. The case of defense, in particular, makes that clear: Erving Goffman's *Stigma* (1963) substantiates it abundantly. The "agreement" that has to be the goal of all "persuasion" (even of self-persuasion) is the congruence — which is endangered in all situations and always has to be secured afresh — between one's role consciousness and the role expectations that others have of one. Perhaps "agreement" is too strong a term, because approval would always already go beyond what is called for. Fundamentally, what is important is not to encounter contradiction, both in the internal sense, as a problem relating to consistency, and in the external sense, as a problem relating to acceptance. Rhetoric is a system not only of soliciting mandates for action but also of putting into effect and defending, both with oneself and before others, a self-conception that is in the process of formation or has been formed. Viewed in terms of scientific methodology, the metaphorically conceived "role" performs the function of a hypothesis, which is "verified" by every act that does not falsify it. The residue that still remains of all the rhetoric about the teleological value of "consensus" as something guaranteed by nature is the ensuring of the non-contradiction, the non-breakage of the consistency of what is accepted — which people therefore like to call, in the current political jargon, a "platform." It is understandable, in view of this state of affairs, that a need for a "basis of shared convictions" becomes virulent again and again, and in the form of one new proposal after another. People may go on calling "consensus" an "idea"[i] of the effect aimed at by rhetoric, but in the anthropological analysis of rhetoric's function it is redundant.

Rhetorical substitution, in situations in which we are compelled to act, and the rhetorical shielding of self-presentation as "self-preservation" have in common the fact that while they do indeed presuppose creative acts (the creation of symbols, the conception of roles), nevertheless as pure creativity they remain impotent and without any function. Here the question immediately arises whether the connection, so sought-after today, between the aesthetics of production and the aesthetics of reception[j] does not point to an analogous structure. "Every art has a rhetorical level," Nietzsche wrote in 1874 in a fragment on Cicero.[4] The "invention" of the substitutive symbol, for example, can be the most harmless, the least imaginative act in the world; it has to be brought to the point where it is recognized, and for this — in contrast to the aesthetic product — it contains, materially, not the slightest inducement. But this recognition is, in effect, everything; only it has consequences. Remember the classical political formula that trade follows the flag; today one can reverse it and say that the flag follows trade: states that do not even maintain diplomatic relations conclude trade agreements in the expectation that the other mode of relations will follow. The reversal of the old proposition is at the same time an expression of the complete devaluation of the symbol of the "flag," which is finally only able to ornament the realities. When it is said (as it used to be) that the respect shown to substitutions is based on "convention," that is both correct and tautological. The convention is a result. How does it come about? Doubtless by being offered and canvassed for. This holds even for the most abstract case in the history of science, the successful promotion of symbolic systems for formal logic; the canvassing rhetoric goes into details or consists of asserting in public, regarding national forms that one does not like, that one will never comprehend them. The less it is the case that political realities can still be "created" outside the sphere of economics, the more important become "diplomatic recognition," questions about names of countries, treaties in which one relinquishes what is in any case no longer possible, and proceedings in which one struggles mightily about what is in any case already well established. As soon as what was once considered to be "real" no longer exists, the substitutions themselves become "the real."

In aesthetics, with the surrender of all kinds and degrees of relation to an object, the proposal that something should be accepted as a work of art — or even only as what is "called for" after the end of all art — can only succeed at the cost of a great expenditure of rhetoric. It is not primarily the work's need for commentary that asserts itself in texts that accompany and come after it, but rather its being declared a work of art or a work of what has succeeded art; to that extent, harsh criticism by a competent critic is still acceptance into a relationship to a history in which art has again and again been produced against art, with the rhetorical gesture of making an end of what has been and a beginning of what is to come. Even the disavowal of rhetoric, here, is still rhetorical; even the kick that is administered to the conventional viewer who strives to "understand" demonstrates to him that what he doesn't understand is legitimate and indeed that it occupies the "position" of what one was once supposed to understand, or what is now understood by competent authorities. The "reoccupations"[k] of which history is composed are carried out rhetorically.

Rhetoric also has to do with the fitting together of actions in time. Acceleration and retardation are elements in historical processes that have so far received too little attention. "History" is composed not only of events and the connections between them (however these may be interpreted) but also of what one could call the "overall situation" with regard to time. What has been designated in our tradition as "rationality" has almost always benefited the element of acceleration, of the concentration of processes. Even dialectical theories of history accentuate the factors promoting acceleration, because they propel the process toward the critical point where it makes its sudden turning and thus bring it noticeably closer to its final state (thus confirming the law that is asserted to govern the process). The many-layered phenomenon of technicization[1] can be reduced to the intention of saving time. Rhetoric, on the other hand, is, in regard to the temporal texture of actions, a consummate embodiment of retardation. Circumstantiality, procedural inventiveness, ritualization imply a doubt as to whether the shortest way of connecting two points is also the humane route from one to the other. In aesthetics, for example in music, we are quite familiar with this type of situation. In the modern world excessive demands result not only from the complicatedness of circumstances but also from the increasing divergence between the two spheres of (on the one hand) material exigencies and (on the other) decisions in regard to their temporal texture. A disproportion has arisen between the acceleration of processes and the feasibility of keeping a "feel" for them, of intervening in them with decisions, and of coordinating them, through an overview, with other processes. Certain auxiliary functions that technical equipment can perform for human action have an assimilating effect: Where all the data are quickly available, a quick decision seems to have a special appropriateness to the case.

The desire to keep developments under one's control, or to get them under our control again, is dominant in our critical reflections on progress, to the extent that they are not pure romanticism. Operations analyses supply optimal problem solutions, but they never also eliminate doubts as to whether the problem was correctly posed — and such doubts already characterize action as something that goes before its theory and does not follow from it as a mere result. There is a clearly recognizable increased accent on delaying factors in public dealings. It is not an accident that such an outmoded word as "reflection" could be renewed as a catchword. There is a need for an institutionalized catching of breath, which sends even majorities that are competent to make decisions on long rhetorical detours. One wants to make it evident that one is not "driven" (by whatever it might be) and that one does not intend merely to sanction what has been decided long since. The acceleration of processes is after all only a variant of the "stimulus overload" that the biologically impoverished creature, man, is constitutionally exposed to and that he deals with by institutionalizing his behavior. Here verbal institutions are by no means a zero-grade instance of more massive regulatory processes; their potency must be measured against the ideal of decisionistic theories, which consists in taking up only a point in time.

There is something like the expediency of what is not expedient. Today we observe an extremely rapid dismantling of "obsolete" forms by critical proceedings in which everything that exists carries the burden of proving that its existence is justified; but at the same time we see at work an exuberant inventiveness in the fresh construction of intricate procedures, which are only distinguished by soberer titles like "rules of procedure," "supervisory agencies," "operational systems," and the like. Whatever time is saved is always immediately used up.

We must increasingly abandon the idea of a model of education or culture [*Bildung*] that is governed by the norm that man must always know what he is doing. In former times a doctor was supposed to know not only the conditions of the functioning of the organs, conditions whose failure constitutes illness, and the mode of operation of the therapies and medications that he prescribed, as well, but also the derivation of the foreign words that he continually used to label all of this and the use of which was evidence of his being initiated into the guild. A captain was not only supposed to be able to use the sextant and the trigonometric formulae that went with it but also had to know how the instrument functioned and how the formulae could be derived, so that he would be a potential Robinson Crusoe who could start out *ex nihilo* [from nothing] if the already manufactured auxiliary means were lost. As opposed to this, the idea has for a long time been gaining ground that the technical world needs trained functionaries who react appropriately but do not understand its functional connections in every respect. Fewer and fewer people will know what they do in the sense that they know *why* they do it that way. Action shrinks to reaction the more direct is the path from theory to practice that is sought. The cry for the elimination of "useless curricular material" is always a cry for "facilitating" functional implementation. Of course the circumstantiality that goes with the claim to know what one is doing is not in itself a guarantee of humane or moral insight, but as a pattern of delayed reaction it is potentially also a pattern of "conscious" action.

I suggest that "education and culture," whatever else they may still be, have something to do with this delaying of the functional connections between signals and reactions to them. The result is that their contents, their "values" and "goods," become secondary. The discussion about these values is usually conducted with an unexamined distribution of the burden of proof: one who defends traditional cultural "goods" is supposed to prove what they are still worth. If we assume that in themselves they are worth nothing at all, their "rhetorical" character becomes evident: they are figures, required exercises, obligatory detours and formalities, rituals, which impede the immediate utilization of man and obstruct (or perhaps only slow down) the arrival of a world of the shortest possible connection between any two given points. If classical rhetoric essentially aims at a mandate for action, modern rhetoric seeks to promote the delaying of action, or at least the understanding of such delay — and it does this especially when it wants to demonstrate its capacity to act, once again by displaying symbolic substitutions.

The axiom of all rhetoric is the principle of insufficient reason (*principium rationis insufficientis*). It is a correlate of the anthropology of a creature who is deficient in essential respects. If man's world accorded with the optimism of the metaphysics of Leibniz, who thought that he could assign a sufficient reason even for the fact that anything exists at all, rather than nothing ("cur aliquid potius quam nihil"), then there would be no rhetoric, because there would be neither the need nor the possibility of using it effectively. The rhetoric that by its dissemination is the most important in our history, the rhetoric of prayer, already had to rely — contrary to the theological positions associated with rationalistic or voluntaristic concepts of God — on a God who allowed himself to be persuaded, and this problem recurs in the case of anthropology: the man whom it deals with is not characterized by the philosophical overcoming of "opinion" by "knowledge."

But the principle of insufficient reason is not to be confused with a demand that we forgo reasons, just as "opinion" does not denote an attitude for which one has no reasons but rather one for which the reasons are diffuse and not regulated by method. One has to be cautious about making accusations of irrationality in situations where endless, indefinitely extensive procedures have to be excluded; in the realm of reasoning about practical activities in life, it can be more rational to accept something on insufficient grounds than to insist on a procedure modeled on that of science, and it *is* more rational to do this than to disguise decisions that have already been made in arguments that are scientific in form. It is true that euphoria about the provision of scientific advice in public affairs has faded away somewhat; but the disappointments in regard to this alliance are due to a failure to understand that lacking definitive evidence of the truth of their findings, committees of scientists themselves cannot proceed differently from the institutions they advise — that is, they must proceed rhetorically, aiming at an actual consensus, which cannot be the consensus of their theoretical norms. It is also a norm of science that one should clearly indicate the modality of one's statements. If one affirms apodictically, or even merely assertorically, what can only be affirmed problematically, one violates this norm. Anyone who is affected by public actions or who has to agree to them has a right to know what is the dignity of the premises that are presented as the results of scientific consultation. Rhetoric teaches us to recognize rhetoric, but it does not teach us to legitimate it.

What is at stake is not only the relation between science and political authorities but also a realm of statements that have very important practical consequences, consequences that cannot be suspended, although in their theoretical status these statements are based, perhaps forever, on an insufficient rational foundation, or may even be demonstrably incapable of being verified. The positivistic proposal, that questions and statements that contain no directions as to how they could be verified should then be extirpated, involves bringing practice — which depends on such premises — to a standstill, and thus becomes illusionary. A decision in such questions as whether

man is by nature good or bad, whether his character is determined by his heredity or by his environment, whether he makes
or is made by his history, can indeed be deferred by science,
but cannot be deferred in practice and cannot be declared to
be meaningless. Thus every kind of pedagogy is already in the
midst of a practical process and cannot wait for the delivery of
its theoretical premises, so that it is forced to accept quasi-
results from among the theoretical generalizations offered by
biology, psychology, sociology, and other disciplines. In this
boundary zone remarkable processes of a rhetorical type take
place, processes in which rationality and realism seem to diverge; for here one is not only compelled to act (as before),
one is also forced to make axioms of premises without which
a theory that is meant to apply to situations in which one is
compelled to act would be paralyzed and condemned to steril-
ity. I think, however, that these decisions have nothing to do
with the cynicism of a *liberum arbitrium indifferentiae* [free will
of indifference], and certainly nothing to do with existentialist
self-positing.

In the realm in which the principle of insufficient reason
holds, there are rational decision rules that do not resemble
science in their form. Pascal provided a model of this in his
argument du pari [argument of the wager], an argument that
we no longer find convincing because (and only because) it
compares the prospect of a transcendent infinite gain with the
risk of a finite stake,[m] but that remains valid in that man has
to wager the whole stake of his practice, at whatever risk of
error, on the particular prospect, as between two theoretical
alternatives, that is favorable to his self-assertion and self-de-
velopment. No theoretical doubt about the validity of the principle of causality or about the possibility of proving it
conclusively can alter in any way the fact that in our conduct
we wager on its unrestricted validity. One of the most momen-
tous declarations from the realm of various sciences would be
an answer to the question of the extent to which man's modes
of behavior are determined by, and therefore modifiable
through, endogenous or exogenous determinants. Although
one may regard this complex question as scientifically still
largely undecided, still it is easy to see that methodological

considerations favor an endogenous determinism — just as, quite independently of empirical findings, they imply, in the theory of evolution, that Darwinism will be preferred to the various kinds of Lamarckism. The theory that restricts itself to a few kinds of factors that, methodically, can be neatly isolated and exhibited has a better chance to become a "paradigm" in Thomas Kuhn's sense than the theory that has to offer a range of factors that cannot be separated out as well and that are diffusely distributed. That science will draw closer to a result of the kind typified by the Darwinistic theories seems to me to be inevitable and theoretically well founded.

This development would have far-reaching effects in many areas of public and private life: in education and the administration of justice, in social prophylaxis, even in people's everyday dealings with each other. In fact, however, the preference that is given to certain practical axioms seems not to be governed by what scientific theories are predominant. This is a fact that Kant discovered when, in the doctrine of the "postulates," in his *Critique of Practical Reason,* he assumed the independence of moral positings from theoretical proofs. For Kant it is the classical chief principles of all metaphysics — man's freedom, the existence of God, immortality — that, in the form of postulates, "are inseparably attached" to the practical law. The logic of this inseparability becomes clearer when one sees that only someone who disregards the law has an interest in citing his unfreedom and the futility of law-abiding behavior as far as well-being is concerned. We would count the postulates, entirely apart from metaphysics, as part of the rhetoric of ethics: they sum up what makes up the consensus of practical axioms, through persuasion and self-persuasion — what produces assent to public and private efforts and gives meaning to improving the conditions for a life that is free of crime and conflict and to trusting in the possibility of repairing backward or misguided lives. We act "as though" we knew that efforts and expenditures of this sort, for the benefit of man, are not in vain and are not called in question by science. In our practice we turn into an axiom, as a "postulate," what provides a motive for taking advantage of the more favorable prospects for humanity. Here rhetoric is also the art of persuading ourselves to ignore what speaks against betting on these prospects. The depressing results of genetic research on twins have not been able to discourage the adherents of theories of the influence of environment — and properly so. However narrow the zone of the uncertainty of scientific statements may become, it will never disappear entirely, and we will bet on it where theory appears to be more than can be demanded of, and intolerable for, practice. Since Kant, the practical postulate stands against the overwhelming determinism of the world of possible scientific objects.

Rhetoric has to do not with facts but with expectations. That which, in its whole tradition, it has called "credible" and "verisimilar" has to be clearly distinguished, in its practical valence, from what theory can call "probable."[5] That man "makes" history is a prospect on which, after detours through philosophy of history, the modern age has wagered. What this proposition means can only be understood if one perceives the "reoccupation" that is accomplished by means of it. I introduced and explained this concept in my *Legitimacy of the Modern Age* (1966 [English translation, 1983]), but I did not yet see that it implies a rhetorical transaction. In our tradition's system of the explanation of reality there is a "position" for this historical subject, a position to which vacancy and occupation refer. The accomplishment and establishment of the reoccupation are rhetorical acts; "philosophy of history" only thematizes the structure of this process, it is not the agency responsible for it.[n] Not accidentally, the act by which the subject of history is determined and legitimized has borne the name of a fundamental rhetorical figure, as *translatio imperii* [transfer (or: trope, metaphor) of power]. "Carryings over,"[o] metaphorical functions, again and again play an essential role here. Alexander conceives his historical project by reversing Xerxes's march across the Hellespont. The God of the Old Testament transfers his sovereignty in history by means of a covenant. The citizens of the National Convention, in the French Revolution, take metaphors of the Roman Republic literally, in their costume and their speech. "Men make their own history, but they do not make it just as they please; they do not make it under circumstances chosen by themselves, but under circumstances directly encountered, given and transmitted from the past," Marx writes in the *Eighteenth Brumaire*.[6] The deeper the crisis of legitimacy reaches, the more pronounced the recourse to rhetorical metaphor becomes — it is not inertia that makes tradition but rather the difficulty of living up to one's designation as the subject of history. So one contents oneself more easily with participating in the role of the subject of history: one *is* not the subject, but one is *part* of it, or one would have to be part of it if only things went properly. Rhetorically, both attributions of responsibility and excuses are always equally readily available.

I am not celebrating rhetoric here as an innate creative gift that man possesses. To illuminate it anthropologically is not to demonstrate that it gives man a special "metaphysical" distinction. As a behavorial characteristic of a creature that lives "nevertheless" [trotzdem], it is literally a "certificate of poverty." I would hesitate to call it a "cunning of reason"; not only because it would then be in even more questionable company but also because I would like to hold to the idea of seeing in it a form of rationality itself — a rational way of coming to terms with the provisionality of reason. It may be that the provisionality of theory that it avails itself of and profits from is only a grace period for it, if it does not prove to be the case that there is no irrevocability in theory. Against all rhetoric that is not "an elegant and clear expression of the conceptions of the mind," Hobbes recommended the use of "right reason." This phrase resembles the one that is going around currently: "critical reason." That is all very well, but what else could judge whether the "right" reason is being employed in each case, except reason once again — except "right reason," in fact? For Hobbes, one of the most important objections to democracy is that it cannot manage without rhetoric, and consequently arrives at decisions more *impetu animi* [by a certain violence of the mind] than *recta ratione* [by right reason], because its orators are guided not by the "nature of the things they speak of" but by the passions of their listeners. "Nor is this fault in the *man*, but in the nature itself of *eloquence*, whose end, as all masters of rhetoric teach us, is not truth (except by chance), but victory; and whose property is not to inform, but to allure."[7] A remarkable proposition, which explicitly absolves men of responsibility for the effects of an instrument that they invented and use only on account of those very effects. An especially remarkable proposition when one confronts it with the type of rationality that Hobbes's theory of the state represents: self-preservation, as the rational motivation of the contract of submission, risks, in the undetermined and undeterminable will of the absolute ruler, every *impetus animi* [violence of the mind] that Hobbes disparages as the correlate of rhetoric.

Hobbes's pathology of rhetoric traces the excitement of the passions back to the "metaphorical use of words." For him, too, metaphor is the distinctive element of rhetoric; in his opinion it is "fitted to the passions" and thus "separated from the true knowledge of things."[8] What is the basis of this relationship between metaphor and the passions, which Hobbes suggests to us here as something self-evident? For him, metaphor is opposed to concepts; by excluding the instruments of reason, metaphor opens the field to everything that traditionally is curbed and controlled by reason, everything that likes to escape from the exertion of concepts into the ease of orientation by images. In this passage Hobbes admits an eloquence (*eloquentia*) that abstains from metaphor and arises "from the contemplation of the things themselves," an eloquence that consists only in the elegance with which one expresses what one has grasped. When it is compared to the "nature of the things," as something that one could possess, rhetoric does indeed appear as an eccentric and artificial means. Yet if one considers Hobbes's theory of concepts, one is surprised to find that his rejection of metaphor depends on crediting the human intellect with more than he is able to grant it in this theory. For the concept, too, is only an artificial means, which has nothing in common with that "nature of the things."

It is not incidentally, here, that I point out this inconsistency in Hobbes's critique of metaphor as the essential element of rhetoric. It suggests the conjecture that Hobbes's critique of metaphor with reference to its affinity to the passions is based on the contradiction between the idea of the absolute state and a rhetoric that Hobbes describes, in opposing it, as "necessary to a man born for commotions." Now metaphor is in fact not only a surrogate for concepts that are missing but possible in principle, and should therefore be demanded; it is also a projective principle, which both expands and occupies empty space — an imaginative procedure that provides itself with its own durability in similes. As Alrich Meyer has recently shown,[9] the absolute state that is rationally deduced from the principle of self-preservation is caught between metaphors of the organic, on the one hand, and of mechanism, on the other. Such key metaphors have their own power of persuasion, which reacts, precisely through its possible extensions, on the core metaphor: for example, the possibility of an organic philosophy of history reinforces the organic model of the state. Hobbes himself overlooked the contradiction between his organic metaphor of the "state as a person" and the artificiality of the state's origin — and this is especially instructive, because the prohibition of metaphor makes it more difficult to perceive its actual background function.[p] Even the prohibition of rhetoric is a rhetorical transaction, which, then, only the others perceive as such. The example of Hobbes shows that in the modern age antirhetoric has become one of the most important expedients of rhetorical art, by means of which to lay claim to the rigor of realism, which alone promises to be a match for the seriousness of man's position (in this case, his position in his "state of nature").

Rhetoric is an "art" because it is an epitome of difficulties with reality, and reality has been pre-understood, in our tradition, primarily as "nature." The reason there is so little perceptible rhetoric in a surrounding reality that is extremely artificial is that it is already omnipresent. The classical antirhetorical figure of speech, "Res, non verba!" [Things, not words!] then points to states of affairs that themselves no longer have any of the sanction of what is natural, but instead already have a rhetorical tincture. On the other hand, this easily makes the emphatic recommendation or presentation of rhetoric's stylistic means a little (or more than a little) ridiculous. One then ascribes this difficulty to one's higher degree of realism. Rhetoric's modern difficulties with reality consist, in good part, in the fact that this reality no longer has value as something to appeal to, because it is in its turn a product of artificial processes. Thus one enters the specifically rhetorical situation of securing an exhortatory cry for oneself so as not to let the others have it: "Ad res"; "Zur Sache und zu den Sachen!" [To the matter at hand, to the things themselves!] It is rhetoric when one suggests to others, as a premise, that it is necessary to think and to act once again — or to do so for the first time ever. If reality could be seen and dealt with "realistically," it would have been seen and dealt with that way all along. So, much more than with the reality that it promises, the attitude of the *retour au réel* [return to the real] has to concern itself with the explanation of the illusions, deceptions, and seductions that have to be disposed of in connection with it. Every rhetoric of realism needs the conspiracies that have prevented it until now. Plato's allegory of the cave, in which because of the shadows playing on the wall the captive people never come to know what is truly real unless they are freed from the cave by force, is the model of such unmasking. It is directed against rhetoric, because the machinators of the shadow world are the Sophists, as "makers of images"; and it is itself rhetoric, since it is based on an elementary metaphor of "coming into the light" and expands it into a simile for an absolute reality, whose promise of definitive evidence cannot be fulfilled. Philosophy's turning from the shadows to reality was usurped by rhetoric and then by aesthetics. Jean Paul reflected this, ironically, in two sentences in the *Unsichtbare Loge* [invisible lodge]: "Alas, we are only trembling shadows! And yet one shadow wants to tear another one to pieces?"

In the *Critique of Judgment* Kant declares that rhetoric, as "the art of playing for one's own purpose upon the weaknesses of men, . . . merits no respect whatever."[10] This "insidious art" deals with "moving men in important matters like machines to a judgment." Now it is not at all in dispute here that man's constitutive dependence on rhetorical actions is always also a susceptibility to being influenced by rhetoric; there are enough dangers of and pressures toward his becoming a machine. The theory of rhetoric has always exposed people's intentions of taking advantage of these "weaknesses of men," at the same time that it served them. In an anthropological localization of rhetoric the issue is these weaknesses, not those intentions. In that connection, anthropological approaches to rhetoric converge on a central descriptive statement: Man has no immediate, no purely "internal" relation to himself. His self-understanding has the structure of "self-externality." Kant was the first to deny that inner experience has any precedence over outer experience; we are appearance to ourselves, the secondary synthesis of a primary multiplicity, not the reverse. The substantialism of identity is destroyed; identity must be realized, it becomes a kind of accomplishment, and accordingly there is a pathology of identity.

What remains as the subject matter of anthropology is a "human nature" that has never been "nature" and never will be. The fact that it makes its appearance in metaphorical disguise — as animal and as machine, as sedimentary layers and as stream of consciousness, in contrast to and in competition with a god — does not warrant our expecting that at the end of all creeds and all moralizing it will lie before us revealed. Man comprehends himself only by way of what he is not. It is not only his situation that is potentially metaphorical; his constitution itself already is. Montaigne's formulation of the result of his anthropology as self-experience is that the worst place that we could choose is in ourselves ("la pire place, que nous puissions prendre, c'est en nous").[11] He refers to the Copernican revolution, which as a trauma of man's interiority in the world metaphorically strengthens skepticism about his interiority in himself. Self-persuasion underlies all rhetoric in external relations; it makes use not only of the very general, practically effective propositions of which I spoke earlier but also of self-understanding through self-externality. So the most daring metaphor, which tried to embrace the greatest tension, may have accomplished the most for man's self-conception: trying to think the god absolutely away from himself, as the totally other, he inexorably began the most difficult rhetorical act, namely, the act of comparing himself to this god.[q]

Notes

1. Friedrich Nietzsche, *Gesammelte Werke*, ed. R. Oehler, M. Oehler, and F. C. Würzbach (Munich: Musarion, 1920–1921), vol. 6, p. 105.

Blumenberg: An Anthropological Approach to Rhetoric

2. Aristotle, *Nichomachean Ethics* 1172b36–37, trans. W. D. Ross, in *Basic Works of Aristotle,* ed. R. McKeon (New York: Random House, 1941), p. 1095.

3. Thomas S. Kuhn, *The Structure of Scientific Revolutions* (Chicago: University of Chicago Press, 1962).

4. Nietzsche, "Cicerofragment," *Gesammelte Werke,* vol. 7, p. 385.

5. On this see H. Blumenberg, "Paradigmen zu einer Metaphorologie," *Archiv für Begriffsgeschichte* 6 (1960) (reprint Bonn: Bouvier, 1960), pp. 88–105.

6. Karl Marx/Friedrich Engels, *Selected Works* (New York: International Publishers, 1968), p. 97; original: Marx/Engels, *Werke* (Berlin: Dietz, 1957–1972), vol. 8, p. 115.

7. Thomas Hobbes, *De Cive,* X, 11; from Hobbes's own English version [which has also been used for the bracketed translations of quotes from the Latin original], in *Man and Citizen,* ed. B. Gert (Garden City, New York: Doubleday Anchor, 1972), p. 231.

8. Hobbes, *De Cive,* X, 12; pp. 253–254.

9. Alrich Meyer, "Mechanische und organische Metaphorik politischer Philosophie," *Archiv für Begriffsgeschichte* 13 (1969): 128–199.

10. Immanuel Kant, *Critique of Judgment,* sec. 53, trans. J. C. Meredith (Oxford: Clarendon Press, 1911), p. 193.

11. Michel Montaigne, *Essais* II, 12 ("Apologie de Raimond Sebond"), *Oeuvres complètes.* ed. R. Barral and P. Michel (Paris: Seuil, 1967), p. 236.

Translator's Notes

a. "Gratuitous action": André Gide's famous notion.

b. Mängelwesen, a term introduced by Arnold Gehlen in his *Der Mensch. Seine Natur und seine Stellung in der Welt* (1940; 4th ed. Bonn: Athenäum, 1950).

c. Institution is used by Blumenberg in a special sense (introduced by Arnold Gehlen in his *Urmensch und Spätkultur* [Bonn: Athenäum, 1956]) that stresses the "pre-given," habitual, unquestioned character of certain behavior patterns and modes of thought (as in the Latin *institutio,* "custom") — rather than, and as opposed to, their being intentionally "founded" (as in one of the main senses of *Institution* or "institution" in ordinary usage). Awareness of this special usage should clarify the contrast here between "institutions" and norms that are based on what is "evident" (and with which one's compliance is presumably conscious and intentional).

d. Blumenberg has *consensus* in italics throughout this piece — even though the term is used not uncommonly in contemporary German — because he wants to remind us that it is a technical term, which was introduced into philosophy and rhetoric by Cicero: I have used quotes for the same purpose.

e. A "radical" in a sense analogous to that in linguistics, where the term refers to a root word or word element, a base to which other things are added.

f. Destruieren, here, is not the usual German word for "destroy" (which is *zerstören*) but instead is the same Latinate term that Heidegger used for what he wanted to do to the history of ontology. It has been rendered, not inappropriately, by the French *déconstruire*, "to deconstruct."

g. Blumenberg makes his own view of this question (and the distinction between his own concept of "institutions" and Gehlen's "absolutism" of them) clear in part 2, chapter 1 of his *Work on Myth* (Cambridge, Massachusetts: MIT Press, 1985). See especially page 166: "What the heading of 'institutions' covers is, above all, a distribution of burdens of proof. Where an institution exists, the question of its rational foundation is not, of itself, continually urgent, and the burden of proof always lies on the person who objects to the arrangement that it carries with it."

h. Some of these "questions relating to the concept of reality" are discussed in the author's "Wirklichkeitsbegriff und Staatstheorie," *Schweizer Monatshefte* 48 (1968): 121–146.

i. I.e., an unattainable guiding idea. (This is Kantian terminology.)

j. Rezeptionsästhetik, the aesthetics of the "reception" of works of art by audiences, critics, and so on, is the central concern of a school of literary theory in Germany of which Hans Robert Jauss and Wolfgang Iser are leading spokesmen. It contrasts, of course, with the traditional focus on the work itself or on the process of its "production" as the key to its meaning and status.

k. The idea of "positions" in a mental space, which are "reoccupied" during changes of epoch, is the central idea of the author's *The Legitimacy of the Modern Age* (Cambridge, Massachusetts: MIT Press, 1983). See especially pp. 65–69, where it is introduced.

l. On this phenomenon see the author's "Lebenswelt und Technisierung unter Aspekten der Phänomenologie," *Filosofia* (Turin) 14 (1963): 855–884, reprinted in his *Wirklichkeiten in denen wir leben* (Stuttgart: Reclam, 1981), pp. 7–54.

m. Blumenberg discusses this aspect of Pascal's "wager" argument in *Work on Myth*, p. 233.

n. "Philosophy of history," *Geschichtsphilosophie*, here and earlier in this paragraph refers — as it usually does in contemporary German writing — to the classical philosophies of history of writers like Condorcet, Saint-Simon, Hegel, Marx, and Comte, who all posit an overall necessary progress in history. Blumenberg's point is that abandoning this kind of philosophy of history need not prevent one from accepting the kind of "reoccupation" that he is describing here.

o. Übertragungen. Metaphor is, in its Greek etymology, a "carrying over." "Transfer" and *translatio* [translation] are Latin versions of the same thing.

p. On "background metaphors" see Blumenberg's *"Paradigmen zu einer Metaphorologic"* (cited in his note 5), p. 69.

q. In the original, this "god" could just as well be read as "God," since all nouns are capitalized in German.

14

Charles Taylor

Introduction

In the introduction to his recently published *Philosophical Papers*, Charles Taylor describes his work as a contribution to philosophical anthropology. His initial approach was largely polemical. He attacked the view that the natural sciences should serve as a model for the methods and procedures of the human sciences. Whether in the form of classical behaviorism, functionalism, AI-based psychology, or any other reductivist explanatory strategy, "naturalism," Taylor argued, is inappropriate to the "sciences of man," because they must incorporate into their explanations the common meanings that are embedded in social institutions and practices, as well as in agents' self-interpretations. Thus, in contrast to Rorty and others who contend that "there is no interesting split between the *Natur*- and the *Geisteswissenschaften*," Taylor revives this classical distinction on the grounds that the latter necessarily include a hermeneutic dimension in a way the former do not. At the same time, Taylor's critique of naturalism and its underlying conceptions of the self, language, and knowledge has led to the development of an alternative that draws heavily on the expressivist tradition of Hegel and Romanticism.

Taylor's defence of the autonomy of the human sciences depends importantly upon his conception of human agents as "self-interpreting animals": who and what we are is partly constituted by our self-understandings and self-descriptions, by our aspirations, desires, aversions, admirations, and the like. On this view, the self is connected to its purposes and projects in a "strong sense" and is not simply the "bearer of preferences" to which it strategically relates. By contrast, this latter, "thin" conception of the self behind naturalism is that of a disengaged subject representing to itself an independent world over which it seeks to gain control. In opposition to this "performance" model, Taylor characterizes human beings as "subjects of significance" (*Philosophical Papers, Vol. 1*, 97–114). What distinguishes us from other animals (and from computers) is not simply that we can do certain distinctive things, but that we are beings for whom things matter in a distinctive way. This is particularly evident in experiences of pride and shame, love and envy, moral goodness and evil, and the like, which, he notes, defy description in terms of a disengaged self, calculative reason, and instrumental goods. "The center is no longer the power to plan, but rather openness to certain matters of significance. This is now what is essential to personal agency" (105).

If reductive naturalism must disregard basic features of our everyday experience and if, as Taylor claims, it has had such meagre success in the human sciences, to what does it owe its wide appeal as a research paradigm? Taylor suggests that the answer is to be found in its spiritual roots, that is, in the notions of human agency, freedom, and self-responsibility closely connected to it. The expressivist critic should be able to show that naturalism derives its plausibility from a background of "strong evaluations" and "distinctions of worth" and that the hermeneutic standpoint can provide a better account of these than competing standpoints. Taylor focuses on the idea of "liberation through objectification," that is, on the notion that subjects of knowledge and action are capable of disengaging themselves from the world by objectifying it, by making it the object of accurate representations and effective actions, and that this disengagement is what grounds human freedom, dignity, and power. It is this same "modern disengaged identity," which centers everything on the subject and sets up a "quite unreal model of clarity and control" (*Philosophical Papers, Vol 1*, 11), that is behind the hegemony, in the modern period, of atomistic, utilitarian, instrumentalist, and formalist modes of conceptualizing human thought and action. "Overcoming" naturalism, then, is more than a matter of criticizing a particular methodological approach. It involves deconstructing the anthropology-cum-moral-and-spiritual-values that carry it — not, to be sure, in the sense of simply rejecting them, but of "purging" them of their "atomistic distortions" and "illusory pretensions" by showing the subject to be essentially constituted by intersubjective meanings, his or her freedom to be essentially situated, and his or her identity to be essentially rooted in community.

Similarly, the present essay explores the pictures, motivations, and evaluations underlying the "epistemological standpoint" that has so dominated modern philosophical thought. In contrast to Rorty, Taylor believes that the heart of the modern epistemological project is not foundationalism but the even more central commitment to a "representational model" of knowledge, and that this in turn is rooted in the same picture of agency and the same moral-spiritual ideals that were seen to underlie naturalism. Accordingly, to "overcome epistemology" means not only to give up foundationalist ambitions (as Quine, for instance, has done) but also to develop a deeper and more adequate conception of human agency (something Quine's behaviorism does not do). The path to this conception leads through a "kind of transcendental argument" that discloses the indispensable conditions of experiencing a world, that is, of intentionality. Pursuing this path in the footsteps of Heidegger, Wittgenstein, and Merleau-Ponty immediately reveals the untenability of the picture of the self as disengaged and disembodied, punctual and atomistic, related to the natural and the social worlds, and even to parts of the self, only as objects of disinterested knowledge and instrumental control. It reveals that we are first and foremost embodied agents in a natural and social world. Our propositional knowledge of this world is grounded in our dealings with it; and there can be no question of totally objectifying the prior grasp we have of it as agents within it. The task of philosophy is the unending one of articulating elements of this largely unarticulated background, of disclosing what it involves, thus making partial detachment and revision possible.

Philosophy as a clarification of the conditions of intentionality is a continuation-through-transformation of the "tradition of self-critical reason." It leads to a better, deeper, and more valid understanding of what we are as knowing, speaking, and acting subjects, and thereby provides insight into the anthropological questions that often underlie our moral concerns. In this sense it is a continuation-through-transformation of the idea of philosophical self-responsibility based on philosophical self-clarification.

Suggested Readings

Connolly, William. "Taylor, Foucault and Otherness," *Political Theory* 13 (1985), 365–376.

Habermas, Jürgen. "Entgegnung" (Reply to Taylor), in *Kommunikatives Handeln: Beiträge zu Habermas' Theorie des kommunikativen Handelns,* ed. A. Honneth and H. Joas. Frankfurt: Suhrkamp, 1986.

Hoy, David. "Hegel, Taylor-Made," *Dialogue: Canadian Philosophical Review* 16 (1976), 715–730.

Rorty, Richard. "Reply to Taylor and Dreyfus," *Review of Metaphysics* 34 (1980), 39–46; followed by a discussion between Rorty, Taylor, and Dreyfus.

Rorty, Richard. "Method, Social Science and Social Hope," in *Consequences of Pragmatism,* 191–210. Minneapolis: University of Minnesota Press, 1982.

Scarrow, David. "The Causality of Reasons: A Survey of Some Recent Developments in the Mind-Body Problem," *Metaphilosophy* 12 (1981), 13–30.

Schmitz, Kenneth. "Embodiment and Situation: Charles Taylor's Hegel," *Journal of Philosophy* 73 (1976), 710–723.

Soll, Ivan. "Charles Taylor's Hegel," *Journal of Philosophy* 73 (1976), 697–709.

Taylor, Charles. *The Explanation of Behavior.* New York: Humanities Press, 1964.

Taylor, Charles. *Hegel.* New York: Cambridge University Press, 1975.

Taylor, Charles. *Hegel and the Modern State.* New York: Cambridge University Press, 1979.

Taylor, Charles. "The Validity of Transcendental Argument," *Proceedings of the Aristotelian Society* 79 (1978–1979), 151–165.

Taylor, Charles. "Understanding in Human Science," *Review of Metaphysics* 34 (1980), 25–38.

Taylor, Charles. "Understanding and Explanation in the *Geisteswissenschaften*," in *Wittgenstein: To Follow a Rule*, ed S. Holtzman and C. Leich, 191–210. Reply by Philip Pettit, "Reply: Evaluative 'Realism' and Interpretation," 211–245. London: Routledge and Kegan Paul, 1981.

Taylor, Charles. "Political Theory and Practice," in *Social Theory and Political Practice*, ed. C. Lloyd. Oxford: Clarendon, 1982.

Taylor, Charles. "Rationality," in *Rationality and Relativism*, ed. M. Hollis and S. Lukes, 87–105. Cambridge, Massachusetts: MIT Press, 1982.

Taylor, Charles. "Philosophy and Its History," in *Philosophy in History*, ed. R. Rorty, J. B .Schneewind, and Q. Skinner, 17–30. New York: Cambridge University Press, 1984.

Taylor, Charles. *Human Agency and Language: Philosophical Papers, Vol. 1*. New York: Cambridge University Press, 1985.

Taylor, Charles. *Philosophy and the Human Sciences: Philosophical Papers, Vol. 2*. New York: Cambridge University Press, 1985.

Taylor, Charles. "Connolly, Foucault and Truth," *Political Theory* 13 (1985), 377–385.

Taylor, Charles. "Justice after Virtue," in *Kritische Methode und Zukunft der Anthropologie*, ed. M. Benedikt and R. Berger, 23–48. Vienna, 1985.

Taylor, Charles. "Sprache und Gesellschaft," in *Kommunikatives Handeln: Beiträge zur Habermas' Theorie des kommunikativen Handelns*, ed. A. Honneth and H. Joas. Frankfurt: Suhrkamp, 1986.

Turner, Stephen. "Social Theory without Wholes," *Human Studies* 7 (1984), 259–284.

Walsh, W. H. "Review of Taylor's *Hegel*," *Canadian Journal of Philosophy* 6 (1976), 785–796.

Warnke, Georgia. "Hermeneutics and the Social Sciences: A Gadamerian Critique of Rorty," *Inquiry* 28 (1985), 329–357.

Overcoming Epistemology

Charles Taylor

Epistemology, once the pride of modern philosophy, seems in a bad way these days. Fifty years ago, during the heyday of logical empiricism, which was not only a powerful movement in philosophy but also immensely influential in social science, it seemed as though the very center of philosophy was its theory of knowledge. It seemed evident that that had to be philosophy's main contribution to a scientific culture. Science went ahead and gathered knowledge; philosophical reflection concerned the validity of knowledge claims. The preeminence of epistemology explains a phenomenon like Karl Popper. On the strength of his reputation as a theorist of scientific knowledge,[1] he could obtain a hearing for his intemperate views about famous philosophers of the tradition, which bore only a rather distant relation to the truth.[2] It is reminiscent of a parallel phenomenon in the arts, whereby the political opinions of a great performer or writer are often listened to with an attention and respect that their intrinsic worth hardly commands.

Of course, all this was only true of the Anglo-Saxon world. On the Continent the challenge to the epistemological tradition was already in full swing. Heidegger and Merleau-Ponty had a wide influence. It would be too simple to say that this skeptical stance has now spread to the English-speaking world. Rather it seems true to say that epistemology has come under more intensive critical scrutiny in *both* cultures. In France the generation of "structuralists" and "poststructuralists" was if anything even more alienated from this whole manner of thinking than Merleau-Ponty had been. In England and America the arguments of both generations of Continental thinkers have begun to have an impact. The publication of Richard Rorty's influential *Philosophy and the Mirror of Nature*[3] helped both to crystallize and to accelerate a trend toward the repudiation of the whole epistemological enterprise.

In some circles it seems to be rapidly becoming a new orthodoxy that the whole enterprise from Descartes, through Locke and Kant, and pursued by various nineteenth- and twentieth-century succession movements, was a mistake. Within this new agreement, however, what is becoming less and less clear is what exactly it means to overcome the epistemological standpoint or repudiate the enterprise. Just what exactly is one trying to deny?

Rorty's book seems to offer a clear and plausible answer. The heart of the old epistemology was the belief in a *foundational* enterprise.[4] What the positive sciences needed to complete them, on this view, was a rigorous discipline that could check the credentials of all truth claims. An alleged science could only be valid if its findings met this test; otherwise it rested on sand. Epistemology would ultimately make clear just what made knowledge claims valid, and what ultimate degree of validity they could lay claim to. (And, of course, one could come up with a rather pessimistic, skeptical answer to the latter question. Epistemology was not necessarily a rationalist enterprise. Indeed, its last great defenders were and are empiricists.)

In practice, of course, epistemologists took their cue from what they identified as the successful sciences of their day, all the way from Descartes's infatuation with mathematics to the contemporary vogue for reduction to physics. But the actual foundational science was not supposed itself to be dependent on any of the empirical sciences, and this obviously on pain of a circularity that would sacrifice its foundational character. Arguments about the source of valid knowledge claims were not supposed to be empirical.

If we follow this description, then it is clear what overcoming epistemology has to mean. It will mean abandoning foundationalism. On this view, Quine would figure among the prominent leaders of this new philosophical turn, since he proposes to "naturalize" epistemology, that is, deprive it of its a priori status and consider it as one science among others, one of many mutually interacting departments of our picture of the world.[5] And so Rorty does seem to consider him, albeit with some reservations.[6]

But there is a wider conception of the epistemological tradition, from whose viewpoint this last would be a rather grotesque judgment. This is the interpretation that focuses not so much on foundationalism as on the understanding of knowledge that made it possible. If I had to sum up this understanding in a single formula, it would be that knowledge is to be seen as correct representation of an independent reality. In its original form it saw knowledge as the inner depiction of an outer reality.[7]

The reason why some thinkers prefer to focus on this interpretation, rather than merely on the foundationalist ambitions that are ultimately (as Quine has shown) detachable from it, is that it is bound up with very influential and often not fully articulated notions about science and about the nature of human agency. Through these it connects with certain central moral and spiritual ideas of the modern age. If one's aim is, in challenging the primacy of epistemology, to challenge these latter as well, then one has to take it up in this wider — or deeper — focus, and not simply show the vanity of the foundational enterprise.

1

I'd like now to try to trace some of these connections. One of them is very evident: the link between this representational conception and the new, mechanistic science of the seventeenth century. This is, in fact, twofold. On one side, the mechanization of the world picture undermined the previously dominant understanding of knowledge and thus paved the way for the modern view. The most important traditional view was that of Aristotle, according to which when we come to know something, the mind (*nous*) becomes one with the object of thought.[8] Of course, this is not to say that they become materially the same thing; rather, the idea is that they are informed by the same *eidos*.[9] Here was a conception quite different from the representational model, even though some of the things Aristotle said could be construed as supporting this latter. The basic bent of Aristotle's model could much better be described as participational: being informed by the same *eidos*, the mind participated in the being of the known object, rather than simply depicting it.

But this theory totally depends on the philosophy of forms. Once one no longer explains the way things are in terms of the species that inform them, this conception of knowledge is untenable and rapidly becomes close to unintelligible. We have great difficulty in understanding it today. The representational view can easily then appear as the only available alternative.

This is the negative connection between mechanism and modern epistemology. The positive one obtrudes as soon as we attempt to explain our knowing activity itself in mechanistic terms. The key to this is obviously perception, and if we see this as another process in a mechanistic universe, we cannot but construe it as involving as a crucial component the passive reception of impressions from the external world. Knowledge then hangs on a certain relation holding between what is "out there" and certain inner states that this external reality causes in us. This construal, valid for Locke, applies just as much to the latest AI-inspired models of thinking. It is one of the mainsprings of the epistemological tradition.

The epistemological construal is, then, an understanding of knowledge that fits well with modern mechanistic science. This is one of its great strengths, and certainly this connection contributes to the present vogue of computer-based models of the mind. But that's not all this construal has going for it. It is in fact heavily overdetermined. For the representational view was also powered by the new ideals of science, and new conceptions of the excellences of thought, that arose at the same time.

This connection was central to Descartes's philosophy. It was one of his leading ideas that science, or real knowledge, does not just consist of a congruence between ideas in the mind and the reality outside. If the object of my musings happens to coincide with real events in the world, this doesn't give me *knowledge* of them. This congruence has to come about through a reliable method, generating well-founded confidence. Science requires certainty, and this can only be based on that undeniable clarity which Descartes called *évidence*. "Toute science est une connaissance certaine et évidente," runs the opening sentence of the second of the *Rules for the Direction of the Mind*.

Now certainty is something that the mind has to generate for itself. It requires a reflexive turn, where instead of simply trusting the opinions one has acquired through one's upbringing, one examines their foundation, which is ultimately to be found in one's own mind. Of course, the theme that the sage has to turn away from merely current opinion and make a more rigorous examination that leads him to science, is a very old one, going back at least to Socrates and Plato. But what is different with Descartes is the reflexive nature of this turn. The seeker after science is not directed away from shifting and uncertain opinion toward the order of the unchanging, as with Plato, but rather within, to the contents of his own mind. These have to be carefully distinguished both from external reality and from their illusory localizations in the body, so that then the correct issue of science, that is, of certainty, can be posed — the issue of the correspondence of idea to reality, which Descartes raises and then disposes of through the supposition of the *malin génie* and the proof of his negation, the veracious God.

The confidence that underlies this whole operation is that certainty is something the thinker can generate for himself, by ordering his thoughts correctly — according to clear and distinct connections. This confidence is in a sense independent of the positive outcome of Descartes's argument to the existence of a veracious God, the guarantor of our science. The very fact of reflexive clarity is bound to improve our epistemic position, as long as knowledge is understood representationally. Even if we couldn't prove that the *malin génie* doesn't exist, Descartes would still be in a better position than the rest of us unreflecting minds, because he would have measured the full degree of uncertainty that hangs over all our beliefs about the world, and clearly separated off from these our undeniable belief in ourselves.

Descartes is thus the originator of the modern notion that certainty is the child of reflexive clarity, or the examination of our own ideas in abstraction from what they "represent," which has exercised a powerful influence on Western culture, way beyond those who share his confidence in the power of argument to prove strong theses about external reality. Locke and Hume follow in the same path, although the latter goes about as far in the direction of skepticism as any modern has. Still, it remains true for Hume that we purge ourselves of our false confidence in our too-hasty extrapolations by focusing attention on their origin in our ideas. It is *there* that we see, for instance, that our beliefs in causation are based on nothing more than constant conjunction, that the self is nothing but a bundle of impressions, and so on.

This reflexive turn, which first took form in the seventeenth- and eighteenth-century "way of ideas," is of course indissolubly linked to modern representational epistemology. One might say it presupposes this construal of knowledge. If Plato or Aristotle were right, the road to certainty couldn't be inward — indeed, the very notion of certainty would be different: defined more in terms of the kinds of being that admit of it, rather than by the ordering of our thoughts. But I believe that there is also a motivational connection in the *other* direction: the ideal of self-given certainty is a strong incentive to construe knowledge in such a way that our thought about the real can be distinguished from its objects and examined on its own. And this incentive has long outlived the original way of ideas. Even in an age when we no longer want to talk of Lockean "ideas" or of "sense data," where the representational view is reconstrued in terms of linguistic representations or bodily states (and these are perhaps not genuine alternatives), there is still a strong draw toward distinguishing and mapping the *formal* operations of our thinking. In certain circles it would seem that an almost boundless confidence is placed in the defining of formal relations as a way of achieving clarity and certainty about our thinking, be it in the (mis)application of rational choice theory to ethical problems or in the great popularity of computer models of the mind, which I referred to earlier.

This latter is an excellent example of what I called above the "over-determination" of the epistemological construal. The plausibility of the computer as a model of thinking comes partly from the fact that it is a machine, hence living "proof" that materialism can accommodate explanations in terms of intelligent performance; but partly too from the widespread faith that our intelligent performances are ultimately to be understood in terms of formal operations. The computer, it can be said, is a "syntactic engine."[10] A great controversy rages over precisely this point. The most perspicuous critics of the runaway enthusiasm with the computer model, such as Hubert Dreyfus,[11] tirelessly point out how implausible it is to understand certain of our intelligent performances in terms of a formal calculus, including our most common everyday ones, such as making our way around our rooms, streets, and gardens, picking up and manipulating the objects we use, and so on. But the great difficulties that computer simulations have encountered in this area don't seem to have dimmed the enthusiasm of real believers in this model. It is as though they had been vouchsafed some certain revelation a priori that it *must* all be done by formal calculi. Now this "revelation," I submit, comes from the depths of our modern culture and the epistemological model that is anchored in it, whose strength is based not just on its affinity to mechanistic science but also on its congruence to the powerful ideal of reflexive, self-given certainty.

For this has to be understood as something like a moral ideal. The power of this ideal can be sensed in the following passage from Husserl's *Cartesian Meditations,* all the more significant in that Husserl had already broken with some of the main theses of the epistemological tradition. Husserl asks in the first meditation whether the "Trostlosigkeit" of our present philosophical predicament doesn't spring from our having abandoned Descartes's original "Geist des Radikalismus philosophischer Selbstverantwortlichkeit." And he continues:

Sollte die vermeintlich überspannte Forderung einer auf letzte erdenkliche Vorurteilslosigkeit abgestellten Philosophie, einer in wirklicher Autonomie aus letzten selbst erzeugten Evidenzen sich gestaltenden und sich von daher absolut selbstverantwortenden Philosophie nicht vielmehr zum Grundsinn echter Philosophie gehören?[12]

This ideal of "self-responsibility" is foundational to modern culture. It emerges not only in our picture of the growth of modern science as the fruit of the heroism of the great scientist, standing out against the opinion of his age on the basis of his own self-responsible certainty — Copernicus, Galileo (he wobbled a bit before the Holy Office, but who can blame him?), Darwin, Freud. It is also closely linked to the modern ideal of freedom as self-autonomy, as the passage from Husserl implies. To be free in our modern sense is to be self-responsible, to rely on one's own judgment, to find one's purpose in oneself.

And so the epistemological tradition is also intricated in a certain notion of freedom, and the dignity attaching to us in virtue of this. The theory of knowledge partly draws its strength from this connection. But also reciprocally, the ideal of freedom has drawn strength from its sensed connection with the construal of knowledge seemingly favored by modern science. From this point of view it has been fateful that this notion of freedom has been interpreted as involving certain key theses about the nature of the human agent; we might call them anthropological beliefs. Whether these are in fact inseparable from the modern aspiration to autonomy is an open question, and a very important one, to which I will return briefly below. But the three connected notions that I would like to mention here are in fact historically closely connected with the epistemological construal.

The first is the picture of the subject as ideally disengaged, that is, as free and rational to the extent that he has fully distinguished himself from his natural and social worlds, so that his identity is no longer to be defined in terms of what lies outside him in these worlds. The second, which flows from this, is a punctual view of the self, ideally ready qua free and rational to treat these worlds — and even some of the features of his own character — instrumentally, as subject to change and reordering in order the better to secure the welfare of himself and other like subjects. The third is the social consequence of the first two: an atomistic construal of society as constituted by, or ultimately to be explained in terms of, individual purposes.

The first notion emerges originally in classical dualism, where the subject withdraws even from his own body, which he is able to look on as an object; but it continues beyond the demise of this dualism in the contemporary demand for a neutral, objectifying science of human life and action. The second originates in the ideals of the government and reform of the self that have such an important place in the seventeenth century and of which Locke develops an influential version;[13] it continues today in the tremendous force that instrumental reason and engineering models have in our social policy, medicine, psychiatry, politics, and so on. The third first takes shape in seventeenth-century social contract theories, but continues not only in their contemporary successors but also in many of the assumptions of contemporary liberalism and mainstream social science.

One does not need to unpack these ideas any further to see that the epistemological tradition is connected with some of the most important moral and spiritual ideas of our civilization — and also with some of the most controversial and questionable. To challenge these is sooner or later to run up against the force of this tradition, which stands with them in a complex relation of mutual support. Overcoming or criticizing these ideas involves coming to grips with epistemology. But this means taking it in what I identified as its broad focus, the whole representational construal of knowledge, not just as the faith in foundationalism.

2

When we turn to the famous, now classic critiques of epistemology, we find that they have, in fact, mostly been attuned to this interpenetration of the scientific and the moral. Hegel, in his celebrated attack on this tradition in the introduction to the *Phenomenology of Spirit,* speaks of a "fear of error" that "reveals itself rather as fear of the truth,"[14] and he goes on to show how this stance is bound up with a certain aspiration to individuality and separatedness, refusing what he sees as the "truth" of subject-object identity. Heidegger notoriously treats the rise of the modern epistemological standpoint as a stage in the development of a stance of domination to the world, which culminates in contemporary technological society. Merleau-Ponty draws more explicitly political connections and clarifies the alternative notion of freedom that arises from the critique of empiricism and intellectualism.[15] The moral consequences of the devastating critique of epistemology in the later Wittgenstein are, naturally, less evident. Wittgenstein was strongly averse to making this kind of thing explicit. But those who have followed him have shown a certain affinity for the critique of disengagement, instrumental reason, and atomism.

It is safe to say that all these critics were largely motivated by a dislike of the moral and spiritual consequences of epistemology and by a strong affinity for some alternative. Indeed, the connection between the scientific and the moral is generally made more evident in their work than in that of mainstream supporters of the epistemological standpoint. But an important feature of all these critiques is that they establish a new moral outlook *through* overturning the modern conception of knowledge. They do not just register their dissidence from the anthropological beliefs associated with this conception, but show the foundations of these beliefs to be unsound, based as they are in an untenable construal of knowledge.

All four of the authors I have mentioned — whom I take to be the most important and influential critics of epistemology, the founders of the most influential forms of critique — offer new construals of knowledge. Moreover, in spite of the great differences, all four share a common basic form of argument, which finds its origins in Kant, and which one might call "the argument from transcendental conditions."

By this I mean something like the following: We argue the inadequacy of the epistemological construal, and the necessity of a new conception, from what we show to be the indispensable conditions of there being anything like experience or awareness of the world in the first place. Just how to characterize this latter reality, whose conditions we are defining, can itself be a problem, of course. Kant speaks of it simply as "experience"; but Heidegger, with his concern to get beyond subjectivistic formulations, ends up talking about the "clearing" (*Lichtung*). Where the Kantian expression focuses on the mind of the subject and the conditions of his having what we can call experience, the Heideggerian formulation points us rather toward another facet of this same phenomenon, the fact that anything *appears,* or comes to light at all. This of course requires that there be a being *to* whom it appears, *for* whom it is an object; it requires a knower, in some sense. But the *Lichtung* formulation focuses us rather on the fact (which we are meant to come to perceive as astonishing) that the knower-known complex *is* at all, rather than taking the knower for granted as "subject" and examining what makes it possible for him to have knowledge or experience of a world.[16]

For all this extremely important shift in the center of gravity of what we take as the starting point, there is a continuity between Kant and Heidegger, Wittgenstein, or Merleau-Ponty. They start from the intuition that this central phenomenon of experience, or the clearing, is not made intelligible on the epistemological construal, in either its empiricist or rationalist variants. These offer an account of the stages of the knower that consists of an ultimately incoherent amalgam of two features: (*a*) these states (the ideas) are self-enclosed, in the sense that they can be accurately identified and described in abstraction from the "outside" world (this is, of course, essential to the whole rationalist thrust of reflexive testing of the grounds of knowledge); and (*b*) they nevertheless point toward and represent things in that outside world.

The incoherence of this combination may be hidden from us by the existence of things that seem to have *a,* such as certain sensations, and even of states that seem to combine *a* and *b,* such as stable illusions. But what clearly emerges out of the whole argument of the last couple of centuries is that the condition of states of ourselves having *b* is that they cannot satisfy *a.* This already began to be evident with classical empiricism in its uncertain shuffling between two definitions of the "idea" or "impression": on one reading, it was simply a content of the mind, an inner quasi-object; it called for an object-description; on another, it had to be a *claim* about how things stood; it could only be captured in a *that*-clause.

Feature *b* is what later came to be called in the Brentano-Husserl tradition "intentionality"; our ideas are essentially "of" or "about" something. Here is another way of characterizing a central condition of experience or the clearing. What Kant calls "transcendental" conditions are conditions of intentionality, and the lines of argument that descend from Kant can be seen as exploring what these have to be.[17]

Kant already showed that the atomistic understanding of knowledge that Hume espoused was untenable in the light of these conditions. If our states were to count as experience of an objective reality, they had to be bound together to form a coherent whole, or bound together by rules, as Kant conceived it. However much this formulation may be challenged, the incoherence of the Humean picture, which made the basis of all knowledge the reception of raw, atomic, uninterpreted data, was brilliantly demonstrated. How did Kant show this? He established in fact an argument form that has been used by his successors ever since. It can be seen as a kind of appeal to intuition. In the case of this particular refutation of Hume (which is, I believe, the main theme of the Transcendental Deduction in the first edition of the *Critique of Pure Reason*), he makes us aware, first, that we wouldn't have what we recognize as experience at all unless it were construable as of an object (I take this as a kind of proto-thesis of intentionality), and second, that their being of an object entails a certain relatedness among our "representations." Without this, Kant says, "it would be possible for appearances to crowd in upon the soul, and yet to be such as would never allow of experience." Our perceptions "would not then belong to any experience, consequently would be without an object, merely a blind play of representations, less even than a dream."[18]

I think this kind of appeal to intuition is better understood as an appeal to what I want to call our "agent's knowledge." As those effectively engaged in the activities of getting to perceive and know the world, we are capable of identifying certain conditions without which our activity would fall apart into incoherence. The philosophical achievement is to define the issues properly. Once this is done, as Kant does so brilliantly in relation to Humean empiricism, we find there is only one rational answer. Plainly we couldn't have experience of the world at all if we had to start with a swirl of uninterpreted data. Indeed, these wouldn't even be "data," because even this minimal description depends on our distinguishing what is "given" by some objective source from what we merely supply ourselves.[19]

Now the four authors I have mentioned push this argument form farther, and explore conditions of intentionality that require a more fundamental break with the epistemological tradition. And in particular, they push it far enough to undermine the anthropological beliefs I described in the previous section: beliefs in the disengaged subject, the punctual self, and described atomism.

The arguments of Heidegger and Merleau-Ponty put paid to the first. Heidegger, for instance, shows — especially in his celebrated analysis of being-in-the-world — that the condition of our forming disengaged representations of reality is that we be already engaged in coping with our world, dealing with the things in it, at grips with them.[20] Disengaged description is one special possibility, realizable only intermittently, of a being (which Heidegger calls *Dasein*) who is always "in" the world in another way, as an agent engaged in realizing a certain form of life. That is what we are about "first and mostly" (*zunächst und zumeist*).

The tremendous contribution of Heidegger, like that of Kant, consists in having focused the issue properly. Once this is done, we cannot deny the picture that emerges. It becomes evident that even in our theoretical stance to the world we are agents. Even to find out about the world and formulate disinterested pictures, we have to come to grips with it, experiment, set ourselves to observe, control conditions. But in all this, which forms the indispensable basis of theory, we are engaged as agents coping with things. It is clear that we couldn't form disinterested representations any other way.

But once one takes this point, then the entire epistemological position is undermined. Obviously foundationalism goes, since our representations of things — the kinds of objects we pick out as whole, enduring entities, for instance — are grounded in the way we deal with these things. These dealings are largely inarticulate, and the project of articulating them fully is an essentially incoherent one, just because any articulative project would itself rely on a background or horizon of nonexplicit engagement with the world.

But the argument here cuts deeper. Foundationalism is undermined, because you can't go on digging under our ordinary representations to uncover further, more basic representations. What you get underlying our representations of the world — the kinds of things we formulate, for instance, in declarative sentences — is not further representations but rather a certain grasp of the world that we have as agents in it. This shows the whole epistemological construal of knowledge to be mistaken. It doesn't just consist of inner pictures of outer reality, but grounds in something quite other. And in this "foundation" the crucial move of the epistemological construal, distinguishing states of the subject — our "ideas" — from features of the external world, can't be effected. We can draw a neat line between my *picture* of an object and that object, but not between my *dealing* with the object and that object. It may make sense to ask one to focus on what one *believes* about something, say a football, even in the absence of that thing; but when it comes to *playing* football, the corresponding suggestion would be absurd. The actions involved in the game cannot be done without the object; they include the object. Take it away and we have something quite different — people miming a match on the stage, perhaps. The notion that our understanding of the world is grounded in our dealings with it is equivalent to the thesis that this understanding is not ultimately based on representations at all, in the sense of depictions that are separately identifiable from what they are of.[21]

Heidegger's reflections take us entirely outside the epistemological construal. Our reflections on the conditions of intentionality show that these include our being "first and mostly" agents in the world. But then this also ruins the conception of the agent as one whose ideal could be total disengagement. This turns out to be an impossibility, one that it would be destructive to attempt. We cannot turn the background from which we think into an object for us. The task of reason has to be conceived quite differently: as that of articulating this background, "disclosing" what it involves. This may open the way to detaching ourselves from or altering part of what has constituted it — may, indeed, make such alteration irresistible; but only through our unquestioning reliance on the rest.

And just as the notion of the agent underpinning the ideal of disengagement is rendered impossible, so is the punctual notion of the self. Heidegger and Merleau-Ponty both show how the inescapability of the background involves an understanding of the depth of the agent, but they do so by exploring the conditions of intentionality in complementary directions. Heidegger shows how *Dasein*'s world is defined by the related purposes of a certain way of life shared with others. Merleau-Ponty shows how our agency is essentially embodied and how this lived body is the locus of directions of action and desire that we never fully grasp or control by personal decision.

This critique also puts in question the third anthropological belief I singled out above, that in atomism. I have just mentioned how Heidegger's notion of *Dasein*'s way of life is essentially that of a collectivity. A general feature of all the paradigm-setting critiques I am discussing here is that they strongly reject this third view and show rather the priority of society as the locus of the individual's identity. But crucially this point is made through an exploration of the role of language. The new theory of language that arises at the end of the 18th century, most notably in the work of Herder and Humboldt, not only gives a new account of how language is essential to human thought, but also places the capacity to speak not simply in the individual but primarily in the speech community.[22] This totally upsets the outlook of the mainstream epistemological tradition. Now arguments to this effect have formed part of the refutation of the atomism that has proceeded via an overturning of standard modern epistemology.

Important examples of arguments of this kind are Hegel's in the first chapter of the *Phenomenology of Spirit*, against the position that he defines as "sensible certainty," where he shows both the indispensability of language and its holistic character;[23] and Wittgenstein's famous demonstrations of the uselessness of private ostensive definitions, by making plain the crucial role played by language in identifying the object and the impossibility of a purely private language.[24] Both of these are, I believe, excellent examples of arguments that explore the conditions of intentionality and show their conclusions to be inescapable.

It is evident that these arguments give us a quite different notion of what it is to overcome epistemology from those that merely eschew foundationalism. We can measure the full gulf by comparing any of the four — Heidegger, perhaps, or Merleau-Ponty — with the Quine of "Epistemology Naturalized." It is plain that the essential elements of the epistemological construal have remained standing in Quine, and not surprisingly therefore the central anthropological beliefs of the tradition. Disengagement emerges in his "taste for desert landscapes,"[25] the punctual self in his behaviorism;[26] and atomism seems to inform Quine's particular brand of political conservatism. In face of differences of this magnitude, a question arises concerning what it means exactly to "overcome epistemology."

3

A picture has been emerging in the previous sections of what this ought to be — a tendentious one, I freely admit. This accepts the wider or deeper definition of the task: overcoming the distorted anthropological beliefs through a critique and correction of the construal of knowledge that is interwoven with them and has done so much to give them undeserved credit. Otherwise put: through a clarification of the conditions of intentionality, coming to a better understanding of what we are as knowing agents — and hence also as language beings — and thereby gaining insight into some of the crucial anthropological questions that underpin our moral and spiritual beliefs.

For all its radical break with the tradition, this kind of philosophy would in one respect be in continuity with it. It would be carrying further the demand for self-clarity about our nature as knowing agents, by adopting a better and more critically defensible notion of what this entails. Instead of searching for an impossible foundational justification of knowledge or hoping to achieve total reflexive clarity about the bases of our beliefs, we would now conceive this self-understanding as awareness about the limits and conditions of our knowing, an awareness that would help us to overcome the illusions of disengagement and atomic individuality that are constantly being generated by a civilization founded on mobility and instrumental reason.

We could understand this as carrying the project of modern reason, even of "self-responsible" reason, farther by giving it a new meaning. This is how Husserl, for instance, conceived the critical project in his last great lectures on the "crisis of the European sciences," given in Vienna in 1935. Husserl thinks of us as struggling to realize a fundamental task, that of the "europäischen Geist," whose goal is to achieve the fullness of reflexive clarity. We should see ourselves as "Funktionäre der neuzeitlichen philosophischen Menschheit." The "Urstiftung" of the European tradition points to an "Endstiftung," and only in this latter is the goal we have been pursuing ("Urstiftung") fully revealed:

nur von ihr [sc. der Endstiftung] aus kann sich die einheitliche Ausgerichtetheit aller Philosophien und Philosophien eröffnen, und von ihr aus kann eine Erhellung gewonnen werden, in welcher man die vergangene Denker versteht, wie sie selbst sich nie hätten verstehen können. [27]

Husserl's hope here sounds ridiculously overstated; and this may have something to do with his having failed to push through his critique of foundationalism to the very end. This overstatement has played an important role, as we will see below, in casting discredit on the task as I have outlined it. But if we purge Husserl's formulation of the prospect of a "final foundation" where absolute apodicticity would at last be won, if we concentrate merely on the gain for reason in coming to understand what is illusory in the modern epistemological project and in articulating the insights about us that flow from this, then the claim to have taken the modern project of reason a little farther, and to have understood our forbears a little better than they understood themselves, isn't so unbelievable.

What reflection in this direction would entail is already fairly well known. It involves, first, conceiving reason differently, as including — alongside the familiar forms of the Enlightenment — a new department, whose excellence consists in our being able to articulate the background of our lives perspicuously. We can use the word "disclosure" for this, following Heidegger. And along with this goes a conception of critical reasoning, of especial relevance for moral thinking, that focuses on the nature of transitions in our thought, of which "immanent critique" is only the best-known example.[28]

In moral thought, what emerges from this critique is a rejection of moralities based purely on instrumental reason, viz., utilitarianism; and also critical distance from those that are based on a punctual notion of the self, such as the various derivations of Kant. The critique of Rawls's theory by Michael Sandel, in the name of a less "thin" theory of the agent, is an excellent example of this.[29] In social theory, the result is a rejection of atomist theories, of reductive causal theories (such as "vulgar" Marxism or sociobiology), and of theories that cannot accommodate intersubjective meaning.[30] Social science is seen as being closer to historiography of a certain kind. In politics, the anti-atomist thrust of the critique makes it hostile to certain forms of contemporary conservatism, but also to radical doctrines of nonsituated freedom.[31] I believe there is a natural affinity between this critique, with its stress on situated freedom and the roots of our identity in community, on the one hand, and the civic humanist tradition on the other, as the works of a number of writers, from Humboldt to Arendt, testify.[32]

It might seem from the above as though everything should run on smoothly, toward a set of anthropological conclusions with a certain moral-political hue. But in fact all this is hotly contested, not just by those who wish to defend the epistemological tradition, which would be well understandable, but by those who also consider themselves its critics. Foremost among these are a range of thinkers who have defined themselves in relation to a certain reading of Nietzsche. The most interesting and considerable of them, in my opinion, is Michael Foucault. In keeping with the themes of this paper, we can perhaps get most directly to the basis of their dissent if we go to the moral or spiritual outlook they wish to defend. In the case of Foucault this became relatively clear at the end of his life. He rejected the conception of the punctual self, which could take an instrumental stance toward its life and character — this is indeed what arises out of the practices and "truths" of the disciplinary society, which he painted in such repellent colors (whatever protestations of neutrality accompanied the depiction). But he could not accept the rival notion of a deep or authentic self that arises out of the critical traditions of Hegel and, in another way, Heidegger or Merleau-Ponty. This seemed to him another prison. He rejected both of these in favor of a Nietzschean notion of the self as potentially self-making, the self as a work of art, a central conception of an "aesthetics of existence."[33]

Something analogous, but on a much more frivolous level, seems to animate some of the "poststructuralist" thinkers — Derrida, for instance. Paradoxically, for all the talk of the "end of subjectivity," one of the strong attractions of this kind of position is precisely the license it offers to subjectivity, unfettered by anything in the nature of a correct interpretation or an irrecusable meaning of either life or text, to effect its own transformations, to invent meaning. Self-making is again primary.

Nietzsche's insights into the way in which our language imposes order on our world, into theory as a kind of violence, was hence crucial to all views of this kind. It offers an alternative to the kind of possible critique of epistemology in which we discover something deeper and more valid about ourselves in carrying it through — the kind I have been describing. Instead it attacks the very aspiration to truth, as this is usually understood. All epistemic orders are imposed, and the epistemological construal is just another one of those orders. It has no claim to ultimate correctness, not because it has been shown inadequate by an exploration of the conditions of intentionality, but just because all such claims are bogus. They mistake an act of power for a revelation of truth. Husserl's "Urstiftung" takes on a quite different and more sinister air.

It is clear that this is the critique of epistemology that is most compatible with the spiritual stance of self-making. It makes the will primary in a radical way: while the critique through the conditions of intentionality purports to show us more of what we really are like — to show us, as it were, something of our deep or authentic nature as selves. So those who take the Nietzschean road are naturally very critical of the understanding of critique as *gain* in reason. They would rather deny that reason can have anything to do here with our choices of what to be.

This is not to say that they propose the end of epistemology as a quite radical break. Just as the critique through conditions of intentionality represents a kind of continuity-through-transformation in the tradition of self-critical reason, so the Nietzschean refusal represents a continuity-through-transformation of another facet of the modern identity — the primacy of the will. This played an important role in the rise of modern science and its associated epistemological standpoint; in a sense a voluntaristic anthropology, with its roots in a voluntaristic theology, prepared the ground over centuries for the seventeenth century revolution, most notably in the form of Nominalism. It is a crucial point of division among moderns, what we think of this primacy of the will. This is one of the issues at stake between these two conceptions of what it means to overcome the epistemological tradition.

Although this represents perhaps the most dramatic opposition among critics of epistemology, it is far from exhausting the field. Jürgen Habermas, for instance, has staked out a position equivalent to neither. Against the neo-Nietzscheans, he wants strongly to defend the tradition of critical reason, but he has his own grounds for distrusting Heideggerian disclosure and wants instead to hold on to a formal understanding of reason, and in consequence a procedural ethic, although purged of the monological errors of earlier variants. He has drawn heavily on the critique of epistemology in the four main authors mentioned above, but fears for the fate of a truly universal and critical ethic should one go all the way with this critique.[34]

How does one adjudicate this kind of dispute? How does one decide what it really means to overcome epistemology? I cannot hope to decide the issue here, only to make a claim as to how it must be settled. In order to define this better, I want to return to the most dramatic dispute, that between the neo-Nietzscheans and the defenders of critical reason.

It seems to me that, whoever is ultimately right, the dispute has to be fought on the terrain of the latter. The Nietzschean position too stands and falls with a certain construal of knowledge: that it is relative to various ultimately imposed "regimes of truth," to use Foucault's expression. This has to show itself to be a superior construal to that which emerges from the exploration of the conditions of intentionality. Does it?

Certainly the Nietzschean conception has brought important insights: no construal is quite innocent, something is always suppressed; and what is more, some interlocutors are always advantaged relative to others, for any language.[35] But the issue is whether this settles the matter of truth between construals. Does this mean that there can be no talk of epistemic gain in passing from one construal to another? That there is such a gain is the claim of those exploring the conditions of intentionality. This claim doesn't stand and fall with a naive, angelic conception of philosophical construals as utterly uninvolved with power. Where is the argument that will show the more radical Nietzschean claim to be true and the thesis of critical reason untenable?

I regret to say that one hears very little serious argument in this domain. Neo-Nietzscheans seem to think that they are dispensed from it since it is already evident, or alternatively, that they are debarred from engaging in it on pain of compromising their position. Derrida and his followers seem to belong to the first category. The main weight of argument is carried here by an utterly caricatural view of the alternative as involving a belief in a kind of total self-transparent clarity, which would make even Hegel blush. The rhetoric deployed around this has the effect of obscuring the possibility that there might be a third alternative to the two rather dotty ones on offer; and as long as you go along with this, the Derridian one seems to win as the least mad, albeit by a hair.

Others try to argue on behalf of Foucault that he couldn't enter the argument concerning construals of knowledge without already abandoning his Nietzschean position, that there is nothing to *argue* between them.[36] True enough, but then the issue whether there is something to argue itself demands some kind of support. Something can surely be said about that. Indeed, lots *has* been said, by Nietzsche for instance, and some also by Foucault — in talking for instance of "regimes of truth"; the question is, whether it is really persuasive or involves a lot of slippery slides and evasion.

In short, the arguments for not arguing seriously are uniformly bad. And in fact, Foucault did on one occasion make a serious attempt to engage with the exploration of the conditions of intentionality, and that was in the latter part of *Les Mots et les choses,* where he talks about the invention of Man and the "transcendental-empirical double."[37] This was admittedly prior to his last, much more centrally Nietzschean phase, but it can be seen as preparing the ground for this, as indeed Dreyfus and Rabinow see it.[38]

The arguments here seem to me much more to build on the Heideggerian and Merleau-Pontyan critique against Kant than to be a challenge to this critique. And the arguments, if valid, would have the consequence that nothing coherent could be said at all about the conditions of intentionality. I can't see how this could fail to undercut the Nietzschean view as well. In *Les Mots et les choses,* Foucault takes refuge in a species of structuralism, which is meant to avoid this question altogether. But he abandons this soon afterwards; and we are left uncertain where this argument is meant to take us. In general among neo-Nietzscheans, however, an atmosphere reigns in which this issue is felt as already settled. We are exhorted by Lyotard not to take metanarratives seriously any more, but the argument for this seems to rely on something of a caricature.[39]

If I am right, the issue is far from settled. And yet at stake in this struggle over the corpse of epistemology are some of the most important spiritual issues of our time. The question, what it is to overcome epistemology, turns out to be of more than just historical interest.

Notes

1. K. Popper, *Logik der Forschung* (Vienna, 1935).

2. Cf., e.g., *The Open Society and Its Enemies* (Princeton, 1950).

3. Princeton, 1979.

4. Rorty, chap. 3, p. 132.

The Transformation of Philosophy: Hermeneutics, Rhetoric, Narrative

5. "Epistemology Naturalized," in *Ontological Relativity and Other Essays* (New York, 1969), pp. 69–90.

6. Rorty, chap. 4, pp. 173ff.

7. Cf. Descartes's statement in his letter to Gibieuf of 19 January 1642, where he declares himself "assuré que je puis avoir aucune connaissance de ce qui est hors de moi, que par l'entremise des idées que j'ai eu en moi." The notion that the modern epistemological tradition is basically dominated by this understanding of representation was pioneered by Heidegger in his "Die Zeit des Weltbildes," in *Holzwege* (Frankfurt, 1972), pp. 69–104; and the transition from the earlier view is brilliantly described by Foucault in the opening chapters of his *Les Mots et les choses* (Paris, 1966).

8. Cf., e.g., *De Anima* III, 430a20, also 431a1 and 431b20–23.

9. Cf., e.g., *De Anima* III, 430a9 and 431b32.

10. Daniel Dennett coined the term "semantic engine" to describe the computer, in "Three Kinds of Intentional Psychology," in R. A. Healey (ed.), *Reduction, Time and Reality* (Cambridge, 1981). But it can, of course, only deserve this description because its functioning first of all matches certain formal operations, which are then understood as *interpreted* in some way. Cf. the discussion in John Haugeland's "Semantic Engines," the introduction to a volume he edited, entitled *Mind Design* (Cambridge, Massachusetts, 1981).

11. *What Computers Can't Do,* second ed. (New York, 1979).

12. *Cartesianische Meditationen* (The Hague, 1950), p. 47.

13. Cf. the penetrating analysis of James Tully, in his "Governing Conduct," in E. Leites (ed.), *Conscience and Casuistry in Early Modern Europe* (Cambridge, 1986).

14. Miller translation (Oxford, 1977), p. 47.

15. Cf. *La Phénoménologie de la perception* (Paris, 1945), part 3, chap. 3.

16. It is in terms of this notion of the clearing, I believe, that one has to interpret Heidegger's famous invocation of the Leibnizian question: "Warum ist überhaupt Seiendes und nicht vielmehr Nichts?" *Einführung in die Metaphysik* (Tübingen, 1966), p. 1.

17. In a sense, this question becomes an inevitable one in the modern age. As long as the Platonic or Aristotelian construals were dominant, the question couldn't arise. The universe itself was shaped by *eide*, which were in a sense self-revealing. The clearing, to use Heidegger's word, was grounded in the nature of the beings known. Once this answer no longer becomes available, the question, What are the bases of intentionality? is ready to be asked. It takes an insensitivity, which is largely generated and legitimated by the epistemological tradition, to avoid raising it.

18. *Critique of Pure Reason*, A111, 112.

19. I have discussed this argument form at greater length in "The Validity of Transcendental Arguments," in the *Proceedings of the Aristotelian Society* 79 (1978–1979), pp. 151–165.

20. *Being and Time*, division I, chaps. 2 and 3A.

21. Of course, a proponent of a computer-based model of human performance would contest this latter claim and try to explain our skilled performances on the football field in terms of some computation on bits of informational input, which have the same role as the representations of the classical theory. But this would be in fact to challenge the grounding of our understanding in our dealings with things. It is to say rather that this order of grounding is merely apparent, merely how things look in experience, whereas the real order is the reverse: skilled performance is based on computation over explicit representations — albeit on an unconscious level. This can't be ruled out by an a priori argument, of course; but its implausibility has been well shown in H. Dreyfus, *What Computers Can't Do*.

22. I have discussed this at greater length in "Language and Human Nature" and "Theories of Meaning," both to be found in my *Human Agency and Language: Philosophical Papers, Vol. 1* (Cambridge, 1985).

23. Cf. my discussion in "The Opening Arguments of the *Phenomenology*," in Alasdair MacIntyre (ed.), *Hegel: A Collection of Critical Essays* (Notre Dame, 1976).

24. Cf. the *Philosophical Investigations* (New York, 1958), I. 28ff., I. 258ff.

25. Cf. *From a Logical Point of View* (New York, 1955), p. 4.

26. Cf., for instance, *Word and Object* (Cambridge, Massachusetts, 1960).

27. Cf. *Die Krisis der europäischen Wissenschaften und die transzendentalen Phänomenologie*, Felix Meiner (Hamburg, 1977), sect. 15, pp. 78, 80.

28. I have tried to characterize this further in my "Explanation and Practical Reason" (forthcoming).

29. Michael Sandel, *Liberalism and the Limits of Justice* (Cambridge, 1982).

30. I have explored this in my "Interpretation and the Sciences of Man," reprinted in my *Philosophy and the Human Sciences: Philosophical Papers, Vol. 2* (Cambridge, 1985).

31. I have discussed this in my *Hegel and Modern Society* (Cambridge, 1979), chap. 3.

32. Cf. the latter's *The Human Condition* (Chicago, 1958). I have tried to deal with some of the issues connected with this understanding of politics and modern society in "Legitimation Crisis?" in my *Philosophy and the Human Sciences: Philosophical Papers, Vol. 2*.

33. Cf. the interview published as an appendix in the second edition of Herbert Dreyfus and Paul Rabinow, *Michel Foucault: Beyond Structuralism and Hermeneutics* (Chicago, 1983).

34. I have discussed the motives and limitations of this kind of procedural ethic in my "Sprache und Gesellschaft," in A. Honneth and H. Joas (eds.), *Kommunikatives Handeln: Beiträge zur Habermas' Theorie des kommunikativen Handelns* (Frankfurt, 1986); and in "Justice after Virtue," in M. Benedikt and R. Berger (eds.), *Kritische Methode und Zukunft der Anthropologie* (Vienna, 1985), pp. 23–48.

35. These points are well made by William Connolly in a debate with me about Foucault. See his "Taylor, Foucault and Otherness," *Political Theory* 13, no. 3 (August 1985), pp. 365–376.

36. Cf. Connolly, "Taylor, Foucault and Otherness."

37. *Les Mots et les choses* (Paris, 1966), chap. 9.

38. Herbert Dreyfus and Paul Rabinow, *Michel Foucault: Beyond Structuralism and Hermeneutics* (Chicago, 1982), chap. 2.

39. *La Condition postmoderne* (Paris, 1979), p. 7. The "postmodern," according to Lyotard, is characterized by "l'incrédulité à l'égard des métarécits."